SOCIAL AND CULTURAL DIMENSIONS OF INDIAN INDENTURED LABOUR AND ITS DIASPORA: PAST AND PRESENT

Social and Cultural Dimensions of Indian Indentured Labour and its Diaspora: Past and Present

Edited by

MAURITS S. HASSANKHAN,
LOMARSH ROOPNARINE AND
RADICA MAHASE

MANOHAR
2016

This edition is for sale in India, Sri Lanka, Nepal,
Bangladesh, Afghanistan, Pakistan and Bhutan

First published 2016

ISBN 978-93-5098-129-0

Published by
Ajay Kumar Jain *for*
Manohar Publishers & Distributors
4753/23 Ansari Road, Daryaganj
New Delhi 110 002

Typeset by
Kohli Print
Delhi 110 051

Printed at
Salasar Imaging Systems
Delhi 110 035

Contents

Introduction

BACKGROUND

This volume is the third publication originating from the conference *Legacy of Slavery and Indentured Labour: Past, Present and Future*, which had been organized in June 2013 by the Institute of Graduate Studies and Research (IGSR) of the Anton de Kom University of Suriname, in collaboration with a number of government and non-government organizations.[1]

The aim of the conference was to connect historical specificities of slavery, indentured labour and migration to contemporary issues of globalization, diaspora, identity formation, nationalism and transnationalism. A second aim of the organizers was to promote new perspectives and approaches in the study of forced and free migration and their impact on the society. By bringing scholars together from various parts of the world – senior scholars as well as new promising talents – they wanted to stimulate exchange of ideas, set up new networks and strengthen existing ones.

Some questions that were answered during the conference were:

- What are the legacies of slavery and indentured labour in social, economic, cultural and political fields?
- How did post-slavery identity formation occur in different parts of the world in general?

[1] The partners who organized the conference were Institute of Social Science Research Institute (IMWO), the National Archives Suriname (NAS), the Advanced Teachers' Training College (IOL), and the following cultural organizations: NAKS, Federasi fu Afrikan Srananman, Cultural Union Suriname (CUS), the National Foundation for Hindustani Immigration (NSHI), the Association for the Commemoration of Indonesian Immigration (VHJI) and the Committee 10th October. The conference was subsidized by the Government of Suriname.

- What has been the psychological impact of slavery and indentured labour?
- How are transnational identities developing in the world today?
- How is the process of identification related to the imaginary relation with the country of origin and with other 'partners in distress' in the Diaspora?
- In the case of the second migration or the twice Diaspora, what is perceived as country of origin? In other words, what kind of homeland perspectives do people have and what impact will this have on their relation with the former homeland?
- In which ways did the various groups adapt to the new environment? What has been the policy or attitude of the receiving countries or societies?
- How are localizing processes ('Creolization') expressed in migrant cultures?
- What kind of transnational ties exist among descendants of immigrants in the Caribbean? Are alternative transnational identities in the Caribbean real or imagined?
- How are transnational ties and identities recognized and institutionalized by the State in the former homelands?
- What has been the policy of the countries of origin regarding their former citizens living in the Diaspora?
- How and why are local processes of identity formation related to emotional and practical identification to the countries of origin, and how do these countries feature in these processes?
- Which are the social, economic, cultural and political consequences of migration and Diaspora in modern times?

The participants were invited to review their respective papers and submit them to the organizers of the conference. Some presenters opted to not publish their papers for various reasons. The conference organizers then selected from the available papers and these were grouped according to topics. As a result, four volumes are now in the publication planning stage.

The first one is *Legacy of Slavery and Indentured Labour: Historical and Contemporary Issues in Suriname and the Caribbean*, edited by Maurits S. Hassankhan, Lomarsh Roopnarine, Cheryl White and

Radica Mahase. The second one is *The Legacy of Indian Indenture: Historical and Contemporary Aspects of Migration and Diaspora*, edited by Maurits S. Hassankhan, Lomarsh Roopnarine and Hans Ramsoedh. The third book is titled *Social and Cultural Dimensions of Indian Indentured Labour and its Diaspora: Past and Present*, edited by Maurits S. Hassankhan, Lomarsh Roopnarine and Radica Mahase. The last one is on a neglected area of the Indian Diaspora and is titled *Indentured Muslims in the Diaspora: Identity and Belonging of Minority Groups in Plural Societies*, edited by Maurits S. Hassankhan, Goolam Vahed and Lomarsh Roopnarine.

STRUCTURE OF THIS BOOK

We have grouped the articles in this book as follows:
Part 1: Women, Labour and Narratives.
Part 2: Social Issues among Hindustani Immigrants in the Netherlands.
Part 3: Religion, Arts and Identity.
Part 4: Indian Musical Traditions and Identity.

SUMMARY OF CHAPTERS

Part One: Women, Labour and Narratives

The three chapters in this part examine Indian women during and after indenture in India, Suriname and Sri Lanka. Although the geographical focus varies, the chapters provide new insights into how women were treated in a predominantly patriarchal plantation system. Moreover, the focus also reveals the little attention paid to women who were left behind while their spouses migrated overseas for employment.

Rachel Kurian and Kumari Jayawardena's chapter 'Plantation Patriarchy and Structural Violence: Women Workers in Sri Lanka' argues that plantations were patriarchal institutions that perpetuated structural violence against women workers through the systematic and long-term denial of their life chances with regard to economic, social and political entitlements. 'Plantation patriarchy' incorporated social hierarchies and gender biases stemming from colonialism, race, caste, ethnicity, religion and cultural practices into the structure of the labour regime and in the social organization on plantations. Women workers were placed under male authority at all levels and exposed to physical and sexual violence in their work and lives, their subordination ideologically justified by caste and religion. They were paid lower wages while working longer hours than their male counterparts and were largely responsible for the reproductive chores in the household. At the same time, they experienced discrimination with regard to their basic capabilities, labour rights and political opportunities. Physical and cultural violence reinforced structural violence against women, normalizing the lower status of women in the plantation hierarchy. Kurian and Jayawardena espouse that the tight controls under plantation patriarchy, and the relative isolation of the workers from the wider society allowed structural violence against women workers to be a durable characteristic of Sri Lankan plantations.

Nivedita Singh's chapter 'My Life My Story: Narratives of the Women Left Behind' examines how migration has from time immemorial always created a distance from home and hearts as well as heavy emotional loss for the poor (both inland/overseas). Singh argues that indentured migration from India (especially from villages of the Bhojpuri and Awadhi regions) to Suriname, Mauritius, Fiji, Trinidad and British Guiana has ceased, but other forms of migration are still dominant in these regions even in contemporary times. Migration still continues from the same villages to internal and foreign destinations such as Mumbai, Surat, Noida, Ghaziabad where marginalized people migrate as seasonal labourers to countries of the Middle East, Australia, USA, Canada and the UK. Women are the worst sufferers of the whole phenomenon of migration. The departure of these migrants have caused untold grief to the women who were left behind. Singh documents the suffering of people who were left behind in the villages to suffer the pain of separation. Through the narratives of women, Singh portrays their psychological sufferings and sociological alienation in spite of the accessibility to new technology, cellular networks and new modes of communications. Women have to live alone with their pain and fight with the mundane drudgery of everyday life. Furthermore, other are the narratives of women whose husbands are seasonal migrants who go every year to work in internal destinations. The chapter documents in these 'my life and my stories' their psychological sufferings and sociological alienation and how different cultural forms help them in their struggle of loneliness and survival. The emotion, or *bhav* that was produced by this separation gave birth to a distinct folk culture *Bidesia* in the Bhojpuri region which expressed the pain of the migrants and the women/loved ones left behind through songs, drama, stories and art forms.

Tanya Sitaram examines the role and position of Indian women during indenture in Suriname. Sitaram essentially revisits the binary opposite arguments of women during indenture and posits that women form a special group, who when seen from the historical angle, takes an interesting position, namely that it is not easy to determine their role, since the role and position of women in general and in this case the British-Indian (Hindustani) female indentured women has often been marginalized. Moreover, Sitaram argues that the position of women in history is not viewed from the standpoint of the women themselves, but always from the standpoint of the men. The invisible contribution of these women had to be made visible in the history of Suriname. Sitaram's chapter departs from the reliance on the reports produced by the planter class since they were written from the perspective of the colonialists. Instead, she uses the perspective of the women from their own status to write her chapter on indentured women in Suriname, which re-constructs the role and position of the Hindustani female indentured women in this former Dutch colony. To achieve this goal she uses, among other sources, the Archives of the Immigration Department and re-interprets the reports and correspondence of colonial officials as well as uncovers the experiences of the indentured women. She uses also a unique source which has not been explored yet, namely the registers of the court cases of Itinerary Judges (Ommegaande Rechters), from where the voice of the subalterns can be heard. Her analysis of the position of the female indentured workers reveals a complex situation in which female labourers were exploited by the colonial system and by their male partners and superiors, but at the same time the scarcity of women gave them the opportunity to negotiate their position and role. They were able to choose their own partner, although in many cases it instigated violent actions from their partners or husbands.

PART 2: SOCIAL ISSUES AMONG HINDUSTANI IMMIGRANTS IN THE NETHERLANDS

The four chapters in this part examine the Suriname Hindustani experience in the Netherlands. While an overwhelming body of literature on the Indian Diaspora in Europe and North America has focused on issues relating to assimilation, accommodation, identity formation and remittances, these chapters probe deeper into the hidden aspects of Hindustani life in the Netherlands. Three chapters analyse health issues while one chapter addresses educational challenges and concerns among the Hindustanis in the Netherlands. The findings, based on intensive ethnographic research, reveal a deeper understanding of challenges this immigrant group has faced over the preceding decades with regard to mental health, alcoholism, depression, suicide, emotional loss and educational achievements. The chapters go further and provide suggestions and solutions on how to improve the lives of Hindustanis in the Netherlands.

Indra Boedjarath's chapter focuses on the prevalence of diabetes, heart and vascular diseases in the area of physical ailments as they relate to the mental afflictions, suicidal behaviour and alcoholism among the Indo-Surinamese in the Netherlands. Boedjarath examines mental health challenges and the underlying aspects of suicidal behaviour and excessive alcohol use as self-destructive coping strategies. She reveals that Hindustani women tend to deliberately harm themselves, mostly non-lethally, while Hindustani men tend to end their lives. Furthermore, she argues that interconnected patterns of social, cultural, and personal factors such as the ability and right to act autonomously are not the only causes for social illness, but also conflicting life choices and the cultural values of self-sacrifice and protection of honour. The loss of status, loss of attachment, the inability to express emotions, the pressure to perform, feeling disconnected, a sense of shortcoming in worthiness, and the consequences of a culture-specific upbringing are factors that contribute to deliberate self-harm. Boedjarath suggests that effective prevention and care will therefore demand connecting with the experiences and cultural background of Hindustani risk groups. Professionals working with this group should have a good command of intercultural skills resulting in a culturally sensitive treatment aimed at increasing the subject's resilience and problem-solving ability, and teaching other coping strategies to eventually improve vitality.

Nirmala Birjmohan-Gobardhan's chapter poses some serious health questions: what effects does migration have on family relations, and what is the physical and mental state of the Hindustani elderly in the Netherlands? She answers these questions using individual case histories. Sixty Hindustanis who immigrated to the Netherlands just before Suriname's independence in 1975 are studied with regard to their loss of culture, home, property and social contacts. Birjmohan posits that a shift has occurred from a social-oriented culture to an individual-oriented one, a significant departure from their traditional joint family system. Migration has caused a change in all family member's roles in the larger system. The traditional expectation is that children should to take care of their parents in old age. But members may have disputes about issues like the financial situation including inheritance, and the care for the parents. Dramatic events like migration itself, loss of partner, physical and mental deterioration, loneliness, nostalgia, low income, poor housing, poor command of the Dutch language and ignorance of available care options may produce psychological complaints like depression and anxiety in the Hindustani elderly. The progressive ageing of the community will increase the incidence of dementia. Brijmohan concludes with recommendations to improve the general well-being of Hindustanis in the last stages of their often eventful lives.

Rahina Hassankhan examines the experiences of loss among Hindustanis from the perspective of systemic work and the healing potential of family constellations as well as several building blocks of systemic constellations. Three main forms of emotional loss are presented with their corresponding causes, that is, loss by migration, loss by early death of a loved one, and loss suffered because of a forbidden first love. The double migration the Dutch Hindustanis experienced in almost one hundred years does not reveal a rewarding experience, but rather one that engenders mourning as families were left behind, longing for the native soil and a general, unspecified feeling of loss. Hassankhan through a number of vivid case descriptions argues that emotional loss can be healed by applying family constellations therapy. She espouses that family constellation, including its supportive rituals, may contribute to the uncovering and processing of unprocessed loss among Hindustani people, and serve to reconnect them with the resilience of their ancestors and the nurturing force of the 'Mother Country' to improve the descendant's everyday life.

Anita C. Nanhoe's chapter addresses a partinent question: what have gender-related factors contributed towards the upward educational mobility of Dutch academics of Moroccan, Hindustani and Dutch descent with lower socio-economic backgrounds in the Netherlands? In her study she pays attention to factors within economic, cultural and social capital and addresses the influences class, ethnicity and gender have had on the aforementioned factors. The study focuses on 18 academics of Moroccan descent, 20 of Hindustani descent, and 17 native Dutch academics from lower socio-economic backgrounds. The non-native respondents were first-generation immigrants. Each respondent was interviewed according to the biographical interview method. The results show that within economic capital the group's different visions on the origin of the family income and the division of financial responsibilities appear to be essential for success. Nanhoe shows that access to libraries, student grants and subsidized jobs promoted success especially among women who continued their educational career later in life. She confirms that within cultural capital, the attention given to education in the upbringing is of paramount importance. The results show that the parents of the Moroccan and Hindustani respondents initially did not value educational qualifications for the future prospects of their daughters. Also Moroccan and Hindustani parent's educational ambitions for daughters gradually increased, but did not replace other upbringing targets. Within social capital, the fact that at least one parent encouraged the educational career was of major importance to all respondents, but especially to women. The Moroccans and Hindustanis also referred to their siblings and family members as sources of positive social capital. After residence in the Netherlands, educational qualifications tended to become a source of competition within families and in the social environment for men and women. The results also showed that teachers and peer groups proved to be of greater importance for non-native schoolchildren because they usually had fewer information sources available at home and that their families frequently failed to appreciate higher educational qualifications, especially for girls. The interviews cited innate strength as a factor that explained why under the same conditions one individual persevered whereas another quit. Nanhoe urges that innate strength is a part of cultural capital. Immigrants fight for better living standards and value upward mobility highly in the upbringing of their children.

Part 3: Religion, Arts and Identity

Part 3 consists of three articles dealing exclusively with religion, arts and identity in Suriname. Two of the articles are unique in the sense that they deal with a comparison of blues with *birhá* (*biraha*) a form of traditional music brought from India to Suriname. The comparison of these two forms of arts and music, dealing with feelings of pain, loss and separation can be an eye opener for many readers. The other unique essay is on body markers of different ethnic groups in Suriname as identity markers. The last article in this part deals with the position of churches and religion in Suriname's history. The focus is on Christian churches and how they dealt with the Surinamese society.

In the first paper of this part, the authors J.S. (Mitra) Rambaran and R. Safdar Zaidi are trying to look at the history of slavery and indenture from the perspective of blues and *birhás.* According to them the gospel and blues are twin modern aspects of ritual of survival via music. While the gospel is the religious side, the blues is the secular side of Afro-American music. In their paper they address the blues, since it is assumed that West African slaves would have brought it to the Americas. According to them the lyrics of the blues are written by slaves, who elaborated their lives under the agency of slavery. A famous phrase says that '*history is written by the conquerors or by the masters*'. However, in the case of 'the blues', the history is written by the slaves. The blues reflects the socio-political scenario, as do the *ghazals* of the last Moghul Bahadur Shah Zafar. This is also the case with the *alhā*, *birhā* and *Rāmāyan* songs brought by indentured labourers to the Caribbean. The authors focus on the *birhā.* They try to answer the question whether the blues and the American-African spirituals are not similar to the *birhā* and *Rāmāyan* that the forefathers of the Hindustanis brought with from India and incorporated in Suriname in their new lives? They argue that the *birhā* is similar to the blues. They describe the development of these music and poetic genres and turn our attention to the similarities between them. About the blues they say:

> The only support for their painful souls was songs and music. It was music without instruments but created by the soul. When songs and music are created out of the depths of the heart and soul, they do not depend upon traditional instruments. They used whatever they could to create a sound, for example a spoon, fork or piece of wood. These were transformed to produce a joyful composition that eased the soul.

Birhā is widely used for the painful separation of the beloved. In Indian culture, love has a wide aspect such as love with God, love with a goddess, love with the mother, love with the village, love with pets or with the homeland. The authors explain that the people of India have created *birhā* lyrics to reflect love affairs and other social issues, such as separation from the village or river or complaining against oppression. According to them the *birhā* was very popular among the Indian immigrants in Suriname. Citing Arya (1968) they say that the *birhā* could be composed by any person on any subject and that it was a kind of a protest song. 'In former days birhā competitions were held and two parties were singing, competing with each other in questions and answers. It may be sung on a dholak or without any instruments at all' (Arya, 1968: 29).

Rambaran and Saidi conclude that they found similarities between blues and *birhās* on six items.

Hilde Neus' article deals with body art as an identity marker. Her main questions deal with how the body was seen in the past, how is it reviewed today and how would it develop into the future. According to her the intersection of body, institution and memory in art history or cultural studies can be the ground for research into the body as imagined, historicized and made part of the cultural process, accessed from both material and intangible angles. Referring to Menke (2008) she states that body art is a form of nation creation. 'From the bottom up, representatives from different ethnic groups share their forms of body decoration'. Her argument is that 'all ethnic groups had their own identity markers when they arrived in Suriname, albeit in the mode of make-up, tattoos, jewellery and hairdos or nail decoration. Over the years, however, groups have adapted to other customs and started using each other's ways of decorating the body.' Neus deals with the following aspects of body markers for the different ethnic groups: make up, tattoo, piercing, jewellery, hair and nails.

She gives examples of tattooing by Maroons and Hindustanis, each with their own characteristics and meanings.

Piercing existed traditionally among the Amerindians, but it has become a fashion. Neus deals extensively with jewellery of different ethnic groups, with their own cultural rituals and religious meanings. She gives also examples of different forms of hair dressings and decorations.

In his article on the role and position of religions and churches in Suriname, Joop Vernooij distinguishes five periods since the take-over of the colony by the Dutch in 1667. The focus is on the relationship between Church and State and between different religions since the arrival of Asian indentured labourers.

During the first period from 1667 to 1873 the Calvinist church was a state-church, with exclusive privileges. In 1735 the Moravians got permission to do missionary work, in 1741 the Lutherans got permission to build a congregation, while in 1785 the Catholics were allowed under certain conditions. In practice the Moravian and Catholic churches became people's churches that were active among the slaves, the indigenous people and the Maroons while the Calvinist and Lutheran churches were for the whites. Vernooij mentions the position of the churches regarding slavery and its abolition. He describes also the struggle of the churches regarding the non-Christian values and traditions, such as marriage practices among the Afro-Surinamese.

After the arrival of the Asian indentured labourers Suriname became a multi-cultural society and it was a challenge for the Christian churches to convert the Asian immigrants and decide how to treat their culture. The solution was categorical pastoral for different groups in order to let them feel at home within the new churches. They translated the Bible in the local languages, which contributed to develop Surinamese languages such as Sranan (Creole language of the slaves and their descendants) and Sarnámi (a Creole language of the Hindustanis in Suriname). Vernooij also deals with serious problems the churches faced during unstable developments in Suriname around the time of independence in 1975, the military coup of 1980 and the military period since 1980. One of the aspects was how to deal with the process of decolonization. According to Vernooij the Roman Catholic church struggled with its own identity. A new phenomenon is the rise of the Pentecostal churches that are growing very fast. These churches are making converts among all ethnic and cultural groups and are a challenge for traditional churches and religious organizations.

Part 4: Indian Musical Traditions and Identity

The three chapters in this part focus on various aspects of the cultural legacy of the Indian indentured labourers which was transported to the Caribbean during the period of Indian indentureship. One article looks at the Indo-Caribbean in general while two focus specifically on aspects of culture in Trinidad and Tobago. The cultural legacy that was transported from India to the Caribbean has remained rich and the musical instruments continue to exist until today.

Satnarine Balkaransingh's article, 'The Role of the Tassa Drum Ensemble in Trinidad and Tobago's Cultural Identity Formation', examines the role of the tassa drum ensemble since its introduction to Trinidad and Tobago. Drumming has always been an important cultural art form in the Trinbagonian landscape; the indigenous people used it in their rituals and worship and it was a very important means of communication during the period of African enslavement. The tassa drums, were introduced to the twin island nation by Indian indentured labourers and became very popular in a variety of cultural activities such as weddings and other celebrations. In this article, Balkaransingh looks specifically at the role of the tassa drums in the Muharram mourning. Although Muharram or Hosay was a Muslim occassion, participation went beyond religion and it developed as a pan-Indian celebration. The tassa drums became an integral part of it and they always accompanied the processions. The different rhythms of the tassa drum ensemble were used to evoke various emotional responses from the participants. The drums tell the story of Muharram and various beats are used to portray different scenes from the story. Listeners, for example, can often tell when a battle is taking place.

The tassa drums are made in Trinidad and Tobago and over the years, the designs as well as materials used, have changed. There have also been changes in the rhythms of the drums. These are similar yet different in many ways to the original drums that were introduced by the Indian indentured labourers. In recent times, there have been many competitions developed amongst the tassa drummers in terms of design, rhythm, stamina (which tassa ensemble can play longer the other) and many of the tassa drum ensemble move to different parts of the country to participate in various festivities. Balkaransingh has effectively illustrated the different drums in the ensemble through the use of photographs and a detailed look at the actual beats of the drums. In this article, the author has compared the tassa drums in Trinidad and Tobago to those in northern India, from where Indian indentured labourers immigrated and where Muharram is celebrated, showing the manner in which the drum ensemble has evoked a deep emotional response to bother drummers and participants.

In 'The Mike Men of Trinidad: Cultural, Social and Political Influences', Primnath Gooptar explores the impact of the mike system, a mobile public address system, used for information and entertainment purposes in Trinidad and Tobago. These mike systems were imported into the country in the 1930s and from the 1940s onwards they were used mainly by the Indo-Trinibagonian community for cultural celebrations such as weddings. In fact, they have risen to such prominence that they play an integral role in Indo-Trinbagonian cultural activities. The mike systems had the greatest impact in Indian weddings, playing Indian film songs at wedding venues. Weddings were one of the main social functions, well-attended by the Indo-Trinbagonian population and they provided a space for the mike systems to grow. These weddings were three-day functions and the mike systems often dominated the Saturday night, serving as one of the main forms of entertainment.

As the importance of the mike systems grew at Indian weddings, they acted as a medium whereby Indian movies and Indian film songs could dominate Indo-Trinbagonian cultural activities. Not only were Indian film songs played through the mike systems' loudspeakers but cinemas also used the mike systems to advertise their Indian movies in the villages. The mikes would play the songs and distribute flyers in smaller villages occupied mostly by people of Indian ancestry. Consequently, this influenced the creation of an identity that was centred on India. It was also instrumental in the creation of an Indian religious identity. Later on their function was extended to the wider non-Indian community as government and political organizations started using the mike systems to get their messages out to the communities.

In Ananya Kabir's 'The Dhantaal's Irreverence: Off-beat as the In-between Time of Indenture', the musical and philosophical role of the Dhantaal is examined. The author speculates that the musical instrument may have come from the Bhojpuri area of India – an area that has influenced much of the Indo-Caribbean cultural traditions. However, this is yet to be proven and it is still not known if the Indian indentured labourers brought the instrument with them or if they developed it when they came to the Caribbean. In this article, the author gives an explanation of the beats and rhythms of the Dhantaal. The paper draws on cultural traditions of the Bhojpuri region in India to explain the role and function of the Dhantaal in the Indo-Caribbean and there is an attempt to locate the dhantal within a theoretical framework rich in resistance and colonialism.

EDITORS

PART 1

WOMEN, LABOUR AND NARRATIVES

CHAPTER 1

Plantation Patriarchy and Structural Violence: Women Workers in Sri Lanka

RACHEL KURIAN AND
KUMARI JAYAWARDENA

INTRODUCTION

Plantation production in Sri Lanka was initiated in the early nineteenth century under British colonialism, with the government undertaking political and economic reforms in line with commercialization of agricultural production and thereby promoting laissez-faire capitalism. The planters, keen to lower the costs of labour, directly recruited labour from neighbouring districts of the Madras Presidency in south India. These were workers who were affected by the widespread famine and indebtedness in the region, were prepared to migrate to work on the plantations. While women formed a small proportion of the early pattern of migration, their numbers subsequently increased and, by the twentieth century, they comprised half the now-permanent workforce on the plantations. The plantation workers constituted the single largest and organized segment of the working class in the country.

The significance of plantation production to the economic development of the country has been highlighted by many academics, politicians and planners, and attention has been given to the recruitment patterns, conditions of work and life, as well as the political rights of plantation labour.[1] The discussion has, on the whole,

[1] These include both historical and contemporary analysis – see for example, see Corea, 1975; Peebles, 2001; Meyer, 1992; Roberts and Wickremeratne, 1973; de Silva, 1982; Snodgrass, 1966; Wesumperuma, 1986.

however, tended to ignore the exploitation of women workers, reflecting a male bias through subsuming their experiences within the wider category of workers.[2] Using a historical and contemporary perspective, this paper analyses the social, economic and political opportunities and entitlements of women workers on the plantations in Sri Lanka and shows how these have changed over time. It deals with the role of different actors and institutions, including colonial government, the management, the trade unions and the community, in influencing these possibilities. It pays attention to the ways in which women have been constrained and supported in their struggles for upward mobility and empowerment. How were women workers incorporated into the labour regime on the plantations, and what implications did this have for their lives as workers, members of the plantation community as well as women? Did these women experience class and gender discrimination with regard to pay and benefits? How did patriarchal norms and gender biases in the prevailing social hierarchies, such as those based on class, ethnicity, caste, religion and other cultural traditions influence the capabilities, labour rights and political achievements of women workers? These are some of the questions which will be asked.

This paper argues that plantations were, by origin, patriarchal institutions characterized by a strict hierarchical order and male domination at all levels. The power of 'plantation patriarchy' extended beyond the boundaries of the unit of production, and planters exerted their influence on the state and wider society, gaining favourable concessions and legal support. Women workers on the Sri Lankan plantations were subjected to structural violence through the systematic denial and discrimination with regard to their economic, social and political rights. The argument is developed as given below.

In the case of Sri Lanka, gender prejudices and patriarchal norms stemming from colonialism, race, caste, ethnicity, religion and cultural practices were incorporated into the structure of the labour

[2] A few authors that have paid attention to the situation of women workers include Amali Philips (2003; 2005), Kurian (1982; 1998); Kurian and Jayawardena (1984); Kanapathipillai (1992; 2006).

regime and the organization of life on plantations. Norms and practices promoting male domination pervaded all classes in the plantation sector, including the planters, management, recruiters and workers (including women themselves) reinforcing the traditional view that the subordination of women was justified by custom, religion and law. Under these conditions, the subordination of women was normalized ideologically and structurally; their work was exploited as 'cheap' labour; they were disadvantaged with regard to education, health and income; and they were excluded from the leadership of plantation trade unions and political parties, as well as national and local government. As a relatively isolated sector of the country, it was possible to sustain these forms of discrimination for nearly two centuries, reflecting a form of structural violence against women workers on plantations.

PLANTATION PATRIARCHY AND STRUCTURAL VIOLENCE

While 'patriarchy' literally means the 'rule of the father', the concept has been used to analyse norms and practices promoting male domination in structures and institutions in society (Barrett, 1980; Beechey, 1979; Bhasin, 1993; Lerner, 1986; Mies, 1986; Walby, 1990). The existence of caste and religious-based discrimination against women have led some feminists to develop the notion of 'multiple and overlapping patriarchies'. This term was initially used by Kumkum Sangari (1995: 3287) in analysing the politics of religious-based personal laws and their impact on women. Given the influence of class, race/ethnicity, caste and religion in the lives of women from the plantation community in Sri Lanka, this paper suggests that multiple patriarchies is a useful framework to understand how the different influences combined to limit women's opportunities and entitlements on the Sri Lankan plantations.

Plantations were, by origin and structure, fundamentally patriarchal institutions. The Portuguese developed the first plantations for the large-scale production of sugar in the fifteenth century with the use of slave labour and incorporated features of the prevailing patriarchal feudal household of the period.[3] The early plantations maintained a strict hierarchical social order and a division of labour that was based on race and colour differences, and reflected on the fields, as well as in the segregation of living quarters and social distance (Durant et al., 1999: 11). At the highest level was the white planter (manager) supported by white staff. Lighter skinned slaves, usually the children of black slaves with either the owner or the managers were maintained as house servants. All persons in authority on the plantations (planters, overseers, recruiters, and even inspectors and other government bureaucrats) were men reflecting hegemonic masculinity at all levels. The planters were linked to the dominant class and supported by the colonial political and legal systems, as plantations were important sources of finances for the exchequer.

Women slaves, while essential labour on plantations, were subject to severe punishment (Patterson, 1967: 67) and 'harshly, physically damaging violence' (Reddock, 1985: 73). These practices of male domination were retained even after slavery was abolished. Women remained at the bottom of the plantation hierarchy and under male domination at all levels of fieldwork and within the household, with sexual exploitation and violence persisting even with indentured labour (Hyman, 1990: 14). In addition, women workers did the unpaid household chores, as well as sexually servicing the men (Shameem, 1998: 54). This overall system of controls on women workers, incorporated in the labour regime and in the organization of plantations, and supported by the wider society, could be characterized as plantation patriarchy. The latter reflected the discriminative norms and practices in colonialism, race and gender relations, as well as other cultural practices to enforce women's subordinate position in the plantation hierarchy. These 'multiple patriarchies' legitimized a gender division of labour where women workers were allocated the labour-intensive tasks on the fields and their household, and were constantly under male supervision and control. It justified women being paid lower wages while working

[3] Familiar with the use of slaves for domestic labour, they used greater numbers of slaves for the large-scale cultivation of sugar, providing a 'model' of slave plantations in the subsequent period (Curtin, 1998: 23-4).

longer hours than their male counterparts, and being largely responsible for the familial chores, including taking care of the children, the sick and the elderly. As most workers resided within the boundaries of the plantations, and interaction with 'outsiders' was relatively limited, plantation patriarchy proved to be fairly durable.

Under these circumstances, it is not surprising that women workers on plantations were exposed to different forms of gender bias and discrimination, which affected their opportunities and entitlements as women, as workers and as members of the plantation community and society. The processes and the outcomes of these disadvantages can be captured by the notion of structural violence. The most well-known author of this concept is Johan Galtung, who defined structural violence as violence that is 'built into the structure' and reflected in a groups' unequal power, unequal life chances and social injustice (Galtung, 1969: 171). It is reinforced through physical/direct violence and cultural violence, the latter making structural violence 'look, even feel right' (1990: 291) and 'legitimized and thus rendered acceptable in society' (Galtung, 1969: 292). According to him, 'a violent structure leaves marks not only on the human body but also on the mind and the spirit' (ibid: 294).[4] Patriarchy he argued, combined 'direct, structural and cultural violence in a vicious triangle'. While 'direct violence, such as rape, intimidates and represses; structural violence institutionalizes; and cultural violence internalizes that relation, especially for the victims, the women, making the structure very durable' (Galtung, 1996: 40). At the same time, as argued by Catia Confortini, direct violence can influence both cultural and structural violence, preventing women from accessing their social, economic and

[4] In his lecture, 'Religions, Hard and Soft' (1994), he identifies the religious sanction given to the caste system in Hinduism as a form of structural violence manifested in both economic exploitation and political repression of those on lower rungs of the caste ladder. The low status of women within the caste system left them exposed to what Galtung has referred as 'culture violence' where religious ideology is used to 'justify or legitimise direct or structural violence' (Galtung, 1990: 291).

political rights, thereby being 'a tool to build, perpetuate and reproduce structural violence' (Confortini, 2006: 350). Domestic violence for instance can be closely linked to wife abuse and structural violence against women, and rape need not be a deviant activity of an individual but closely related to promoting male supremacy and gender inequalities in society (ibid.: 350).

The concept of structural violence has particular relevance in analysing the experiences of women workers on the Sri Lankan plantations. It is widely acknowledged that physical violence was, since its inception in the fifteenth century, embedded in the labour relations on plantations. The physical cruelty of planters, the management and overseers on slaves, and subsequently on indentured labour and so-called 'free' labour has been well-documented (Wolf, 1959; Tinker, 1974; Breman, 1989).[5] In addition, as will be discussed in the subsequent sections on Sri Lanka, plantation patriarchy in Sri Lanka was supported by gender biases in caste and religion, resulting in a form of structural violence that discriminated against their economic, social and political capabilities and denying them equal life chances for nearly two centuries.

WOMEN WORKERS ON COLONIAL PLANTATIONS IN SRI LANKA

Women were part of the labour force that planters recruited from the 1830s, from the famine-prone districts of the Madras Presidency in south India. These women belonged to the lowest classes

[5] Eric Wolf has argued that the plantation was 'an instrument of force, wielded to create and to maintain a class structure of workers and owners, connected hierarchically by a staff line of overseers and managers' (1959: 136). Plantations were characterized as 'total institutions' with workers on a plantation often being restricted from having contact with outsiders, while the planters exercised authority over 'all aspects of the lives of people within its territory' (Beckford, 1972: 9). In analysing the plantations on Sumatra's east coast under Dutch colonial rule, he observed 'the relationship between the planter and the coolie, which was so imbued with the use of public and private violence, represented an extreme form of the lack of freedom of colonized labour under Dutch rule' (Breman, 1989).

and castes in the villages and like their male counterparts suffered from chronic indebtedness and sought some form of remuneration for their survival. They migrated to work on the plantations only when the monsoons were insufficient for rice cultivation in south India, leaving them unemployed and living under precarious conditions. In the early period, they formed a migratory labour force, with approximately 56,000 men, 10,300 women and 8,000 children travelling across as plantation workers between 1843 and 1877; although the proportion of departures to arrivals was nearly 60 per cent (Kurian, 1989: 61). According to the Census of 1881, the estate population was 206,495 persons, with about 125,000 men and 82,000 women (Ferguson, 1883: 250). The workers were, as noted by Sir Emerson Tennent, the Colonial Secretary in-charge of Ceylon in 1847, caught between the dictates of plantation capitalism and debt bondage and had little choice of place of work or seasonality of employment (SLNA 3/34 Pt. I Tennent to Grey, Dispatch No. 6 (misc). 21 April 1847).

Women formed a very small proportion of the workforce during the initial stage, just 2.6 per cent of the labour force in 1843, and 27 per cent by 1866. Their conditions of travel were dismal; they were vulnerable to all kinds of dangers, including diseases, exposure to wild animals and sexual abuse. W.C. Twynam, Government Agent of Jaffna, commented on the fact that the few women accompanied the workers during the initial period of migration, indicating that the migrant workers formed '. . . miserable gangs of coolies of 1843 and 1845, with one or two women to 50 or 100 men, strangers in a strange land, ill-fed, ill-clothed, eating any garbage they came across (more however from necessity than choice. . .).'[6]

The planters were keen to recruit women workers and the Secretary of the Immigrant Labour Commission in 1860 asked the Agent in India to look for more labour, 'either on long or short engagements, and who, if required, would bring their wives and families with them' (SLNA, 6/2144: Dawson to Graham: 6 March

[6] London, Colonial Office, CO 54/475, Letter to Colonial Secretary, Henry T. Irving in 'Correspondence on the Condition of Malabar Coolies in Ceylon', p. 16, Enclosure No. 8, 30 September 1869.

1860). The planters were motivated by economic as well as labour control advantages in recruiting women. First, women workers in south India were paid less than their male counterparts, a principle that was adopted in the recruitment of women as workers to the plantations. As such, the Commission was willing to pay relatively higher rates for 'able-bodied' men, with 'women and youths at some proportionally lower rate' (SLNA, 2/2644: Dawson to Graham: 6 March 1869). Second, women workers were viewed as more controllable and according to the Agent, women were generally 'the more steady and regular labourers' (SLNA, 6/2644: Graham to Hansbrow: 24 March 1859). Both these elements stemmed from the patriarchal norms and practices in their home regions and were used on the plantations in Sri Lanka. The recruitment of women workers and the maintenance of discrimination against them with regard to payments and control were clearly in the interests of plantation profitability.

The system of recruitment through the so-called *kangany* system further reinforced patriarchal norms and practices. *Kanganies* were Indian recruiters who were given advances by the planters to go to their villages in India and bring back persons, usually friends and relatives, to work on the plantations. Under these circumstances, the workers who migrated were aware of the backgrounds of the others, and carried over the prevailing caste and religious norms to the plantations. In this process, the subordinate position of women in Hinduism, as well as the caste hierarchy in the prevailing Indian society, was transferred virtually intact to the plantations. As mentioned previously, these attitudes were consciously retained by the planters, as they justified paying women lower wages than their male counterparts.

Few regulations governed the recruitment process as it was considered the movement of 'free' labour. In reality, however, these workers were not afforded even the minimal protection that was provided for workers on indenture, the latter viewed by Lord John Russel as a 'new form of slavery' and analysed in the seminal work by Hugh Tinker (1974). Workers often fell ill, fever and dysentery prevailed on the estates, and workers were not sent to hospitals or given treatment by medical advisors.[7] The active recruitment of women resulted in their increasing numbers as workers on the plantations, and by the early decades of the twentieth century, they constituted the majority of the labour force on the plantations.

THE PATRIARCHAL AND HIERARCHICAL LABOUR REGIME

The labour regime on the Sri Lankan plantations retained the hierarchical features of the earlier slave plantations in the Caribbean and Latin America. The British Superintendent, or the *periyadorai* (big master), like his counterpart under the slave plantations, was at the top of the hierarchy, wielding ultimate authority over every aspect of estate life. He commanded all those below him and was helped by some assistants, generally British, as well as the *sinnadorais* (small masters). Below them were the office staff, such as the accountants who tended to be Tamils or Euro-Asians from outside the estate, and who viewed themselves as superior to the workers. Below the management were the workers; men and women who worked and lived most of their lives within the confines of the plantation. Similar to the race, class and gender hierarchies of the slave plantations, women occupied the lowest rungs and were subordinated to men at all levels of the estate hierarchy. According to the Superintendent of Police in Kandy, J.S. Colpepper, in 1847, the treatment of plantation workers was 'exceedingly arbitrary and cruel' and worse than 'Negro slavery' (quoted in Roberts, 1966).

The patriarchal order on the Sri Lankan plantations was further strengthened through the *kangany* system of recruitment, and more particularly the role of the head *kangany* in the estates. Over time, as *kangany* gangs increased in number and new *kangany* gangs came into existence (Majoriebanks and Marakkayar, 1917: 2) a hierarchy also developed on the estates with a head *kangany* controlling several sub-*kanganies* (Wenzlhuemer, 2008: 250).[8] The head kangany

[7] SLNA. 5/34. Pt. I, Disp. No. 6 (Misc.) Tennent to Grey, Colombo, 21 April 1847.

[8] Roland Wenzlhuemer, 2008, *From Coffee to Tea Cultivation in Ceylon, 1880-1900: An Economic and Social History*, Leiden, Koninklijke Brill NV.

usually belonged to a relatively higher caste than the workers, and functioned as the intermediary between them and the management, using his position to control most of the 'domestic affairs of his gang'. This included settling their disputes and dealing with their grievances (Majoriebanks and Marakkayar, 1917: 2). He also supervised the workers on the fields for which he was paid a 'head' money. The workers were further split in smaller groups under their own patriarch or *silarakangany*, and lived in 'line room', which were barrack-like structures, debt-ridden to the *kangany* and the planters. Their line rooms were often arranged, in consultation with the *kangany*, along caste lines. In these ways, the patriarchal norms associated with Indian caste and religious practices were retained in women's lives on the plantations. According to the *Report of the Labour Commission*, in 1908, however, the plantation workforce divided to enhance the 'family principle', workers at each level exercising rights on those below them and paying respect to those higher in the hierarchy. In reality, women remained on the lowest ring in this social ladder as well as within the 'families' (*Report of the Labour Commission*, Colombo: 1908).

Physical violence was, as in the case of the slave plantations, also meted out to workers by the planters, with women experiencing, in addition, threats of or actual sexual abuse.[9] The planters also used watchers and guards to prevent workers from absconding the estates, even employing Sinhalese villagers to arrest workers on the roads outside the estate (*Report of a Commission*, 1916, op. cit., para 55.). Condemning such practices as a 'form of slavery' the social reformer and politician P. Arunachalam, in 1916, wondered 'that the Superintendent of the Estate was not ashamed to insert

[9] Writing in 1878 P.D. Millie noted that 'cuff and a kick' were sometimes used to settle disagreements, and corporal punishments were also used (Jayawardena, 2007: 66). These forms of physical violence were evident even in the twentieth century and the Sabaragamuwa Commission in 1914 noted that 'some superintendents are averse to the practice, but others have admitted that castigation was resorted to whenever the occasion demanded it' (*Report of the Commission to Inquire into the Conditions of Immigrant Tamil labourers in Sabaragamuwa 1914*, cited in Jayawardena, 1972: 22).

such an advertisement and to organize a hunt for a poor sickly woman with a baby in arms and burdened with two more children' (1936: 217). The Labour Ordinance of 1865 enabled magistrates to return workers, who 'bolted' from the estate including women and children, to the estates. In 1916, following many protests, the Attorney General Anton Bertram drafted a bill to exempt women from imprisonment, but a female over sixteen years could be imprisoned for drunkenness, insolence or misconduct, as 'women may be quite as capable of giving trouble as a man'. The penal provisions of this ordinance were only abolished in 1922 (Jayawardena, 1972: 209).

PHYSICAL, CULTURAL AND STRUCTURAL VIOLENCE UNDER COLONIALISM

In addition to the harsh working conditions on the plantations, women workers, like their slave counterparts, were also exposed to sexual abuse, harassment and domestic violence. The planters, like the other males on the plantations, could subject the women workers to sexual exploitation with impunity. As early as in 1848, Governor Torrington noted these 'most objectionable' ways of the coffee planters with regard to women (cited in K.M. de Silva, 1965: 98). British bureaucrats, soldiers and minor officials also sexually exploited the workers, as well as local women. The children from these liaisons were sent to Catholic convent schools, or to the Paynter Homes, established for 'rescuing' the Eurasian children (Jayawardena, 2007).[10] This violence was built into the labour regime and the household as women workers were constantly under the control of male authorities, whether they were the planters, the *kanganies* or their fathers and husbands.

The subordinate position of women in the plantation hierarchy was also justified through what could be viewed as 'cultural violence'. Hinduism, the religion followed by the vast majority of the planta-

[10] Little has been written on Eurasians by researchers, but there are some references in fiction set in Ceylon (Jean Ararasanayagam, Lorna Wright, William Knighton), and also some in Indian writing on Anglo-Indians (Jayawardena, 2007).

tion workers, espoused the notion that to be born a woman was a sign of a bad *karma* or the negative consequence of bad deeds in the past. Therefore, women had to fulfil their *dharma* or duty, which was to be obedient to the male members of their family, including the father, husband and son and thereby hope for a better rebirth. In addition, such a woman had also to be deferential and respectful to those above her in the social hierarchy. Women workers were in the lowest rungs of this social pyramid, with religious rituals and norms pressurising them to abide by their rules in their daily existence. Strong female deities, such as Kali, Saraswati and Lakshmi were also worshipped on the plantations, and women were highly involved in organizing religious festivals. Thus, while religion was viewed as an important source of solace and strength for women workers, and participating in religious activities noted as a meritorious deed that could enable them to be reborn at a high level, it also endorsed the fatalistic belief that women's injustices stemmed from actions in the past, and were therefore deserved. In a similar manner, the so-called low castes in society were pressured to accept their fate and not attempt to challenge their situation. Planters, on their part, actively encouraged religion on the plantations, viewing it an important form of controlling the workforce (Jayawardena and Kurian, 2015).

Physical and cultural violence informed the structure of the plantations, including the division of labour in the fields and households. Women were allocated labour-intensive and time-consuming tasks on the fields and the households, and in spite of these activities being amongst the most important, were considered to be of low or no value. Women were involved in the plucking of tea because they had 'nimble fingers', they were 'patient' and 'controllable'. As befitting the norms and practices of plantation patriarchy, they were paid less for their work, while contributing significantly to the profitability of production. They were always under some form of male control, either by the *kanganies*, office staff or planters. The latter were aware of the benefits of recruiting more and preferring women. A planter in 1839, during the early migration when relatively few women migrated for plantation work, pointed out that plucking had become expensive as it was done by men, who could not pluck 'as cheaply as the women and children' with the latter also 'working at it steady'.[11] This inequality remained a form of structural violence for two centuries. It was incorporated by the state into the minimum wage legislation in 1929, and continued until rectified by law in 1984, because of mass trade union action and mobilization of workers (see later discussion).

In addition to their work on the fields, women workers were also responsible for a wide range of household tasks, such as cooking, cleaning, and caring for the children and other family members, fetching the water and firewood. This was the accepted traditional gender division of labour and as it was unpaid (or even acknowledged as work). Like their work on the fields, the women were under male authority in their households, and were supposed to, by culture and practice, take care of the needs of the different males (husbands, fathers and at times, even the *kangany* and the planters). Overall, the tasks undertaken by the women were labour-intensive, repetitive and placed them under male supervision and control. Finally, the different activities provided them with little time for either social contacts or sustained political activity, and the nature and intensity of estate and household work placed them in a well-defined, limited and highly controlled situation.

While perpetuating discrimination in wages, the state and the planters also did little to improve the capabilities of girls through providing education. The primitive estate schools were mainly for boys and little effort was made to raise women's literacy. While literacy was, on the whole, very low for both males and females, the statistics for 1911 showed that women fared significantly worse than the men. The literacy rates for women among the Indian Tamil population in the Principal Planting Districts were between 1 and 3 per cent (the equivalent figures for males was between 13 and 21 per cent) (Denham, 1912: 409). While educational facilities improved after the enactment of the Education Ordinance of 1920, girls did not have equal access to education as boys, the latter often joining the trade unions in the 1930s. The structure of

[11] Report by Rettie of the Spring Valley Estate, reporting on the Uva Estate on 4 July 1893; Spring Valley Estate.

work on the estates and the patriarchal norms served to restrict educational opportunities for girls, as they were expected to help their mothers with their choice in the household. This division of labour prevailed even after the country gained independence in 1948, with plantation women workers having the lowest levels of literacy in the country (Socio-economic Survey of Ceylon 1969/70). Fieldwork done in the late 1970s and early 1980s showed that daughters, often as young as eight or nine years old, helped clean the house and prepare the food, and looked after the siblings, often at the expense of education. This resulted in the vast majority of women being unable to read or write, and thus even unable to discern if the weight of tea they picked or the rubber they tapped was correctly recorded by the management (Kurian, 1982: 109-10).

PATRIARCHY IN POLITICS: HISTORICAL AND CONTEMPORARY INJUSTICES

While the colonial government and the planters did their best to isolate the plantation workers from the wider working-class movement in the country, trade unionism developed on the plantations from the 1930s onwards. These were able to mobilize a significant proportion of the workers, undertake militant strike action in alliance with the Left, and take up their demands for better working conditions, pay and other benefits with the planters and the government. There were also important women leaders like Meenachi Ammal who, in the 1930s, called for women's franchise and equality, and chastized more conservative male leaders for their lack of attention to this problem. Women workers had a high level of trade union membership and their fees were automatically deducted from their payroll. They also participated in large numbers in strikes and supported the plantation political parties.

Furthermore, as part of the process of increasing local government in Sri Lanka, the British colonial government granted universal franchise rights in 1931 to all the plantation workers who could show that they had resided in the country for five years or longer. The franchise rights of the plantation workers were, however, severely curtailed shortly after Sri Lanka gained independence in 1948, when the new elected government passed acts that denied citizenship to the vast majority of plantation workers, rendering them 'stateless'. The agreements between India and Sri Lanka in 1964 and 1974 allowed individuals to gradually register as citizens in Sri Lanka, but it was only in 1986, that the government finally passed an act granting citizenship to all the 'stateless'.[12]

The fact that all the citizenship acts up to the twenty-first century reflected a gender bias, stipulating the grant of citizenship to be based on male descent, and used only the masculine pronoun to refer to both women and men is illustrative of the strength of patriarchy.[13] No reference was made to the mother, grandmother or the great-grandmother who might have been born in the country. This gender inequality was premised on the patriarchal notion that a woman's nationality depended on that of the man. The Indian and Pakistani Residents (Citizenship) Act of 1949, provided the right to apply for citizenship only to male heads of households. Women were able to apply independently only if they were widows, or unmarried and more than twenty-one years old (Kanapathipillai, 2009: 45). Even the 1986 Act, which effectively removed the 'stateless' problem, contained this gender bias, reflecting the continuing association of women as dependents on men. This anomaly was finally removed in 2003, in response to pressures and campaigns from women's groups, lawyers and the National Committee of Women on the broader issue of gender injustice in the grant of citizenship.

Women workers were rarely included in the leadership of the trade union and political parties in spite of the high degree of their involvement in strikes and political action.[14] The exclusion of women

[12] The struggles of the plantation workers for their basic franchise and citizenship rights have formed an important part of the labour movement of the country (Jayawardena and Kurian, 2015).

[13] According to the Sri Lankan Citizenship Act, a person born in the country needed to show that her or his father was also born in the country, or that her or his paternal grandfather and paternal great-grandfather were born in the country.

[14] Women in Sri Lanka in general have a poor representation in parliament and are seldom more that 5 per cent of members in parliament and 2 per cent or less in the provincial councils, municipal councils and *pradeshiyasabhas* (ADB, 2008: 6).

from leadership had both ideological and structural dimensions. Gender biases that informed plantation patriarchy continued the normalization of the subordinate position of women in society. As a result, the leadership of trade union as well as political parties – almost entirely composed of men – simply did not view women as capable to represent their interests and few women were even nominated, and even fewer represented in the political hierarchy. In addition, as we have seen previously, the gender division of work was maintained well into the twenty-first century, with a normal working day for women workers beginning at 4 a.m. and their household chores completed usually late in the evenings. In some contrast, men were involved in 'task' jobs that were completed by about 2 p.m. and political meetings were held usually in the afternoons and the evenings, during which time the women were either busy or too tired to participate in political discussions. According to Amali Philips, women on plantations were treated like children who needed to be controlled and guided by men at home and at work (2003: 21). Even the *Matha Sangams*, which were women's wing of the trade unions, were according to Amali Philips, 'limited to traditional religious, cultural and ritual events' (Philips 2003: 27).

Up to the second decade of the twenty-first century, there are just a handful of women who have come up the ranks of the trade union and political leadership. Menaha Kandasamy, the first woman to lead a plantation trade union in the country, namely, the Ceylon Plantation Workers' (Red Flag) Union, has argued that trade unions were male dominated and women's leadership was essentially a 'non issue' for them (2002: 37). Women were 'active members and "nominal" leaders', and of 'use value only so far as it suited the male agenda of the trade unions' (2002: 51).[15]

[15] In line with these concerns, the RFWF organized an Asian regional conference held in Kandy in December 2011 on the significant theme 'Can We be Democratic without Women's Leadership?' (RFWM, 2012). The participation of women in trade union leadership and local, regional and provincial councils, even if it is minimal, has brought about discussion and debate on the obstacles that women experience in politics.

CONTINUATIONS IN STRUCTURAL, CULTURAL AND PHYSICAL VIOLENCE

Given the persistence of plantation patriarchy and the poor representation of women in the political leadership, it is not surprising that many of the disadvantages women workers experienced persisted for long periods. Plantation workers, on the whole, were amongst the lowest in terms of quality of health and level of income, a historical legacy that continued to the twenty-first century. This can be seen from the report 'National Plan of Action for the Social Development of the Plantation Community'. This report noted the persistent problems of housing, water supply and sanitation, as well as 'over-crowding of line rooms', which were 'obsolete housing . . . unfit for human habitation' (NPA, 2007: vi; 2). In addition, all health indicators were below the national average 'with infant and maternal mortality and malnutrition amongst pre-school children more than double the all-island rates'[16] and public health preventive facilities not always available to plantation workers (World Bank, 2007: vii). Also, women workers have been doubly affected as part of the marginalized plantation community, as well as women with lower levels concerning both income and health.

In contrast, and in response to increasingly better facilities for education, women have improved their educational capabilities. S. Thondaman, the leader of the CWC, became a minister in 1978 in the UNP-led government and put great effort into improving the educational opportunities for children on the estates, even mobilizing foreign donors to support schools on the plantations (Little, 2003: 254). In response to these facilities, male and female literacy rates on the estates increased from 80 and 58.1 per cent respectively in 1986-7, to 88.3 and 74.7 per cent respectively by 2003-4 (World Bank, 2007: 90) as seen in Table 1.1. While the performance of women continues to be less than that of men, these figures suggest girl children also greatly benefitted in this process.

[16] The World Bank cites figures from the DHS (2000) indicating that 37 per cent estate children were stunted as compared to 14 per cent of rural children and 48 per cent of estate mothers had a low body mass index compared to 23 per cent of rural mothers (World Bank, 2007: xvii).

Cultural violence, as manifested in the low status assigned to women in caste and religion, was continued and helped in legitimizing inequality in terms of life chances and power. In the case of the plantations, this cultural violence against women workers has been worked into the structure of work and life on the plantations. In analysing the kinship, marriage and gender experiences of Tamil women on six tea plantations in Sri Lanka in 1999-2000, Amali Philip noted the continued controls placed on their work and opportunities through the importance of religion in the daily lives of the women. According to her: 'Women bear their double burden of work at home and in the fields with poignant sarcasm, calling it the "fulsome boon we have received from the gods" (*ithu engalukku pongi vantha varam*), while men attribute women's burdens to their karma and the "sin of female birth" . . .' (2005: 119).

Philips further describes the domestic rituals that reinforce their role as carers for their families.

> As if to thank the gods for their plight, women are assigned the tasks of praying and performing domestic rituals such as decorating the front step (*kolam*), lighting oil lamps, offering flowers to and garlanding sacred pictures and idols, sanitising the home with cow dung, and offering prayers for their husbands and family members. Prayer and worship are intermingled with domestic tasks. Women pray to the gods for a successful day, and they pray before lighting the hearth, cooking the rice meal, and cleaning the pots and pans at the end of the day. (2005: 119)

The subordinate position in society, idealized in religion, was reflected in rituals on plantations. While women were enthusiastic and did voluntary work on religious occasions, they were 'not allowed to serve on the estate temple boards'. The excuse for this exclusion was that women were incompetent and stupid, and that management was a man's job (2005: 115, 119). The management also continued their support for religion, viewing it as a useful outlet for the feelings of the workers, and thereby helping them to accept their situation. Philips noted that in spite of complaints by the management that religious activities 'cut into the busy work schedules' on the estates, the management 'actively participates in the rituals and deducts money from workers wages for the expenses incurred in organising them' (ibid.: 115). At the same time, religious rituals, while embodying the 'concerns and anxieties of workers who live and work under adverse conditions', are especially relevant as a 'form of escape from the drudgery of work' and for women 'a release from the monotony of repeated picking' (ibid.). Women were able to use these religious ceremonies for their own purposes and they were occasions for women to get together and socialize outside their work (Philips, 2005: 119 and Kurian, 1998: 79). They also enjoyed the dances and songs associated with religious events and participated in their own dance forms such as the women's *kummi* dance. No doubt, they also took pleasure in the songs and dramas performed by estate workers where sly hints could be made about their grievances (see Jayawardena and Kurian, 2015).

In addition to structural and cultural violence, physical violence against women continued to remain a feature of plantation life. According to a study in 2001 by Kamalini Wijayatilake and Faizun Zackariya, women from the plantation community remained targets of verbal and physical abuse. This violence was prevalent 'within the family, the work place and in society reflecting unequal gender relations in these three spheres' (2001: 17).

> If the women showed anger or resentment at the passes the Kangani would make, or not acquiesce with his demands, he would reduce the weight of the leaf plucked and increase it for those who he favoured or those women who give in. When we protest about the short weight, he throws our card away and abuses us – Responses of women workers on tea plantations in Sri Lanka. (Wijayatilake and Zackariya, 2001: 13)

Prevention of domestic violence and sexual harassment did not appear to be of high priority for the management and the unions, with women even losing confidence in the unions to take up their cause (ibid: 26). Physical violence or even the threat of violence also contributed to the low participation of women from the plantation community in politics, as it was unlikely that a woman would join politics if she were under physical or psychological threat.

COUNTERING PATRIARCHAL CONTROLS

The Sri Lankan state has taken several measures to counter violence against women and to promote gender equality. The 1978 Constitution (Amendment) included principles of gender equality and non-discrimination in the amendment. The country also ratified the United Nations Convention on the Elimination of All Forms of Discrimination against Women (CEDAW) in 1981 and subscribed to the Beijing Declaration and Platform for Action (1995). It passed laws to combat sexual harassment in 1995, and under Section 345 of the Penal Code of 1995 identified sexual harassment as 'unwelcome sexual *advances* by words or action used by a person in authority, in a working place or any other place'. Another important legislation put into operation in 2005 was the Prevention of Domestic Violence Act of 2005. In spite of these progressive enactments, physical violence against women continues to be a pervasive feature of the plantations. It would appear that the relevant information is not sufficiently provided to these workers, and their fallback situation also does not encourage them to resort to supportive legislation. It is equally important to acknowledge that male authority has been normalized and internalized in the plantation community, with serious repercussions (including condemnation by her own family) if a woman should recourse to taking up legal action against domestic violence. Furthermore, the police and those in authority who should take action are often imbued with patriarchal norms, often encouraging the women to return to their traditional roles and accepting their situation rather than seriously taking up their concerns.

At the same time, it would be incorrect to assume that women workers completely accepted their subordinate role as ascribed by the hegemonic ideology. To the contrary, they expressed their anger at domestic violence indicating that it hurt and humiliated them both physically and emotionally. Several of them also passionately said that they would not allow their daughters to be victims of such situations (even if they felt that they could do little to change their own lives on this score). Such attitudes reflect an awareness of the wrongs that are being done to them even if these are not articulated as direct or open protests (Kurian, 1989). Discussions undertaken by the authors in 2014 with A.P. Kanapathipillai, a lawyer working in Nuwara Eliya, a plantation district, indicate that there have been increased numbers of separations, divorces and lawsuits by women for maintenance, in the twenty-first century, suggesting that women are taking more direct action in challenging male domination.

Women have always participated in strikes and protest actions on the plantations. One typical way of threatening the *kangany* was to 'crowd' him with their baskets, thereby not allowing him much movement (fieldwork). Another method of 'go-slow' was to collect the leaves and throw them on the floor before the weighing machine, so that time would be spent on gathering the leaves, thus resulting in delay in production. These are methods used to resist the system without having to face formal punishment. A major strike involving collective action was undertaken in 1984, with the massive involvement of women workers. It resulted in equal wages for women and men on the plantations, removing an inequality that that had characterized plantations for the previous 150 years.

Women have also started to make inroads in the plantation political hierarchy, a domain from which they had previously been virtually excluded. A few of them such as Anushiya Sivarajah of the Ceylon Workers' Congress and Saraswati Sivaguru of the National Workers' Union have been elected to local and provincial councils, the latter in particular highlighting the problems of underage pregnancies, sexual harassment and rape prevalent on the plantations. We have also previously noted the role of Menaha Kandasamy, who, as leader of the Ceylon Plantation Workers' (Red Flag) Union, has fought against patriarchy in politics through teaching and taking action to improve the leadership skills of women; expanding their knowledge of basic labour and human rights; and leading campaigns against domestic violence. All these reflect ways and means by which women workers, individually and collectively, have challenged the conventional attitudes of female subordination and have asserted their agency under multiple forms of patriarchal oppression.

PLANTATION PATRIARCHY AND STRUCTURAL VIOLENCE

Plantation patriarchy has endured for nearly two centuries, perpetuating structural violence against women workers and denying them equality with regard to their basic capabilities, labour rights, political opportunities and even basic survival. Cultural and physical violence informed and shaped the structural violence against women. More insidiously, the different forms of violence sustained one another, to the extent that it was not possible to separate the influence of one on the other, but rather recognize their cumulative effect on the lives of women workers. Those in power, including the state, planters, the unions and even the male members of community had stakes in keeping them in a subordinate position, and either through active intervention or neglect, played their roles in the violence that characterized plantation patriarchy.

REFERENCES

Asian Development Bank (2008). Country Gender Assessment: Sri Lanka, Metro Manila, the Philippines, Asian Development Bank.

Barret, Michele and Mary McIntosh (1980). 'The "Family Wage": Some Problems for Socialists and Feminists', *Capital and Class*, no. 11, Summer: 51-72.

Beechey, V. (1979). 'On Patriarchy', *Feminist Review*, 3: 66-82.

Beckford, G.L. (1983). *Persistent Poverty: Underdevelopment in Plantation Economies of the Third World*, London, Zed Press.

Bhasin, K. (1993). *What is Patriarchy?* New Delhi, Kali for Women.

Breman, Jan, (1989). *Taming the Coolie Beast: Plantation Society and the Colonial Order in Southeast Asia*, New Delhi, Oxford University Press.

Confortini, Catia C. (2006). 'Galtung, Violence, and Gender: The Case for a Peace Studies/Feminism Alliance', *Peace & Change*, vol. 31, no. 3, July 2006.

Corea, Gamini (1975). *The Instability of an Export Economy*, Colombo: Marga Institute.

Curtin, Philip, (1998). *The Rise and Fall of the Plantation Complex: Essays in Atlantic History*, Cambridge, Cambridge University Press.

Denham, E.B. (1912). *Ceylon at the Census of 1911: Being the Review of the Results of the Census of 1911*, Colombo, Government Press.

Durant, T.J. and David J.D. Knottnerus (eds.) (1999). *Plantation Society and Race Relations: The Origins of Inequality*, Westport (USA), Praeger Publishers.

Fernando, Nimal (1978). *Land Reform in Plantation Agriculture: An Analysis of the Case of Sri Lanka with Special Reference to Tea Plantations*, Madison, Wisconsin, Land Tenure Center, University of Wisconsin-Madison.

Galtung, Johan (1969). 'Violence, Peace and Peace Research', *Journal of Peace Research*, vol. 6, no. 3, pp. 167-91.

—— (1990). 'Cultural Violence', *Journal of Peace Research*, vol. 27, no. 3, pp. 291-305.

—— (1994). '*Religions, Hard and Soft*' essay given at the 1994 UNESCO Conference in Barcelona on the contribution of religion to world peace. Available at http://www.crosscurrents.org/galtung.htm

—— (1996). *Peace by Peaceful Means: Peace and Conflict, Development and Civilization*, London and New Delhi, Sage.

Hyman, R. (1990). *Empire and Sexuality: The British Experience*, Manchester University Press.

Jayawardena, Kumari (1972). *The Rise of the Labour Movement in Ceylon*, Durham, N.C. Duke University Press.

—— (2007). *Erasure of the Euro-Asian: Recovering Early Radicalism and Feminism in South Asia*, Colombo, Social Scientists' Association of Sri Lanka.

Jayawardena, Kumari and Rachel Kurian (2015). *Class, Patriarchy and Ethnicity on Sri Lankan Plantations: Two Centuries of Power and Protest*, Hyderabad, India, Orient BlackSwan.

Jayawardena, L.R. (1960). 'The Supply of Sinhalese Labour to the Tea Industry in Ceylon', *Research Study*, Cambridge, made available by author.

Kanapathipillai, V. (2009). *Citizenship and Statelessness in Sri Lanka: The Case of the Tamil Estate Workers*, London and New York, Anthem Press.

—— (1992). *A Decade of Change in the Plantations: The Implications for Women Workers*, International Centre for Ethnic Studies, ICES monograph series.

Kandasamy, Menaha Vijayaluxmy (2002). *The Struggle Continues: Women's Leadership in Plantation Trade Unions in Sri Lanka*, Institute of Social Development.

Kurian, Rachel (1982). 'Women Workers in the Sri Lanka Plantation Sector: An Historical and Contemporary Analysis', *Women, Work and Development*, 5, Geneva: International Labor Office.

—— (1989). 'State, Capital and Labour in the Plantation Industry in Sri Lanka 1834-84', Ph.D. thesis, University of Amsterdam.

Kurian, R. and K. Jayawardena (1984). *The Exploitation of Women on the*

Plantations: Tamil Women Workers on Tea Plantations, Colombo, Women's Education Centre.

Labour Commission 1908, *Report of the Labour Commission*, Colombo, Ceylon Labour Commission Handbook, p. 193.

Lerner, G. (1986). *The Creation of Patriarchy*, New York, Oxford University Press.

Little, Angela (2003). *Labouring to Learn, Towards a Political Economy: Plantations, People and Education in Sri Lanka*, Colombo, Social Scientists' Association.

Majoriebanks, N.E. and A.R. Marakkayar (1917). *Report on Indian Labour Emigration to Ceylon and Malaya*, Government of India.

Meyer, Eric (1992). ' "Enclave" Plantations, "Hemmed-In" Villages and Dualistic Representations in Colonial Ceylon', *Journal of Peasant Studies*, 19 (April/July 1992): 199-228.

Mies, M. (1986, 1998). *Patriarchy and Accumulation on a World Scale: Women in the International Division of Labour*, London and New York, Zed Press.

National Plan of Action (NPA) for Social Development of the Plantation Community (2006-15), 2007.

Patterson, O. (1967). *The Sociology of Slavery: An Analysis of the Origins, Development and Structure of Negro Slave Society in Jamaica*. Mac Gibbon and Kee, London.

Peebles, Patrick (2001). The *Plantation Tamils of Ceylon: New Historical Perspectives on Migration*, London and New York, Leicester University Press.

Philips, Amali (2003). 'Rethinking Culture and Development: Marriage and Gender among the Tea Plantation Workers in Sri Lanka', in *Gender and Development*, vol. II, no. 2, Taylor and Francis Ltd.

—— (2005). 'The Kinship, Marriage and Gender Experiences of Tamil Women in Sri Lanka's Tea Plantations', in *Contributions to Indian Sociology*, 39: 1, pp. 107-42.

Reddock, Rhoda (1985). 'Women and Slavery in the Caribbean: A Feminist Perspective', *Latin American Perspectives*, vol. 12, no. 1, pp. 63-80.

Report of the Labour Commission (1908), Colombo.

Report of the Labour Commission (1916), Colombo.

Roberts, Michael (1966). 'Indian Estate Labour in Ceylon during the Coffee Period, 1830-1880', *Indian Economic and Social History Review*, vol. 3, no. 2, pp. 1-52.

Roberts, M. and L.A. Wickremeratne (1973). 'Export Agriculture in the Nineteenth Century', in K.M. de Silva (ed.) *University of Ceylon, History of Ceylon*, vol. III, Colombo, University of Ceylon.

Sangari, K. (1995). 'Politics of Diversity: Religious Communities and Multiple Patriarchies', *Economic and Political Weekly*, vol. 30, no. 51, 23 December, pp. 3287-3310 and vol. 30, no.52, 30 December , pp. 3381-9.

Shameem, S. (1998). 'Migration, Labour and Plantation Women in Fiji: A Historical Perspective', in *Women Plantation Workers*, Oxford, Berg, pp. 49-65.

Silva, S.B.D de (1982). *The Political Economy of Underdevelopment*, London, Routledge and Kegan Paul.

SLNA 3/34 Pt. I, Tennent to Grey, Dispatch No. 6 (misc). 21 April 1847.

SLNA. 6/2644: Graham to Hansbrow: 24 March 1859.

SLNA. 6/2144: Dawson to Graham: 6 March 1860.

SLNA. 2/2644: Dawson to Graham: 6 March 1869.

Snodgrass, D. Ceylon (1966) *An Export Economy in Transition*, Homewood, IL. Richard D. Ifwin.

Tinker, H. (1974). *A New System of Slavery: The Export of Indian Labour Overseas, 1830-1920*, London, Bombay, New York, Oxford University Press.

Walby, S. (1990), *Theorizing Patriarchy*, Oxford, Blackwell.

Wenzlhuemer, Roland (2008). *From Coffee to Tea Cultivation in Ceylon, 1880-1900: An Economic and Social History*, Leiden, Koninklijke Brill NV.

Wesumperuma, Dharmapriya (1986). *Indian Immigrant Plantation Workers in Sri Lanka: A Historical Perspective, 1880-1910*, Kelaniya, Vidyalankara Press.

Wijetilake, Kamalini and Faizun Zackariya (2001). *Sexual Harassment at Work: Sri Lankan Study on Plantation Sector*, Colombo, ILO.

Wolf, E.R. (1959). 'Specific Aspects of Plantation Systems in the New World: Community Sub-Cultures and Social Classes', in *Plantation Systems of the New World*, Washington D.C., Pan American Union.

World Bank (2007). *Sri Lanka Poverty Assessment: Engendering Growth with Equity: Opportunities and Challenges*, 23 January 2007, produced by the Poverty Reduction and Economic Management Sector Unit, South Asia Region, Report no. 36568-LK.

CHAPTER 2

My Life My Story: Narratives of the Women Left Behind

NIVEDITA SINGH

Bidesia (from the word 'bides' meaning 'foreign') was the term used to refer to migrant labourers by the people who were left behind. Bidesia folk culture is the name given to this cultural tradition and is represented in many forms like *nautanki* (musical theatre), drama, folk songs and folk paintings. It is a holistic folklore tradition which revolves around the theme of the departure of the migrant Bhojpuris (Narayan, 2005: 34). Under the indentured migration system the labourers who were migrating left their home to come back, while there were others who remained behind to start a new life. How many of them left with the intention to settle permanently in the country of destination is not known and so they did not leave their own story. They were going away to a far-off land from where it was difficult to communicate. That is why these migrants were addressed as *bidesia* which meant those who had become foreigners. The migration of indentured labourers from the Bhojpuri region started in the year 1834 and the Bidesia folk culture also seems to have developed around this time since the word 'bidesia' for migrant labourers in Bhojpuri folk songs started being used after the phenomenon began.

Today Bidesia folk culture has come to imply a holistic folklore tradition revolving around the theme of departure and separation and also includes other folk forms like *biraha (birha), kajari, jantsar, barahmasi* and so on. These particular folk songs originated in the pre-colonial period since migration from this region took place even before that time, causing the same *bhav* both in the migrants and in their family members, especially women who were left behind, as in the colonial and in the contemporary period (Deva, 1989: 236) .

In the colonial period when the European colonial countries like the United Kingdom, France and the Netherlands were extending their domain across the globe transforming regions into their colonies, they set up a large number of sugar, coffee, cocoa, jute and other plantations in some of the Caribbean countries like Suriname, Fiji, Mauritius, Guyana, and Trinidad. These plantations, which were owned and overseen by Europeans from the colonial countries needed labourers to work on them. During the first decade of the nineteenth century, the entire Bhojpuri region had emerged as a cane tract area and a very strong centre for sugar plantation and production of molasses (*gur*), *raab* (*liquid form of gur, syrup*). In the entire region cane fields, *kolhu, tawa* and *chulha* to cook ground cane were visible. The labourers engaged in cane cultivation and *gur-raab* production were highly trained and skilful. That is why the Bhojpuri region had become a big labour market where one could get labourers skilled in sugar plantation.

There is an entire folk culture and ritual system around the cultivation of cane, which is still alive and thriving among the local people. Bihar and Gorakhpur had also become important centres for sugar plantations and sugar manufacture in northern India during 1830-50, catering to the big boom in sugar exports from eastern India to London via Calcutta (Amin, 1984: 27).

This boom led to the flourishing of contractors or middlemen who functioned in the sugar plantations and sugar mills in the Gorakhpur region. The sugar mills required a large amount of raw materials and also labour to work in them. The middlemen were used for recruiting labour from the villages and also buy *gur* (molasses) from the cultivators growing sugar cane. Due to the presence of a large number of mills, owned by both Indians and colonial masters, there was strong competition to recruit labour and buy *gur* at the lowest possible price. These middlemen who worked for the sugar plantations were known as *arkatias* in the entire Bhojpuri region in the early nineteenth century (ibid.: 85, 139).

After the abolition of slavery in the British colonies the Bhojpuri region of India that includes parts of Uttar Pradesh and Bihar was viewed by the British colonial government as a potential source of cheap labour. This was met by the development of a system of indentured labour from population-rich regions of India, especially from the Bhojpuri region, where the peasants were skilled in sugar production.

Emigration from the Bhojpuri region to Mauritius started in 1834, to Guyana in 1838 and in 1845 to the other British Caribbean colonies. The number of migrants in the different colonies varied. Mauritius received more than 453,000 immigrants, followed by Guyana (238,900), Natal (152,184), Trinidad (143,930), Fiji (60,965), Jamaica (36,400) and Suriname (34,300) (see Figure 2.1). The other British West Indian islands received smaller numbers

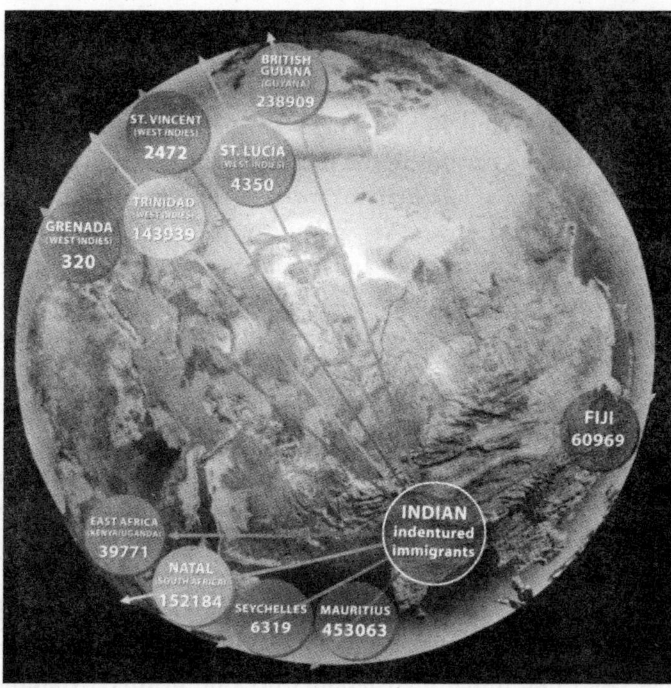

Source: Bidesia Gallery, G.B. Pant Social Science Institute, Allahabad.

Figure 2.1: Map on Indian Diaspora

(Lal, 2006: 75; Roopnarine, 2007: 6). Most of the indentured labourers were introduced in countries where there was enough fertile soil available to cultivate to crops (Engerman, 1986: 225). They were pushed out from the Bhojpuri region to these colonies in the aftermath of the 1857 revolution that had drained the region of all its resources, leaving the maximum population in poverty and misery (Buckland, 1863: 765-6). The frequent famines and droughts affecting the region also brought abject scarcity and destitution in their wake and left the entire region reeling under acute unemployment and penury. After the first Indian war of Independence, peasants were being made to pay rent in cash rather than kind. There was also a decline of the indigenous handicraft industry because of competition from British products (Lal, 1980: 61). The resulting economic hardships affected everyone, but the lower caste tenants and labourers suffered the most (ibid.: 62; Roopnarine, 2003). A main 'coolie depot' was opened in Calcutta and many sub-depots were scattered throughout north India located in key centres such as Allahabad, Kanpur, Lucknow, Faizabad, Benaras, Ghazipur and Buxar. These sub-depots were run by the sub-agents. The key persons in the migration story were the *arkatiyas* or recruiters of Indian labourers to work in the sugar plantations of Suriname, Mauritius and other European colonies. The *arkatiyas* were the direct recruiters of Indian labourers who had a wide network in the villages and *kasbas* of north India and operated during feasts, open-air traditional shows, pilgrimages where a large number of people gathered looking for employment. Thus, under an agreement between the British government and the governments of France (1860) and the Netherlands (1870), the period between the late nineteenth century and the early twentieth centuries saw huge populations of Indians, who were mostly Bhojpuris but who also included people from the Braj, Awadh and the Magahi regions of Bihar and Uttar Pradesh, being sent to work in overseas plantations as indentured labourers for a period of five years. Later when India got Independence and made many laws for the protection of labours, cases like indentured labours became history (Majumder, 2008: 5-8).

The sense of 'disappearance' which occurred during the indentured period, due to lack of awareness among the affected people about their destinations, was the chief reason for the strong emotional base of this kind of migration. They understood that people were going to Calcutta but found it difficult to comprehend fully where they were going from there.

EXPERIENCE OF TOTARAM SANADHYA (FIJI)

Totaram Sanadhya, who migrated to Fiji as indentured labour and lived there for twenty-one years, published his story after his return to India in 1914 in 'My Twenty-one Years in the Fiji Islands'. He was born in Hirangau in Firozabad in 1876. After the death of his father his elder brother left home to work in Calcutta, but the family remained poor, notwithstanding the remittances they received from Calcutta. In 1893, Sanadhya left for Allahabad in search of work. After a few months when he still was unable to find a job, he thought of returning home, but did not do so as he was wary of being a burden on his mother. Here is his story about his recruitment (Hassankhan, 2013: 12-13).

> One day when I was in a market near the kotwali (police station), engaged in worrying about finances, a man I didn't know came up to me and asked, 'Do you want employment?' I said 'Yes'. Then he said, 'Good I can get you a very good job. It's the sort of work which will make your heart joyful'. To this I said, 'I will work but I won't be able to work for more than six months or a year'. He said, 'Good! You should come. When you wish, then quit working. Nothing will happen. Come, you should visit Jaganathji'. 'My mind was not mature. On these words I came along! Deceived in this way, high class Indians come and bear hardships for their whole lives'.

Sanadhya eventually registered in Allahabad as a Thakur, although he was a Brahmin, and was taken to Kolkata (Sanadhya, 2003: 10, 34). There, the immigration officer explained to the emigrants that they were going to Fiji for five years and that if they chose to return after ten years they were entitled to a free return passage. Further, that they would earn much more money than 12 *annas* a day. Sanadhya was ultimately taken to Fiji. He contends, however, that he never had done field work before, did not want to go to Fiji, was taken away and isolated from the other emigrants until he was forced to agree to go to Fiji (Sanadhya, 2003: 37-8).

Some knew that their loved ones had gone to Suriname, as is evident from the letters that did not reach their destinations and were intercepted by the postal department, and have been preserved in the Suriname National Archive, Paramaribo. Similar letters were sent to other colonies. These letters reveal the depth of emotional pain within migrants and their loved ones back home.

A letter by Shiv Mangal of Asauli village, district Ahmadpur in district Rae Barelli of Uttar Pradesh, to his brother Bajrangbali

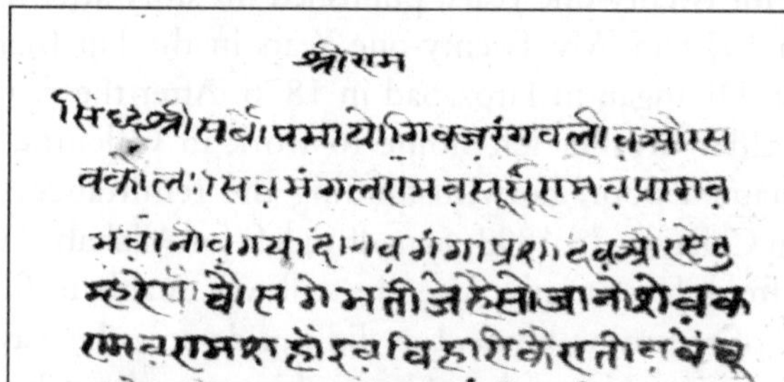

Figure 2.2: Part of a letter to a migrant in Suriname urging him to return[1]

[1] This letter is a part of an original in the National Archives of Suriname (NAS), provided by Maurits Hassankhan who found it in 2009 in the archives of the Immigration Department, Suriname, Correspondence 1902, when he was doing research on Resistance of Indentured Labourers in Suriname. I thank him for making this letter available for my article.

who was working at Sarmacca plantation in Suriname, strikingly brings out the emotional pain resulting from separation.

Greetings to Siddh Sri Sarvoprasayog Bajrangbali from Shivmangal Ram, Suryaram, Bhavani, Gayadin, Gangaprasad and your five nephews and Sevakram, Ramsahai, Bihari, Kairati, Benchu, Chhedi, Mandas, Chandi, Seetal and Bhikhari. May all their 'Ram Ram' (a form of greeting used in rural areas of UP) reach you. Further we are well and we are happy to hear that you are also well. The further news is that please know that we have received Rs. 48 in the month of Kartik. And your mother and sister-in-law and your woman (wife) and your five nephews are all well. You asked about the cultivation so please know that we have a farming of two oxen. By God's grace everything is going well. It is the desire of all of us in the house that you return home. Your mother thinks about you day and night which you should come and see. And we have received the letter which you had sent and have informed about the reply of each person. I don't know whether you will receive it or not.[2]

This letter makes several things clear. Bajrangbali left his wife behind when he emigrated to Suriname. The entire family seems to be missing him and strongly urges him to return.

To Bhojpuri people, mass indentured migration was a heavy emotional loss as many tender relationships were torn apart – wives from husbands, sisters from brothers, children from ageing parents. In the emerging folk tradition, the question underlying all songs was *kahegaile bides* (why did you go overseas?). For various reasons, few indentured ever returned. This is why these migrants were addressed as 'bidesia', that is, those who had become foreigners. Since very little folk tradition is written and published, it is difficult to fix the exact time period when it emerged, but in 1858 a prostitute named Sundari, who came to Benaras from Delhi, used the word 'bides' as a form of address. Pandit Beni Madhav Ram, a resident of Kashi, composed a folk song which was published in

[2] The digitized copy of this letter has been made available to us by the kind cooperation of Maurits Hassankhan, who has done extensive research on the experiences of indentured labourers in Suriname. The original is in the archives of the Immigration Department in Suriname and according to Hassankhan it is between other correspondence. The digitized copy is available in the Documentation Centre of the Bidesia Project at G.B. Pant Institute in Allahabad and in the private collection of Hassankhan (Suriname).

1884 in which the word 'bidesia' was used to address a person who had gone away (Narayan, 2005: 62)

Kahe mori sudhi bisaraye re bidesia
Tarhpi tarhpi din rain gavayo re
Kahe mo se nehiya lagae re bidesia.

(Why did you make me lose my consciousness, O Bidesia?
I am suffering constantly day and night.
Why did you lock your eyes with mine, O Bidesia?)

The compositions depict the ontology of the pain of the migrants centered on separation, due mainly to the need for the money earned by migrants. Those left behind suffered as much as those who emigrated, hence the wage of migrants was the family wage. The wives left behind suffered many hardships since they were likely to be ill-treated (regarded as 'widows') and acquiring the necessities of life may be a struggle, especially when husbands did not send remittances. In the joint family system, a woman expected support from the brothers of her husband and other members of the family, but prolonged absence often put too much strain on the system.

A touching *Jantsar* (grinding mill) song is:

I cooked puris for every body
but that food became poison
as the prince went away to a foreign land (bides).
My mother-in-law asked me 'on whose earnings will you live?'
My mother-in-law's offspring is Lakhan devar,
I shall live upon his earnings.
'I have a married woman myself', the devar said.

Thus, the woman is told bluntly by her husband's younger brother (*devar*) that he is unable to support her. Later, in the same song, it emerges that more and more people refuse to help her on one pretext or the other. Her brother's wife (*bhaujai*) plainly tells her: 'O *Nand*, the loaf that I might give you, will be eaten by my children' (Narayan, 2005: 73-4).

During the colonial period Kolkata was the most important departure point for migrants going overseas. Not only did the pain of separation haunt these women, but also the fear of adultery by the husbands. A man who stayed away for a long time was likely to develop relations with some other woman. Many woman songs express this apprehension and warn men to be careful not to fall prey to the machinations of the women of Calcutta, which was the port from where the migrants sailed.

This fear psychosis syndrome of co-wife usually recurs in the Bhojpuri folklore:

Wheat was sown but ankari grew
My lord laments sitting on the road
O Lord, do not lament, do not, kill yourself lamenting
I shall exchange ankari and grind wheat
My wife, you have become thin due to grinding and pounding
If you like I shall bring a maid for you
He went for a maid, but brought a co-wife. How shall I undo
this bargain of the co-wife. (Singh, 1988: 21)

The folk songs demonstrated that the separation of human bonds is not a mere description of the loneliness of the separated ones but are also expressions of various social and cultural animosities within and without the family, like the increasing burden of the loan in the absence of the husband, the intimidation by the landlords, moneylenders and *sahukar* (shopkeepers), and the inner family conflicts in which the wife is dominated by her in-laws (Singh, 1988: 21).

In the folk psyche in the Bhojpuri region this overseas migration was sometimes perceived as a kind of imprisonment or *kalapani*, which was an island in the Andamans where Indians were imprisoned by the British as it was difficult to escape from there. The following folk song reveals this similarity:

Pal Ke Jahajua men roi-dhoipaithiho
Kaisi hoi kalapani par re videsia
Jiaradirae Ghat Kyannahi aaeho'
bita din kaibhae mas re videsia.

(Weeping and sitting in the ship with a sail,
Anxious to know the journey to the fearful place,
the heart is sinking and the mind is disturbed,
as the destination is not visible.) (Narayan, 2005: 76-9).

In all such compositions there are two implications. Firstly, the migration is a kind of punishment for engaging in anti-British activities on a large scale, and secondly, a severe punishment is inflicted on those accused of treason. Hence, migration represents a highly frightening punishment at a distant place from where there would be no news. In Bhojpuri folk consciousness there is an imagined perception that *kalapani* is located in the east. There is a belief in Bhojpuri folk consciousness that everyone who leaves their place goes to the countries of *purub* (east). In fact, Calcutta is situated in *purub*. Most of them went to Assam, Mauritius, Fiji via Calcutta. Not only is there a *kalapani* but it is also located in *purub*.[3] *Topiwala* (*arakati, dalal*) [agents of Colonial Sugar Refinery Company (CSRC)] and others used to come from the *purub* (east) and take Nagar (a wrestler of Banaras) towards *kalapani*. The ship also multiplies the degree of pain because it was used to take the loved ones to the *kalapani*. Around 1899 when the above mentioned song was composed, the ship was perceived to be an enemy by those who were left behind. The following folk song suggests this:

Purub ke desawa se aile topiwalawa, Rama
deradale sunder ke aanganawa re Hari
Bharibhari kurui sona debo topiwalawa, Rama
Nagar naiyyamat le ja kalapaniya re Hari.

(A topiwala (agent) has come from Purab, O Rama
And has planted himself in the courtyard of a beautiful woman (called Sundar).
I will give you (topiwala) a lot of gold, O Rama,
but please do not take Nagar to Kalapani, O Hari.) (Kamlesh, 1999: 99)

Apart from these Bidesia folk songs another tradition developed during this period which was part of the same genre. This was the Bidesia folk theatre tradition and the person who is believed to be the creator of this tradition is Bhikhari Thakur. Bidesia plays are a mixture of prose and poetry and are still popular in the Bhojpuri

[3] On the tea plantations of Assam there were tens of thousands of unfree labourers, who were also recruited in Bihar and UP (see, for instance, R. Behal; P. Mohapatra).

area. The entire play is filled with Bidesia songs set to folk tunes like *lorikayan, jantsari, sorthi, birha, barahmasa, poorvi, alha, pachra, nirgun, chaupai and kavita.* Bhikhari Thakur, popularly known as the 'Shakespeare of Bhojpuri', was also the first person to cast male actors in female roles wearing female clothes and other folk songs. Thakur's Bidesia theatre drew large audiences. His style became so popular that people started calling other *nautankis* Bidesia (Narayan, 2005: 84-5). The storyline of the plays were usually related to the sorrow of a young bride whose husband has been forced to leave her in the village and go to *pardes* or foreign land to look for a job. It developed in the form of Sundari sending a message through a messenger to her husband and telling the messenger to bring her husband back to the village after releasing him from the clutches of another woman in the city. The entire story develops in such a fashion that even the most stonehearted person will feel like crying. Bidesia theatres were, however, not only the story of grieving young women, but also narrated the feelings of young men who returned to their village after roaming hither and thither in the city looking for work. The plays were based on the *nautanki* style and all characters, from the king to the yogi, sang and danced on the stage. The characters of the Bidesia theatre entered the stage singing, and then started dancing to the beats of the musical instrument *duggi.* Apart from these other musical instruments like *dholak, sarangi, harmonium, jhaal, kartal* and *jori* were also used. There were no curtains or stage and the plays were usually enacted on benches inside tents or in the open on wooden planks covered with a *durrie.* The Bidesia theatres drew huge audiences when enacted by Bhikhari Thakur and his party and because of them Bhikhari, called Bhikhariya by the common folk, became known to millions of people. Alongside other theatre companies also started enacting Bidesia theatre (Dwivedi, 2000: 25).

Thus from the folk genre which developed in the Bhojpuri region at the time when the indentured migration system was prevailing it is evident that the going away of the migrants caused a heavy emotional loss which was the basis of the *bidesia bhav* that pervades the entire region even today.

CONTEMPORARY MIGRATION

Migration is a dominant phenomenon within the country (*Pardesia*) even in contemporary times. A large number of labourers (unskilled workers in factories or as farm labourers) migrate from Awadhi and Bhojpuri regions to cities like Kolkata, Mumbai, Delhi, Noida, Gurgoan or as farm labourers to Punjab. These poor people leave their homelands and go to different destinations to earn money. During the colonial period Kolkata was the most important destination for migrants from where they were shipped overseas. Today Punjab has emerged as the single largest destination for migrants from Bihar and UP. Apart from Punjab, some labourers also migrate to Delhi, Kolkata, Assam, Mumbai, Surat and other big cities in India. In Punjab there is a tremendous demand for labourers to work in the big farms in rural areas and in the factories in cities like Ludhiana, Amritsar, and Jalandhar. Women again are the worst sufferers. This pain and suffering is still being experienced by the migrants of this region who are migrating in the present period to places like Delhi, Mumbai, Kolkata, and Surat. The oral tradition and cultural heritage that emerged in the colonial period as an outcome of the heavy emotional loss and were handed down over generations, are still being used as coping mechanisms to cope with the pain and suffering that the present-day migrants and their family members experience (*Bidesia National Report* 2005: 236-7).

TYPES OF INTERNAL MIGRATION IN INDIA

Labor migration flows include permanent, semi-permanent, and seasonal or circular migrants. Much of the available data polls migrants in the permanent and semi-permanent categories, and considerably less large-scale statistical data are available on the numbers and characteristics of circular migrants.

Semi-permanent migrants are those who are likely to have precarious jobs in their destination areas, or lack the resources to make a permanent move. While they may reside in their destination cities for years or decades, they likely have homes and families in their sending district.

Seasonal or circular migrants, by contrast, are likely to move from place to place in search of employment, or continue returning to the same place year after year. Such circular flows encompass migrants who may stay at their destination for six months or more at a time and hence need social services at their destination. Scholars have long characterized this migration as a type in which the permanent residence of a person remains the same, but the location of his or her economic activity changes.

Many of the women who migrate for marriage are also participants in the labor market, even if their primary reason for migration is marriage. The domestic maid industry in urban areas, for example, is a rapidly growing sector that employs women, most of whom are rural-to-urban migrants.

Source: Rameez Abbas and Divya Varma, 2014.

The north Indian states of Uttar Pradesh and Bihar have the highest percentages of rural populations, with 18.6 and 11.1 per cent of people living in villages, respectively, as per the 2011 census. These states are also the largest migrant-sending states. Substantial flows of labour migrants relocate from Uttar Pradesh to Maharashtra, Delhi, West Bengal, Haryana, Gujarat, and other states across northern and central India.

The cities of Mumbai, Delhi, and Kolkata are the largest destinations for internal migrants in India. Many of the migrants to these cities are intrastate migrants relocating from rural areas of Maharashtra and West Bengal. All three cities also absorb large numbers of people from other states across India (Abbas and Varma, 2014).

The expression of pain, sufferings and separation present in this *bidesia bhav* were expressed through folk forms like *biraha, kajari, jantsar, barahmasi* and other folk songs. Separation and waiting are the keynotes of *bidesia* emotionality since there was always a distant and remote hope that the loved one might return. The migrants in the destinations too constantly felt that only 'half the self' was living as the other half had been left behind in their homelands. Though it helped them stay rooted to their traditions, the sense of loss and the search for the other half always loomed large. The uprooting was so unsettling that internally they often felt that they had been exiled. Their destinations were their encampments, but their home was where their people were. This feeling meant that psychologically they felt rooted in their homelands where the 'other

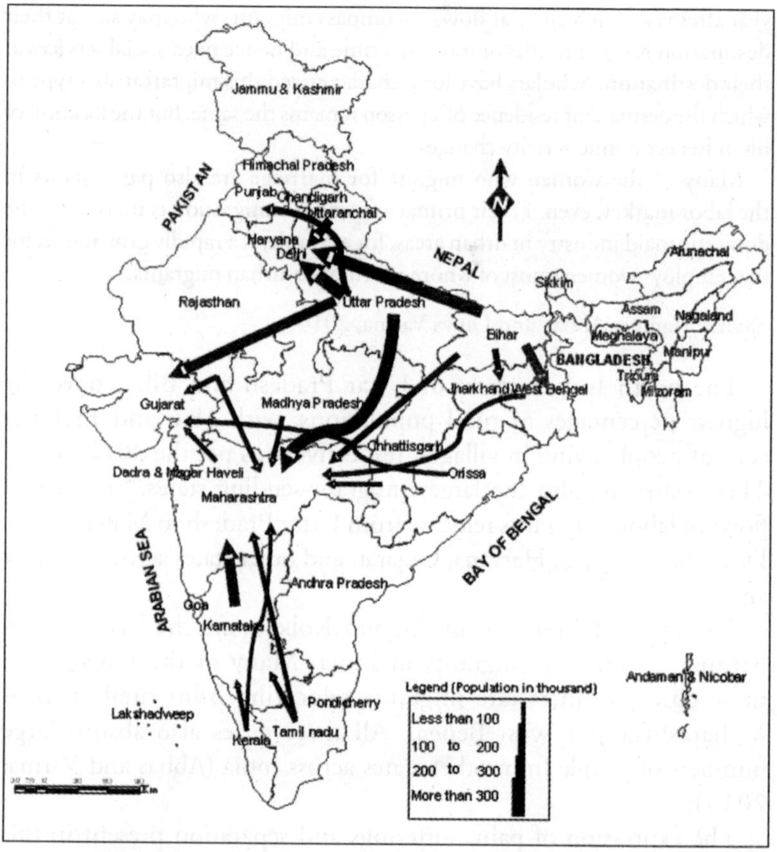

Source: R.B. Bhagat and S. Mohanty (2009). 'Emerging Pattern of Urbanization and the Contribution of Migration in Urban Growth in India', *Asian Population Studies*, vol. 5, no. 1: 5-20.

Figure 2.3: Major Net Internal Migration Flows in India, 2001.

half' still was. This grief, pain and anguish which erupted in the hearts of those left behind in the homelands as well as the migrants is can be termed as the *bidesia bhav* (emotionality). This grief at the separation was expressed in various forms in the daily lives of the migrants at their destinations like their lifestyle, rituals, religious practices, language, and also their cultural expressions like folk songs, which enabled them to hold on to memories of their homeland and also imagine a homeland in their destinations. In the

Bhojpuri region the cultural productions that were composed as an expression of the grief at the separation of the migrants led to the emergence of a distinct folk culture which was given the name Bidesia folk culture (Upadhyaya, 1989: 3). In the destinations the cultural productions of the migrants in the form of songs, poems and literary compositions including autobiographies reveal the underlying grief at leaving behind their homeland and loved ones.

The wrath of a young wife and her agony is stark in the following song. Her aching heart cries for her husband, her lover and man, whom money (read better prospects and livelihood) has snatched away. Interestingly, this young wife's heart-rending call is not a one-off case. It depicts a deeper malaise of mass migration of working men to distant lands (*bides*), as depicted in this song of separation and longing.

Railiya bairan more piyake le jai
Jone sahariya mein piya more naukar
Agiya lage sahar jarijae re
Jone sahib wake piya more naukar
Naagin dase sahib mari jaere
Jone tikatwa se piya more jai hain
Pani pare tikat galijaere
Railiyana bairi se jahajwana bairi se paisawa bairina
mor saiyanke bilmawe se paiswa bairina

(Sung by Maya Singh, village Barwaripur,
district Sultanpur, age 30, on 5 June 2005)[4]

My foe is the train that snatched my husband
To a city where he works,
Let that city burn to ashes.
May snake sting the sahib*
For whom my man works.
Let the train-ticket get soaked and perich in water
It takes my lover away from me.
The train and the ship that snatched my lover aren't my foe
My foe is money that lured and stole my man.
(*Note*: * The 'big man' or the employer)

[4] Interview of Maya Singh by Nivedita Singh, 5 June 2005.

If we analyse Bidesia, we will find that it is both a *bhav* and a folk cultural tradition of the Bhojpuri region (UP and Bihar), that has evolved around the agony of migration. We are using it as a metaphor which encompasses many other similar folk forms on migration like Bidesia *nach* (folk theatre tradition), and folk songs within its fold (Singh, 1955: 216). It also includes motifs and wall paintings which depict a parrot with a letter in its beak, to showcase the theme of migration. And there are several folk stories and folk deities that have evolved around migration in this region, where women left behind used to pray for the well-being of their loved ones who left them. Thus, it represents an inclusive repertoire of cultural legacy. These oral traditions depict the agony of separation, which is still alive in the folk memory and popular culture of Bhojpuri people.

The rich folk tradition, Bidesia, is not static, but constantly evolving. The agony of separation gave rise to a new folk form. When the migrants return to their homelands, they bring new experiences and sensibilities with them, which are then woven into the folk tradition, thereby completing the cycle. The cultural tradition helps those left behind in the homelands, as well as the migrants during their journey to, and stay, in the distant lands. By singing these songs the migrants and those in the homeland purge themselves of the pain of separation and continue with the mundane drudgery of everyday life. Bidesia is used both as a metaphor of the distance and separation as well as a folk repertoire. These folk forms are élan vital of the migrants and those left behind, as it helps them survive, sustain and adjust to the pressures of everyday life. Bidesia that is constantly evolving undergoes a process of change – older forms decay and die and are replaced by newer forms of interpolations (Narayan, 2005: 42-3).

It is a truism that migrants all over the world take with them their cultural baggage which includes songs, stories, art, paintings and so on when they leave their homelands. This cultural repertoire helps the migrants and women left behind to purge themselves of the pain of separation and continue with the mundane drudgery of everyday life in their destination points. This holds true for Bhojpuri migrants (also called *pardesis* in the local language) too, who leave their native villages to work in far-off places and return for a short visit every year. While it is their economic need which drives them out from their native lands it is their culture which helps them to be emotionally connected and rooted to their homeland. After a hard day's gruelling labour when they get together in their slums or ghettoes and sing songs they are able to mitigate some of the pain at separating from their native villages and loved ones. To the people who are left behind in the homeland too, like the wives, children, parents and siblings, this cultural repertoire provides solace and helps them to surmount the pain and anguish at the going away of their loved one.

Geeta Nishad

In the Bidesia project we have interviewed a number of people in the Bhojpuri area. In the following section we will present two narratives as examples of the *bidesia bhav.*

NARRATIVE 1
GEETA NISHAD, VILLAGE BARWARIPUR[5]

My name is Geeta Nishad and I live in Barwaripur village. I have five children and my husband is a migrant who goes for eight months every year to Mumbai to work as a fisherman. I came to this village nearly 15 years ago after my marriage, with dreams in my heart like every new bride has. My new family was very small. There was only my father-in-law, my mother-in-law, my brother-in-law and my sister-in-law, apart from the two of us. The day-to-day needs of our family were somehow being fulfilled. My father-in-law did not own any land but sustained the family by doing small-time menial labour work wherever he could find it in the village. There was only one earning member and five stomachs to fill. How long could this situation continue? Nearly every day there used to be quarrels between my husband and his father. My husband wanted to leave the village to search for work but my father-in-law wanted him to work inside the village. My husband felt that working in the village meant losing his honour since he would be working as someone's servant. Besides the work should be such that he could get a good amount of money in return for his hard labour. In the village there was no scope of work except working in the fields of the

[5] Interview of Geeta Nishad by Nivedita Singh, 12 May 2005.

Thakurs. The daily wage rate in the village was very low and in addition he would also have to suffer the ill-treatment of the Thakurs. All these considerations made my husband decide against working in the village.

These constant quarrels made me very anxious about the future. I could not get rid of the haunting fear that I would soon be separated from my husband. At that time many women of our community told me that their husbands were leaving the village for *pardes* in search of jobs. Finally what I was scared about happened. I heard the news from people that my husband was leaving for Mumbai along with other men of the village. I also understood that they would have to stay there for eight months at a stretch. The *malik* stopped work for four months when the labourers were given leave to go home.

The very thought of separating from my husband made my blood run cold. All kinds of things kept running through my mind. I used to make up all kinds of excuses to prevent him from going. But there was no way to stop him. To make him understand my feelings better I sang the following song to him:

Piya mat jaa bideshwa rahab kaise
Piya mat jaa bideshwa rahab kaise
Sasura ke batiya to sahi sun lebe
Sasura ke batiya to sahi sun lebe
Saas ke boliya sahib kaise
Piya mat jaa bideshwa rahab kaise
Piya mat jaa bideshwa rahab kaise
Dewra ke batiya to sahi sun lebe
Dewra ke batiya to sahi sunlebe
Nanadiya ke boliya sahib kaise
Piya mat jaa bideshwa rahab kaise
Piya mat jaa bideshwa rahab kaise

O my husband don't go to *bides*, how will I live
O my husband don't go to *bides*, how will I live
My father-in-law's words I can stand
My father-in-law's words I can stand
But my mother-in-law's words how will I stand?
O my husband don't go to *bides* how will I live.
My brother-in-law's words I can stand
My brother-in-law's words I can stand
But my sister-in-law's words how will I stand?
O my husband don't go to *bides* how will I live?
O my husband don't go to *bides* how will I live?

Geeta lamented that her pathos ridden song did not have any effect on her husband. She continued, 'The need of the house and the family members was money which could be met only by leaving the village. The preparations for his departure began in early Magh (January). Soon the time came for him to leave.

Without enough words to express her difficulties, Geeta sang another folksong narrating the hardships which a migrant's wife has to face in different seasons:

My sorrow, my pain and my sufferings
without my husband cannot be expressed in words.
My husband also did not think of my feelings
since he did not bother to send me even a single letter
in all the eight months he was away,
which I could read and console myself.
At night I used to lie tossing and turning in my bed,
praying to God for my husband's well-being
and to send him back to me soon.
I understood that it was essential for him to leave
me and the village to earn money
but my heart refused to be pacified.

Somehow the eight months passed and soon it was time for him to return. One by one the men of the village who had also gone to Mumbai started returning. From these men I understood that my husband too would be coming back soon. The village had already started getting a festive look with each household from where men had gone to *pardes* brimming with laughter and joy. All the women who had been waiting eagerly for their husbands felt their patience had been justified. Each one's husband had brought new clothes and gifts for them and their children, which they proudly showed to the other women. My husband was one of the last to return and I waited impatiently for him to come back.

Soon one day my impatientce ended. It was time for my husband to arrive. I got up early in the morning to clean the house with cow dung. Then I took my bath and started preparing different kinds of food items to welcome my husband. I then wore a bright saree, put on whatever little ornaments I had and waited for him.

The first time my husband had brought back Rs. 8,000 as savings from his earnings in Mumbai. He had also brought new clothes for everyone in the house and a saree and a pair of earrings for me. The entire money was spent in buying cereals, pulses to last the whole year, repairing the house, buying a few extra sets of clothes for the family, and repaying some of the outstanding debts which I had accumulated when I was short of money. My husband spent the first month after his return in eating, sleeping, relaxing and doing odd jobs in the house. The next three months he spent in working as a daily labourer in the village to earn some money for the house. Somehow the four months went off and soon it was time for him to leave again for Mumbai. Last time when he went I was a new bride and did not have the courage to talk to him freely. This time I broke my earlier shyness and made him promise that he would write to me.

Now his arrival and departure has become a routine thing in my life. But now in addition to worrying about my husband's living in *pardes*, I also have to worry about the upbringing of my children single-handedly with no one to share the trials and tribulations of their growing up. Earlier when my family was small the savings which my husband brought back from Mumbai seemed a large amount. But now that we have a large family to support this amount is barely adequate. Another thing that has affected us adversely is that now the competition for work with the contractor in Mumbai has greatly increased. More and more people from our village and other adjoining villages are desperately seeking work there. Since the supply of workers is greatly exceeding the demand, the contractors have decreased the contract amount. For the last few years my husband is being paid only Rs. 5,000 as the contract amount for eight months, out of which he is able to save only Rs. 3,500.[6] This amount is too small to sustain such a large family for the whole year. So I have to supplement it by twining more and more ropes to sell in the market.

One thing that is helping to comfort me is that with the spread of communication technology in villages, I am in direct touch with my husband over the phone. On the last day of every month he rings up at a fixed time at the *bania's* (grocer) shop where I wait to receive his phone call. I now feel less distant from him since I can hear his voice and we can share each other's problems. The distance from our village to *pardes* now does not seem so far any more. Letters do not serve the same purpose since they take a long time to reach and often get lost in transit. Also the news becomes stale by the time it reaches its destination. I sing Bidesia songs in the absence of my husband which helps me to express my emotions and this outburst of emotions helps me fight against the destitution.

The departure of the migrants, who were referred to as *bidesia*, caused an emotional vacuum both in the homelands and destinations, as mentioned in the aforementioned narrative, which resulted in the emergence of the *bidesia bhav* (emotionality). This emotionality could be said to be the outcome of the fact that the migrants were

[6] These are the amounts given by Geeta Nishad. They earn money below the market value because they do not know the correct amount of market value. Therefore labour exploitations are still prevalent in some rural areas.

often thought to have been unfaithful to their homeland by leaving it, somewhat like traitors, even though the migration was involuntary and beyond their control. As Ranajit Guha (1995) says, the migrant as a diasporan is almost like an apostate, since the breaking of ties with the home as the guardian and propagator of values associated with parenthood to the extent of investing the latter with sanctity akin to religiosity, makes the desertion amount to transgression. The *bhav* (emotionality) that arises within the migrants as diasporans in their destinations is reflected in their analytical criticality of their everyday life, both in the diaspora and in their homeland. The *bidesia bhav* also works as an antidote for the negative colonial memories which erupt in their everyday lives despite enjoying all the benefits of living in the country of the colonizer.

Anara

This whole folk genre was a device to help women left behind to come out of their pain and agony even in cases of internal migration.

Another woman of village Barwaripur is Anara whose husband Om Prakash has been away working in different places for many years. She narrated the story of her trials and tribulations and her joy and sorrows in the following words

NARRATIVE 2
ANARA, BARWARIPUR[7]

My natal house is in Jaunpur. I got married at a very early age and my *gauna* (ceremony which takes place after the bride attains puberty when she is sent off to her husband's house) took place after nine years. In those nine years I had no conversation with my husband but after going to his house we used to take each other's *haal-khabar* (asking after one's wellbeing). A few months after my *gauna* my husband went to *pardes.* At that time I was in my natal home. A few months later he came to visit me. At my parent's house I could not talk much with him so could not request him not to go but next time when he returned I was at my in-law's house. Then I begged him not to go by telling him that we will manage on whatever little we have here but my husband did not heed my words. Now he has been living away for the last 17 or 18 years and I have become used to his absence.

[7] Interview of Anara by Nivedita Singh, 13 May 2005.

It is difficult to narrate in a few words the condition of a woman whose husband is away. My heart felt that it would burst the first time that he went. The first few days I consoled myself by chanting in my mind over and over again that he has gone to *pardes* because he needs to earn money. He has a large extended family to support. He could not have managed by living in the village, so he had to go. By repeating these lines to myself I gradually overcame my sorrow. The next time when he came I requested him to take me with him. Since I had no children then he took me to Assam, Kanpur, Delhi, etc., wherever he found work. Now that we have children it is not possible for him to take all of us with him.

Earlier there was no facility for telephoning so I could not communicate with him. Being illiterate I could not write myself, neither could I ask someone else to write them for me since I was afraid they would fall into the hands of the elders of my house. Sometimes when he wrote letters in Inland letters, I used to get them read by my younger sister-in-law. I used to also ask her to write my '*haal-khabar*' and that of the children. Sometimes I used to ask her to write *Dohas* (couplets) or *sher-o-shairi* (love poems in Urdu). I would send them through the hands of a very reliable courier without the knowledge of my own parents or his parents. Now he rings up once in a while so we can take each other's *haal-khabar* directly.

My husband works as a welder in Delhi. He joins scooter parts, makes nets, etc. Here we have around one *bigha* land (around 1600 square metres) which is too small to sustain our big family. Only a small amount of cereals and vegetables grow in it. There is no work available in our village to supplement the output from the land. My husband's earnings from his stay in *pardes* helps us to fulfil our requirements. In my spare time I weave baskets to fill my loneliness. Sometimes when my sisters-in-law (*nanad*) come over for a visit we discuss our husbands and share our joys and sorrows.

When my husband comes he usually stays for around 15 days. Sometimes he even stays for two months at a stretch. I have become very superstitious about my husband since his departure. There are many superstitions which the people of this village believe in and which I too have started believing. It is believed that when a bird called '*shuklain*' calls, the husband will come bearing money and gifts. When a green spider climbs up one's left shoulder then the husband will bring items for make-up (*shauk-shringaar ke samaan*). A black spider does not specify anything special. If a woman's left palm itches it is a good omen. If a woman dreams of small fish or of a snake striking someone, it is a good sign. All the women of this village whose husbands are away take these dreams and superstitions very seriously since they are all worried about the well-being of their men and would like them to return soon bearing gifts for them.

In the absence of my husband I feel very lonely. All the worries of my house are on my shoulders. To escape from these anxieties I sing Bidesia songs and dance with the other women of the *basti* (neighbourhood).

CONCLUSION

Migration is undoubtedly an economic activity, as no one leaves home and hearth without the promise of a better livelihood. It is wrong to divorce economics from culture as Bidesia is woven around the social displacement that is caused by economic necessity. A two-way process is observed: firstly, culture develops and is often shaped around economic activity, triggered by the necessity of migration. And secondly, economic activities also get a fillip from the cultural repertoire, as migrant labourers carry on with the drudgery of everyday life with the help of these cultural forms.

Traditionally economic activities and culture are watertight compartments, where these two are distinct and distanced from each other. However, the study of Bidesia establishes a link between economic activities and culture, which is a paradigm shift in this project. We find that economics, sociology, politics, literature and culture are woven closely and intertwined like small strands of strings that twirl around each other to make a strong rope.

The departure of the migrant causes untold agony, both to the persons who are left behind and to those who are willy-nilly leaving their homeland either for distant shores or far-away cities. The 'journey without' – in spatial time or the actual travel away from home and hearth – causes the people affected by it to search for answers within their selves. It is another kind of a travel – a 'journey within'. The resultant schism finds expression in the literary form Bidesia. It was, and is, a distinct folk culture in the Bhojpuri region.

List of Interviews

1. Maya Singh: Maya Singh (30 years) lives in the village Barwaripur, district Sultanpur. Her husband's name is Lalji. He has been living in Meerut for the last seventeen years. Interview of Maya Singh by Nivedita Singh, 5 June 2005.

2. Geeta Nishad: Geeta Nishad (28 years) lives in the Nishad hamlet in village Barwaripur, Dt. Sultanpur. Her husband's name is Ram Saran. He has been living in Mumbai for the last ten years. Geeta looks much older than her actual age. She is dark-skinned and short in stature. She is happy and cheerful and has an extroverted personality. Interview of Geeta Nishad by Nivedita Singh, 12 May 2005.
3. Anara Devi: Anara Devi (34 years) lives in the Chamar hamlet in village Barwaripur, district Sultanpur. Her husband's name is Om Prakash. He has been living in Delhi for the last twelve years. Anara is short and stout and has a cheerful, outgoing nature. She is a good singer of Bidesia songs, which she sang before the Bidesia team without any inhibitions. Interview of Anara by Nivedita Singh, 13 May 2005.

Archival Sources

- Bihar State Archives
- Uttar Pradesh State Archives
- Bidesia Project Collection, Interviews, Audio, Video CDS, (GBPSSI, Allahabad)

GLOSSARY

Biraha	*Biraha* songs are based on the theme of painful separation of the beloved from her lover.
Kajari	*Kajari*, is a genre of semi-classical singing, it describes the longing of a maiden for her lover as the black monsoon cloud come rolling in the summer skies.
Jantsar	*Jantsar* songs, sung while women are at the 'Chhakki' (flour grinding stone), describe their deepest sorrows or desires.
Barahmasi	*Barahmasi* is the song of the twelve months of the year. These are simple rustic songs describing the cycle and moods of the seasons.
Kala pani	The 'black sea' which had to be crossed in order to be brought to the Andaman's.
Kolhu	Oil mill
Chulha	Stove

REFERENCES

Abbas, Rameez and Divya Varma (2014). 'Internal Labor Migration in India Raises Integration Challenges for Migrants', http://www.migrationpolicy.org/article), accessed on 3 March 2014.

Amin, S. (1984). *Sugarcane and Sugar in Gorakhpur: An Enquiry into Peasant Production for Capitalist Enterprise in Colonial India*, New Delhi: Oxford University Press.

Arun, Neerja (2010). *Summarising History of Indian Diaspora*, Ahmedabad: Ashok Prakashan.

Bhagat, R.B. and S. Mohanty (2009). 'Emerging Pattern of Urbanization and the Contribution of Migration in Urban Growth in India', *Asian Population Studies*, vol. 5, no. 1: 5-20.

Bose, P.S. (2009). 'Home and Away: Diasporas, Developments and Displacements in a Globalising World', in W. Safran, A.K. Sahu and Brij V. Lal (eds.), *Transnational Migrations: The Indian Diaspora*, London, Routledge, pp. 136-63.

Buckland, C.E. (1863). *Bengal Under Leiutenant Governors*, Delhi.

Deshpande, Sudha, (1983). *Migration to Bombay: Problems and Policies*, Bombay: C.P. Prakasan.

Deva, Indra (1989). *Folk Culture and Peasant Society In India*, Jaipur: Rawat.

Dwivedi, B.P. (2000). *Bhikhari Thakur*, Allahabad.

Engarman, Stanlay L. (1986). 'Economic Change and Contract Labour in the British Caribbean: The End of Slavery and Adjustment to Emancipation' in David Richardson (ed.), *Abolition and its Aftermath: The Historical Context*, London: Routledge, 1986, pp. 225-44.

Gopal, S. and Hetukar Jha (1983). Caste and Profession: A Case Study of Rural Bihar in the First Decade of the Twentieth Century, *Man in India*, 63: 3, Ranchi.

Grierson, G.A (1885). *Bihar Peasant Life being a Discursive Catalogue of the Surroundings of the People of that Province* (rpt. 1975), Delhi: Cosmo Publications.

Guha, R. (1995). 'The Migrants Time', in P. Chatterjee, *Small Voices of History: The Collected Essays*, New Delhi: Orient Longman.

Gulati, Leela (1993). *In the Absence of Their Men: The Impact of Male Migration on Women*, New Delhi: Sage.

Hassankhan, M.S. (2013). 'Kahe Gaile Bides – Why Did You Go Overseas? An Introduction in Emotional Aspects of Migration History: A Diaspora Perspective', in Kumar Mahabir (ed.), *Caribbean Issues in the Indian Diaspora*, Delhi: Serial Publications, pp. 3 -35.

Kamata Kamlesh (1999). 'Pravasi Hindi Lokgeeton men Vedana ke Swar', *Manav,* 22: 1, Lucknow, pp. 2, 99.

de Klerk, C.J.M. (1953; 1998). *De Immigratie der Hindoestanen in Suriname.* (*The Immigration of Hindustanis in Suriname*). The Hague: Amrit.

Lal, Brij V. (1980). 'Approaches to the Study of Indian Indenture Emigration with Special References to Fiji', in the *Journal of Pacific History,* 15(1): 52-70. London: Leicester University Press.

Majumder, Mousumi (compiler and editor) (2010*). Kahegaile Bides, Why did You Go overseas?: On Bhojpuri Migration since the 1870s and Contemporary Culture in Uttar Pradesh and Bihar, Suriname and the Netherlands,* Amsterdam: KIT Publishers.

Mishra, S. (1971). *Bhojpuri Loksahitya: Sanskritik Adhyayan,* Allahabad: Hindustani Academy.

Narayan, B. (2005). *Bidesia: Migration, Change and Folk Culture,* Allahabad: NCZCC.

National Indian Report (2005). 'Bidesia: Exhibition and Research Project on the Dynamics of Migration, Social Development and Cultural Identity in the Bhojpuri Region of India, in Suriname and the Netherlands', Allahabad: GBPSSI, pp. 236-8.

Roopnarine, Lomarsh (2007). *Indo-Caribbean Indenture: Resistance and Accommodation,* Kingston: University of the West Indies Press.

Roopnarine, Lomarsh (2004). 'East Indian Indentured Emigration to the Caribbean: Beyond the Push Model' *Caribbean Studies,* vol., 31, no. 2, pp. 97-134.

Singh, Kamla (1991). *Purvanchal ke Shram Lokgeet,* Allahabad: Parimal Prakashan.

Singh, N.P. (1988). *Bhojpuri Sammelan Patrika,* Patna.

Singh, Durga Shankar Prasad (1958). *Bhojpuri Ke Kavi Aur Kavya,* Patna.

Srivastava, S. (1937). *Prayag Pradeep,* Allahabad: Hindustani Academy.

Tiwari, Badri Narayan (2012). 'Separation, Emotion and History: A Study of Bidesia Bhav in Indentured Migration', in *Man In India,* 92 (2), New Delhi: Serials Publications, pp. 281-97.

Tripathi, R. (1923). *Kavita Kaumadi, Teesra bhag,* Sultanpur: Hindi Mandir.

Upadhyay, H.S. (1989). *Bhojpuri Folk Songs from Balia,* Varanasi: Indian Enterprises.

CHAPTER 3

Tracing the Past of Hindustani Indentured Women in Suriname, 1873-1921[1]

TANYA SITARAM

INTRODUCTION

Slavery in Suriname was abolished on 1 July 1863, and as a consequence, the planters began to search for a solution to the loss of free labour. Because of the past ill-treatment, it was very unlikely that the freed slaves would continue to work on the plantations. The planters then imported indentured labourers from China, Madeira, Indonesia, and British West Indies to replace the slaves but this labour experiment turned out to be unsuccessful. The government then decided to bring British Indians, which had proven to be a huge success in the British territories. In the beginning, the supply of indentured workers was conducted through private initiative. After some problems, the government in British India demanded that the immigration of these workers be of concern to the government (Meel, 1985: 122, 124; Hassankhan, 1993). Subsequently, negotiations between the Dutch and British governments led to a treaty on 8 September 1870 (known as the Coolie Treaty), with which the recruitment of Hindustani workers for Suriname became possible. This treaty was ratified in 1872, and the purpose was to send a ship with labourers the same year to Suriname, but

[1] This article is a part of a larger research which I am doing for my Master's thesis which is a research about the Hindustani female indentured worker in Suriname during the indentured period 1873-1916.

that did not succeed. So the first vessel, *Lalla Rookh*, arrived with Hindustani immigrants on 5 June 1873, a year later than planned (Colonial Report, 1873: 13).

THEORETICAL FRAMEWORKS

The theoretical frameworks which have been used have a gender perspective. While these theoretical frameworks are important, I would like make a mind-shift and look at situations from a decolonized perspective. What Sandew Hira said during his Masterclass in Suriname in 2011, has really made me think: 'What do you see in the information, what you actually do not see? Search more behind a situation'. However, before the method of reading against the grain can be applied, it is necessary to first look at the archives and information from along the grain method. In this way one can understand the thinking of the colonial officials. I agree with Margriet Fokken (2011: 3) and Anna Stoler (2009: 50) that it is important to have a top down (along the grain) and a bottom up (against the grain) perspective about situations if you want to have a complete understanding of them.

METHODOLOGY AND RESEARCH QUESTION

As mentioned before, the method used for this study is primarily based on archival research, the study of information from archives in Suriname. So in theoretical research it is thought of as primary written source.[2] This article is descriptive-analytical so that on the basis of the information found further research can be done.

[2] We are fortunate that the archives are more accessible at present; there is much information which has not yet been used. Examples are: the archive of the Agent General for the Immigration (Immigration Department), the correspondences between the colonial officials, the various reports as well as the archive of the Governor, the Colonial Reports, the archives of the District Commissaries and the judicial archives.

RESEARCH QUESTION

There was a shortage of female Hindustani workers during the indentured period in Suriname. This imbalance had many consequences for women. Also there were many complaints by and against women. Focusing on these issues, the central questions for this article are: What were the consequences of the imbalance between men and women in the indentured period? And what kinds of complaints were logged by and against the Hindustani female indentured workers?

LITERATURE REVIEW ON INDENTURED WOMEN

It should be noted that there is a lot of interest in the history of women and female indentured workers in other countries. Scholars from the Caribbean and other areas where contract labour existed have done much research. Some of them are: Patricia Mohammed, Rhoda Reddock, Verene Shepherd, Bridget Brereton, Radica Mahase, Lomarsh Roopnarine and Aisha Khan for the Caribbean and Marina Carter for Mauritius.

In Suriname there is a lack of in-depth research on this matter. However, the discussion in the 1980s between Pieter Emmer and Rosemarijn Hoefte about the position of women in Suriname is well known. One of the issues they discussed was whether or not the arrival of indentured women from India in Suriname was a *great escape* for them with regards to their depressed socio-economic background.

In his article, Emmer (1984: 218; 1986: 250) stated that the indentured labourers (especially the women) were not victims of deception or fraud but that they rather used the indenture system to escape hunger and misery. He also highlighted the (positive) aspects of the indentured labour system, and how it was beneficial to women, namely freedom. He supported this by various arguments, some of which are: the emigration offered women the opportunity to escape hunger and misery; the contract migration offered the opportunity to increase the low income compared to the wages in India; to escape 'personal problems' which could not be resolved within the Indian society; the sad fate of unmarried women in India as well as the almost insurmountable obstacles with which divorced women and widows in India were confronted; after the indentured period two-thirds of the Indian indentured labourers decided to stay in Suriname as well as only a few women signed a second contract.

Hoefte (1987: 121-4) opposes Emmer and argues that indentured labour meant no freedom for the female indentured workers in Suriname. She argues that indenture system was twice as difficult for women and that they experienced double oppression. They had to work on the field and in the household, so they had double duty. Hoefte indicates that the wages of women were also very important for the household income. So instead of having the option of staying at home, women were 'forced' by circumstances to work on the plantations as well in an attempt 'to make ends meet'. When women came home after the fieldwork, they were saddled with the role of being a housewife and mother. They were responsible for cooking, cleaning and taking care of the children. They had to do all this work after working on the plantations in the late afternoon or in the evening. Only in cases where the partner was a very good worker and earned much could the household be kept running without the financial contribution of women. Hoefte furthermore notes that the low income of women was a reason why they could not return to India after the indentured period rather than that they did not want to go (1987: 66). It was much more difficult for the women to return to India than men. She also mentioned that fewer women signed a second contract because the planters did not want to sign a second contract with female workers. Additionally, Roekminie Debipersad (2001), Bea Lalmohamed (2001) and Sharita Rampertap (2011) have done a lot of research on Hindustani female indentured workers in Suriname using oral history. They interviewed (grand) children of the Hindustani immigrants. In this way not only the part of the archives which Emmer and Hoefte have studied can be analysed but also the other side of the story by the use of oral testimonies. The last three authors have highlighted the perspective of the women themselves.

RECRUITMENT, KIND OF WOMEN RECRUITED, GENDER RATIO AND NUMBER OF EMIGRATED WOMEN

How Did the System Operate?

Since immigration had been a government matter, the Governor advertised in the Colonial Advertisement Paper if planters needed workers. Referring to this publication the planters gave their application or their 'order' for immigrants to the Governor. The planters also guaranteed that they would pay for the cost and the partial cost of the return passage of the immigrants. Then the Governor passed orders to the Agent General (AG), who was in-charge of the immigration on behalf of Suriname. The AG wrote to his colleague the Emigration Agent in Calcutta/India to start the recruitment of the requested number of emigrants. The Emigration Agent in Calcutta was responsible for the recruitment of Hindustani labourers in British India (Coolie Treaty 1872, Article 5). According to the agenda of the AG letter no. 82 dated 29 July 1872, the Governor had published two such advertisements for the first transportation of British Indians to Suriname. He had received eight orders for a total of 647 British Indian immigrants (NAS: Archive of the AG, inv. no. 516).

It was not easy to meet the needs of the plantation managers regarding the orders for indentured labourers. There is much correspondence between the Emigration Agent and the AG about the difficulties and progress of the orders and recruitment. There were times when recruitment went very well and times when recruiting people was very difficult, especially the recruitment of female labourers. In 1893, for instance, there were many difficulties with the recruitment of females workers for Suriname. The head recruiter of Fyzabad, Abdool Hayee, wrote to the Emigration Agent on 25 July 1893 that:

> The females are not seen in many districts to be recruited for. I have 35 men and 3 women ready this time at Fyzabad . . . females scarce this time. I have sent my recruiters every side in my surrounding districts and other places to look for females, but I regret to write that I will not be able to complete the order of coolies of the 1 August. I hope you will be kind enough to give me time up to

the end of August to complete the order of women being short in my challan, otherwise I can send the whole number of my agreement without the proportion of females by the first week of August. (NAS: Archive of the AG, correspondence 1893)

The year 1893 was probably a very difficult year to recruit female immigrants. Also the AG and the Emigration Agent were very concerned about this when they wrote to each other. Some parts of their correspondences are:

15 August 1893: It is especially difficult to obtain women, even if one is willing to spend more for her than the men; currently we already have a short of 12 women, which shortage we are trying to fulfil, in any way.

22 August 1893: 'There are still problems in the recruitment of females. The recruiters are unable to fulfil their contracts'. Because of these circumstances the Emigration Agent had to send a baboo (as the native clerks were called in India) to 'try every way to recruit emigrants, especially women'. Of course he would be obliged to pay more for the coolies, than thought. Recruiters wanted 35 rupees for the females and some demanded even 40, but 'those extra expenses must be taken for granted, because they otherwise could not obtain the emigrants'.

19 September 1893: . . . that he had been 'forced' to pay more for coolies than he had thought, because some recruiters with whom he had a contract were not able to fulfil their contracts. Moniram, one of the recruiters, had delivered only 85 out of the 200 and Lachman 77 instead of 100. I had to turn to other recruiters and also sent my baboos to the districts to attempt to recruit emigrants, especially women. The baboos had tried their best but could not obtain them for 28 rupees for men and 35 for women, but I had to pay eight coolies even 40 rupees per head.

18 October 1893: Women are very difficult to obtain, and we will be forced to pay more than the previous trips.

15 November 1893: At the moment it is still very difficult to obtain emigrants especially women. That's why I will have to send one of my clerks who knows the recruiting, up country to see what he can do.

(Correspondences of different months in the archive of the AG, 1893)

So it can be assumed that the recruitment of Hindustani women was costly because the recruiters were given a double commission to recruit them. For a recruited woman, 35 rupees, or sometimes even 40 rupees were paid as opposed to a premium of 25 rupees for men (De Klerk, 1953: 55). But as the Emigration Agent Reelfs wrote to A.G. Granada, these additional expenses should be taken for granted otherwise they could not meet the required number of women who were very scarce.

Another problem was that the Surinamese planters were looking for a special group of women. In previous studies these women are described as *'right kind of woman', 'honorable women', 'moral types'* and *'useful women'* (Hoefte, 1987: 57; Reddock, 1994: 30). The recruited women were from the lower castes and according to the colonial government had low morality. So the government tried to prevent these *'types'* of women from entering the colony. Within the Indian community the behaviour of economically active and independent women was linked to debauchery, immorality and prostitution (Reddock, 1994: 30). Suitable field workers could only be obtained from the lowest classes, for example, from the so-called *'immoral'* classes of society but such women would be useless in the fields (Debipersad, 2001: 21).

Article 16 of the Treaty of 1870 stated that with each shipment the number of women had to be half the number of men. However, the Emigration Agent could not fulfil this required minimum of 50 per cent, so the quota for women was set for 40 women to 100 men. But even this requirement could not be met and the Emigration Agent repeatedly pointed to the difficulties he encountered in fulfilling the transports with the standard quota set by the British Government (Letter of Emigration Agent Van Cutsem to AG Cateau van Rosevelt, 15 January 1884, in the Archive of the Governor, Government Resolution 1884, no. 1346).

On 11 March 1884, the AG proposed to the Governor of Suriname to take necessary steps as soon as possible to improve this situation. Both the AG and the Emigration Agent felt that if the required quota for women was 25 instead of 40, the numbers would be easily recruited. This would allow them to concentrate more on the recruitment of the better class of women and in case they were to obtain more than 25 per cent, they would not keep to this minimum but would make it 40 per cent (Letter of the AG to the Governor, 11 March 1884, in Government Resolution 1884, no. 1346).

The AG, Emigration Agent and the Governor of Suriname requested the Minister of Colonies in the Netherlands to take the necessary steps to reduce the minimum quota of 40:100 to 25:100. This request was not met; the quota stayed at 40 women to 100 men (Letter of the Governor of Suriname to the Minister of Colonies, 6 September 1884, in Government Resolution 1884, no. 1346). Also the delegation from India, Mr. James McNeill and Mr. Chimman Lal (1915), had advised to increase the existing quota of 40 women per 100 men to 50 women per 100 men. Their advice was based on the unfavourable relationships between the women and the men.

The argument of A.G. Roosevelt was that they could not meet the quota and too often women were sent to the colony that should never have come to Suriname. He describes them as 'women of the worst kind, the foam of Calcutta, Benares and other large cities that are good for nothing, only a curse for the coolie men. Instead of salvation flows nothing but mischief' (Government Resolution 1884, no. 1346). The image that the authorities had of women was not good. In the Colonial Reports of 1874 and 1876 are many such erroneous statements about the Hindustani women and their 'low point of morality'.

How Many and What Type of Women Emigrated?

Despite the many problems in the recruitment of Hindustani female workers, women arrived continuously in Suriname but with every arrival there were fewer females than males.

TABLE 3.1: RATIO BETWEEN HINDUSTANI FEMALE AND MALE INDENTURED WORKERS

Year	Ratio of Women to Men
1880-1900	± 300:1000
1901-2	± 260:1000
1905-7	± 300:1000
1908-12	± 400:1000
1913-16	± 370:1000

Source: Colonial Reports, 1880-1916.

This imbalance led to a very big difference between the British Indian men and women in Suriname. The consequences for the men were that it was difficult for them to find a wife/partner. As a result, the women were given a certain degree of freedom, but this freedom was very 'expensive'. Emmer (1984: 222) indicates that a total of 21,237 males, 8,527 females (28.6 per cent) came from British India to Suriname. The difference of 12,710 gives an indication of the imbalanced sex ratio between women and men. This imbalanced sex ratio is also evident from Table 3.1 which shows that during the entire indentured period the ratio between men and women never reached half or more, but stayed at an average of 300 women per 1,000 men. Although this was a very unfavourable ratio, it was not seen as such by the colonial authorities. The AG wrote in his report for the immigration in 1892 that 321 women per 1,000 men was a favourable ratio. Also in the reports of 1893 and 1895 is written, 'Once again in 1893, as in the year before, the ratio between men and women was more favourable than in 1892, namely 335 women per 1,000 men (in 1892 it was 321 women by 1,000 men)', and 'The ratio between men and women in 1895 was slightly better than in 1894, namely 344 women per 1,000 men' (Colonial Reports 1892: 19; 1893: 5; 1895: 28).

Emmer (1984/7) states that from this population of Hindustani women, approximately half were married. According to De Klerk (1953: 147) from this total of married women, one-third emigrated with their husbands. The rest were widows, young women, people with a 'forbidden' love relationship and a minority were prostitutes.

OCCUPATIONS OF THE HINDUSTANI FEMALE IMMIGRANTS IN BRITISH INDIA

Upon arrival of the indentured immigrants in Suriname, the AG had to write some information about each of them with regard to their occupation in British India. Everyone was recruited for work on the plantations or in the factory, but most of them were not fieldworkers. Figure 1.1 gives an overview of all the noted occupations which the female emigrants had in British India.

FIGURE 1.1: LIST OF ACTUAL NOTED OCCUPATIONS OF WOMEN FROM BRITISH INDIA, 1873-1916

All-rounder, baker, basket maker, broker of women, cake/candy maker, cleaning woman, clothes washer, dancer, factory worker, farmer, female barber, field worker, fire stoker, fisher woman, grass cutter, health woman, herdswoman, homemaker, housemaid, midwife, milk seller, mud seller, nurse, oil preparer, porter, pottery maker, rice cutter, rice pestle, seamstress, singer, shop keeper, shop servant, spinner, swineherd, vegetable seller, water carrier, weaver, worker in a company/craft and women without any occupation.

Source: Colonial Reports, 1873-1916.

The list in Figure 1.1 shows that women did different kinds of work but were used in Suriname and other countries as indentured workers in the fields. The most common occupation was fieldworker and some had been given other kinds of occupation. There were also a great number of women who had been never worked before in India. It is difficult to know whether or not most of the women who stated that they were fieldworkers in India had really done this work. Work on the plantation was so difficult for many immigrants that they even got sick and tired. This is odd since many had said that they were fieldworkers in India. Plantation work was only demanding and difficult for the small group house servants, singers, *prostitutes*, shopkeepers, midwives, milk sellers and for all the women. There were many types of women (married, divorced, disowned, widows, single women, fieldworkers, housemaids, weavers, mud sellers, seamstresses, rice pestle workers, oil preparers, clothes washers, female barbers, grass cutters, milk sellers, water carriers) that were recruited from British India to work on the plantations. In the Hindustani immigrant registers (1873-1916) it is also mentioned that women were with and without children.

COMPLAINTS

Although the group of Hindustani women in Suriname was small, there were many complaints about them. From their side the women also had many complaints. Generally the British Indian immigrants had many complaints about their living conditions, wages and the seriousness of the tasks that they had to do (NAS: Archive of the AG, inv. no. 1032). In addition the archives of the AG, the Governor, District Commissioners (DC), Judicial Archives and Colonial Reports contain many reports of other types of complaints, both against women as from women.

Complaints against Women

A frequent complaint from British Indian men against British Indian women was that the women left their men/husbands to live with another man. These 'abandoned' men always complained that when the women left their homes, they took with them all the money and jewellery which the men had given them. They also took away the children. The consequence of the decision of a woman who left her man could be fatal for her.

In such cases the husband would complain at the office of the AG or the DC and ask for help so that the woman would return home. If she did not want to come back, the husband had the right to demand that she return the jewellery, money and children to him.

Manglho 1784/Ll complained to the AG that Inundi 1326/N (with whom he was living in close relationship), had left him and had taken 'a golden coin and 4 silver bracelets' with her (NAS: Archive of the AG, inv. no. 1035).

Nepal Sing also complained that his young wife Gangadye (with whom he had lived together for seven years), had left him to live with the free British Indian Srabjit on plantation Rust en Werk. Nepal Sing claimed that she had taken all the jewellery with her. When Gangadye was asked she said that the jewellery was given to the administrator of plantation Rust en Werk for safekeeping. He had returned the jewellery, which consisted of 'a golden nose ring, a pair of silver foot bracelets, eight pairs of flat bracelets, a pair of round bracelets and a silver necklace' (Letter of the DC Beneden Commewijne to the AG, 19 December 1912 no. 2032, Archive of the AG, inv. no. 1035).

On 30 October 1912, Olimahomed 269/P also complained that his wife Sewradjie had left him, taking with her a large amount of money and much jewellery. There were 'four golden coins on a string, four golden fingerings (of which only two were found at Sewradjie) and 10 pairs silver flat bracelets, a pair of silver upper arm bracelets and a necklace with dimes'. Sewradjie claimed that the last sets of jewellery were given by Olimahomed to the wife of Mangroo, Maherenia. Sewradjie also indicated that she had taken no money and that she had gotten a couple of the jewellery from Raghoobersing and Mohan (Letter of the DC Nickerie to the AG no. 2247, Archive of the AG, inv. no. 1035).

Research in the judicial archives showed that there was another frequent complaint, namely the use of inappropriate statements, insults and morally offensive words from the Creole language that the women used toward the British Indian men as well as towards the officials of the plantation (planters, colonial authorities, supervisors, overseers, etc). Statements like *'jo beest, moerskont, ma mapima'* (words of abuse) already existed in the indentured period. A woman could be punished by law for the use of these words. She could receive a penalty in money which was replaceable with imprisonment (NAS: Archive of the AG, inv. no. 1032).

On 1 August 1888, the British Indian man Gungoo 697/G complained that a British Indian woman had said the words *'jou moerskont, jo ma mapima'* to him (Complaint register of District Coronie, 17 July-17 August 1888, Archive of the AG, inv. no. 1032).

Luchmoneea (not yet 25 years, field worker and living at Plantation de Resolutie) lamented on 13 October 1881, that she had threatened the planter of de Resolutie (Jacques Bueno Arrias) in the field with a cutlass and had publicly said the offensive words *'joe ma mapima (je moerskont) je moerskont'* to him. The judge declared that Luchmoneea was guilty and she had to pay a fine of two guilders for the first offence and for the second offense a fine of 50 cents. If she was unable to pay the money within a certain period, the penalty would be replaced by a prison sentence of one day every time. She was also sentenced to pay the costs of the lawsuit which was 93 cents (43 cents for the Hindustani interpreter + 50 cent court fee). If the money could not be recovered from Luchmoneea, she could get a subsidiary imprisonment of one day.

It should be noted in which way justice was done and the high costs to be paid taking into account the low wages women earned (NAS: Archive of the Ommegaande Rechter, 17 November 1881).

Another such case was of Louis Andries Malmberg (manager of plantation Meerzorg) against Dilbaseea (not yet 25 years old and field worker) and Sookhit (30 years and field worker), both indentured workers at plantation Meerzorg. Dilbaseea had opposed planter Malmberg and used offensive words in public on 16 November 1881. Dilbaseea denied the accusation but the court found it legally and convincingly proven that when Malmberg ordered her to carry sugar, Dilbassea had replied with anger in a violent tone 'I'm not going to carry sugar' . . . 'your mother sleeps with two men'. Dilbaseea was found guilty, and for the first offence she got imprisonment of four days hard labour and for the second offence she had to pay a fine of 15 guilders which could be replaced by four days imprisonment (NAS: Archive of the Ommegaande Rechter, 26 November 1881).

Land border issue was another common complaint in the archives of the AG. The boundaries of most of the land that was given to British Indian immigrants, were unclear. On 13 January 1913, Ramchurn 457/W complained about this issue at the office of the DC of Saramacca and the AG. His complaint was that because of these unclear boundary issues, he experienced a lot of trouble from his neighbour Duyi. The DC had tried several times to resolve the border issue but all attempts failed because of the unwillingness of Ramchurn. According to the DC (Letter of 23 January 1913, no. 195 in the Archive of the AG, inv. no. 1036), Ramchurn was wrong in this matter, but he did not want to acknowledge it. The AG finally decided that land surveyor Ront would have to go to Saramacca during February 1913 to measure the plots in this case. Meanwhile, the AG had asked the DC that both parties 'would not make the life of each other unpleasant' (Letter no. 53/V, Archive of the AG, inv. no. 1036).

As will be shown further in this article, there were also many complaints by males against their mothers-in-law because they took away their wives (the daughters) after the wedding/engagement, to promise them to other men.

Women were not only involved in minor matters but were complicit in cases where crime had occurred. The eighteen-year-old Hindustani woman Somaria, also known as Bhagwantia, daughter of Rogho 301/N, was complicit in the murder of her husband. Together with her father Rogho and their servant Tikait 145/Ee were subjected to the death penalty as they had murdered Mahadeo, the husband of Somaria. The court called this crime which had been committed at plantation De Goede Verwachting, a horrifying drama. Rogho issued on 6 July 1912, to AG Van Drimmelen and the Governor that what had happened was the result of a bad relationship between Mahadeo (his son-in-law) and himself (Petition of AG Van Drimmelen to the Governor, 6 July 1912, in Government Resolution 5 August 1912, no. 3891). Mahadeo was frequently ill-treating his daughter and did not take care of her and by theft and other crimes he brought shame to his in-laws. In the application of S. Queno Qibar (Petition of S. Queno Qibar to the Governor, 15 July 1912, in Government Resolution 5 August 1912, no. 3891) (representing Somaria), he suggested that Somaria was only eighteen years old and that she like 'the case with Coolie girls in general, was under the influence of the father who terrified her to participate in the crime against Mahadeo. That applicant feels deep remorse about her crime, as was revealed through her tears in Court'.

Attorney General S.D. De Vries mentioned in his letter of 26 July 1912, to the Court of Justice that this crime should be counted as one of the most horrible one ever presented in Court (Letter of Attorney General S.D. De Vries, 26 July 1912, in Government Resolution, 5 August 1912, no. 3891). He indicated that Tikait and Somaria had in fact slaughtered Mahadeo. They had first let Mahadeo drink too much and eat. In his drink they had mixed an intoxicating fluid (*dhatour*). After Mahadeo was intoxicated and was leaning forward Tikait gave him the first terrible hack in the neck.

Under the complaints of crime in 1887, there were four complaints of murder, in two of these cases women were involved. One was committed on a free British Indian at plantation Spieringshoek, with the intention to rob him. Five immigrants were suspected, including the woman with whom the victim lived together. The second incident took place on plantation Sorgvliet where a mother drowned her baby, who was only a few days old, in the river. The reason she gave was that the baby was born with two teeth and this was seen as an evil omen by others. She was acquitted as not attributable (Colonial Report, 1887: 15).

The year 1888 saw a case on plantation Zorgvliet where a man was killed, and the wife and her lover were suspected as the perpetrators. The immigrant was found dead on the floor of his house. The wife of the deceased and a coolie, with whom she had an illicit relationship were arrested as suspects. Due to lack of evidence both were acquitted (Colonial Report, 1888: 13).

COMPLAINTS FROM WOMEN

There were not only complaints against women, but also women had complaints against their fellow countrymen and the authorities. In the archives are many cases of alcohol abuse and beating of women by men. The Hindustani indentured woman Rajdai 650/Ee, wife of Abdoolrazak, living at Meerzorg, complained to the DC of Suriname and the AG that she had left her husband because he drank a lot and made her life intolerable (Complaint Register, November 1932, Archive of the AG, inv. no. 1052).

Debipersad (2001: 82) indicates that the use of alcohol and beatings were an important mechanism to keep the women 'under control'. Choenni and Choenni (2012: 369, 373) indicate that there were various causes of alcohol abuse among the Hindustani men, namely, stress, extreme poverty, hard work and little pay, closet homosexuality, performance and social pressure, fear of failure and inferiority. After consuming liquor, they let their frustrations out on their wife and children by beating them. In the complaint of Nepal Sing against his wife Gangadye, mentioned earlier, she indicated that she no longer wanted to return to him because he had abused her three times and the last time he had even chased her out of the house. Johorah, wife of Fazalalli at Mariënburg, also complained in 1892 that she was abused by her husband and was chased away (Complaint of Johorah, 9 November 1892 at the DC Commewijne and the AG, in the Archive of the AG, inv. no. 370).

Police officer Vaseur had arrested the women Sookhia and Jagwantia at Nieuw Amsterdam Voorburg. Sookhia was drunk and said that she was continually being abused by her husband Raghubar and that she wanted to leave him. She had fl. 88.50 cash and jewellery in her possession. Jagwantia also indicated that she was being abused by the parents of her husband Harkoo (Report of agent Vaseur to the AG, 7 May 1919, in the Archive of the AG, inv. no. 1041). On 28 May 1893, the AG and the DC of Beneden Suriname received a complaint that Bahadur 393/T of plantation Meerzorg had abused his wife Imameen 394/T (Letter no. 279, Archive of the AG, inv. no. 372). Also, the British Indian woman Khuba 449/Ii complained on 30 October 1919, to DC Essed and the AG about the ill-treatment of her husband Gaya 1185/Ii (NAS: Archive of the AG, inv. no. 1041). DC Jessurun of Beneden Cottica had reported on 8 October 1874, letter no. 359 to the AG about the compliant of the Hindustani woman Suffeena 1063/C of plantation de Resolutie. Her husband Lall-Mahomed 1062/C, who was daily in a drunken state and not amenable to reason, was repeatedly beating and abusing her and their children (NAS: Archive of the AG, inv. no. 148).

The judicial archives, archives of the DC and the AG are full with complaints of women beaten by their men/husbands. The 'beatings' were a common complaint. The complaints also show that not only the woman but also the children were beaten along with the mother (Complaint Register 1888, Archive of the AG, inv. no. 1032).

The immigrant Abdool Gaphur who had beaten the woman Sadhu was fined fl. 2, as a punishment; the money was handed over to Sadhu (Report of the AG to the Governor, 5 December 1892 in the Archive of the AG, inv. no. 370). It is notable that if another man had beaten a woman, he was being fined and the amount was handed over to the woman. But in cases where the husband hit his wife he was never fined.

Besides beating and drinking, women also complained that the men did not take enough care of them. Lalkia 1821/M had complained against Radhoo 1820/M that he hit her and did not want to take care of her while she was pregnant and no longer able to work. She also complained that Radhoo had a relationship with another woman and that was the reason why he wanted nothing to do with her (NAS: Archive of the AG, inv. no. 1032). Khatirani 916/V of Kroonenburg complained that her lawful husband Ramsadak Sing 395/V, who was a sirdar at Mon Souci, had left her five years ago. He had agreed to pay fl. 2, as weekly maintenance for her and the children, but the last two weeks he had stopped this and so she and her children were suffering (Complaint of Khatirani to the DC Beneden Commewijne and the AG, 28 April 1912, no. 458/V in the Archive of the AG, inv. no. 1036).

A complaint earlier mentioned in this article is that some Hindustani female indentured women abandoned their men/husbands to live with another man or had more relationships. However, this was not just an act committed by women, as men also left their wives to live with other women. The fisherman Dukhi Sanichara from Nieuw Nickerie left for Paramaribo to sell dried fish. After a month his wife Mangri complained to the DC and the AG that Dukhi had left her and their three children in Nieuw Nickerie. The DC reported to the AG, 'So far we heard nothing from Dukhi Sanichara and as Mangri had learned, her husband lives with a certain woman Betsy Kuaria, daughter of Mahadew Sonar, residing in the Groote Combe No. 75'. The DC had asked the AG to use his influence so that Dukhi Sanichara would return to his wife who was left behind without care with her children (Correspondences between the DC Nickerie and the AG, January-February 1931, no. 167, and no. 208 in the Archive of the AG, inv. no. 1046).

Threats towards women were also common. On 1 November 1911, the British Indian woman Jhinki 276/Ff asked the acting overseer from Kroonenburg for a pass to go to station Nieuw Amsterdam. She wanted to file a complaint at the DC against Jangbahadoor 275/Ff, who had threatened to murder her if she took another man (NAS: Archive of the AG, inv. no. 1036).

An interesting case occurred on plantation de Resolutie, where the overseer logged a complaint at the DC of Beneden Cottica against an immigrant woman Soogeea 131/B (Complaint 21 October 1874, no. 409 in the Archive of the AG, inv. no. 148). According to him and some other Hindustani indentured labourers, Soogeea wanted to set fire to the sugar cane fields on 21 October 1874, 'either from carelessness or malice'. Some women had seen Soogeea at 8 o'clock in the morning that she set fire in the fields. After the fire was extinguished by the overseer, Soogeea had tried again at noon to set fire to the field. Soogeea stated that she was innocent and that the overseer R. Simons had propositioned her to sleep with him and when she refused 'he would have set the coolies against her to put fire on her beds, to get her punished'.

Another complaint which has been noticed in the Colonial Reports is mentioned under the complaints made against tenants etc. in 1893, in Boven, Suriname. It was made by a woman with charges of attempted rape but the case was withdrawn or was declared not amenable to prosecution because there were no grounds to prosecute (Colonial Report, 1893: 13). Munna 1826/M too complained to the AG, the DC of Frederiksdorp and the British Consul on 13 April 1893, that Cheda entered her house on a night when her husband was in the city, and wanted to have physical intercourse with her (Complaint of Munna, Archive of the AG, inv. no. 372).

On 23 August 1874, Luchmeenia 2330/B from plantation Wederzorg was almost raped by the Creole worker, John Huyck. During a Hindustani dance party he offered her fl. 4, to have sex with her but she refused and walked away. The man followed her into her house, grabbed her bodily and threw her on the ground to achieve his goal with violence. Another woman heard her screams and saw her struggling with the Creole worker, who was lying half naked on top of her. The other Hindustanis offered her help, which resulted in a fight, leaving many injured and one dead (Letter no. 165 of the DC Beneden Commewijne to the AG in the Archive of the AG, inv. no. 147).

In the Colonial Report of 1888, (1888: 13) mention is made of two sever cases. On plantation Nieuw Clarenbeek the woman Ropoah was assaulted by the man Chlinkowree with whom she lived in 'illicit relation'. In a fit of jealousy, he hacked her causing serious wounds, which made her unfit for work. The other incident took place on plantation Goudmijn, where in the early morning of 15 October 1888, two British Indians Thakoor and Kobair, attacked a young coolie woman who had gone outside her house, with a bat. It is mentioned that they robbed all her jewellery and 'after that they threw her on the ground, and while one was holding her by the throat, they alternately had raped her and had badly beaten her'. The above listed complaints deal with the safety of the British Indian women. Threats, beatings, not taking care and rape indicate that women, although they were in the minority and therefore had a certain 'dominance', were constantly in danger and had to be on guard.

It weren't just the Hindustani men who had complaints against women, women too had complaints against one another. On 17 April 1888, Neori 694/G had logged a complaint against Sugia 683/G because she had insulted her with words like 'you sleep with Sookdhan. I have seen you with him under the tree'. Sugia was convicted for this and she had to pay a fine of fl. 10, plus cover the costs of fl. 2.30. If she did not pay this amount she could be imposed with a second imprisonment for three days with forced labour (Complaint register of District of Coronie, 17 April-16 June 1888, in the Archive of the AG, inv. no. 1032). Thus, the use of expletives and morally offensive language or words was not only addressed to men but also to women.

There were even quarrels between neighbours and among sisters. The British Indian woman Rekobia 1654/M of Huwelijkszorg complained that she had much trouble with her neighbours Rasiawon and Ramkhelawan. She said that there was not one day when she was not teased and disturbed. Rekobia wished to put an end to this intolerable situation, and she wanted the help of the AG and the DC. The DC reported to the AG that the complaint of Rekobia was not entirely correct. It turned out that Rasiawon's wife and Rekobia were sisters and that between them was a very long enmity whereby both parties had the same unforgiving attitude. Attempts to reconcile were only for a very short time because both parties always tried to tease each other again with all sorts of petty trifles which Rekobia started. Also the two very brute sons of Rekobia were very annoying and always contributing to the quarrels of their mother. Because of their carelessness they had created a fire in a cocoa field belonging to their other neighbour Ramkhelawan, in which about two acres, already bearing cocoa, were lost. The damages were worth fl. 100, and Rekobia had still not paid the money. Since then, she also quarrelled with this neighbour in order to take revenge. She regularly logged complaints at the office of the DC and the AG against both her neighbours, but upon investigation it was revealed that she had concocted the whole case (Correspondence between the DC Saramacca and the AG, February-March 1912, no. 192/V and no. 414 in the Archive of the AG, inv. no. 1036).

The overseers also had a number of complaints against women for unwillingness to work and leaving the plantations without permission. In contrast, many women logged complaints that they earned less wages and that the work was too heavy for them (Colonial Reports, 1873-1921). Two women, Golab and Mohadai, complained against the colonial authorities. Golab no. 10, who came to Suriname in 1884 with the *Peshwa*, stated after arrival that she was cheated, deceived and kidnapped. She said she was not presented before the authorities and had therefore not agreed to leave for Suriname. Golab refused to leave the depot and to work on the plantations and insisted that she be sent back to India. Her statements were taken in doubt but the Governor and the Attorney General decided that she had to pay the expenses of her return passage to Calcutta by herself and with the assistance of the compounders of the *Peshwa*. After the inquiry of the Emigration Agent it showed that the whole story was fabricated, probably with the help of one of the assistants on board, to get the woman back to Calcutta (Bhagwanbali, 2010: 65).

The other case involved the Hindustani woman Mohadai no. 276 who came to Suriname with the *Grecian* in 1894. Upon arrival she asked for the termination of her contract, which was subsequently terminated with the approval of the Governor. She had to refund the amount of fl. 260. She said that she was not contracted for Suriname but wanted to sign an agreement for Demerara where she had relations whom she wished to join. The 'recruiting woman' who approached her said that she was recruiting for the colony of Demerara, so she felt deceived and cheated (Colonial Report 1884: 3).[3]

[3] See also Archive of the AG, inv. no. 639.

SCARCITY OF HINDUSTANI FEMALES AND THE CONSEQUENCES

It is already stated that the number of women transported to Suriname was fewer than that of the contracted men. Throughout the indenture period there was a shortage of Hindustani females, because the quota of 40:100 women to men could not be met. Because of their fewer number, women were in demand and had a certain freedom, power and bargaining ability. However, this freedom was not without consequences. It gave rise to much hassle for women which resulted in attacks on them. The unbalanced sex ratio had different, sometimes far-reaching consequences. An important immediate consequence was polyandry which impacted on the lives of the immigrants.

For single women it was quite easy to find a life partner. Also widows could take a new partner and even remarry. Take the case of the Hindustani immigrant Rehman Mahomed Khan 452/Aa. When a single woman had forced herself on him, he had called her a 'bitch' (Hira, 2003: 145). Some women simultaneously had intimate relationships with different men and regularly exchanged their partner. So it was up to the women to decide for themselves whether they chose a relationship with a certain man or not. She could decide for herself if she wanted to abandon her husband for another, or to have simultaneous relationships with several men. Debipersad (2001: 134, 135 and fn. 32) confirms through two cases in her research that polyandry occurred in the indentured period. A couple of persons intervied on plantation Kronenburg told about their *adjie* (grandmother from father's side, an immigrant) who lived with three men in her house. Another respondent told about an old woman who lived with two (old) men.

The archives also confirmed the occurrence of polyandry during the indentureship period. Attorney General De Vries had discussed a case on 12 March 1912,[4] where two British Indians, Lautan

[4] Letter of Attorney General S.D. De Vries to the Court of Justice, 12 March 1912, no. 1441 about the replacement of the death penalty for Lautan 186/Ll and Jaganath 1386/Ll in Governments Resolution, 25 March 1912, no. 1424. See also the Archive of the AG, inv. no. 1048.

186/Ll and Jaganath 1386/Ll had killed their compatriot Kishun in an 'extremely abominable and animal way'. The motive was jealousy because all three men had a relationship with Sanichari 1393/Ll. Lautan and Kishun also had an intimate relationship with the wife of another immigrant Behari. They were given the death penalty which was changed to hard labour for twenty years, in chains.

Not only were there many attacks on women, but also in the cruellest ways such as dousing them with petroleum and then burning them, cutting their arms, hacking with a cutlass etc.[5] A case at plantation Rust en Werk in 1887 showed that in a fit of jealousy, a man had poured petroleum on the woman whom he lived with and then burned her (Colonial Report, 1887: 15). The woman died the next day. In 1886, there was among the repatriated British Indians, a woman 'whose both forearms were cut off by her husband out of jealousy' (Colonial Report, 1886: 4). On 8 July 1893, Surjballi 548/U murdered his lawful wife Ramdai/Ramdaya 549/U, because she left the marital home to live with another man in adultery (Government Resolution, 27 July 1893, L.B. no. 5395).[6] The British Indian immigrant Jodha 402/I had requested the AG and the DC of Boven Cottica on 19 September 1892, to intervene that his wife Roopoa, who according to him, lived in close relation with the coolie Chundun, return to him. Chundun was a boatsman at the station of the DC Boven Cottica (Letter no. 832 in the Archive of the AG, inv. no. 369).

The DC of Beneden Commewijne had sent a telegram message to the AG on 30 October 1892, in which he reported that the 'Coolie woman Janaki of Wederzorg is not yet deceased, had obtained very serious injuries and the condition is perilous. She left her lawful husband and went to Sobadra. She got a quarrel about this with her husband and he injured her in the field' (Archive of the AG, inv. no. 369). Hira 777/Oo was also sentenced to death on 4 June 1913, for the murder of his wife on 14 September 1912 (Government Resolution 1913, no. 563).

[5] Bhagwanbali (2010: 105, 106) also mentioned some cases he found in the Archives of the Minister of Colonies in the Netherlands.

[6] See also the Archive of the AG, inv. no. 1048.

Sometimes the colonial government was very concerned about the attacks but in most cases the attacks were seen as legitimate jealousy on behalf of the man. Apart from the fact that the death penalty was not carried out in Suriname, it was on this basis, that many men who had killed their wives got pardon from the colonials. The Hindustani woman, Tetree, was assassinated on 21 November 1885, by the British Indian Toofani 205/M. For his deed, he was sentenced to death penalty but his punishment was changed to six years of hard labour. The reasons for the pardon/modified punishment was: 'The act was committed of justified jealousy as the defeated would abandon the marital home to live with a certain Ballah, which situation in other cases could be taken by the Court as mitigation' (List of convicted murderers, 1875-1913 in the Archive of the AG, inv. no. 1048).[7]

On 12 May 1886, Behari 667/M murdered Duye 1664/M the decision of the Governor the death penalty changed into penal servitude for fifteen years, of which the first ten years would be in chains.The reason for pardon was that 'The condemned was led to the crime by his wife who had left him to live with another man of a lower caste' (List of convicted murderers, 1875-1913 in the Archive of the AG, inv. no. 1048).[8]

The AG had expressed his concern about the attacks in a letter (17 October 1893, no. 713) to the DC of Beneden Suriname. He had written about the immoral way of life of married and unmarried coolies and the consequences of these actions. He wrote that he objected to the relations between and the transfer of the adulteress Jumurti 1112/S and Sumbhos 1636/M to plantation Eendracht. The AG was convinced that her lawful husband Mirabakash 1095/S, would react someday to the relationship of his lawful wife Jumurti to Sumbhos and that he would find a way to punish Jumurti in a real Indian way (Archive of the AG, inv. no. 374).

Jugessur was murdered on 24 June 1885, by the British Indian man Sewtohul 465/M. For this crime he was sentenced to death. However, a request was filed, pardon was granted and the sentence

[7] See also Government Resolution, December 1885, L.B. no. 1328.

[8] See also letter of the Attorney General to the Court of Justice, May 1886 no. 349. See also Government Resolution, June 1886, L.B. no. 3215.

was changed to twenty years of hard labour; the first five years in chains. The reason for the change was that the convict was motivated by his wife to commit the murder as she led an illicit life. In fact, he had repeatedly complained to the DC about her. (List of Convicted Murderers, 1875-1913 in the Archive of the AG, inv. no. 1048).[9]

The DC Beneden Cottica reported to the AG, in a letter of 16 August 1893, a case which had occurred at plantation Pieterszorg on 16 August 1893. The British Indian immigrant Karimbux 68/U had killed his wife Rahimun 65/U. The DC went to the plantation with the District Surgeon Wesenhagen. When questioning Karimbux he said 'that his wife was scolding him many times in a day and that she clearly stated that she had a forbidden relationship with the coolie Ori'. Karimbux said that he never liked the relationship so he made a plan to kill his wife. On Sunday they quarrelled again, so he shifted to another house, but Rahimun kept taking care of him and giving him food. The morning before, when he went to the house to eat, she had not cooked anything for him. When he asked her why, she had answered 'I do not want to cook for you anymore; I am going to live with Ori'. After hearing this he immediately executed his plan to kill her. He attacked her with his cutlass, hit her on her left arm and then on her neck. When he thought that she must be dead, he stopped hacking. A Creole worker chased him to the road and handed him over to the police. The people on the plantation had told the DC that Karimbux and Rahimun quarrelled frequently and that Karimbux had abused his wife several times. The report of Wesenhagen stated that because of the many blows, Rahimun died of heavy blood loss. The reports also stated that she was 5½ months pregnant (Archive of the AG, inv. no. 18).[10]

Not only married or women living in concubinage became victims of murders, but also single women who were coveted by a man. Because of the uneven number of men and women, not every man could find a woman and so some forced women to have

[9] See also Government Resolution, 23 July 1885, L.B. no. 5.

[10] See also the Archive of the AG, inv. no. 1048. Also see GR January 1894 no. 68.

relationships with them. If the woman refused she could be killed out of frustration, as in the case of plantation 't Vertrouwen, where the woman Kanchi was murdered in a horrible way with a cutlass by her lover Chuuderbeer. Kanchi was a widow and wanted nothing to do with Chuuderbeer because she had already taken another man (Colonial Report, 1888: 13). If it was not possible for a man to murder his unfaithful and cheating wife, there were cases where he would commit suicide. In 1908, a Hindustani immigrant had committed suicide and it was noted as 'hanging arising out of unfaithfulness of his wife. Despair through jealousy' (Archive of the AG, inv. no. 1129).

Analysis

It is not about the number of attacks or murder cases, but the mere fact that these attacks occurred which explained much and gave the impression that something was wrong. The shortage of women led to frustration and attacks on the British Indian women. The situation in which the British Indian men lived can also be explained by this. Jealousy and frustration meant that there were attacks committed on women. Not only did women bear the brunt of these acts but also men who had a relationship with the same woman. In this way, there was a certain rivalry and competition among men. The fact that a woman could leave, and in fact, left her husband, was seen as a loss of prestige by the men. Even after many tries (with the help of the AG and the DC) return home, the man was not always successful in getting the woman (and children) back in the house. In the archive of the AG are cases recorded where the woman returned, but after some time left again with the same or another man with whom she had a relationship before she returned to her lawful husband. Because of their bargaining position, the women were able to let other men commit a crime, in many cases, the murder of her husband or lover. It may be assumed that the British Indian women had a certain power during the indentured period because they were in the minority. But this 'power' also resulted in many attacks being perpetrated on them. What certainly should not be lost sight of is that the shortage of women and their bargaining did not give the men the right to murder the women.

Child Marriage as a Consequence (Misuse of Child Marriages)

The imbalance in the sex ratio between males and females also caused major shifts in the traditional practice pertaining to marriage. Women from lower castes could now marry men from higher castes and girls were often married at a younger age. An indirect consequence of the shortage of women was the 'misuse' of the phenomenon of child marriage that was brought from India by the immigrants. With child marriage, the life partner for the child was chosen by the parents or other adults. Such a marriage was arranged when the children were young. De Klerk (1953: 169, 170) indicates that the main principle was that one had to marry within one's caste, so marriage within their own *gotra* and family was not allowed. But because of the shortage of women, it was common for women from lower castes to marry men from higher castes. Bhagwanbali (2010: 106) mentioned that due to tradition and because of the shortage of women, girls were married off at a young age. The female immigrant Ramlali Jhagru, known as Ramlal adjie, said that at the age of three years she was already married according to Hindu tradition. 'It was the intention that I would live with his parents in the future, but it never happened' (Dalhuisen et al., 2007: 113).[11] There are many cases to be found in the archive of the AG, where this scarcity of women led to young girls being promised to a certain family but when another family offered more money to the parents, they would marry their daughter into the other family. Also the parents of the girl would not return the gifts and money to the first family.

In a letter from Paramaribo, dated 16 June 1913, the former British Indian immigrant Goness (then a shopkeeper) had requested the AG to help him with a problem. Two years earlier, his fourteen

[11] See also *De laatste kantraki*, a documentary film from 1988 by Ramdjan Abdoelrahman, colour, 29 minutes, produced by Feduco Tv.

years old son Danrath, got married to twelve-year old Calapdea, the daughter of Bhagwandee. In his request Goness had stated that:

> On this occasion I have spared no expense to give the party a magnificent sight according to Hindu rites, especially because I am well-off and the mother of the bride is poor. For this purpose I had spent an amount of six hundred guilders. Besides this, gifts and jewellery for the bride namely 10 pairs silver bracelets, 2 pairs of thick silver bracelets, 1 pair foot bracelets, 2 golden nose ring, 1 silver neck bracelet, 1 pair silver earrings, 1 broad golden nose ring, 1 silver head ornament and various precious sets of clothes.

Six weeks after the marriage Bhagwandee, who was an alcoholic, took away the girl in a mysterious way and without any reason or offence and without telling or asking someone from the in-laws. She also took away all the valuables. Goness told the AG that he had repeatedly tried to get the girl back but his attempts were fruitless 'because the mother, who was living a bad life, wanted to 'sell'/engage the child again to another man' (Petition of Goness to the AG, 16 June 1913, in the Archive of the AG, inv. no. 1036).

Also Motilal 123/P, of plantation Lust en Rust, got married in Indian style with Mungree, daughter of Tekney. His wife did not want to live with him, so Motilal asked the AG to help him to get her to live with him, or return him the fl. 190, which he had spent on her for their wedding 'from which pleasure he is now deprived of' (Letter to the AG, 13 October 1892, in Archive of the AG, inv. no. 369). On 9 July 1913, police officer Kortram of station Poelepantje also made report of such a case (Report of officer Kortram of DC Beneden Suriname and Beneden Para, 26 July 1913, no. 1027 in the Archive of the AG, inv. no. 1036). Matai had filed a complaint against Soodial. Matai's son and Soodial's daughter had got married three years ago. For the marriage Matai contributed fl. 300. He also gave gifts to the girl such as 10 pairs flat silver bracelets, 2 necklaces and 2 neck bracelets. The girl had grown up and her family was refusing to send her to Ramklawan, Matai's son.

Similarly, the daughter of Bandhu 1149/Y, Jaipali, had married in the Hindustani way with Madho, son of Sankar. She was given a lot of money and jewellery but afterwards the girl did not want to go back to Madho. In a letter of 29 March 1917, the DC of Nickerie wrote to the AG (Letter no. 638 in the Archive of the AG, inv. no. 1022), wondering whether the girl had been hiding and did not want to go to her husband, or had a baseless reason or was it because of speculation for a second wedding gift. According to the DC, that was the deciding factor. Jaipali insisted that she did not want to go to the man, so Madho wanted to have his jewellery back which was withheld by Bandhu. According to Jaipali the jewellery consisted of: '8 silver bracelets (tjoeria), 1 silver neck bracelet (hasoeli), 1 necklace with silver coins – 20 half and one whole guilder – (hamél), 2 silver upper arm bracelets (bajoe) and 1 golden nose ornament (tjuhtji)'.

Another case is the complaint of the British Indian immigrant Ghoolab 1027/Ee, which was filed in 1921 with the AG, and the DCs of Beneden Commewijne and Beneden Suriname. Ghoolab and his family reported that their son Basalie 1025/Ee got married according to Hindustani tradition with Phatumun, daughter of Abdul Rahiman. But both father and daughter did not want her to return to her husband. Phatumun told the DC of Beneden Commewijne that she did not want to go to Basalie. As a reason she stated 'that before the Hindu marriage she had never seen the man and that she did not like him and so did not want him'. The DC demanded then that she return all the jewellery, which she willingly returned (Letter of the DC Beneden Commewijne to the AG, 8 August 1921, no. 2135 in the Archive of the AG, inv. no. 1042).

Analysis

Taking into account the shortage of Hindustani women, the many attacks on them and the misuse of child marriage, DC Van der Feen from Nickerie wrote on 8 May 1919 (Letter no. 1102, Archive of the AG, inv. no. 1041), expersing his concerns to the AG. In his letter, he mentioned that: 'in the recent times it repeatedly occurred that young British Indian girls, for example of eleven years, were married in Hindustani way, are taken home again by her parents. This gives rise to constant quarrels and many complaints at the district office. The last murder of the twelve years old British Indian girl Boodia was also the result of such a case'.

The DC said that the cases had to do with corrupt parents who wanted to successively marry off their daughters to several men.

Also Mac Neill and Lall (Report of Mac Neill and Lall, 1915: 14) were informed that parents who had engaged their daughters often refused to honour their promises if they were offered a better 'match'. Both gentlemen indicated that this was not an unknown phenomenon in India, and suggested that the best way to solve this social problem was to immigrate more girls in families to Suriname. DC Van der Feen called the situation with the child marriages and the promise of the girls to several men not good and indicated that this led to misuse, quarrels and worse. Also, that this habit of the British Indians had to be changed and that they must behave better at this point in particular, taking into account that the treaty between the Netherlands and Britain had been terminated and therefore no large flow of people would come anymore to the colony.

It is not incorrect to say that child marriages were a way for British Indians to already 'reserve' a woman for themselves or their sons for the future. Families made use and misuse of the shortage of women. Taking all these aspects into account, the question that can be asked is why did parents (mis)use their girl children. An explanation can be found in the low wages that the immigrants earned. The marriages of the daughters could be seen as a way to 'earn' some extra money to supplement the low income. The immigrants already earned so less and they had to work very hard, so the early marriage of girls can be seen as an additional source of income. Another question is what could the colonial authorities have done to minimize the shortage of Hindustani females in Suriname? For now it can be said that they have showed their concerns only through correspondences. It is known that Hindustani families desired/preferred male children over female children. But because of the shortage of women during the indentured period, it is not incorrect to state that the families would apparently have preferred females instead of males. Life on the plantations was very difficult, so in this way these girls/females could provide some additional finances.

Another aspect noticed from the cases mentioned above is that the family of the man had given money and jewellery to the family of the girl. It can be seen as a kind of 'reservation' of the girls for the man, so that he already had a wife for himself in the future. To compare this with the phenomenon of *dahej* (dowry), we see that *dahej* is where the family of the girl has to give the in-laws gifts and money. But the scarcity of women in the indentured period reversed this custom so that now the family of the groom had to give the bride gifts and money; in this case to probably 'reserve' her for the future.

CONCLUSION

If we look at the manner in which the immigrants came from India to Suriname, it can be stated that the system of immigration of the Hindustani indentured labourers had been set up by the planters who needed workers for the plantations. The immigrants were ordered for this work because they were needed to help keep the plantation sector alive. Women formed a special group who had an interesting position. It is not easy to determine a women's role, since the role and position of women in general and in this case the British Indian/Hindustani female indentured women, had often been forgotten. Thus while in history and in the literature books the role of the male workers is very well represented, that of the women lacking. Different types and numbers of women had been recruited from British India to work on the plantations in Suriname. There were also women with and without children. From the 34,304 Hindustani immigrants who came from India to Suriname, 21,237 were males and 8,527 were females. Consquently, there was a scarcity of women and this scarcity of the Hindustani female indentured women had positive as well as negative consequences. As positives, we can see the inter-caste marriages and as negatives, we can see the engagement of young girls with several men, jealousy, abuse of the women and wife-chopping or wife-murdering. Due to the shortage of women, it was possible for them to have more freedom in having more than one relationship. This gave women certain dominance, even if it was relative. The result was that both men and women fell into practices which would be impossible and unthinkable under normal circumstances and according to Indian standards. In India, women would stay with their husbands even if he ill-treated them as it was their duty and destiny. Having different relationships at the same time gave the Indian women a very negative image.

The use of physical violence seems to have been a way to subdue the woman. Presently there is limited data available about wife chopping and murders in Suriname during the indentured period. That is because there are still many archives (judicial archives and some archives of the DCs) which are not accessible at present. For now, the phenomenon of wife chopping is not quantified by exact numbers, but it definitely occurred. It can be noted that the competition for women was strong. If a woman had been suspected of adultery it could have a cruel end. The use of physical force was a traditional means to subjugate women.

During the indentured period the British Indian immigrants had many complaints; not only against the colonial authorities and the planters, but also amongst themselves. There were many kinds of complaints against women such as the use of bad words, abandoning the man/husband, taking away money, jewellery and children, etc. Their were also complaints of women against other women and men such as rape, adultery, not taking enough care of her and the children, neighbour and sister quarrels, using bad words, etc.

There are still many aspects of the lives of Hindustani female indentured workers which have not yet been researched. Also, more information can be found through the use of oral history and interviews with (grand)children of the Hindustani indentured workers. Oral history provides an opportunity to decrease the reliance on the archives and other documents as evidence. Otherwise we will be left with a history written by the colonial rulers. If we also want to know the other side of the story, we must make use of oral history; record the stories of the 'living proofs'.

REFERENCES

PRIMARY SOURCES

National Archives of Suriname (NAS):

Archive of the Agent General (AG) for the Immigration (known as the Immigration Department), 1853-1946, Paramaribo, NAS, inventory numbers: 18, 147, 148, 369, 370, 372, 374, 1022, 1032, 1035, 1036, 1041, 1042, 1046, 1048, 1052.

Archive of the Governor of Suriname, 1846-1957, Government Resolutions, Paramaribo, NAS.

Colonial Reports, 1870-1921, Paramaribo, NAS.

Immigration Registers of British Indians, 1873-1921, Paramaribo, NAS.

Judicial Archives (Ommegaande Rechters), Paramaribo, NAS, November 1881.

Microfiches of the Immigration Registers of the British West Indies and Chinese Immigrants, Paramaribo (NAS).

SECONDARY SOURCES

Adhin, J.H. (1961). 'Radiotoespraak, De Hindustaanse bevolkingsgroep in Suriname', 24 juli 1961 in *Schakels*. Suriname. Grote volksgroepen. Uitgave van het Kabinet van de Vice Minister President, jaargang volume 1962, no. S 46.

—— (1960). 'Over de joint family der Hindostanen' in *Nieuwe West-Indische Gids (New West Indian Guide)*, 40ste jaargang, juli no. 1.

Bhagwanbali, R. (2010). *Hindoestaanse migranten onder het indentured labour system naar Suriname, 1873-1916. De nieuwe awatar van slavernij*. The Hague, Amrit.

Choenni Chan and Choenni Gharietje (2012). *Sarnami Hindostani 1920-1960,* part 1: *Worteling, identiteit en gemeenschapsvorming in Suriname.* Amsterdam.

Commins, D.W.D. (1982). *Note on Emigration from the East Indies to Surinam or Dutch Guiana.* Calcutta.

Dalhuisen Leo, Maurits Hassankhan and Frans J. Steegh (2007). *Geschiedenis van Suriname,* Walburg Pers, Zutphen.

Debipersad, R. (2001). *Emancipatie van Hindoestaanse vrouwen. Een beschrijving vanveranderingen in het leven van Hindoestaanse vrouwen in Suriname vanaf 1873*. Paramaribo, CERDES.

Emmer, P.C. (1984). 'Een goede keus? De migratie van vrouwelijke contract-arbeiders van Brits-Indie naar Suriname, 1875-1916', in *Oso,* 1984 no. 2.

Emmer, P.C. (1986). 'The Great Escape: The Migration of Female Indentured Servants from British India to Surinam 1873-1916', in *Centrum voor de geschiedenis van de Europese Expansie*: 1-17.

Fokken, Margriet (2011). 'Dutch Interest and South Asian Lives: South Asian Men and Women in the Suriname Colonial Reports between 1873-1917'. MA-thesis, University of Groningen.

Hassankhan, M.S. and S. Hira (1998). *Historische database Suriname. De gegevens over de Hindostaanse immigranten, 5 delen*, IMWO/AMRIT/Nauyuga, Paramaribo/Den Haag.

Hassankhan, M.S. (1993). De immigratie en haar gevolgen voor de Surinaamse samenleving, in L. Gobardhan-Rambocus and M.S. Hassankhan, *Immigratie en ontwikkeling emancipatie van contractanten*, IMWO, Universiteit van Suriname, Paramaribo.

Hira, S. (2009). *Decolonizing the Mind. Een fundamentele kritiek op het wetenschappelijk kolonialisme*. Amrit, Den Haag.

—— (2003). *Het dagboek van Munshi Rakman Khan*. Oorspronkelijke titel: Levenslicht. Amrit, Den Haag.

Hoefte, R. (1987). 'Female Indentured Labor in Suriname: For better or for Worse?' in *Boletin de Estudios Latinoamericano y del Caribe 42*.

—— (1987). 'The position of Female British Indian and Javanese Contract Laborers Suriname: A Last Word' in *Bolletin de Estudios Latinoamericano y del Caribe 43*.

Klerk, C.J.M. de (1953). *De Immigratie der Hindostanen in Suriname, Amsterdam*, Nederland, Urbi et Orbi.

Lalmahomed, B. (1992). *Hindoestaanse vrouwen: De geschiedenis van 6 generaties*, Utrecht, Nederland.

Mc Neill, J. and C. Lal. (1915). *Verslag der Heeren Mc Neill, J. & Lal, C die in het begin van 1913 de kolonie Suriname bezochten in opdracht der Britsch-Indische regeering, teneinde aldaar een onderzoek in te stellen naar den toestand der Britsch-Indische immigranten. Verslag der Heeren* (Uittreksel H. van Ommeren-Paramaribo.

Meel, P. (1985). '*De emigratie van Hindostaanse contractarbeiders naar Suriname 1873-1917*', in *Groniek, Gronings historisch tijdschrift*, no. 92: 120-38.

Rampertap, S. (2011). '"*Ka bhail?" "Wat is er gebeurd?" Veranderende posities van vrouwen in de Hindostaanse gemeenschap in Suriname, 1916-1950*'. MA thesis, Erasmus University, Rotterdam.

Reddock, R. (1994). *Women, Labour & Politics in Trinidad & Tobago: A History*, Ian Randle Publisher, Kingston.

—— (1985). 'Indian women and Indentureship in Trinidad and Tobago 1845-

1917: Freedom Denied', in *Economic and Political Weekly*, vol. 20, no. 43: 79-87.

Stoler, Anna Laura (2009). *Along the Archival Grain: Epistemic Anxieties and Colonial Common Sense*, Princeton and Woodstock; Princeton University Press.

PART 2

SOCIAL ISSUES AMONG HINDUSTANI IMMIGRANTS IN THE NETHERLANDS

CHAPTER 4

Gender-specific Problems among Surinamese Hindustanis: Suicide and Alcoholism[1]

INDRA BOEDJARATH

INTRODUCTION

Four years ago a Surinamese-Hindustani woman died of a perforation of the stomach and peritonitis. She had swallowed concentrated acetic acid. Her suicide was thought to be the result of years of spousal abuse. He is now on trial for wilfully driving her to her death. A special case, as never before in Dutch history someone was accused of inciting to commit suicide.

VOLKSKRANT, A DUTCH DAILY, 24 AUGUST 1992

The radical step with fatal consequences this woman took was meant to escape the tight corset of systematic physical and mental abuse and oppression by her husband whom she married four years before. This suicide emerged from a situation she felt was unbearable, for ending an immediately present experience. Was this step an attempted suicide gone awry or a suicide that succeeded by accident? Was mental illness involved? Was her personality to blame? Was it a

[1] In Dutch parlance, the term 'Hindustani' [Hindo(e)staan(s)] denotes (pertaining to) a person of Indian origin in the diaspora. In international literature the term 'South Asian' is commonly used to refer to descendants of emigrants from India. For clarity purposes, I prefer to use the anglicized Dutch term throughout. I express my gratitude to Mark Eijkman for the translation into English, and for his proof-reading and comments.

lack of healthy coping mechanisms? Or should we look at the cultural background of this woman for an explanation? The opinions around this court case were divided. A Surinamese-Hindustani expert, a male, commented in the same newspaper article: 'The deceased woman made the choice to take her own life herself, and that has to do with her personality rather than her Hindustani background'. He felt that 'abuse is something is common in all cultures, it's not the sole preserve of Hindustanis', but also: 'she could have engaged her family, something she didn't do; that's why it went wrong.' Can a woman who has been taught from childhood to be resigned, and that she *is paraya dhan* or *kisi aur ke amanat* (someone else's treasure) easily turn to her family? The question is, too, whether the reaction of the expert speaking here wasn't just an expression of the silent collective responsibility of the Hindustani community not to wash its dirty linen in public, connected to the social code *manai ka boli?* (what are people going to say?)

Stories like these, from twenty years ago, still exist, albeit under different circumstances. Various studies have shown there are a lot of hidden grief among Hindustanis, as is demonstrated by the following story. A Hindustani man with a successful career, owning an accountancy firm with many clients, is frequently quarrelling with his wife at home, who feels he is drinking too much, and is overly occupied by his work. His two adolescent daughters are extremely rebellious and are constantly behaving disrespectfully towards him. The fights are getting out of hand and the man abuses his wife, especially after he has had a few drinks. One day his wife reports him to the police and the man ends up in a domestic violence reduction programme requiring him to follow a course in 'handling aggression'. He later drops out and there is no change in the domestic situation. The man becomes increasingly quiet and withdrawn, takes to the bottle and his business is going under. After four months his youngest daughter finds him hanging from a rope in the attic. He has committed suicide. Was he depressed? Did he feel his role as a male had been undermined, his role as a provider, as a husband? Had he become too ashamed to face his family? An (attempted) suicide is never an isolated incident. It always takes place in the context of an individual in his or her surroundings. Both biopsycho-social and socio-cultural elements may play a role.

These cases suggest that hidden suffering often results in alcohol abuse, domestic violence, suicide attempts and suicides. Several studies have indicated that the rates of attempted and completed suicide in India and the Indian diaspora (in the UK, the Netherlands, Singapore, Trinidad and Tobago, Guyana, the USA, Mauritius, Fiji, etc.) are very high (Bhugra and Desai, 2002; Mayer 2010; Burger et al., 2005; Bhugra, 2004; Garssen, 2007; Mehta, 1990). In the Netherlands, Hindustani men commit suicide twice as often as males from all other communities (Garssen et al., 2007) and Hindustani women engage in attempted suicide four to five times more than native Dutch women of the same age group (Burger, 2013; Burger et al., 2005; Schudel et al., 1998).

A study analysing the leading causes of mortality in Indians, and differences across age and sex (Palaniappan et al., 2010) concludes that cardiovascular diseases were the leading cause of death for both sexes, followed by diabetes and traumas/accidents/suicides. This analysis confirms the leading causes of death found in other regions with a large population of Indian descent.

The aim of this paper is to take a closer look at the (mental) problems and the underlying aspects of these self-destructive coping strategies. On the basis of a literature search[2] and the life stories of Hindustani men and women who have received mental healthcare, specifically in the author's practice, I will unravel typical interconnected patterns of social, cultural, and personal drivers. First, I

[2] In a literature search about healthcare for migrants, stereotypical generalizations appear to be hard to avoid. To gain an insight and discover connections, making generalizations is imperative. Explanations and points of debate should therefore not be seen as absolute. Within Hindustani society many differences are discernible. When observing (the impact of) Hindustani culture it is important to remind oneself culture is a dynamic concept, and what is being described here doesn't apply to all Hindustani people.

will address parasuicide[3] and suicide among Hindustanis in general. Then I will focus on gender-specific elements relating to Hindustani culture that may lead us to a better understanding of how to prevent parasuicide, suicide and excessive alcohol abuse. Finally, I will consider prevention.

PARASUICIDE AND SUICIDE

Worldwide, every year about a million people die by suicide, which means one death every two minutes. The WHO estimates that every year between 10 and 20 million people attempt suicide and about one in ten succeeds. Thirty per cent of all suicides occur in India and China. In India farmers and students are the groups most at risk to commit suicide (Mayer, 2010). Among young adults worldwide suicide is the third most important cause of death. Most of those who took their own lives decided to do so due to family or personal crises or due to undetected and untreated depression. Each suicide has a serious impact on at least six other people. The psychological, social and financial impact of suicide on the family and society is immeasurable. Suicide originates in a complex interaction of biological, genetic, psychological, social, cultural and environmental drivers.

Hindustanis and Parasuicide

Asha is sixteen years old; she attempted suicide after a row with her brother. Her brother was making comments on the fact Asha spoke with boys, and about the way she dressed. 'You look like a slut'.

The latest figures on parasuicidal behaviour (Burger, 2013) show the Surinamese community in The Hague, together with the Turkish community, in the period 2008 to 2010 having a significantly

[3] Definition of parasuicide: 'An act with non-fatal outcome, in which an individual deliberately initiates a non-habitual behaviour that, without intervention from others, will cause self-harm, or deliberately ingests a substance in excess of the prescribed or generally recognized therapeutic dosage, and which is aimed at realizing changes which the subject desired via the actual or expected physical consequences (WHO, 1993).

higher incidence of parasuicides (Figure 4.1). Most striking in this period is that Surinamese men in the age group of 25-34 years attempt suicide 2.5 times more compared to all other ethnic groups, when in the years preceding 2008 the numbers weren't significantly higher. Surinamese women always scored high, which has remained the case, with a high in this period in the 35-44 years cohort.

Hindustani girls and women who attempt suicide experience serious psychosocial problems, mainly as a result of poor communication with their parents and the fact that they experience little freedom of movement and strong social control (Krikke et al., 2000; Salverda, 2004; van Bergen et al., 2006; Bergen et al., 2010). The same holds for women in the diaspora, where studies have shown that conflict in the family – between parents and daughters, between spouses, between daughters-in-law and her in-laws accultruralization problems and social stress are the most common causes

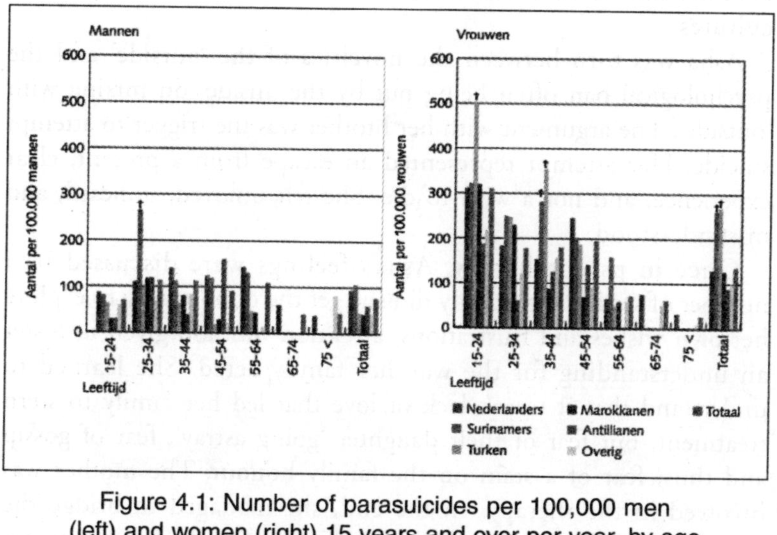

Figure 4.1: Number of parasuicides per 100,000 men (left) and women (right) 15 years and over per year, by age and ethnicity, The Hague 2008-10.
Note the significant elevation compared to native Dutch age and sex peers ($p < .05$) (6). Legend (top down, left to right): Nederlanders = Dutch; Surinamers = Surinamese; Turken = Turks; Marokkanen = Moroccans, Antillianen = people from the Dutch Antilles; Overig = Other.

(Bhugra, 2004; Bhugra and Desai 2002; Mayer, 2010; Mehta, 1990). Only rarely mental disorder seems at play (Burger, 2013; Bhugra, 2004; van Bergen et al., 2011).

In Asha's case, mental disorder wasn't involved either. What did play a role in her case was that she, as a girl, was supposed to abide by a whole different set of rules than her brother was, who enjoyed much more freedom. And then, she would like to go out some time or just hang out in town with her female friends. Often she would ask her mother, who would understand, but would still not give her permission to go out. Many 'migrant mothers' are stuck with a double, somewhat paradoxical role, emanating from family history and their responsibility in raising the children. Frequently this leads to parental inaptitude. On the one hand, they want to indulge their children, whose future will be in the country of migration. On the other hand, they are looking for continuity between the generations and want to impart the appropriate norms and values. Mothers may serve as both a conduit, and a demarcation between cultures.

Asha was torn between the novelties of the 'outside' and the psychological ban often being put by the 'inside' on mixing with 'outside'. The argument with her brother was the trigger to attempt suicide. Her attempt represented an escape from a present, clear experience, and not a wish to die. She felt unloved, unheard, and misunderstood.

Once in psychotherapy, Asha's feelings were discussed in a number of sessions. Not only did she get the opportunity to explore her own wishes and frustrations, attention was also given to foster an understanding for the way her family acted. She learned to understand that it wasn't lack of love that led her family to stern treatment, but fear of their daughter 'going astray', fear of gossip and thus, fear of a stain on the family honour. The mother was involved in the therapy. In the end, she managed to bridge the differences with the rest of the family. She first had to overcome her own 'objections', which meant primarily her heeding to the social code of Manai ka boli (what will people say) I mentioned before. She was encouraged to talk about her own adolescence, which made her recognize her daughter's behaviour. The mother's adolescent behaviour had expressed itself in the 1970s in, for instance, her struggle with her parents to be allowed to wear miniskirts. A recognition evolved in which the yearning for individuality and self-determination established a common ground, and she felt room to face up to her irrational fears and engage in negotiations with her daughter, instead of drawing unmotivated, strict lines. The space was created to really see and get to know each other. Each family member's share in all of this responsibility was also addressed. Asha turned out not to be 'bad' anymore than her mother was, but that had become a label to disapprove of behaviour there was no consensus on in the family. The family proved able to indeed grant Asha more freedom of movement when they became confident she wouldn't go astray. Both the brother, acting as the protector of honour, and the father, who was primarily caught up in alcohol abuse, were in due course able to put the whole situation in a different perspective.

HINDUSTANIS AND SUICIDE

Dew was 49 years old when he took his own life by hanging. Having immigrated to the Netherlands as an adolescent, he followed vocational training without graduating, but managed to find a job as a car mechanic, working since he was 18 years old.

He got married and had four children. His family meant the world to him and he would do anything to make sure his children would get a proper education. He was moonlighting besides his day job to pay for his children's studies. Then, the company he worked for went bankrupt. Dew tried to find a new job for over a year, but was told each time that he didn't have the right diplomas. Even though he had ample experience, he was turned down wherever he went. Meanwhile, the family had to make do with less. Dew regularly mentioned he didn't want his family to suffer the poverty he and his parents had experienced when he was a young boy. One night, after his numerous job applications were rejected, Dew started to drink heavily when he wouldn't normally, and killed himself. He left his family a handsome life insurance payout.

Suicide is relatively common among Hindu Surinamese men in the Netherlands until they reach middle age, while Muslim

Surinamese do not differ much from native Dutch in this respect. Garssen et al. (2007) found significantly higher suicide figures in the Netherlands among Hindustani men aged 35 to 54 years, and among young Creole men aged 15 to 35 years (see Figure 4.2). Among Hindustani women, the numbers at a young age (15 to 34 years) are significantly elevated as compared to Dutch; in other age groups their suicide rate does not differ a great deal from the suicide rate among native Dutch women. Suicide figures of Surinamese men are about three times those of Surinamese women, while among native Dutch men they are about two times those of native Dutch women.

Recent figures on suicides in The Hague (Burger, 2013) show that of all non-native men, the Surinamese are the group most represented with nearly 10 per cent of all suicides in the period 2001 to 2010. In non-native women, the Surinamese have again become the largest group in this period (8.7 per cent of total number of suicides).

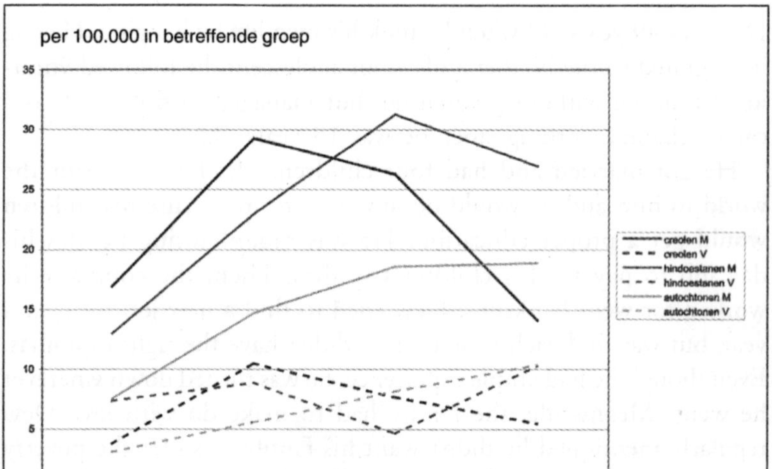

Source: Garssen et al., 2007.

Figure 4.2: Incidence of suicide among Dutch Surinamese by ethnicity, gender and age (1996-2005).

The following elements constitute a possible explanation of elevated incidence in men: migration stress, identity crisis and depression caused by the shift from a collectivist to an individualist society; high expectations men are supposed to meet as concerns education, profession and business success; lack of communication skills as concerns feelings; social control; impulsivity, alcohol and drugs abuse, and aggression when ambitions are frustrated; frustration over failing to achieve life goals (Garssen et al., 2007).

As for Dew, a combination of different drivers played a role in his suicide. Although from a poor family, he had made it, even without a diploma. He admittedly didn't do as well as his older brother, who was a doctor the whole family was showing off with, Dew was satisfied with his life. His parents, who had two sons, called him Lachman, Lord Rama's younger brother, after the story in the Hindu epic *Ramayana*. Dew built up a life living in harmony with his family. The turning point in his life came when he lost his job. When people asked Dew about his job, he would prefer to avoid the subject or become irritated. His wife tried to encourage him and told him it would all be ok. But Dew was consumed by the feeling he couldn't fulfil his role as a provider anymore. He developed fears. His greatest fear was that his family would live in poverty. He shared this fear with no one, but took action, like taking out a good life insurance. Although he was doing fine in his family, he felt his relatives' unspoken pressure was mounting, especially when they were talking about his brother who had been so successful; then Dew felt himself overshadowed by the great 'Rama'.

Suicide numbers of Hindustani men in the Netherlands, and of those in Suriname are about equal. There is, however, a difference in age group; a younger group having the highest incidence (Figure 4.3) in Suriname. According to WHO data published in April 2011 suicide deaths in Suriname were 4.01 per cent of total deaths, ranking the country 8th in the world. Graafsma et al. (2006) identified suicide and attempted suicide as serious mental health problems in Suriname, especially in Nickerie, a rather isolated agricultural town and district in the far west of the country. An epi-demiological study in Nickerie revealed high rates of suicide

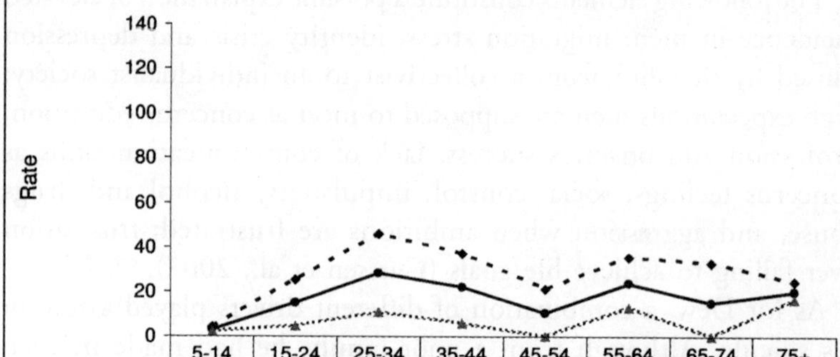

	5-14	15-24	25-34	35-44	45-54	55-64	65-74	75+
Total	3.1	15.1	28.4	21.9	10.4	23.5	14.8	19.8
Male	4.1	25.5	45.6	37.0	21.0	35.2	32.9	24.6
Female	2.1	4.4	10.6	5.7	0.0	12.8	0.0	16.6

Age group

Source: WHO, 2005.

Figure 4.3: Suicide rates per 100,000, by gender, in Suriname (1975-2005).

(48 per 100,000) and attempted suicide (207 per 100,000) on an average in the years 2000-4. In particular, the researchers found remarkably high numbers of attempted suicides among males (49 per cent), and the use of pesticides in both fatal (55 per cent) and nonfatal suicidal behaviour (44 per cent). The high incidence of suicidal behaviour seems to be a reflection of the very poor economic situation of the district, the poverty of most of the population, high levels of alcohol abuse, domestic violence, the rigidity of Hindustani culture regarding family traditions, the accessibility of pesticides, and a lack of perspective.

In Suriname hanging, consuming pesticide, and jumping from the high Wijdenbosch Bridge seem to be the most prevalent methods to commit suicide. Poisoning isn't uncommon among Hindustanis in either Suriname or the Netherlands, mostly involving ingesting bleach or acetic acid. In popular speech, acetic acid is even referred to as *koelie-cola* (coolie coke), not just because of the dark colour of the liquid. Over the last decades, these agents seem to have been replaced with pesticides, notably the herbicide Gramoxone.

Pesticide self-poisoning accounts for about one-third of the world's suicides, mostly occurring in rural areas. Besides Suriname, the highest numbers are found in rural areas in Sri Lanka and India, and in the Indian diaspora in Fiji, Malaysia, Guyana, Trinidad and Tobago and Singapore (Gunnel, 2007). Graafsma et al. (2006) note that healthcare alone cannot tackle this problem. The authors suggest that to prevent suicide in Suriname, one of the most urgent measures would be to store pesticides in locked cabinets with the key held by the proprietor of the farm. Restricting access to this means of suicide seems to be more urgent and more technically feasible than anything and would help to prevent mainly unplanned, impulsive suicide, according to Graafsma and his colleagues.

Newspapers in Suriname regularly report on suicides by Hindustanis, predominantly from Nickerie. Reports like this one, from the online *Dagblad* (Daily) *Suriname* of 24 February 2013 are not uncommon: 'A 14 year old boy, J.W., has taken his own life on Thursday. He put his words into deeds. This little boy hanged himself from a tree using a piece of rope. According to the preliminary inquiry the motive was thought to be related to domestic problems'. Or the following detailed story from the same daily, on 7 May 2012 (translation by the author):

> 29 year-old Maheshwar B., Aka Rajin, hanged himself in the early morning on Sunday at about 00.30 hours. This happened on Sairenweg (Sairen Road) in Paradise, in the neighbourhood of the Corantijnstrand cremation grounds. On Saturday around 21.00 hours he was at his brother's home in the Van Pettenpolder, where he parted with his ring, giving it to his brother Sunil and saying he was leaving forever. He couldn't be stopped. After leaving, he drank some alcohol at a supermarket. He hanged himself with a piece of rope he had taken off a calf grazing in the immediate vicinity'. Remarkably, a lot of media attention is given to suicides; there is even a news site in Nickerie that makes all kinds of (even gruesome) videos and posts them on You Tube.

Intense reporting on suicides can have a contagious effect especially when they are being glamourized, provoking imitation or 'copycat suicides'. This phenomenon has been observed in India on many occasions, especially after the death of a celebrity, most often a movie star or a politician. Copying methods depicted in movies isn't uncommon either. Bollywood films can be socializing, as for instance in the movie *Mohabattein*, that features the heroine committing suicide because her father won't allow her to be with the love of her life. The suicide is not being problematized, but rather romanticized. This has an important socializing effect.

Wide exposure given by the media has led to suicides carried out in a similar manner. The risk of additional suicides occurring increases when the story explicitly describes the method employed, uses dramatic or graphic headlines or images, and when repeated and extensive coverage sensationalizes or glamourizes a death. Several leading experts, some of whom developed reportingon-suicide.org have established guidelines for the media, because carefully covering suicide, even briefly, can help to change public misperceptions and correct myths, which might encourage those who are vulnerable or at risk to seek help.

SUICIDE IN INDIAN HISTORY

An appreciation of the literary, religious, and cultural ethos of the subcontinent is necessary to understand suicide in the Indian context (Bhugra, 2004; Lal, 1985). Ancient Indian texts contain stories in which suicide as a means to avoid shame and disgrace was glorified. Suicide has been mentioned in the great epics of *Ramayana* and *Mahabharata*. In the *Ramayana*, when Lord Rama died, an epidemic of suicide ensued in his kingdom Ayodhya. In Upanishadic period suicide was generally condemned, but it was acceptable for holy men, especially if they had reached the stage in life where they had gained insight into life's problems. Suicide was permitted on religious grounds, as death was seen as the beginning of another life. The *Bhagavad Gita* condemns suicide for selfish reasons and posits that such a death does not allow for *shradha*, the all-important last rites. However, the Vedas permit suicide for religious reasons and consider that the best sacrifice was that of one's own life. Suicide by starvation, also known as *sallekhana*, was linked to the attainment of *moksha* (liberation from the cycle of life and death), and is still practiced to this day, mainly among Jains. *Sati*, which involves a woman immolating herself on the pyre of her husband rather than live the life of a widow, and *jahuar (johar),* in which Rajput women collectively killed themselves to avoid humiliation at the hands of foreign invaders, were practiced until the late Medieval times; a few stray cases of *sati* continue to be reported even now.

Suicide among Indentured Labourers

Suicide attempts were punished during the contract period, even by prison sentences (Choenni and Choenni, 2012), because ending one's life was seen as a breach of contract. Many people at the time attempted or succeeded in suicide, all over the Indian diaspora. The majority of those who committed suicides were males, twice as often or more than Hindustani women would. A striking detail is that the highest number of suicides was to be found among the Brahmin caste (Lal, 1985). The Fiji Indian suicide rate in the period 1900 to 1915 was the highest among all Indian labour importing colonies in Africa and the West Indies, and much higher than in India itself. In Mauritius too, hundreds of indentured Indian labourers committed suicide by jumping from a particular hillock during the indenture period, which acquired the name of 'Suicide Hill', now turned into a monument. The situation was no better in Fiji, though it may have been slightly less hopeless in the Caribbean countries and the Guyanas, including Suriname. Even so, in Suriname too many suicides were witnessed.

In his article 'Veil of Dishonour' Lal (1985) describes what officials tend to point out as the primary cause of the Fiji Indian suicides: sexual jealousy arising from the persistent shortage of women on the plantations. The rate of indentured adult Indian females to males in Fiji was only 43 to 100. The intense competition for women among the indentured men was seen as the main reason for male suicides in Fiji. Lomarsh Roopnarine (2007) also shows high rates of suicides among indentured Indians in British Guiana. Incidentally, not all marital relationships during indenture were monogamous. Polyandry was socially sanctioned and practiced among some castes and ethnicities in India and the practice was reinstated on some of the plantations, in part to cope with the added pressure of the shortage of women. The Hindu epic *Mahabharata* provides a famous example of polyandry with Draupadi, daughter of the king of Panchāla being married to five brothers, the Pandavas.

Although there is no reason to doubt the existence of sexual jealousy, this emphasis on the scarcity of women disregards the arduous circumstances in which the indentured labourers were working, and the disruption of the 'integrative institutions' of society – family, marriage, caste, kinship and religion – as the underlying causes of suicide and other ills afflicting the Indian indentured labour population in Fiji, and indeed all over the diaspora. Additionally, women were more free to leave their husbands than in India, because their relations weren't legally registered and women had their own sources of income. This liberty was traditionally seen as an affront and loss of face for the male. Lal (1985, p. 222) tells us of Ammakanna, who had left her quarrelsome husband, and told the official investigating her husband's suicide on 30 January 1917: 'We were married five years ago. We had quarreled constantly. He had complained constantly of my shortcomings as a housekeeper. He placed a rope on the beam of our room a fortnight ago when I expostulated with him'. Some women left with their share of the earnings and jewellery when domestic life degraded to constant tension and torment, or when their lives were endangered. The women were most often vilified and accused of debauchery by both indentured males and officials. Because the women's perspective is absent in the written records in which, for the most part, 'their faces are shrouded by a veil of dishonour drawn by men', as Lal (1985) puts it. In Suriname, the situation was no different (Choenni and Choenni, 2012). When subsequently the community was reverting to a more regular, traditional social order, women tended to lose the temporarily freer position they held before.

The suicides can be better understood when we look at the circumstances the men lived in, that is, facing unaccustomed problems in unfamiliar surroundings, without the support of family and the guiding hand of an established community. The actual or threatened absence of the family in the lives of deeply depressed young individuals, together with all the disorganization that emigration and indenture caused, probably aggravated the sense of anomy and alienation, both conducive to suicide. Discrimination played a role, too; both among themselves, on the basis of skin colour or caste, and by the white rulers. It remains to be seen to what extent departure from India was voluntary and what effect the recruiting system had on the well-being of the migrants, when deception and kidnapping seem to have been quite common (Bhagwanbali, 2010).

ALCOHOL

The abuse of alcohol is a problem all over the world. It is estimated that 4 per cent of all global deaths and 5 per cent of global disability-adjusted life-years (daly's: a measure of overall disease burden, expressed as the number of years lost due to ill-health, disability or early death) are attributable to alcohol (Rehm et al., 2009). Alcohol may lead to disorders wholly attributed to alcohol, such as acute alcohol poisoning. Chronic alcohol exposure can cause chronic diseases (e.g., liver disease, hypertension and cancers), infections (e.g., tuberculosis), mental illness (e.g., depression and suicide) and road traffic fatalities and injuries. Furthermore, it has damaging social and economic effects, both on individuals themselves (e.g., days lost to work) and their families (e.g., violence) (ibid., 2009). Alcohol use has been identified as a key factor in the incidence of homicide, and domestic violence is also exacerbated by alcohol (Pyne et al., 2002).

Among a certain segment of Hindustanis all over the diaspora alcohol appears to be a problem, with all available evidence pointing to men being the predominant consumers. In the Netherlands, Braam (1998) presented data on inhabitants of Amsterdam of Surinamese descent. Although Hindustani Surinamese tended to be teetotalers more often than Afro-Surinamese (58 per cent to 39 per cent), the percentage of excessive drinkers was almost equal among both groups (Afro-Surinamese: 7 per cent; Hindustani Surinamese: 5 per cent), with binge drinkers and habitual heavy drinkers most often being poorly educated.

A study (Ramlal-Körmeling and Rolsma, 1989) conducted in The Hague, the Hindustani 'capital' of the Netherlands, clearly indicated alcohol use among Suriname's Hindustanis led to psychosocial problems, and alcoholic men tended to ascribe relational problems to women's liberation. The researchers concluded that alcohol performed a clear, positive function in the Hindustani community, as a sign of hospitality and confirmation of group solidarity. This is affirmed by drinking habits at parties, when even if alcohol isn't served, men will congregate in the car park to have a drink from the stash in the boot of their cars.

There is a, somewhat mistaken view in Hindustani communities that their religious and cultural background acts as a barrier to the kind of drunken scenes that are, however, seen so often among Hindustanis. Although it is difficult to stereotype drinking habits among a group as diverse as this, given the differences in language, and cultural and religious practices, there are some recurrent themes that may put Hindustanis at risk for abusing alcohol. Despite the absence of well-controlled longitudinal data currently available to support this, there are some preliminary data to suggest alcohol abuse and binge drinking (O'Hare and Tran, 1998).

With more than half of all alcohol consumers in India meeting the criteria for hazardous drinking, alcohol abuse is emerging as a major public health problem (Prasad, 2009). Studies suggest between 33 and 50 per cent of middle-aged Indian men currently use alcohol (Gajalakshmi, 2009). India's reputation as a country with a culture of abstinence is shifting rapidly to alcohol use as a lifestyle choice. Another shift being reported is women increasingly consuming alcohol regularly and heavily. The main problem is people beginning to drink at an ever younger age.

In a literature review Hurcombe et al. (2010) found that, in the UK, alcohol-related deaths are higher among Indian men than among the general population. Women showed an increased tendency to drink frequently and heavily, especially in the higher income brackets. Hindus and Muslims are less likely to drink if they report that religion is important to them, but, if they do drink, rates tend to be high compared with other religious groups. Sikh men show high rates of heavy drinking, and are over-represented for liver cirrhosis. In the UK a group of Sikh women even started a 'name and shame' campaign aimed at wedding binge drinkers to end the problems associated with excessive drinking. Douds et al.

(2003) studied ethnic differences in the UK in cirrhosis of the liver and concluded that alcohol was the commonest cause of cirrhosis (60.9 per cent) and Hindustani non-Muslim males with alcoholic cirrhosis were over-represented and were younger at diagnosis than their white counterparts. A study in the USA shows that although male Hindustani students consume alcohol less frequently than their American counterparts, they consume larger amounts (Yeramaneni, 2009).

Moderate alcohol consumption is known to be protective against coronary heart disease (Yusuf, 2004). But this does not apply to Hindustanis. A thorough study has revealed that alcohol consumption in Hindustanis was not protective against coronary heart disease, in sharp contrast to other populations who benefit from it (Roy et al., 2010). In fact, Hindustanis who consume alcohol had a 60 per cent higher risk of heart attack, which was more pronounced with local spirits (80 per cent) than branded spirits (50 per cent). The harm was observed in alcohol users classified as 'occasional', as well as 'light', 'moderate', and 'heavy' consumers. Potential explanations for this alcohol paradox include an unfavourable variant of alcohol dehydrogenase, which is known to have an impact on coronary heart disease. Also, the common practice of binge drinking as well as the concomitant use of tobacco are contributors to the paradox (Bagnardi et al., 2008). So the absence of a beneficiary effect of alcohol among Indians is possibly due to unhealthy patterns of drinking.

Younger Hindustanis, being raised in a strict environment, often begin drinking once they enter higher education or become independent from their parents. In addition, many do not feel comfortable speaking openly about emotional problems with their family members and peers, which unfortunately may lead to alcohol use as a source of comfort.

Heavy drinking is nothing new among Hindustanis. Choenni and Choenni (2012) describe alcohol abuse as one of the many problems of indentured labourers. They even see alcohol use and abuse as the 'central theme throughout the history of Hindustanis in Suriname' (p. 367). On the plantations drinking was rampant, to forget problems, combat fatigue, and for relaxation. At the time, women were drinking too, which came to be seen as improper after the contract period was over, unlike the men's drinking habits. Men indulged themselves with rum (*half achtste* – 'one shot') and later whisky. All kinds of conditions to be expected as a result of alcohol abuse ensued, as did domestic violence. Choenni and Choenni (2012, pp. 374-5) relate the story of a young woman who after getting married came to be seriously abused by her husband, a doctor, who could not stand her complaining of him having mistresses. One night, when he came home drunk once again, the fight got so out of hand that he strangled her. Startled to find she was dead, he then hanged her with a piece of rope in the kitchen annex to make it look like a suicide.

SOCIALIZATION

Women and men are always socialized in the specific context of a particular culture with its associated gender roles. One may define culture as the learned values, beliefs, norms and way of life that influence an individual's thinking, decisions and actions in specific ways. Culture is dynamic and constantly developing. Gender roles, too, are subject to change, depending on context, time and place. In the culture and gender-specific socialization of Hindustanis one may not just find more explanations for elevated incidence of (para)suicide and alcoholism, but also clues for solutions.

Culture-specific Socialization

Classical Hindustani culture, just like that of many other immigrant communities with a group-oriented culture, is characterized by strict parameters of what constitutes normal and out of the normal behaviour. Each age group and both genders are burdened by great expectations. These expectations will generally be upheld implicitly and subtly by families and the Hindustani community as a whole, but felt explicitly by the individual and often steered by the social code Manai ka boli. This serves to tacitly keep each other in line, and sometimes in a stranglehold. Getting ahead, success, achievements in society, and honourable behaviour are highly valued, while achieving success may also 'compensate' for certain kinds of problematic behaviour, like a doctor having a drinking problem. In any case, the social code and the corresponding expectations put pressure on all members of the community. Every family and almost every household produces and reproduces that pressure, a pressure that can be traced back to the need for self-preservation, and to fear. Fear of change, of the unknown, of the disintegration of the family and the community, or fear based on one's uncertain position in life. These fears are most often subconscious and deeply embedded, experienced individually and carried collectively (Boedjarath and Eijkman, 2003).

Having children growing up in a different and dominant culture in itself generates intercultural tension in the parent-child relation. A tension that shows in the way affective bonds are shaped, and in the parents' normative authority. Hindustani adolescents find themselves in the new society day in day out, and at the same time experience a mental ban on radically integrating in that society. To many parents, the touchstone for a good upbringing means obedience, and good results in school, good manners, respect for 'superiors', and cultivating a good reputation. For girls, this good reputation mostly resides in an honourable, that is, sexually untainted existence. For boys, it means to stay away from drugs and crime. Now, the insecurity and fear I mentioned earlier express themselves most severely upon encountering elements outside one's culture and familiar conduct. An encounter with a 'stranger' entails insecurity, which expresses itself in the fear of not understanding the other, and at the same time not being understood or even engulfed in oneself. This might explain why Hindustanis married off their daughters at a very early age when confronted with the threat of the advancing Moghuls, but also the current fear of losing their daughters to someone from another culture, or to a Westernized lifestyle. This might bring them to enforce strict and stifling rules.

Living in a multicultural society means the old time day values are no longer self-evident; it turns out there are multiple ways of dealing with the same matters, which renders the 'old' normative style of upbringing inconclusive, which may lead to authority problems (Boedjarath, 2006; Boedjarath and Ferber, 2006). An example of this is the clash in communication styles. The style of communication used most, and that primarily fits in an authoritative household, is not catching on anymore with the wives and children. The children, growing up in Dutch culture, may be more used to negotiating and arguing. Parents who fail to co-emancipate will be 'old-fashioned, traditional and strict' in their children's eyes. The stress will then be on the communication skills of the family to find agreement. Negotiating and convincing will then be the strategy to go by. However, that is opposed to the authoritative household style most Hindustani parents were socialized in. A comparable discrepancy might develop between men and women, when women are emancipating more rapidly than men. The ensuing tensions and clashes may lead to all kinds of excesses like domestic violence, extreme alcohol use and suicidal behaviour.

Individuals experiencing difficulties of any kind with the group will find it hard to talk about it, as the individual is both subordinated to the group, and its ambassador charged with upholding the group reputation and honour. In exchange for this role the group offers shelter and security, a 'deal' rooted in the joint family system. Even if one no longer lives in such a group unit, the social codes and silent control may still apply, despite the eroding force of migration. Even if values in the country of origin continue to evolve, after migration one may, out of self-preservation, try to live up to one's own culture, albeit a petrified form of that culture.

Although the classical version of Hindustani culture is to be encountered less and less in its full flower, and Hindustani group conscience may no longer be strongly present in all families, internalized components can be traced even in the increasing diversity in individual values and behaviour. The civilization Hindustanis inherited may be modified and overlaid by elements specific to the new cultural environment. Yet an underlying sense of Indian identity continues to persist, even into the third or fourth generation of the Indian diaspora around the world, and not only when they gather for a Diwali celebration or to watch a Bollywood movie (Kakar, 2007). An example of this is presented by Faranaz, an emancipated, fairly Westernized, successful Surinamese Hindustani lawyer who from an early age was driven by the will to succeed and was seen as an example by her environment. Until a burnout incapacitated her and she discovered she suffered the effects of Manai ka boli.

Kakar (2007) states using the term 'Indianness' is preferable to using a limited concept like 'Indian identity'. Indianness is omnipresent and multiform. It comprises thoughts, actions, and institutions, and is both dynamic and contextual. It perfectly relates to notions like habitus and cultural understandings. Indianness, then, is about similarities produced by an overarching Indic civilization, pre-eminently but not exclusively Hindu, that has contributed the lion's share to what Kakar calls the 'cultural gene pool' of Indian people.

The high value placed on connectedness does not mean that an Indian is incapable of functioning when he is by himself or that he does not have a sense of his own agency. It implies his greater need for ongoing mentorship, guidance and help from others in getting through life and a greater vulnerability to feelings of helplessness when these ties are strained.

Gender-specific Socialization

Migration doesn't leave gender roles untouched. In most Hindustani families men were traditionally the head of the family and the provider, in accordance with patriarchal norms. The wife used to lead in running the household and upbringing. Girls and boys were – definitely after a certain age – socialized with norms, values and conduct becoming their gender in the context at hand. Usually the boy and future man enjoyed more freedom, and acted as the protector of the family, especially of the honour of the family's female members. Starting at the development of secondary sex differentiation girls were subjected to rules protecting their sexual honour, meaning they should shun boys and avoid indecent behaviour. Hindustani women were for a large part – financially, as well as socially, and in some cases emotionally – dependent on male family members. Possibly that led to Hindustani women's widespread and long-time forbearance and self-sacrifice for the benefit of the family.

Often, the many Hindu writings were and are used as a source for the upbringing of girls as concerns gender roles, but mostly, this serves to put women in their place as the second sex. The cultural implementation of the old traditions thus shows up a selective use of the many role models available in Hindu tradition, like the story of Rama and Sita in the *Ramayana*. However, of all of Sita's qualities and virtues, only those contributing to the image of a subservient, tolerant, self-sacrificing, chaste, honourable, ever friendly woman, even in the face of humiliation and rejection are employed (Boedjarath, 2007). Rama questioning Sita's honour after her abduction by Ravana drove Sita to undergo the trial by fire and endure dismissal and rejection, with her ultimately preferring death. In telling and retelling of Sita's story, women and men learn to read gendered behaviour through this frame (Bhatt, 2008). The association of the feminine with nurturing mother figures is seen by feminists as a patriarchal conspiracy to put women in restrictive and self-effacing roles.

Cultural and religious heritage will always form some part of one's upbringing. Hindustanis, both Hindus and Muslims, are no different; tradition seeps in, sometimes quoted literally from writings, or else by oral tradition. It would be preferable if educators not only highlighted interpretations of stories underscoring women's oppression, but above all stressed the strength of the women in those stories, too. In the Rama and Sita case, that would mean also showing the other side of the story. Mahatma Gandhi used the Sita symbol to advocate the idea of women's strength, autonomy and ability to protect themselves rather than depend on men for safety. His Sita was like a 'lioness in spirit' (Kishwar, 1997). Also, it would help men to emphasize Rama's sensitivity.

Meanwhile, a lot has changed in the role of women. Women are enjoying more education and are active in the workforce, by their own choice or out of financial necessity. Women have become more independent, financially, but also in other respects. In this growing independence and emancipation, women in the Netherlands usually experience more room than in Suriname, resulting from, among others, the right to free speech and sanctions on (sexual) violence, including within marriage. All this doesn't leave men untouched, in both a sociocultural sense and psychological perception. Four general patterns can be discerned in the various coping strategies encountered in practice (Boedjarath, 2010). Firstly, a trend can be observed of men being able to redefine their roles and handle the changes flexibly. These men derive their identity less from the prescribed roles in the community. They intra-psychically construct a 'new' identity in which elements of their own culture, and that of the Dutch-Western one are interwoven.

Other men both fail to achieve a personal, active redefinition of their roles, and firmly retain their old role. This makes them extremely vulnerable, as having a clear identity (no matter how progressive or conservative) constitutes a protective factor in their mental wellbeing. Yet other men stay attached to old role patterns and behaviour, come what may. They are often seen as an 'old-fashioned and strict' father by their children and as a 'traditional' man by their wives. They feel limited in exerting their old authority. One could say the male role has been depleted, which makes these men vulnerable and leads them to crisis after they have failed to redefine their role in the family differently. Incidentally, cross-national and intra-national research has shown there is a clear link between growing equality between men and women, and a decline in the number of suicides (among women), except for the Indian case. In India, on the contrary, a strong correlation was found between an increase in equality of education in men and women, and an increase in suicide in men (Mayer, 2003).

Finally, some men even expand their identity and supplement it with notions, values and norms deemed typical of the culture of origin, in which religion often plays an important part. A revival of a certain partial identity is often witnessed after migration in any case, but this group tends to become more Catholic than the Pope. This gives them a hold, but may also frustrate and isolate them when applied rigorously, and when they fail to connect with their surroundings.

IDENTITY

The development of identity of Hindustani adolescents in the Netherlands is bicultural and multiple, which poses especially difficult tasks for them compared to their native peers. For instance, a Hindustani adolescent has a different problem when building up a separate individuality and autonomy as a result of the stronger vertical bond with the parents that is a feature of the intrinsically hierarchical relations of the we-culture. They are also negotiating the cultural socialization, that all their lives has transmitted the implicit message 'together in the group you are someone, alone, you are lost'. The notion of self is inextricably intertwined with the social environment. In group-oriented cultures *social esteem* and *self-esteem* are often synonymous (Van Dijk and Boedjarath, 2002). Interdependence is an important part of identity formation. In some cultures, interdependence is seen as a sign of maturity, when personal independence is exactly not (Chin et al., 1993). The interpretation of the concept of autonomy (self-determination, assertiveness, self-reflection, self-development, self-reliance) may also be problematic. This concept that takes such a prominent place in Western cultures turns out not to be obviously suitable as a cognitive schema, nor does it by definition hand the therapist any meaningful leads (Boedjarath, 2002). The limited validity of the concept of autonomy shows up especially in the case of women. Their group-oriented socialization leads them to focus on respecting traditional relations in the community for survival. Inside the safe network of relations, opportunities arise for personal growth, without eroding connectedness. With Hindustanis, one should rather depart from the concept of 'autonomy-in-connectedness' (Boedjarath, 1994).

The universal polarities of individual versus relational, nearness versus distance in human relationships are prey to culturally moulded beliefs and expectations. Using a metaphor coined by the philosopher Schopenhauer, Kakar (2007) compares the need for belonging in internally oriented groups to hedgehogs huddling together in the cold to stay warm:

> the hedgehogs approach each other for warmth; get pricked by the quills of the other and move away till, feeling cold, they again come closer. This to and fro movement keeps on being repeated until an optimum position is reached where the body temperature is above the freezing point yet the pain inflicted by the quills – the nearness of the other – is still bearable. The leveling point is different in various cultures. In India, for example, as compared to modern European and North American cultures, the optimum position entails the acceptance of 'more pain to get greater warmth.

In the diaspora, this means even more uncertainty as each family member's optimum may vary between the extremes pointed out above.

Migration and the migrant existence can increase the vulnerability of certain groups to psychosocial stress. It is no coincidence Hindustani girls and young women engage in self-damaging behaviour more often than their native peers, as after all, they have to take two cultures into account that aren't always compatible (Boedjarath, 2010). On the one hand, the girls experience peer pressure to fit in and participate. On the other hand parents may set demands that diametrically oppose the outside world's expectations. Quite apart from that, many girls have to deal with specific cultural problems, such as being married off, forcibly or not, or the requirement to preserve their virginity until marriage. The community may have high expectations and make strict demands of girls. Expectations exist for boys as well, as they too are supposed to keep up the family honour and protect the female members of the family. They too feel the pressure to achieve by getting a good education and a good job.

This kind of socialization might have strong repercussions on identity development, and consequently on coping strategies, as there are several, sometimes conflicting loyalties at work. This may also entail an existential fear the moment a girl or boy chooses to go her or his own way, which is psychologically linked to rejecting the parents. Existential fear (Yalom, 1989) is fear stemming from the realization that life is finite, that our existence could be absurd, and that man is free, and therefore has to take decisions. This fear often emerges when the foundations of existence are threatened, physically (by fate and death), mentally (by emptiness and loss of sense) and morally (by guilt and judgement).

COPING STRATEGIES

Under cultural pressure, girls and boys, men and women, have to meet many requirements: to uphold the honour of the family (mostly translated as the sexual honour of the female members); get a good education with good career prospects; find a respectable job; marry honourably; have children; be a good wife; be a good father and provider; own a home and take care of the elderly, etc. Most cope with these requirements in a healthy way and find an agreeable balance in their lives, whether or not they attain those goals. They are able to handle potential adversity.

The groups that are the subject of this article have difficulty coping with these matters. Any event that upsets the expected course of life will often be seen as failure. Think of a daughter getting involved with a boy of another ethnicity, a son turning out to be gay, a wife deciding to get a divorce, a man losing his role as breadwinner. The failure will be criticized by the community and will be experienced by the individual too, as socio-cultural norms are internalized. The 'victim' feels the community is scrutinizing him or her, and feels he/she is standing alone, a feeling being reinforced by the responsibility resting on him or her towards the family and the group. The family honour has not been upheld, generating shame and guilt. The shame is often felt individually and collectively. Individualist emotions, such as anger and guilt, are secondary (Kakar, 2007).

Often, a psychological ban on transgressing the (group)norms exists, and an actual transgression may lead to isolation, alienation and exclusion, which in turn may lead to despair and low self-confidence, self-reproach and feeling torn by loyalty conflicts. Failure, or deviating from the norms and the (supposed) reactions of the environment may cause intense frustration, anger and grief, fretting, feelings of inferiority, depression, and sometimes self-destructive behaviour like alcohol abuse and suicidal behaviour. The connectedness that plays such an important part in one's identity then turns into feeling a loss of attachment. And such a crisis in identity may lead to alcohol abuse with associated feelings of anxiety, guilt and conflict. Suicidal behaviour then becomes a form of communication. The traditional notion of 'a cry for help' becomes in this group a cry for hope, for connection, companionship and understanding, to be seen as an idiom of distress that expresses a lack of connectedness or belonging (Bhugra, 2004). The person concerned longs for reciprocity, (the recovery of) interdependence and retracing the relational self.

Although there is no single cause for suicide and no two suicides can be understood to result from exactly the same constellation of drivers, there are individual elements regularly recurring in Hindustanis. Murphy (1992) emphasizes loss of attachment as crucial to the alcoholism-suicide link. Alcoholism and suicidal behaviour can be seen as coping strategies to deal with stressful situations. Drivers close to the person that are contributing to that strategy are, among others, biological and psychological determinants like helplessness, low resilience, internalization of problems, low frustration, impulsive and aggressive tendencies and loss of attachment. Environmental elements will be loss of loved ones, copycat behaviour, but also availability of means. Socio-cultural triggers may consist of lack of social support, a taboo on seeking help, and also the inaccessibility of professional care. A group with an enhanced risk of self-destructive behaviour is made up of persons with a history of traumatic experiences, like emotional neglect, a low sense of security (deficient attachment), physical, emotional and sexual abuse.

Impulsiveness often plays an important role here, too. There even seems to be a genetic link between addiction and impulsiveness in men. Stoltenberg (2011) mentions the gene NRXN3 in this connection, a gene already associated earlier with smoking. Murphy (1992) emphasizes loss of attachment as crucial to the alcoholism-suicide link. There is strong evidence to suggest that most suicides among Hindustanis are impulsive (Graafsma, 2007; Bhugra, 2004). Graafsma's (2007) finding that the availibility of substances like pesticides poses a great risk to people with impulsive tendencies (read: *Hindustanis in Nickerie, Suriname*) is confirmed by studies in India indicating many farmers commit suicide using pesticides (Gunnel, 2007). The use of pesticides as a means to commit suicide is seen more in unplanned, impulsive suicides, whereas hanging is seen more in planned suicides (Conner et al. 2003). Durkheim (1951) speaks of impulsive or automatic suicide when it is unmotivated; instead of being produced by a fixed idea obsessing the mind for a shorter or a longer period and only gradually affecting the will, it results from an abrupt, immediate and irresistible impulse to kill oneself. In Hindustanis anomic and fatalist suicide prevail (Dullaart et al., 2006).

On the vulnerability and impulsivity of Hindustani men Spijker et al. (2009) comment that a possible explanation may be found in their upbringing, with boys enjoying instant gratification and not learning to endure frustration. There is indeed a culture of instant gratification, whether in the realm of relationships, career or anything else. Very likely most Hindustani suicides in both Suriname and the Netherlands are to be labeled impulsive. Impulsivity, depressogenic cognitive schemata and disillusion resulting from failure to attain goals are a lethal mixture.

PREVENTION

Suicides can be prevented. If there is a way to alleviate the underlying mental pain, the individual will spring back to active life. Most suicidal people can be helped in getting through their moment of crisis if they have someone who will spend time with them, listen, take them seriously and help them talk about their thoughts and feelings.

Acute suicide risk is generally short-lived. Suicidal behaviour, both actual and attempted suicide, is often impulsive. Most survivors of potentially lethal suicide attempts do not appear to have a very high long-term risk of suicide (Hawton, 2005). There is clear evidence that availability of methods to commit suicide influences the choice of method. And changes in availability of popular methods of suicide, as shown before in the shift from acetic acid to pesticides, can have substantial effects on suicides rates.

Most Hindustanis showing suicidal behaviour do not want to die, but want to end a direct, actual experience (Boedjarath and Ferber, 2010), and that is what prevention should focus on. All risk factors mentioned in this article offer leads for preventive strategies.

When targeting the mental make-up of Hindustanis at risk, the focus should be on increasing resilience. The actual moment someone wants to hurt himself often revolves around a lack of, or indeed an excess of violent and agonizing feelings, like fear, guilt, shame and rage (Boedjarath and Ferber, 2010). Too little, or no feeling at all may lead to self-destructive behaviour in order to feel just anything at all. It is then important to teach Hindustanis from an early age to distinguish between feelings; for instance, if they suffer a bad experience, it doesn't mean they are entirely 'bad' as a person, or that they have failed. They should be supported in increasing their self-esteem. It is imperative to explain how to deal with problems, and how to develop skills to cope with (interpersonal) conflict and frustration. Increasing frustration tolerance and problem-solving ability helps to prevent tunnel vision.

At the level of family and community, good communication with the environment has a protective effect. First and foremost, suicidality should come to be seen as a problem of the community, that should realize that failure to problematize suicide will perpetuate its incidence. A harrowing example of what may happen, from the Dutch daily *Algemeen Dagblad* dated 17 December 2005, about a 13-year-old Surinamese Hindustani girl from Rotterdam who fell victim to gang rape while on holiday in a Spanish holiday resort: 'When the girl spoke out after her rape, her family did not believe her, and was outraged. The pressure on the girl eventually became so strong she decided to end her life. She swallowed acetic acid and was later found dead in her room. She was quietly cremated. The girl's family declines to discuss the matter.'

When people learn at an early age to talk about problems, the pressure can be relieved; even if there is just one person, an aunt, a cousin, who listens and gives support. Close, non-oppressive family ties are also effective in curbing self-destructive behaviour, as is social support in the environment. A debate in the wider community on the impact of the social code Manai ka boli is conducive to internal communication. Websites offering culturally sensitive information can contribute to the debate. Example are www. jestaatnietalleen.nl ('you're not on your own') and www.stopsuicide.nu, aimed at Dutch-speaking Hindustanis. Cultural and religious convictions that reject suicidal behaviour may also be protective, if only out of fear of ending up in hell when committing suicide.

Experiencing no taboos on mental health problems and help seeking, in school, in mental healthcare or anywhere else, is also fortifying. But then, that help must be available, and coupled with knowledge about the cultural background of the person seeking help. Providing accessible care that is both culturally sensitive and effective can reduce and prevent a lot of suffering. It is imperative to consider and connect to the perception of the person and his or her family.

And last but not the least, at the societal level, the availability of alcohol and access to pesticides should be reduced, while the media should follow guidelines when reporting on the subject.

DISCUSSION AND CONCLUSION

Fortunately, the issues surrounding suicidal behaviour among Hindustanis receive a lot of attention in the Netherlands, as well as in Suriname and the rest of the diaspora, and the underlying drivers preventive strategies may be derived from are becoming increasingly clear. It has to be said, however, there hardly seems to be a concerted effort to combine the several multifactorial and multidimensional insights acquired in the diaspora, and that a fitting cultural sensitivity is often lacking. This article is meant to be a modest attempt at doing just that, in the hope that there will be more research into self-destructive and even suicidal behaviour among Hindustanis that comprehensively covers biological, genetic, psychological, cultural, religious, social and environmental factors.

Although the will and wish to engage in comprehensive research appears to be there, only a few researchers like Bhugra (2004) succeed in considering the whole spectre of related aspects. Some researchers are inclined to approach the problems from a Western perspective, using Western instruments, developed for and standardized to the self-centred Western culture. They either highlight one specific aspect, like personality or parenting styles, and draw far-reaching conclusions, like Bergen et al. (2006), who trace the single cause for suicidal behaviour in girls in: 'A parental bonding style of affectionless control that hardly knows emotional nurturance'. These kinds of statements tend to live a life of their own, echoed by many subsequent authors, and ignore the fact that parents may act out of fear, while being perfectly capable of showing affection in other areas. Such an approach also neglects the importance of engaging the parents in solutions, instead of demonizing them, when indeed connectedness, or the loss thereof, is implicated in suicidal behaviour (Boedjarath, 2005). Likewise, based on qualitative research in The Hague into the living conditions of Hindustani girls who had attempted suicide (Salverda, 2004), a docudrama was produced (OHM, 2005) to broach the subject with the wider public. The docudrama completely missed the point by framing the girl as a victim to be saved, and the parents as the big villains of the story.

Only too often a situation develops where caregivers or others moved by the adolescent's suffering want to help out based on their own, i.e. Western, point of view. Such an attitude impedes the person's own power and repels the much needed support from the environment. Effective care is characterized by connecting with the experiences and cultural background of people displaying suicidal behaviour. It is important that professionals working with this group have a good command of intercultural skills and possess knowledge of their cultural background in order to proceed in a culturally sensitive way.

Understanding and treating the problems of internalized negative feelings that find an outlet in alcohol abuse or suicidal behaviour not only require knowledge of the psychodynamics and socio-cultural circumstances at play, but also the historical cultural background (Vijayakumaar, 2006). Seen from this perspective, it should be noticed that suicidal behaviour in Indian historical and religious context may have a positively sanctioned connotation. The strong tradition in the often oral transfer of various stories that do not problematize suicide may lower the threshold for suicidal behaviour, or indeed show a traditionally acceptable way out. Incidentally, a striking bias may be witnessed in the way the stories are told; thus, in the story of Radha and Krishna who are the embodiment of love, passion and devotion, the fact that Radha was married to someone else is blissfully overlooked. And yet, suicidal behaviour does not only occur in persons who have been socialized with those stories, but also with Hindustanis who hardly picked up any of that, and with Muslim Hindustanis too. Frustration turned inwards, and (para)suicide seems to be ingrained in Indianness facilitated by a process of intergenerational transfer of mental, behavioural, social and cultural concepts constituting a kind of collective memory, or morphogenetic resonance, as Rupert Sheldrake (1988) calls it. That may possibly be a wider Asian problem, in view of the high numbers of suicides in China and other Asian countries. In the Netherlands, presently girls and young women of Turkish descent are topping the parasuicide table. Moroccan girls, however, with their roots in northern Africa, are growing up in comparable socio-cultural circumstances, but present no elevated risk. The same goes for impulsivity, playing such an important role in suicidal behaviour in men that supposedly had their needs satisfied instantly in childhood (the so-called little princes); Moroccan boys receive a similar upbringing and share similar socio-cultural circumstances, but they do not present an elevated suicide risk. The difference is to be found in internalizing *versus* externalizing problems and frustration, and the corresponding resulting action: causing harm to oneself, *versus* causing harm to the environment. Acting 'in' *versus* acting out.

It is wise to look into the circumstances causing self-destructive behaviour and what means are employed, but it is wiser not to be obsessed with those subjects. The way in which one handles problems offers more clues for change, like increasing resilience and problem-solving ability, and teaching other coping strategies to eventually improve vitality.

REFERENCES

Bagnardi, V. et al. (2008). 'Does Drinking Pattern Modify the Effect of Alcohol on the Risk of Coronary Heart Disease? Evidence from a Meta-analysis', *Journal of Epidemiol Community Health*, 62: 615-19.

Bhatt, A. (2008). 'The Sita Syndrome: Examining the Communicative Aspects of Domestic Violence from a South Asian Perspective', *Journal of International Women's Studies*, 9: 155-73.

Bhugra, D. and M. Desai (2002). 'Attempted Suicide in South Asian Women', *Advances in Psychiatric Treatment*, 8: 418-23.

Bhugra, D. (2004). *Culture and Self-Harm: Attempted Suicide in South Asians in London*, Hove and New York, Psychology Press.

Boedjarath, I. (1994). 'Vrouwengroepen: Over oude principes en nieuwe doelgroepen', in J. Mens-Verhulst and L. van Schilder (eds.), *Debatten in de vrouwenhulpverlening*, Amsterdam Babylon-De Geus, 55-73.

Boedjarath, I. (2002). 'Gender en etniciteit. Hulpverlening aan zwarte, migranten- en vluchtelingenvrouwen', in E. van Meekeren, R. May and A. Limburg-Okken (eds.), *Culturen binnen psychiatriemuren. Geestelijke gezondheidszorg in een multiculturele samenleving,* Amsterdam:Boom, 204-14.

—— (2005). 'Laat me los, hou me vast: een half verhaal over zelfmoordpogingen onder Hindostaanse meiden'. 16 November. http://forum.indianfeelings.nl/religie-spiritualiteit/1193-ohm-hou-me-vast-laat-me-los.html

—— (2006). 'Klem tussen twee werelden?' *Boekelezing lecture* 6 November 2006. Unpublished.

—— (2007). 'Shakti, de kracht van de vrouw'. *Ohmvani, quarterly of the OHM broadcasting foundation,* 13: 24-7.

—— (2010). 'Gender', in J. de Jong and S. Colijn (eds.), *Handboek culturele psychiatrie en psychotherapie,* Utrecht De Tijdstroom, 215-28.

—— (2011). 'Cultuursensitief werken in de interculturele hulpverlening', in R. Van Dijk, R. Borra and R. Verboom (eds.), *Cultuur en psychodiagnostiek. Cultuursensitief werken met psychologische testen,* Houten: Bohn Stafleu Van Loghum, 23-41.

Boedjarath, I. and M. Eijkman (2004). 'Angst staat integratie in de weg', *NRC Handelsblad,* 16 October 2004.

Boedjarath, I. and M. Ferber (2006). 'Verborgen verdriet. Parasuïcide en zelfbeschadiging bij allochtone jongeren'. *Cultuur Migratie Gezondheid* 3:2-13.

—— (2010). 'Huilen zonder tranen: suïcidaal gedrag bij allochtone jongeren', in *Suïcidepreventie in de praktijk,* ed. A.J.F.M. Kerkhof and J.B. van Luyn, Houten: Bohn Stafleu Van Loghum, 175-189.

Braam, R.V. (1998). *Allochtonen en verslaving; Inventarisatie van de aard en omvang van de verslavingsproblematiek onder allochtonen in Nederland en over de werkwijzen en knelpunten in de zorg voor allochtone verslaafden.* Utrecht: Centrum voor Verslavingsonderzoek.

Burger, I. (2013). 'Resultaten registratie suïcidaal gedrag'. *Epidemiologisch Bulletin* 48: 12-28.

Burger, I. et al. (2005). 'Parasuicides in Den Haag: Meldingen in de jaren 2000-2004', *Epidemiologisch Bulletin,* 40: 2-8.

Chin, J.L., V. De La Cancela and Y.M. Jenkins (1993). *Diversity in Psychotherapy: The Politics of Race, Ethnicity and Gender,* Westport: Preager.

Choenni, Ch. and C. Choenni (2012). *Sarnami Hindostani 1920-1960. Worteling, identiteit en gemeenschapsvorming in Suriname,* Amsterdam: KIT Publishers.

Conner, K.R., A.L. Beautrais and Y. Conwell (2003). 'Moderators of the Relationship between Alcohol Dependence and Serious Suicidal Behavior:

Analyses of Canterbury Suicide Project Data'. *Alcoholism: Clinical and Experimental Research*, 27: 1156-61.

Douds, A.C. et al. (2003). 'Ethnic Differences in Cirrhosis of the Liver in a British City: Alcoholic Cirrhosis in South Asian Men', *Alcohol & Alcoholism*, 38: 148-50.

Dullaart, A., A. Kerkhof and T. Graafsma, (2006). 'Suicide bij Hindoestanen. Mogelijke verklaringen voor een verhoogd suiciderisico', *Cultuur Migratie Gezondheid*, 3: 200-10.

Durkheim, E. (1951). *Suicide: A Study in Sociology*, New York: The Free Press.

Gajalakshmi, V. and R. Peto (2009). 'Smoking, Drinking and Incident Tuberculosis in Rural India: Population-based Case-control Study', *International Journal of Epidemiology*, 38: 1018-25.

Graafsma, T. et al. (2006). 'High Rates of Suicide and Attempted Suicide Using Pesticides in Nickerie, Suriname, South America', *Crisis, The Journal of Crisis Intervention and Suicide Prevention*, 27: 77-81.

Gunnell, D. et al. (2007). 'The Global Distribution of Fatal Pesticide Self-poisoning: Systematic Review'. *BMC Public Health*, 7: 357.

Hawton, K. (2005). 'Restriction of Access to Methods of Suicide as a Means of Suicide prevention', in K. Hawton (ed.), *Prevention and Treatment of Suicidal Behavior: From Science to Practice*, Oxford: Oxford University Press, 279-91.

Hurcombe R., M. Bayley and A. Goodman (2010). *Ethnicity and Alcohol: A Review of the UK Literature*, York: Joseph Rowntree Foundation.

Kishwar, M. (2003). 'Of Humans and Divines. Feminine Role Models in Hindu Tradition'. *Manushi*, 136: 17-30.

Krikke, H., H. Nijhuis and R. Wesenbeek (2000). *Aan de Grenzen. Suïcidaal Gedrag onder Allochtone Meisjes en Jonge Vrouwen*. Den Haag: Bureau Public Health Service.

Lal, B.V. (1985). 'Veil of Dishonour: Sexual Jealousy and Suicide on Fiji Plantations', *The Journal of Pacific History*, 20: 135-55.

Mayer, P. (2010). *Suicide and Society in India*, New York: Routledge.

—— (2003). 'Female Equality and Suicide in the Indian States', *Psychological Reports*, 92: 1022-8.

Murphy, G. (1992). *Suicide in Alcoholism*, New York: Oxford University Press.

O'Hare, T. and T. V. Tran (1998). 'Substance Use among Southeast Asians in the U.S: Implications for Practice and Research', *Social Work in Health Care*, 26: 69-80.

OHM (2005). 'Laat me los, hou me vast: zelfmoord onder jongeren', aired by *OHM Broadcasting Foundation*, on 6 November 2005. Hilversum: OHM.

Palaniappan, L. et al. (2010). 'Leading Causes of Mortality of Asian Indians in California', *Ethnicity & Disease*, 20: 53-7.

Prasad, R. (2009). 'Alcohol Use on the Rise in India', *The Lancet*, 373: 17-18.

Pyne, H., M. Claeson and M. Correia (2002). 'Gender and Alcohol Consumption and Alcohol-related Problems in Latin America and the Caribbean', *Pan American Journal of Public Health*, 12: 59-62.

Ramlal-Körmeling, A. and G.J.J. Rolsma (1989). *Onderzoek naar de aard en omvang van alcoholproblematiek bij Surinamers.* Den Haag: Stichting Surinaams Regionaal Steunpunt.

Rehm J. et al. (2009). 'Global Burden of Disease and Injury and Economic Cost Attributable to Alcohol Use and Alcohol-use Disorders', *The Lancet*, vol. 373: 2223-33. Accessed 1 April 2013.doi: 10.1016/S0140-6736(09) 60746-7.

Roopnarine, Lomarsh (2007). *Indo-Caribbean Indenture: Resistance and Accommodation*, Kingston: University of the West Indies Press.

Roy, A. et al. (2010). 'Impact of Alcohol on Coronary Heart Disease in Indian Men'. *Atherosclerosis* 210: 531-5.

Salverda, E. (2004). *Laat me los, hou me vast. Verslag van een kwalitatief onderzoek naar het psychisch welbevinden van dertig Haagse meisjes van Hindostaanse afkomst.* Den Haag: Bureau Public Health Service.

Schudel, W., H. Struben and J. Vroom-Jongerden (1998). 'Suicidaal Gedrag en Etnisch-Culturele Afkomst Den Haag 1987-1993', *Epidemiologisch, Bulletin*, 33: 7-13.

Sheldrake, R. (1988). *The Presence of the Past: Morphic Resonance and the Habits of Nature*, New York: Times Books.

Spijker, B.A.J. et al. (2009). 'Impulsive but Fatal Self-poisoning with Pesticides among South Asians in Nickerie, Surinam', *Crisis*, 30: 102-5.

Van Bergen et al. (2006). 'Gendered and Cultural Patterns of Suicidal Behaviour: Young Hindustani Immigrant Women in the Netherlands', *Crisis*, 27: 181-8.

—— (2011). 'I Felt so Hurt and Lonely': Suicidal Behaviour in South Asian-Surinamese, Turkish and Moroccan Women in the Netherlands', *Transcultural Psychiatry*, 49: 69-86.

D.D. and S. Saharso.(2010). 'Suïcidaal gedrag van jonge vrouwen. De rol van gezinscontext bij Turkse, Hindostaanse, Marokkaanse en autochtone achtergrond', *Cultuur Migratie Gezondheid*, 7: 62-75.

Van Dijk, R. and I.Boedjarath (2002).'Wat een geluk dat niemand weet dat ik Repelsteeltje heet! Op zoek naar het wezen van transculturele psychotherapie', in van E. Meekeren, R. May and A. Limburg-Okken (eds.). *Culturen binnen psychiatriemuren. Geestelijke gezondheidszorg in een multiculturele samenleving*, Boom, Amsterdam.

Yeramaneni, S. and M. Sharma (2009). 'Predictors of Alcohol Use and Binge

Drinking among Asian Indian Students based on Social Cognitive Theory'. *American Journal of Health Studies,* 24(2): 287-97.

Yusuf, S. et al. (2004). 'Effect of Potentially Modifiable Risk Factors Associated with Myocardial Infarction in 52 Countries (the Interheart Study): Case-Control study', *The Lancet,* 364: 937-952.

Yalom, I. D. (1989). *Love's Executioner,* New York: Basic Books.

WHO, (2005). 'Suicide rates (per 100,000), by Gender, Suriname, 1975-2005'. Accessed 29 April.http://www.who.int/mental_health/media/suri.pdf

—— (1993). *International Classification of Diseases-10,* Copenhagen: WHO.

CHAPTER 5

Elderly Surinamese Hindustanis in the Netherlands[1]

NIRMALA BIRJMOHAN

INTRODUCTION

An 85-year-old Hindustani male living in The Hague is asking day in and day out all passers-by to take him to Livorno (a town in Suriname where he was born) while hanging out of the window. In broken Dutch, he asks a Turkish couple loading groceries into their car whether they might give him a ride to Livorno, because he doesn't own a car himself. The Turkish couple, being at a loss, asks a passing Hindustani lady if she might ask him in his native language what he wants. Then the man explains he is living in his son's house, who went abroad for work. His son should have returned ages ago and then could have taken him to Livorno. But now that his son isn't there, he must go by himself. Only, he forgot how to get there. He asks the Hindustani woman whether it's a long ride, whether she knows how to get there, and if she can take him there that afternoon because he just has to go home, to Livorno.

The elderly man invites the woman in so that he may gather his belongings and she can have a glass of lemonade in the meantime. He has arranged his clothes on the table in the living room: a pair of pants, a shirt, and a pair of socks tied into a bundle with a belt. On the wall, right under the ceiling, are framed

[1] In Dutch parlance, the term 'Hindustani' [Hindo(e)staan(s)] denotes (pertaining to) a person of Indian origin in the diaspora. In international literature the term 'South Asian' is commonly used to refer to descendants of emigration from India. For clarity purposes, I prefer to use the anglicized Dutch term throughout.

I wish to thank Mark Eijkman for the translation of the article into English, and him and Indra Boedjarath for their proof-reading and remarks and recommendations.

pictures of the Ka'aba. The woman asks him whether he has any children. Yes, he has, but they all live far away. His wife passed away six months before. He shows her all kinds of pictures. Wants to show her around the house. The woman then asks for the phone numbers of his children and is handed a notebook with many loose pages with numbers. She reads out the names she sees and asks which ones are his children's. Then she phones a daughter-in-law, whose first reaction, after a short explanation by the caller, is: 'Is he at it again?' The man's son should be on his way over already. The woman then waits for the son who arrives about an hour later and starts to rant at his father: 'I told you to stay inside. You just never listen, you make me crazy!'

The father turned out to live there all right, alone, and the son is the family caregiver, who appears to visit a few hours every day. The old man is confused, and most probably suffering from dementia. But he has received no formal help. Social services hardly invest in this target group, assuming the family will assist him, as 'Hindustanis are so group-oriented'. What is disregarded is that this man may originally be coming from a group culture, but his children and grandchildren have come to be part of the prevailing individual-oriented culture, and simply have no time for (gran)dad, who as a consequence leads an isolated existence. This man was eventually taken care of by social services, thanks to the Hindustani woman who gave ample attention to his situation.

For a long time, Dutch social services have given no attention to the situation of the immigrant elderly and the main reason for this was that their numbers were so small. Over the last decade more research has been done among this group. There is, however, very little literature dealing specifically with the Hindustani elderly. What is available is research on Surinamese elderly in general, mostly without differentiation on ethnicity. Among Surinamese, there are many similarities and differences. The distinction is important because there are significant differences in health problems between Hindustanis and Afro-Surinamese (Bindraban et al., 2008). The various ethnic groups also differ in patterns of social behaviour and social participation (Liemand Veld, 2005; Choenni and Adhin, 2003).

This article focuses on the Hindustani elderly, that is, persons who were between 30 and 45 years of age when they immigrated to the Netherlands around Suriname's independence in 1975, and now have reached old age. I will also compare changes in the family system with the diaspora experience in the United States.The data are based on a literature review, my own practical experience as a psychotherapist, and interviews with the elderly themselves. From time to time the literature research will be illustrated with individual case studies. One has to keep in mind that culture is a dynamic notion, and that Hindustani elderly are a very diverse group and so the contents of this article cannot be viewed as valid for all Hindustani elderly. The article asks on the following questions: What effects does migration have on family relations, and what is the psychological condition of Hindustani elderly?

The first section provides an overview of quantitative data on Hindustanis (including the elderly) in the Netherlands. The second section discusses the Hindustani immigration to the Netherlands. The third examines the influence of immigration on family systems as concerns the duty of care, respect and authority, grandchildren, finances and housing conditions, while the fourth section analyses the symptoms of dementia, depression, loneliness, nostalgia and anxiety, as well as illness perception. Section five delves into their illness experience, and finally the paper shares some conclusions and recommendations.

QUANTITATIVE DATA

At the end of September 2008, some 338,000 people of Surinamese descent were living in the Netherlands. This number had increased to 345,000 as of 1 January 2011. Out of this total, 151,000 were Hindustanis in 2008, constituting the single largest ethnic group among those of Surinamese origin living in the Netherlands. Initially, after the massive immigration in the mid-1970s, Hindustanis were spread out all over the Netherlands, due to the policy at that time to first accommodate immigrants in reception facilities, and assign individual residences in the surrounding areas later on. Later, most immigrants were relocated to the four major Dutch cities (see Figure 5.1), with the largest concentration building up in The Hague (Den Haag), where Hindustanis now make up 10 per cent of the total population, and three quarters of all inhabitants of Surinamese origin. In other cities like Almere, Purmerend and Zaanstad, Afro-Surinamese outnumber Hindustani Surinamese,

Figure 5.1: Geographical Spread of Hindustanis

whereas in Zoetermeer, Utrecht (one of the big four), Leeuwarden and Gouda, Hindustanis outnumber Afro-Surinamese and all other Surinamese groups.

Table 5.1 shows Hindustani women outnumber men in the 55 years and over cohort, by 10,300 to 8,050 respectively. Hindustani elderly women tend to be single more often, with their partners being mostly deceased. In the same cohort Afro-Surinamese women also outnumber men by 10,700 to 8,660. Afro-Surinamese women tend to be single more often.

TABLE 5.1: SURINAMESE ETHNIC GROUPS IN THE NETHERLANDS BY GENERATION, AGE AND SEX

First generation	Hindustanis	Afro-Surinamese	Indonesians	Chinese	Maroons	Other	Unknown	Total
Men								
15 year	510	730	80	30	110	40	30	1,520
15-24 year	2,180	2,390	330	180	310	130	80	5,590
25-34 year	5,250	3,660	880	340	440	270	180	11,010
35-44 year	12,120	7,300	1,560	750	650	420	250	23,040
45-54 year	10,280	8,320	1,590	810	620	420	200	22,230
55-64 year	5,540	5,350	950	510	370	240	110	13,060
65 year +	2,510	3,310	410	390	200	160	100	7,070
Total	38,390	31,040	5,790	2,990	2,680	1,680	950	83,520
Women								
15 year	500	680	90	40	110	50	20	1,480
15-24 year	2,290	2,660	410	180	320	130	70	6,050
25-34 year	6,780	4,220	1,130	420	550	320	100	13,530
35-44 year	14,420	9,200	2,150	800	840	590	130	28,120
45-54 year	12,790	10,370	1,970	960	820	520	110	27,550
55-64 year	6,410	5950	920	610	360	290	60	14,590
65 year +	3,890	4,750	500	480	290	260	120	10,290
Total	47,080	37,830	7,170	3,480	3,280	2,170	590	101,600

Source: CBS Netherlands Bureau of Statistics, 2008 and 2010.

Figure 5.2 predicts the increases in the numbers of non-Western elderly immigrants. The definition of 'non-Western' employed by the Dutch statistics authority CBS (Statistics Netherlands) includes all countries outside Europe, with the exception of the USA, Canada, Australia, New Zealand, Japan and Indonesia, and all people with at least one parent born in one of these countries.

As Figure 5.2 shows, the number of elderly of non-Western origin, including those of Surinamese origin, will increase markedly. Strikingly, especially the number of those 65 years of age and over will increase. This means social services will be confronted by an increase in the number of aging patients.

With the current notable increase in life expectancy of both men and women in the Netherlands, the age limit defining a person as 'old' is shifting too. For native Dutchmen, the age of 65 years is usually employed, but age 55 is defined as old among elderly

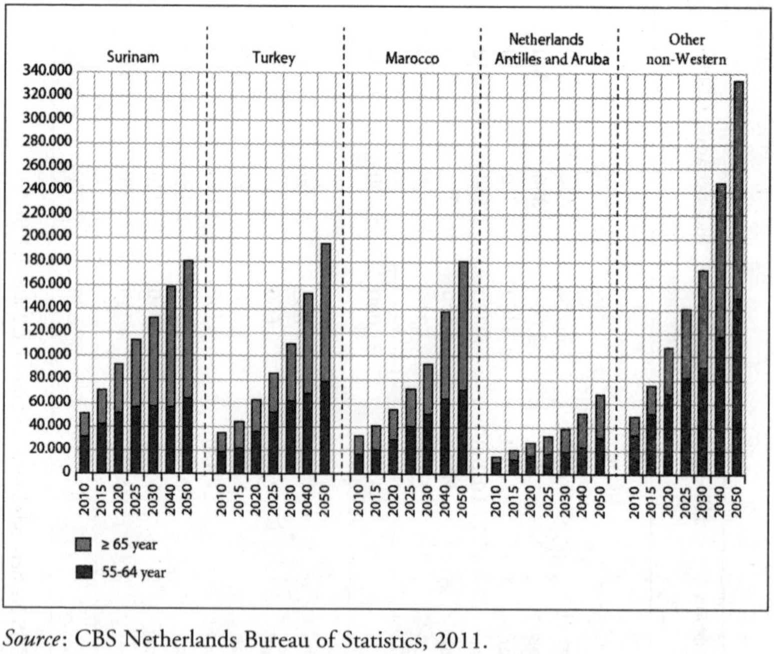

Source: CBS Netherlands Bureau of Statistics, 2011.

Figure 5.2: Numbers of non-Western immigrants, 55 years and over, by country of origin (2010 and prognosis up to 2050)

immigrants. The reason for this definition is that they often have a history of physically exacting labour, and immigration and other dramatic events may have had a profound influence on their health. In addition, they may experience a stressful situation due to their low socio-economic status, poor education, low income and sub-standard housing, which will all impact on their health situation.

EMIGRATION, A LIFE EVENT

Leaving Suriname

The causes of migration can be categorized into pull factors and push factors. According to K. Schermer (Schermer, 2007) pull factors are *reasons* for entering a particular country such as looking for a better future or a better education. Push factors are *forces* that cause people to leave a country. These forces are non-attractive such as poverty, unemployment, war, persecution which drives one out of the country.

Both pull and push factors were the reasons why Hindustanis migrated from Suriname to the Netherlands. Hindustanis are the descendants of British Indian indentured labourers who came to Suriname between 1873 and 1917. Less than a century later their grand children would make the passage to the Netherlands. Already in the 1950s and 1960s, some Hindustanis, predominantly from the higher social strata, moved to the Netherlands. They would tend to live in Paramaribo, the capital of Suriname, and left to pursue higher education (pull). In 1968, an estimated 1,800 Hindustanis were living in Holland (Choenni, 2003). By far the largest group emigrated at the start of the 1970s, just before Suriname gained its independence. Over 36,000 Hindustanis left the country in 1974 and 1975 (ibid., 2003). This surge was caused by fear of an uncertain economic situation, and of, in some cases, the perceived evil of the Afro-Surinamese community acquiring more power (push). Families would persuade each other to leave.

After independence in 1975, Surinamese immigrated to the Netherlands freely up to 1980 as a consequence of an agreement allowing Surinamese citizens to apply for Dutch citizenship for five more years (CBS Netherlands Bureau of Statistics, 2011). A further but limited surge in emigration occurred following the 1980 coup. Once relatives or friends had left, others would soon follow their example. Many had sold their major possessions like homes or land, or left them in the care of relatives staying behind. That created tensions for a number of people when those staying behind, the caretakers, often (mis)appropriated the property under their temporary care.

PREPARING EMIGRATION

The Hindustanis emigrating shortly before independence originated primarily from rural areas and involved young families with their parents. Most of the time, a part of the family would emigrate with the rest of the family members following later. They were not well-prepared for life in the Netherlands and had no idea what to expect. They had heard all kinds of positive stories from relatives and acquaintances about income, educational opportunities for children, employment, luxury items, etc.; in short, they thought they would have a much better life in Holland and they were happy to emigrate to acquire a new future. Some sold their possessions so that they could afford to purchase an airline ticket. People were busy preparing the departure for days on end, not only to provide themselves, for instance with warm clothing for that cold place Holland, but also to supply relatives already living in the Netherlands with fresh Surinamese products like vegetables, fruits, fish and snacks. Families staying behind came by days before departure to say goodbye, even renting coaches to get the intending emigrants to the airport, Zanderij. Hindustani radio stations would announce departures, calling the emigrants by name, and play heart breaking *khás farmáis* – special requests for Bollywood songs (see Majumder, 2010; Hassankhan, 2013).

Upon arrival in the Netherlands, the families were received by relatives or went on straight to government-provided reception facilities that were spread all over the country. From there, they would as a rule be assigned a house in the vicinity. This is why many people still live in smaller towns already mentioned. Meanwhile, a concentration also occurred as the newcomers preferred to live in one of the Netherland's four major cities where they would have relatives and friends and better educational facilities for their children (see Figure 5.1 for the geographical distribution of Hindustanis). In the absence of today's advanced means of communication, contact with relatives in Suriname was conducted mainly by writing letters or special phone-in radio shows. Those with a poor command of Dutch used cassette tapes as a means of communication (source: from individual interviews or field notes, 2014).

Integration

Leaving one's country is a sad event. Spouses, family members and relatives are separated. There is mourning regarding what was lost or left behind and fear of the new environment and experience. The emigration from Suriname to the Netherlands thus engendered loss such as: loss of culture, of home and property, and loss of social contacts. Migration entails a process, a series of events influenced by individual and social factors that eventually define one's appreciation and processing of migration. Individual factors including age, gender, ethnicity, self-concept, psychological, social and biological vulnerabilities shape the reactions to migration (Bhugra, 2004). Or as Kamperman (2005) puts it: 'Migration involves changes in one's physical surroundings, family relations, social network and changes in social status, it also involves changes in (cultural) identity'.

Generally, Hindustanis in the Netherlands are said to have adapted quietly while retaining a recognizable identity in the cultural dimension. On the one hand, Hindustanis have adopted a number of predominantly functional values and norms from Dutch society (there are more women, especially working women, who find that their men should participate in housework). On the other hand they have retained or adapted certain values and norms, as well as cultural orientations (traditional dressing at ceremonies, traditional way of marriage) (Choenni, 2003).

The pluralist structure of Dutch society, which is a result of the traditional 'pillarization' – a typically Dutch phenomenon of social segregation along politico-religious lines involving each group having its own, separate institutions and social life – allowed Hindustanis to integrate without having to give up their own identity. Hindustanis participated in the public sphere, while maintaining their own identity for the most in the private sphere (Choenni, 2003).We see a comparable adjustment in elderly Indians who immigrated to the USA, expressed in interviews with these elderly. 'Life in America can never be the same as an envisioned life in India. People move back and forth between geographic, and conceptual worlds, and in so doing take some values, practices and images from "India" and some from "America". Creating new, complex forms of family and aging across what sometimes appear as gaping divides between generations and nation' (Mehta and Singh, 2008).

THE INFLUENCES OF EMIGRATION

Change in Family Systems

In the diaspora of both Hindustanis in the Netherlands as those in the United States, Britain, Canada, Malaysia, Singapore and East Africa we encounter similarities and the shifting of roles of relatives within the system. A shift is taking place from group-oriented to individually oriented culture, a profound change for Hindustanis, who are traditionally accustomed to the joint family system, a shift informed in large part by the prevalent social structures in the Netherlands that have been internalized over time. Many Hindustanis in the Netherlands experience tensions in the process as Dutch society expects a certain adaptive behaviour while the Hindustani community expects itself to continue the traditional habits in clothing, relations and food preparation (Pot et al., 2007). The contact with the new environment in the host country may initially lead to emotional reactions such as lack of understanding, astonishment, disapproval and stress among the immigrants. Such stressful situations are denoted by the term 'culture shock' and have consequences for both the social functioning of the newcomer and his or her physical and mental well-being. The extent of these feelings and their consequences depend on, among other things, the gap between one's own culture and the new culture, past experiences and personal skills. Culture shock may involve tension as a result of the required mental adaptation to the new surroundings, feelings of loss and deprivation caused by leaving behind relatives, friends, status and property, rejection of and being rejected by members of the newly encountered culture, confusion over new role expectations, and even indignation after becoming aware of the culturally defined feelings of incompetence stemming from the inability to cope in the new environment (Shadid, 2003).

Choenni (2003) maintains that emigration requires redefining internal relations, role models and role expectations within the family system. The family unit is undergoing individualization. Families can no longer live together in one house, due to for instance the smaller size of houses in the Netherlands, leading to extended families breaking up into nuclear families. Less importance is accorded to the group or else old identities are now interpreted in a different way. Also, members of the nuclear family tend to individualize themselves.

Emigration can also be very rewarding on a socio-economic level, and in the encounter with traits of the receiving culture that offers new options. In an interview a Hindustani woman aged sixty-seven years related the difficulties she had with her husband in Suriname because of his frequent infidelity. She did not dare end her relation with him in Suriname because of her financial dependence. When they immigrated to the Netherlands the husband persisted in his behaviour. Empowered by the 'new' opportunities at her disposal in Holland, she chose to go her own way: 'I chucked him out. I was able to apply for welfare and become financially independent. I'll manage.'

The change in the traditional family roles of husband and wife extends to the elderly. When in Suriname the man would be the breadwinner and the wife would tend to run the household and take care of the children, this state of affairs changed somewhat in Holland. Among some elderly who immigrated at an early age we are witnessing women having access to employment too, with some having pursued an education. In cases where both partners were working outside the home, men tend to be more involved in housekeeping.

The Duty of Care

The Surinamese Hindustani community expects the children to take care of their parents. Important elements in the Indian perception of junior-to-senior intergenerational 'service' (called *seva*) are love and respect. These are what many Indian seniors feel to be the most seriously lacking: the failure to return the gift of the sentiments of love and respect that make up close intergenerational ties (Mehta and Singh, 2008). Hindustani elderly expect the same. As an elderly lady I interviewed put it: 'I want my children to give me love, and for us to live in peace'.

Research (Mehta and Singh, 2008) among elderly persons who emigrated to the US or stayed there for a long time indicated that adult children, often a son and daughter-in-law, live with and care for their aging parents out of a profound sense of moral, even spiritual duty to attempt to repay the inerasable debts they owe their parents for all the effort, expense and affection their parents spent on raising them. Children are later obliged to return to their parents the material support, services of caring and sentiments they enjoyed when they were young.

The same goes for Hindustanis living in the Netherlands, but the exact way in which children fulfil their care duties may vary. In the Indian system adult children not only provide material support for their elderly parents but also key services, such as cooking and serving food, tending to household chores, providing companionship and entertainment, and the like (Mehta and Singh, 2008). Children want to perpetuate the age-old intergenerational reciprocity of parents caring for and bringing up children, who will return that care in their parent's old age. However, while some children will do their utmost to grant their parents a comfortable old age, some will eschew those duties almost completely. In between these extremes the duty of care will take various shapes, both incidental and structural. Some families even devise a schedule distributing the tasks, like which child will prepare dinner on what day, or clean the house, or do the shopping, etc. Neighbours too may be involved depending on the family.

In an interview, an elderly lady living in Holland explained: 'I have got four children, one does the shopping, another does the paperwork, the third one cleans, and the last one takes me to see the doctor'. The elderly's expectations concerning the care duty may not always be met as a result of children finding it hard to combine their care duty with working outside the house, not to mention the fact that children often do not live close to their parents. On their part, parents often don't want to be a burden on their children as they are aware they are already quite occupied. Parents understand their children cannot always shoulder the full care owing to the pressures of work, differing values, the travel distance involved or limited living space (*source*: from individual interviews).

Respect and Care

As compared to the situation in Suriname, the relation between most elderly and their (adult) children, grandchildren and partners underwent significant change after the emigration from Suriname to the Netherlands. Their children live more and more compartmental lives embedded in the nuclear family. Therefore, the position of the elder, who traditionally enjoyed great respect as the 'eldest, wisest' member of the family and was consulted in all manner of life matters, has come to be viewed differently. The authority of the elderly has diminished, particularly over the way their children arrange their lives. An elderly lady told me she worried a great deal about her daughter when she became of marriageable age. As a mother, she had always imagined a traditional Hindu wedding for her daughter. She lived in fear her daughter would turn up with a partner from another culture. She would fret a lot about this. She was disappointed and sad when her daughter indeed married someone from another culture (Mehta and Singh, 2008).

In the Indian diaspora in the Netherlands, the US and Britain and we are observing that the traditional role of the daughter-in-law – taking care of the in-laws and household affairs – has changed with the starting to work outside the home. Even if the in-laws are living in, it is often they themselves doing the domestic chores and taking care of their grandchildren. Indian immigrants living in the US even had their parents come over precisely to perform these tasks. For instance, an elderly man who never prepared dinner in

India turned out to have acquired that skill when living with his son in America. He said he had never asked his daughter-in-law to make him a cup of tea. He experienced problems in the food department: 'Every morning he looked in the refrigerator to see if his daughter-in-law had left any prepared food there for his lunch. Rarely did he find any: so he would take the bus to an Indian restaurant, where he was able to buy lunch'. For elderly men, the absence of these services may thus be problematic (Mehta and Singh, 2008).

Members of the family system may have disputes for a variety of reasons, over inheritance, their financial situation, but also over care for the parents. When children take care of their parents, taking them in, they may start to reproach one another over their respective contributions to the parents' care, or lack thereof. The parent may become depressed and start fretting over the matter as a result, which obviously has a negative impact on their mental well-being. Often, they dare not comment as they find themselves in a position of dependency.

Grandchildren

In Surinamese Hindustani families we are also seeing grandparents taking care of the children and, sometimes, preparing dinner. Likewise, there are fears the grandchildren may become Westernized, that the grandparents fail to communicate with the grandchildren, disrupting their relation.

The elderly in the Netherlands, Britain and the US complain that their grandchildren show them disrespect. They have become Westernized and have a problem communicating due to differences in the languages both groups master. Grandparents fail to have children heed their elder's family stories, which prevent them from transmitting their culture's norms and values. They are unhappy with the way the parents treat the children and disagree about the upbringing they receive. The grandparent's role and input become superfluous and they feel they do not belong anymore, which makes them sad and brings them to worry over their grandchildren's identity.

Contrary to the Dutch example, Mehta and Singh (2008) show that elder Indians in the United States assist their working children in taking care of the grandchildren and housekeeping, but also to prevent the grandchildren from becoming 'Americanized'. But when grandparents traditionally were tasked with imbuing grandchildren with the values of their culture, children have come to claim more of a voice in decision-making in the family unit. There is now room for negotiation, which inevitably changes the bond between the grandparent and the grandchild. Traditional values may be exercised less stringently or even give way to new values.

Finances

The Hindustani elderly in the Netherlands often do not receive a full pension as they were not always able to transfer their Surinamese pensions to the Netherlands half way through their working life, as the Dutch public pension system is based on the number of years one has been active in the workforce. Children are willing to support their parents financially and buy them groceries from time to time, or the airline ticket for a holiday. Some elderly living independently don't expect their children to support them. They refuse to be a burden on their children, preferring to be independent.

Housing Arrangements

Hindustani elderly prefer to continue living independently as long as possible, although some of them will live with their children, especially as they grow older. A solution in-between is provided by housing adapted to the needs of elderly persons. When their health situation no longer permits living at home they will often move to a care facility, but only as a last resort. Some, however, profess encountering less conflict with the family when living alone. Although in countries like the US, Indian elderly are inclined to return to India, in the Netherlands, however, the Hindustani elderly often do not want to return to Suriname because their children and grandchildren are settled in Holland, because of the quality of the Dutch healthcare system, and for socio-economic reasons.

The following case illustrates how a dispute in the family system may result in mental affliction. This is the story of a daughter in such a dispute:

> My mother, who is completely dependent on others, lives in with my brother. He got into a quarrel with my sisters and me one day after discussing inheritance matters with my mother, and banned us from visiting her. We are not to contact her in any way, not even by phone or postcard. My mother awfully misses being with her daughters. She'd rather discuss her secrets with us. She's afraid to take the matter up with my brother because she is totally dependent on him and her daughter-in-law. She thinks too much of the past, our upbringing, the good time she had in Suriname. She worries too much and has trouble sleeping. She really has to restrain herself.

The mother can't accept her son telling her that her daughters can't visit her. She feels extremely offended and depressed as a result.

Apart from such problems arising between siblings, taking in parents can cause serious strains between the partners, leading to relational problems and possible collapse of the nuclear family involved. Here are a few stories highlighting conflicts between elderly parents and adult children:

An elderly woman (90 years old, single, lives in a care home) describes how her children are ignoring her: *Jab sapratrahá, bhojanbanáwehke, sabkoiáwatrahá, abkoinaáwehhai*. (When I was still able to do everything, like making dinner, everybody would come over, but now, nobody comes anymore – meaning her children.)

An elderly woman explains in an interview that she is really living between East and West; she thinks like a 'Hindustani mother', she expects her son to call every day and visit her regularly. The son says he won't; she accuses him of being 'Westernized'.

An elderly woman, aged 82, recounts how she used to live in with her son, but preferred to move to a care home because there were differing views on the role of her daughter-in-law and she felt she wasn't free. She was satisfied with the situation now.

A 90-year old woman notes all her children were living in the Netherlands and she was all alone in Suriname. Her children asked her to come over as she was living all by herself there, as she and her husband had separated years earlier. She agreed to immigrate to Holland. Once there, she imagined living in with one of her children, but none of them turned out to be prepared to take her in and so she then rented a house. She was very sad, explaining how she had worked herself to the bone for her children. And now nobody had time, not one of them was looking out for her. One of her children even borrowed money from her and never returned it.

AFFLICTIONS

Dementia

The prognosis is that the number of dementia patients will increase if only due to the progressively ageing population. By 2050, the number of dementia patients will have risen to over half a million persons (of a total population of 16.5 million). The number of elderly immigrants suffering from dementia will rise significantly over the coming years, from 13,750 in 2010 to 30,750 in 2020 (Van Grondelle, 2013) (see Table 5.2).

Dementia is a syndrome characterized by the disruption of information processing in the brain, causing, among others, loss of memory. There are several forms of dementia, with Alzheimer's disease being the most common (70 per cent), followed by vascular dementia (16 per cent) (Alzheimer Nederland, 2011).

TABLE 5.2: BACKGROUND FIGURES ON DEMENTIA PERSONS

Background Figures	2010	2020
Total number of persons with dementia	235,000	292,000
Non-Western immigrants	13,750	30,750
Turkish Dutch citizens	2,800	6,276
Moroccan Dutch citizens	2,534	5,990
Surinamese Dutch citizens	4,387	8,338

In the initial stages of the disease the memory defects are most striking. Dementia involves rapidly forgetting recent events, while earlier memories are retained longer. A patient may suffer verbal problems like aphasia, being at a loss for words, uttering gibberish and inventing things. He or she will become incapable of deliberate action (apraxia), and also confused during daily activities, self care diminishes, for instance, how to dress and in what order. (Oostelaar and Wolfswinkel 2003).

The patient loses control over himself and his surroundings, sometimes virtually living in an alternative reality, and fails to recognize objects (agnosia). Additional symptoms are mental and behavioural changes such as anxiety, apathy, depression, suspicion, claiming or resisting behaviour, and delusions and hallucinations. Elderly suffering from dementia and living at home become a tremendous emotional, physical and mental burden on their environment. Seventy per cent of all elderly with dementia are cared for at home. This rate is much higher among immigrants at 99 per cent. Therefore, informal family caregivers with an immigrant origin are usually burdened much heavier than native informal caregivers (van Grondelle, 2012).

Still, Surinamese and native elderly are employing home care more often than the elderly of Turkish, Moroccan or Dutch Caribbean origin (Pot et al., 2007). When elderly Hindustanis receive professional care, they are not used to just being bathed. Especially elderly men find it hard to be bathed by female home care workers. They want to be bathed with 'respect'. This may lead to a stressful situation.

People around the patient may find it difficult to accept a dementia patient dressing or behaving 'indecently', just as it finds it equally difficult to imagine that the same person that used to be able to do all kinds of things has changed so much. The patient's loss of functions causes anger, sadness, powerlessness and anxiety around him or her. The patient himself, who initially enjoy brief periods of clarity, is wondering what is happening too, fails to understand, and becomes anxious, sad, angry and depressed. Especially in the initial stages of the disease, those closest to the patient failing to understand dementia is involved and having no clue on how to deal with the patient, may encounter serious problems, and may react with anger and incomprehension (Oostelaar and Wolfswinkel, 2003).

Diagnosing incipient dementia in elderly immigrants is fraught with difficulty. Language problems and cultural interpretations, including cultural bias, may render examination complicated. Relatives and care professionals who do speak the patient's language can make an important contribution in this respect. The Parnassia Psychomedical Centre has developed a Cognitive Screening Test specifically for Surinamese Hindustani elderly. According to the researcher the test is very reliable, but more research is necessary (Laurens-van Weelden, 2006).

Hindustani elderly and those close to them often are not familiar with the affliction. The partial or complete loss of memory is mostly ascribed to the trappings of old age. In addition, it is a taboo among Hindustanis to discuss the subject. Those close to the patient are ashamed of the behaviour and language the patient displays. 'What will people think?' People are afraid of gossip, afraid of the shame. 'You have to be crazy to walk around in the street in pyjamas and slippers. Imagine him speaking gibberish, what are people going to say? That's crazy'. Especially the elderly living alone, with children far away, are struggling, like the case of the man wanting to return to Livorno I mentioned earlier. The neighbours will notice the person's behaviour and contact the children who often just come to make dinner and leave afterwards. The patient forgets to eat, and sometimes the food will linger in the fridge for days, with the high probability of the patient then eating stale food.

Depression

Everyone feels tired, listless, dejected or sad from time to time, and when these feelings are short-lived, there is no problem. When the condition persists, however, one may wonder if it amounts to depression. The elderly often suffer from depression. Dutch studies reported a relatively high prevalence of anxiety and depression in elderly immigrants (Pot et al., 2007).

Many circumstances may play a role in the development of depression, including dramatic events, the loss of a partner, physical and mental deterioration, illnesses, and the loss of social contacts, nostalgia or loneliness. Hindustani elderly, in addition, experience much stress caused by their low income, poor housing, poor command of the Dutch language and ignorance of the care options available. Furthermore, they are dealing with immigration stress and the impact of immigration on the family system.

The elderly and their environment will not recognize depression easily because the symptoms are supposed to be related to old age. In elderly Hindustanis, depression is often expressed in somatic symptoms, as they are not used to thinking in terms of psychological causes, accepting somatic symptoms more readily than something supposedly being 'all in your head'. Sometimes, shame is the overruling feeling, with the depressed person who feels that their environment will be overwhelmed to say *paglá hai* (he is mad) or *okar muri nakamá hai* (he is not right in his mind). Often they will have a 'smile' on their face despite feeling depressed. In Hindustani culture, one may not always express what one feels, and keep smiling when all is not right. This may confuse outsiders, who will think nothing is amiss, as the person looks cheerful. To soothe their suffering, the Hindustani elderly may draw strength and comfort from religion, that are seen as positive, protective agents to fortify well-being. Religion is thus employed as a coping mechanism.

The following case illustrates how shame and isolation play a role in depressive symptoms. A 70-year old Hindustani woman is presented with depressive symptoms. Her husband has died one year before. She explains she feels very lonely, when before she was very active, looked after her grandson, and was occupying herself with countless activities. She is suffering fits of sobbing, feels dejected and has trouble sleeping. Sometimes she will stand in the doorway of her house to talk to passers-by. During our conversation she cries a lot and asks me to do something about her situation. She wants to become active again, like she was before. She takes antidepressants, which reduces her feelings of gloom. She thanks me several times for the trouble I am taking to listen to her story. She wouldn't dare discussing her problems with her children and doesn't want to bother them, for fear of her daughter-in-law's reaction, considering the way things are in the family. In the course of the therapy she indicates being up to an adult day care activities programme, in which she consequently enrols. She ends up in a group of elderly of mixed cultural backgrounds. As she is not pleased with that, she moves to a programme for the Hindustani elderly exclusively, which she says she really enjoys.

LONELINESS AND NOSTALGIA

The Hindustani elderly were accustomed to living in with relatives. But the close-knit network of mutual support has collapsed into nuclear families often living far away from the elderly. Elderly in the Indian diaspora in the US and UK experience a similar essential problem: 'The problem is not a matter simply of who provides the material support, or who performs the labour of household services, but of a lack of closeness, a loneliness, a being caught in a house all day surrounded by cold fog' (Mehta and Singh, 2008).

Some elderly Hindustanis are filled with nostalgia for their former homeland. Nostalgia is a kind of mourning. Now they are living alone, they constantly reminisce their lives in Suriname, the time they lived in an extended family, their farmland where the cattle was grazing, a bench under the mango tree by the roadside, the marquee they would dine under when visitors came, the holidays, listening to certain songs.

To return to Suriname or not may be a topic of discussion between the husband and wife in some families. Conversations with elderly persons suggest men are usually prepared to return, while women are not. Even at this advanced age this might lead to relational problems. The woman will feel more attached to her children and grandchildren. Some elderly, mostly the fairly healthy, will travel back and forth regularly between the Netherlands and Suriname.

To fight loneliness, fortunately, all kinds of day activities are being organized for elderly Hindustanis in the Netherlands, allowing them to maintain a social network. Taking part in these activities reduces the risk of depressive complaints and loneliness. They have a feeling of belonging, being appreciated, and not being left to their own devices, although there are a few instances of someone being bullied into leaving the activity group. There is ample choice of activities offered by day-care centres that often serve meals as well: moving to music, yoga, religious gatherings, bingo, handicrafts, etc. One 76-year-old lady told me she learned to swim in the Netherlands.

When elderly persons feel lonely they may find strength and support in religion, reading the holy scriptures and saying prayers. Most of the time they will have a display cupboard or a room specially arranged for prayers. The research literature gives no statistics on the number of people visiting places of worship. The availability of Indian satellite TV networks is a great help. Many interviewees reported watching these stations when bored.

Anxiety

As I mentioned before, prevalence of anxiety and depression among elderly immigrants is relatively high. Elderly persons may experience a fear of falling, a fear of developing dementia, of losing their partners and having to carry on with life alone, and of loss of independence and autonomy (Pot et al., 2007). When the elderly live alone they fear nobody will be around when something will happen to them. A 73-year-old woman living independently speaks out in the interview I conducted with her about her fear that 'nobody will be there if something would happen to her'. She has one child; 'If I'd had more children they could take turns in coming to see me'.

Incontinent elderly may be afraid other people might smell them, leading them to avoid social situations, afraid to go anywhere where they know there is no toilet available (ibid.). Hindustanis may often be too ashamed to discuss the subject openly.

Recognizing anxiety symptoms in elderly isn't always easy. Just as with depression, anxiety symptoms will often be translated in somatic symptoms, and may be expressed as palpitations, dizziness and feeling constricted. Comorbidity may occur with depression. As an example I mention an elderly person who, after having fallen down, doesn't go out for fear of something happening again. The environment will often be very understanding, and dissuade them to go out, thereby confirming the evasive behaviour by doing someone's shopping. That also serves to prevent gossiping as people might think they aren't taking good care of their parents. Fear of falling and of going out has negative consequences for physical social contacts. Three-quarters of elderly having experienced a fall at least once suffer from fear of falling, which is indeed conducive to actually falling (ibid.). Osteoporosis increases the risk of elderly persons breaking a bone when falling.

Because of poor illness insight Hindustanis may develop negative thoughts that increase their fear the worst might happen. They tend to fret over other relatives' or acquaintances' ailments. Just an example: a 73-year-old woman heard an acquaintance was going to have her leg amputated due to diabetes. She has got diabetes herself and imagines this could happen to her too, so she has all kinds of negative feelings and worries about her future.

Traumatic Experiences

Anxiety symptoms may also be linked to past traumatic experiences that included feelings of anxiety. Apart from emigration itself being a dramatic, sometimes traumatic event, earlier traumatic experiences may resurface when getting older. Oostelaar and Wolfswinkel (2003) describe how these feelings may be experienced as a new loss, and may be tied to earlier loss, when aging results in physical or mental limitations, for example, the inability to walk.

The next case reflects the story of such a traumatic experience in a 65-year-old Hindustani woman who is seeking therapy upon referral by her GP. The conversations take place in Dutch, occasionally switching to Sarnámi, the daily language of the Hindustanis from Suriname. She is living with her divorced daughter with whom she has good relations, and who helps her with housekeeping and offers a patient ear. As an only child, the client was beaten a lot by her mother in Suriname and was forced to do a lot of domestic chores. She wasn't always fed on time, but the neighbour would sometimes stealthily give her some food. Her mother rejected her, being a child from an earlier marriage, when she remarried. The patient relates how she was sometimes tied to a tree and beaten. Her mother would occasionally feed her just rice that was hardly cooked. She was a shy child that was bullied by her stepsisters.

Later, when she got married, her alcoholic husband abused her. From time to time he would lock her up in a room and severely beat her up. One time, he went after her with an axe. She feels inferior and rejected and suffers many somatic symptoms. She still has flashbacks of her husband's regular beatings and his going after her with an axe, still experiencing unpleasant memories, images and thoughts, and nightmares. She suffers physiological reactions which include trembling, sweating and palpitations. Sometimes, when seeing images on TV or overhearing conversations triggering memories of the trauma sustained she relives the fear and helplessness, but less poignantly than at the time. The therapy involved treatment of her panic attacks and an EMDR (Eye Movement Desensitization and Reprocessing) session. The panic attacks have since subsided.

Illness Insight and Illness Perception

The Hindustani elderly have a limited insight into illness and often fail to recognize they are depressed, or are showing beginning signs of dementia. This causes them to only seek help when the symptoms have worsened. And once referred for care they tend to drop out of therapy because they fail to see a rapid change in their psychological situation. This may be either the result of the caregiver lacking the intercultural skills to correctly diagnose the condition, or of the immigrant patient failing to properly express the symptoms, which might be due to poor command of the Dutch language, or the use of words and expressions wrongly interpreted by the care professional. This process may be confounded by the apparent disconnect, if only in the diagnostician's perception, between the actual suffering and the smile it is presented with. Another factor is that the physical complaints presented may be intricate and subject to multiple interpretations. As we have seen before, comorbidity, somatization, and an unwillingness to discuss complaints with the children may constitute further complications.

In some cultures being ill is interpreted in a way that differs from the corresponding Western idea. For instance, someone who is depressed may be advised not to go out and stay in bed all day long. The family system is ready to do anything for the patient because someone who is ill should be treated in the best way possible. In some cases the patient accords a special status to the caregiver who will be seen as someone who knows everything. A case in point: A 70-year-old man suffers a stroke and ends up in a rehabilitation centre. He immediately wants to return home, as the doctor treating him, a Dutch native, tells him 'he should work on rehabilitation himself and exercise'. Upon hearing this, the man decides he can do the stair-walking exercises at home too, asserting 'he'd just climb the stairs at home, and if he wouldn't manage, his family would carry him upstairs'. The next day, a doctor of Iranian origin addresses him, telling him 'he'd show him what to do, and God willing, he would succeed'. The patient decided this was an excellent doctor and was prepared to stay in the centre after all. The difference is that the Dutch physician imposed autonomy on him. The patient sees him as the expert who should tell him what to do. That is why he reacts differently to the second physician, with the nuance being present in the style of communication and interpretation.

A culturally specific form of insight may involve seeking an explanation for the symptoms experienced in metaphysical causes, leading to migrants seeking help with a religious pastoral worker like a pundit or imam (a Hindu or Muslim priest), who often act as psycho-social caregivers, or in another culturally specific alternative health care circuit available, as for instance *winti*, an Afro-Surinamese belief system, and faith healers (Kamperman, 2005).

Sometimes Hindustanis will externalize their complaints and assume their physical and psychological symptoms are caused by evil forces and will then seek recourse with a pundit or imam (Hindu or Muslim clergyman, pastoral worker, but often also healer), like in the case of a 71-year-old woman. She heard all kinds of sounds in her house, and sometimes someone seemed to be calling her. Doors would open by themselves. She was afraid and had trouble sleeping. Her family told her to go see a pundit as they thought someone had used 'black magic'. The pundit she went to confirmed that, and visited her home to say prayers, and sprinkle the house with a liquid mix of herbs. He then convinced her she wouldn't be bothered anymore as 'all' had been 'chased'. Her fears subsided.

There have been several studies on the utilization of mental health care in the Netherlands, but without proper regard to ethnicity. Little is therefore known about mental health care use by elderly Hindustanis. Some Surinamese think only 'mad people' visit a psychiatrist, which is based on their view of psychiatry back in Suriname. One would 'go to the psychiatric ward' if one was 'mad'. Jokes were told about the subject and the institution was called the 'madhouse'.

CONCLUSIONS

Most Surinamese Hindustanis immigrated to the Netherlands just before Suriname's independence in 1975, involving a changeover from a social-oriented to an individual-oriented society. Consequently, their family systems show up a tension between the norms and values valid in the Netherlands and the Hindustani norms and values. Migration has changed the roles of family members within the system. The roles of husband and wife change, the parent-child relation changes as well as the relationship between grandchildren and grandparents. The Surinamese Hindustani community expects children to take care of their parents. In Dutch society, but, also in the diaspora communities in the United States and the UK children cannot always meet expectations because they are working outside the home and therefore taking care of the elderly may often be incompatible, if only because children may live far away from their parents. The elderly themselves may not want to become dependent, or a burden on their children. Hindustani elderly prefer to continue living independently as long as possible, although some of them will live with their children, especially as they grow older. Care for the elderly may be realized in various ways. Some children share the tasks, others help out only from time to time. The support may consist of doing the shopping and cleaning the house, managing the finances, making dinner, accompanying the parent when visiting his/her GP, but also offering opportunities for relaxation. Care may become a bone of contention in the family system that may collapse as a result and cause depression in the elderly person. Elderly Hindustanis are very susceptible to developing psychological complaints anyway, as a result of dramatic events like migration itself, traumata, loss of the partner, physical and mental deterioration, loneliness, nostalgia, low income, poor housing, poor command of the Dutch language and ignorance of available care options which may produce psychological complaints like depression and anxiety in Hindustani elderly. Dutch studies indeed reported high prevalence of anxiety and depression in elderly immigrants. Hindustani elderly will often express their complaints in somatic form and may differ from native Dutch in the way they experience illness. Discussing psychological symptoms with people in their environment may be taboo, engendering shame.

The progressive aging of the Hindustani community will increase the incidence of dementia, that so far has hardly been studied and hardly any memory tests have been developed that have been validated for this group. The number of day-care centres that cater to the Hindustani elderly and their informal caregivers is insufficient, too. The ignorance, taboo and shame surrounding dementia calls for psycho-education, which might address other mental health subjects too, as well as for briefing on care options available.

In the diagnostic procedure, information about the cultural background, the personal history of the elderly patient and his the perception of illness is of the utmost importance. The relevant professional education does cover several subjects pertaining to migrants, but more thorough coverage should be provided. Measurement tools should be assessed for validity, reliability and applicability for a certain group.

The day-care activities for Hindustani elderly being organized around the country represent a welcome development to deal with loneliness and depression. The family system should encourage the elderly, their state of health permitting, to take part in these activities. The family should not always yield to the elderly's limited mobility and encourage them to go out, accompanied by someone if needed. Empowering by way of motivating or complimenting their ability to do something increases confidence. Successful elderly persons may serve as a role model.

Most Hindustani elderly will not return to Suriname as their children and grandchildren are living in the Netherlands, but also for socio-economic reasons and the availability of health care.

The family system should be more aware of the changes elderly persons are undergoing in the last stage of life called 'old age', how they are dealing with their limitations, and how they react. One person may become quiet and withdrawn while another person may become assertive and quick-tempered. We should really grant oursenior citizens a pleasant old age in the last stage of their lives.

REFERENCES

Alzheimer, Nederland (2011). Factsheet dementie algemeen. Publieksversie. http://www.alzheimer-nederland.nl/media/38133/factsheet%20dementie%20algemeen%20-%20publieksversie.pdf

Bhugra, D. (2004). 'Migration and Mental Health', *Acta Psychiatrica Scandinavica*: 109: 243-58.

Bindraban, N.R. et al. (2008). 'Prevalence of Diabetes Mellitus and the Performance of a Risk Score among Hindustani Surinamese, African Surinamese and Ethnic Dutch: A Cross-sectional Population-based study', *BMC Public Health.*

Centraal Bureau voor de Statistiek (2011). 'Omvang en spreiding van Surinaamse bevolkingsgroepen in Nederland'. Last accessed 1 April http://www.cbs.nl/NR/rdonlyres/E77E4C63-775E-4708-B347-1D1DA392B119/0/2011k2b15p97art.pdf

Choenni, C. and K. Adhin (2003). *Hindostanen, van Brits-Indische emigranten via Suriname tot burgers van Nederland.* Den Haag: Sampreshan.

Den Draak, M. and M. de Klerk (2011). *Oudere migranten, kennis en kennislacunes.* Den Haag: Sociaal en Cultureel Planbureau.

Hassankhan, M.S. (2013). 'KahegaileBides? Emotional Aspects of Migration History', in K. Mahabir (ed.), *Caribbean Issues in the Indian Diaspora,* New Delhi: Serial Publications, 3-35.

Kamperman, A.M. (2005). *Deconstructing Ethnic Differences in Mental Health of Surinamese, Moroccan and Turkish Migrants in the Netherlands,* Amsterdam: Vrije Universiteit.

Laurens-van Weelden, C. (2006). *Ontwikkeling van een Cognitieve screeningtest voor Surinaams-Hindostaanse ouderen,* ParnassiaPsycho-Medisch centrum, Den Haag.

Liem, P. and T. Veld (2005). *De integratie van Surinamers:voortgang en stagnatie.* Instituut voor Sociologisch-Economisch Onderzoek, Rotterdam, 2005.

Majumder, M. (2010). *Kahe Gaile Bides. Why You did Go Overseas?* Allahabad: Mango.

Mehta, K. and A. Singh (2008). *Indian Diaspora, Voices of the Diaspora Elders in Five Countries.* Sense Publishers, Rotterdam/Taipei.

Oostelaar, D. and G. Wolfswinkel (2003). *Ouderen in de samenleving,* Bussum: Coutinho.

Pot, A.M, Y. Kuin and M. Vink (2007). *Handboek Ouderenpsychologie,* Utrecht: de Tijdstroom.

Shadid, W.A. (2003). *Grondslagen van interculturele communicatie.* Alphen aan den Rijn: Kluwer.

Schermer, K. (2007). *Interculturele samenwerking en communicatie.* Noordhoff Uitgevers Groningen/Houten.

Van Grondelle, N. (2013). 'Je bent tweemaal kind en eenmaal volwassene', *Phaxx*: 5-7.

CHAPTER 6

Emotional Loss among Hindustani[1] Migrants in the Netherlands[2]

RAHINA HASSANKHAN

INTRODUCITON

On my nephew Raoul's seventh birthday, in February 2010, his mother, my *chhoti bahan* (younger sister), told him how when she was seven years old she experienced the 'big move'. In October 1974, the whole family departed by plane from tropical Suriname, and arrived, after a fourteen-hour flight, in autumnal Netherlands. It was exciting; she got a warm overcoat and new shoes and marvelled at the streetcars zooming by. She also told her son how her grandmother, Raoul's great-grandmother, had made a 'big move' at seven years of age as well. *Dadi* (paternal grandmother) had left India together with her parents and brother. In 1912, after a sea passage lasting months, they had set foot on Suriname's shores.

Today, a part of the Indian diaspora has taken root in the Netherlands as the second leg of a journey that started in India over two centuries ago. Dutch Hindustanis' family history involves crossing two wide oceans in little over a century. The distance bridged isn't just a geographical distance, but a time warp too (Ramdas, 2000,

[1] In Dutch parlance, the term 'Hindustani' [Hindo(e)staan(s)] denotes (pertaining to) a person of Indian origin in the diaspora. In international literature the term 'South Asian' is commonly used to refer to descendants of emigration from India. For clarity purposes, the anglicized Dutch term is used throughout.

[2] My heartfelt thanks go out to Indra Boedjarath and Mark Eijkman. I couldn't have written this article without their contributions, proofreading and comments. I also want to thank Mark Eijkman for his meticulous translation.

12). My forebears had no idea what to expect when they made the crossing as indentured labourers. Just like my parents, who knew the Netherlands mostly by the stories of relatives and friends who had left earlier. They could not have foreseen the far-reaching impact migration would have on the family, focusing instead on their dreams and ambitions only. Migration, however, constitutes a rift in the stories of people's lives, necessitating a reconnecting of a person's, and a family's past, present and future (Van Dijk, 2006: 66).

This study is a modest contribution to the well-being of the present generation of the Hindustani community, by honouring the stories of our parents' and ancestors' lives. Insight into the motives and feelings of the historical actors enhances our general understanding of history. This article focuses on experiences of loss among Hindustani migrants based on a systemic perspective and the healing potential of family constellations, a form of short-term therapy and supervision involving the individual always being positioned in the context of the family. It describes three main causes and corresponding forms of emotional loss, that is, loss by migration, loss by early death of a loved one, and loss caused by a forbidden first love. I have regularly encountered these three forms of loss in the family constellations I am facilitating. The central question will be: how can we heal emotional loss by applying family constellations therapy? Based on both theory and experience, I will explain the process of a family constellation using examples from my practice. I will finish with a discussion of supportive rituals that may contribute to uncovering and processing unprocessed loss among Hindustani people, and serve to reconnect with the resilience of the ancestors and the nurturing force of the mother country to improve the descendants' everyday life today.

DOUBLE MIGRATION

First Leg: Indentured Labourers from India to Suriname

Indians are, alongside the Chinese and the Jews, one of three major ethnic groups to establish diaspora communities all over the world (Bhatia, 2001: 271). At the end of the nineteenth and the start of the twentieth centuries, after the abolition of slavery, Indians started to work as indentured labourers on the plantations in European colonies. From 1873, Indian workers were transported from Calcutta to Suriname. There was a total of 64 voyages of shiploads of labourers. These migrant workers predominantly hailed from Uttar Pradesh and west Bihar (Bakker et al., 2007: 97).

While much has been made, traditionally, of the forceful nature of recruitment, recent research suggests many of those recruited were already migrants within India (Hassankhan, 2013: 12) and had various motives to embark on such an adventure. Meanwhile, the main reason for migration was poverty, as a result of agricultural land being scarce in densely populated areas, and the cottage industry being substituted by factory produce. So workers on sugar cane plantations and textile weavers in particular were prone to leave. Less prominent reasons included family conflicts, the ban on marrying outside one's caste, the shame of pregnancy out of wedlock, and the subordinate position of unmarried women and widows, with about half the women emigrating to Suriname being unmarried (Bakker et al., 1993: 98).

The indentured labourers from India arrived to end up in terrible circumstances. Hira (1982: 194) described how the working day and the work rhythm of the indentured labour hardly differed from that of the slave, while housing conditions, food and health care were very similar, too. 'The old putrid slave barracks were taken over by the indentured labourers together with the unhygienic mud pool and the diseases. Malnutrition was no exception.'

Women suffered even more, as they were burdened with the care for the children, apart from the work on the land, and were living in isolation as they could not acquire a pass to leave the plantation unaccompanied by their husbands, and were abused on top of all that (ibid.: 194-5). Of the women who came from India 35 per cent came as married women, 10 per cent were children under 10, and the rest consisted of unmarried women who used overseas emigration to both escape economic hardship and acquire more personal freedom. This included widows, who were bullied and oppressed in India (Bhagwanbali, 1997: 97-100).

During the labourers' temporary contract they were offered a piece of land to encourage permanent settlement, while retaining the right to a free passage back home. But over time, a large majority decided to settle.

SECOND LEG: FROM SURINAME TO THE NETHERLANDS

In the 1960s, predominantly young Hindustanis left Suriname for the Netherlands for work or study. I personally recall a number of my mother's cousins moving to Holland to start a career in nursing. That migration at the same time meant a move towards more freedom, as they were moving away from the stern eyes of the joint family's granddad, uncles and brothers, to the freedom to establish their own lives in the Netherlands, including the freedom of choice of partners, who wouldn't necessarily be other Hindustanis. The second, and main wave of Surinamese Hindustani emigration occurred around the country's independence. Scores of Hindustanis, and others, left the country to settle in the Netherlands, driven by the uncertain political situation, the fear of tension between the ethnic communities, the economic prospects in Holland and the educational opportunities for their children. Some of those who stayed behind would see those leaving as traitors of sorts, forfeiting their right to call themselves Surinamese. Later on, after the 1980 coup and the ensuing political unrest culminating in the 1982 killings of a number of prominent citizens, a further number of Surinamese fled the country. While most emigrants chose the Netherlands as their destination, many settled in other countries as well mainly the United States.

On 25 September 2011, The Hague mayor Jozias van Aartsen opened the Indian Diaspora Day (Pravasi Bharatiya Divas). He said in his speech in 2011:

> The fact that The Hague may once again host this important meeting is a pleasure for me, all the more so in view of the Netherlands and India's shared history. (. . .) The extensive attention for Indian culture in the Netherlands and The Hague isn't surprising. The Netherlands is home to the largest Hindustani community on the European continent. And The Hague is, with its Hindustani population of 50,000 souls, without a doubt the Hindustani capital of the Netherlands. (Van Aartsen, 2011, translation by the author)

The Surinamese Hindustanis have experienced dramatic changes over the last century and a half, both in a positive and a negative sense. The two great migrations, with their concomitant problems of transition and adaptation, entailed both loss and enrichment. Hindustanis were able to develop a uniquely rich cultural mixture that resembles those of their forebears, but yet is quite different. Acculturation, creolization, secularization, modernization and urbanization have resulted in the formation of a unique Indo-Surinamese culture that is not simply a degraded version of the culture of the mother country, but is unique, having its own richness and depth (Majumder 2010: 86).

Migration and Nostalgia

Migration is a process and experience characterized by separation, by time and place, within the life story of the migrant. It inevitably entails loss, loss of loved ones, home, property, status, and country. Loss of the native soil, family roots, support system, social status, language and friendships.

Pravási Yádgár

Vahi dinvá jab yád ávelá, ankhiyá me bharelá páni re,
Hindustán se bhágkar aili, yahi hai apni kaháni re,
Bhái chutá, báp chutá, aur chuti mahatári re.
Arkatiyá khub bharmavlis, kahai paisá kamaibu bhar-bhar tháli re,
Vahi cakkar má par gaili, bacvá yád áy gail náni re.

Immigrant's memory

When that day comes to mind, the eyes get filled with water,
Fleeing Hindustan, I've come (here) – this is my personal story.
Brother got separated, father got separated and my wife got separated.
The recru[i]ter deceived me badly, saying that I would make much money.
I got stuck into that web, O dear, and suffered tremendous pain.

(Majumder, 2010: 159)

Migration and settling in the new country may be a drawn out process starting long before the actual move and lasting many years after arrival in that new country, but the concomitant emotional process is not necessarily synchronous. A number of factors may influence the exact way and pace people overcome the experience, like the ability of an individual or family to cope with new and changing circumstances. This makes each experience of migration unique (St. Joseph's WHC, 2007, website). Arriving in the new country, they often experience culture shock, usually followed by some measure of acculturation, which has a significant impact on the mental health of parents and children and thus provides inter-generational consequences. Unprocessed emotions stemming from migration may lead to stagnant mourning and neglected, chronic complaints.

Nostalgia

'Migration also engenders an affliction like nostalgia, which may encompass three aspects: mourning over the lost homeland, separation stress, and a disconnect hard to describe, involving sensory and archaic aspects. Also, we should not forget that nostalgia is linked to the extent to which someone feels attached to the country he or she emigrated to' (Edrisi, 2010: 5). Discontinuity is the most serious problem for migrants, as Anil Ramdas so aptly tells us in his essay *Heimwee* ('Nostalgia'):

> When memories fade, when we start to forget details, because of migration, being uprooted, because of relocation in space and time, we face a difficult continuity problem, which is another word for identity problem. That is the real immigration problem. The problem of integration, that is, integrating our past experiences into those of today. The problem of adaptation, that is, adapting our former selves to our present selves. Or indeed remarking we were different before, and thank god we aren't like that anymore today.
> (Ramdas, 2000: 28)

Of course, apart from creating tensions, migration also promises new opportunities. Many families concentrate on providing their children with a better future, after all they went through themselves. This takes quite a bit of resilience, a resilience Hindustanis had to employ to survive and settle both after migrating from India to Suriname, and after migrating from Suriname to the Netherlands.

SYSTEMIC WORK AND FAMILY CONSTELLATIONS

Systemic work and family constellations are powerful tools to work with individuals and groups on problems one encounters in everyday life. Systemic work is a method that understands the individual in the context of the interrelated system of the collective. A system is the whole of mutual bonds within a group of people, from one's school, the neighbourhood one grew up in, the ethnic community one belongs to, the country one was born in or is living in at the moment, and the family of origin, the most important of them all.

The method employed to visualize the mutual bonds in a system is called constellation. A constellation serves to uncover what is beneath the surface. In such a constellation, the client proposes a theme or aspect of his or her life that he or she struggles with. These may be symptoms like vague physical ailments, addiction, loss of power or a death wish. A constellation is like a *tableau vivant*: a client's inner issue is represented in the physical space by using stand-ins, called representatives, exposing the underlying relations, patterns and entanglements in a tangible form. Constellations show how we are connected to ourselves, our family and our environment.

BERT HELLINGER AND SYSTEMIC CONSTELLATIONS

Systemic work and family constellations have been developed by the German Bert Hellinger, who worked for years as a priest in South Africa. In his work as a family therapist, he developed his own therapeutic approach, based on various movements and methods available.

Hellinger distinguished and described different hidden patterns that allow love to start flowing again in a family, calling them 'Orders of Love'. If the Order of Love is disrupted and fails to be restored, later generations will experience all kinds of problems of a mental or physical nature (Hellinger, 2001:12).

Three Essential Concepts: Position, Bonding and Conscience

'Every member of a family or a system has his or her own position and knows the position the other members hold. Our position is defined by our relations with other family members, including earlier generations, and with the wider society. There is an order that each member of the system relies on and there are natural laws everyone should heed and *bow* to' (Veenbaas, 2002: 55). In the healing process, a number of rules apply. Each member of the system stays a member, regardless of any event. There is no distinction between good or bad. All matters may belong to a system: birth, death, bonding, detachment, war and peace. The firstborn have more rights than those who came after, who in turn have no responsibility and should feel no guilt for the fate of an ancestor.

In systemic work every person is bonded within a (family) system where everyone has (an equal right to) a position, even if that right is denied. There is bonding between children and their family, but also, in the wider world, bonding through sexuality, violence in the relation between victim and perpetrator, and through trauma (Veenbaas, 2002: 67-79). The notion of conscience in various forms is an essential aspect of family constellations and systemic work (Veenbaas et al., 2007: 129-33). The three most prominent types include the *primary personal conscience*: a type of survival conscience that instinctively seeks to connect with the system as a way of self-preservation; the *group* or *family conscience* that involves the transfer of rules consciously or unconsciously in a group, and the *collective conscience*, which transcends the group, encompasses all contradictions and is beyond right or wrong (Veenbaas et al., 2007, 32-3).

The Process

A family constellation is the visualization of the system discussed above and is usually enacted in a group. The process of such a constellation starts with a question a client has, that arises from his day-to-day life. Questions may arise from symptoms or problems such as rage, feelings of guilt, anxieties, stress, addictions, depression or physical ailments. The facilitator enquires about all relevant information about the client's family, and decides who or what (e.g. a certain emotion) is to be represented by the persons present.

The client intuitively arranges those 'representatives' in the room, who then without fail tune in to the *field*. The field is the notion that we are all connected through various networks and influenced by many types of energy, allowing, in this particular context, the participants to sense the feelings of the persons they represent (Sheldrake and Smart, 1998; McTaggart, 2004). The body language and the reactions of the representatives also give insight into the dynamics and entanglements in the family. The term 'dynamics' refers to the play of forces between guilt and innocence, life and death, or perpetrator and victim. An entanglement indicates the client is caught up in the fate of another member of his family system (Veenbaas, 2006: 54-5).

From a constellation it can be inferred whether the 'laws' of systemic work and the collective conscience are respected, and the entanglements will become visible. The facilitator changes the positions of the representatives relative to each other, lets them pronounce healing phrases and checks its effects on the representatives. Ordering, and honouring, healing or resolving formulas and rituals all serve to produce a new image of the family system. Accepting reality the way it is, along with seeing a different reality in the client's family, is enough to begin the healing process. At the end of the session everyone is positioned in the 'right' place and the relief and relaxation in all concerned is palpable. The client lets this new image sink in quietly, and over time he or she will figure out by him/herself, how to act according to this image. 'After a constellation the soul knows an alternative for previous strategies; and the individual should maintain the freedom to apply, or not to apply that information' (Van Kampenhout, 2001: 146).

Why Systemic Work and Family Constellations

Emotional loss that hasn't been processed will affect newer generations as it is passed on from one generation to the next. This intergenerational loss becomes visible through the family constellation process. In systemic work, people reconnect with their lost story, the story of their family, of their country of birth, their story of life and death, and of longing. A constellation brings important but forgotten people into the picture. With the use of strong statements, tensions are brought to light and resolved through rituals. Ancient tensions that have been passed on from generation to generation may be resolved. This allows for space and above all more freedom to live one's own life.

LOSS EXPERIENCES OF HINDUSTANIS AND FAMILY CONSTELLATIONS

Loss and Mourning

Each and every one of us is familiar with one kind of loss or another, and the ensuing mourning. We attach ourselves to humans, animals and all kinds of inanimate objects and concepts; likewise, there is grieving over their loss. Mourning is a logical consequence and a natural response to loss, any loss. The pain of loss is active at physical, psychological and spiritual levels (Veenbaas et al., 2007: 392; van Kampenhout, 2007: 158). Just like loss, mourning also comes in all kinds of shapes; it may be light, recent, profound, acute, delayed, entrenched, or even determine one's identity, like second-generation war victims suffering from the loss of their parents in war.

Mourning is present in all stages of life. One may mourn the little brother one lost at age four, mourn the forcible departure from the beloved homeland because one's parents envisaged a better future elsewhere, mourn for an unknown person who jumped to his death in front of a train, and one sheds many tears over one's lover when a decade-long relationship comes to an end. Mourning does not just entail tears; it also involves anger, the missing, the shock, the black hole felt, and the helplessness. A 53-year Hindustani explains:

> When I was 32, when I was grieving over losing my beloved, I was amazed expressions like 'feeling a black hole' was actually so palpable. Apart from the tears that kept coming, whether I was on a train or in a meeting, I was somehow happy to experience this new feeling, it was enriching. By the way, the thought that mourning is the flip side of love was soothing too; I had loved him so much. Over the years I have learnt that mourning and saying goodbye also means saying thank you for all that has been.

Part of the grieving process is that the story wants to be told over and over, allowing the grief to become less painful. A recent loss can be shared with family, friends, a teacher, a therapist or whoever is available. But in certain circumstances grief is swallowed, when discussing it is out of the question, as in the case of a forbidden love or a secret abortion. Alternatively, when circumstances are such that grief has to be postponed, for lack of acceptance by the environment, or for sheer survival, for example, in the case of a political assassination in a society that oppresses certain groups. Finally, there is grief that is not recognized, as in the case of a 14-year-old emigrating with the parents, and surreptitiously and chronically suffering nostalgia for the homeland, that may be felt more severely when triggered later on by certain life events. Mourning means becoming conscious, experiencing and processing longing for what or who is missing. If this feeling isn't completely followed through it may very well disappear beneath the surface and cause insidious trauma. The grief is directed inwards, thereby weakening the subject, resulting in loss of interest in life and possibly depression. Other consequences may be inability to experience intimacy or bond with fellow humans or places, homes, jobs, creations, ideals, or even one's own body – in short to open up and reach out, all of which serve to hinder development and utilizing one's own strength (Van Kampenhout, 2007: 159; Veenbaas et al., 2007: 393). A special instance of loss is intergenerational loss, where persons who are suffering from grief passed on throughout the generations in the family system of origin (Veenbaas et al., 2007: 392).

Migration and Family Constellations

Veenbaas (2007: 392) explains how people can suffer the grief of unprocessed loss that is transferred throughout the generations in the family system of origin. This type of transgenerational loss is a recurring theme in constellations with Hindustanis, where the children are bearing the grief and loss of the forebears. Themes like oppression may pervade generations, and may reverberate in the family's whole field, and the soil one is standing on. One can often sense in a client there were themes in the ancestral soil involving oppression and trauma that still influence the client's life here and now. Having been intertwined with the tradition of the ancestors' pain, grief and suffering for so long, the client loses the ability to shine light on his or her own themes; he lacks a reference to act differently himself. This may for instance involve a son suffering from his father having been abused by his grandfather, with the son consequently being boundlessly indulgent with his own children. A young woman who finds herself unable to bond in a relationship might find the cause in the fact her mother was born after a brother who died as a baby, after which the young woman's *nani* (grandmother) grieved in silence for her first born and kept longing for her own mother, whom she lost when still a little girl, all lifelong.

Entanglements and adopted feelings from the system of origin have their effects on the individual and his/her relationships. 'Entanglement and adopted feelings are systemic causes that frequently initiate behaviour in a partnership. When these relationships are disturbed, regardless of the reason, then this will have an inhibiting effect on the present relationships' (Ulsamer, website 2). In systemic work, a distinction is made according to *tertiary feelings.* A tertiary feeling arises out of identification with another member of the system; a shift in position takes place allowing the transferral of feelings belonging to an earlier generation. A tertiary feeling may determine a person's basic feeling; it is an 'improper', out-of-place feeling (Veenbaas, 2007: 537). 'Children rarely, if ever, dare to lead happier or more fulfilling lives than those of their father and mother: out of loyalty to their parents, children repeat the parents' mistakes and misfortunes' (Ulsamer, website 2).

Out of loyalty, children may often carry the suffering of their parents and forebears, like the woman in the following case: a daughter is standing opposite her mother. The mother says: 'I am your mother and you are my daughter'. The daughter replies: 'You are my mother and I am your daughter'. The facilitator asks her to pronounce the following phrase to her mother and gives her a symbolically heavystone to hold: 'What I am carrying with me here represents grief; it belongs to you and I carried it out of love'.

The daughter is now in tears and cannot utter the words, exclaiming instead: 'But I am so much stronger than my mother, I can carry this'. Here is a daughter who imagines herself bigger than her mother. Out of blind love and loyalty she has been carrying her mother's grief around. The grandmother is positioned behind the mother. When questioned what she feels she answers: 'I feel very sad (and from behind she makes a repelling gesture), I feel a tsunami of grief engulfing me'. The grandmother experienced a lot of grief herself and therefore, fails to be completely supportive of her daughter. In case of untold and unprocessed, past suffering that prevents an earlier generation from supporting the next, the archetypical 'forefather' (or foremother) is positioned behind the client as a resource. It is important for a woman to receive the female energy from the female line, and for a man to receive the energy from the male line.

In such cases it is important to trace the force in the ancestral lineage, and to connect with the force and love already present. Here, a perfectly applicable exercise, described by Daan van Kampenhout (2007: 53-5), is 'connecting with the unbroken force of the ancestors'. An exercise inspired by Van Kampenhout's constellation in the course of a workshop I conducted produced a remarkable experience for the participants. The client was standing in front of his parents. He paid tribute to them by pronouncing, among other words: 'I respect you and the choices you have made in your lives' and expresses the need to connect to the unbroken energy of the ancestral roots, so that he may be whole. He asked his parents' permission to open up the path for him. The parents gave their blessing and stepped aside. Then the client came up to the person representing the ancestors (may include a number of generations) and the ritual was repeated. Finally, he was standing face to face with the representative for the unbroken force and the client also paid him his respect. This representative acknowledged him and welcomed him as his offspring. A week later, the client recalled: 'It felt so welcome, familiar and warm; besides power I felt a lot of loving tenderness when I was allowed to embrace the unbroken force and when I was allowed to lean back I felt so supported.'

Another participant told me: 'The unbroken force was warm and nice, and it was wonderful to experience how the ancestors are the source of my fantastic parents. That made me feel strong and I'm grateful for this overwhelming experience'.

Yet another participant felt experiencing the confirmation of the force of the ancestors was so special; it was quite evident. She now realizes she is nourished by generations she doesn't know, and she now knows they are behind her as a source of power.

The Homeland in Family Constellations

The theme 'homeland' comes up in constellations when the homeland has been lost. 'The effect of this loss is similar to the effect of losing a person in the family. If this loss is supressed, it is like an inner wound, which makes one weak. The wound can heal when the pain is allowed a place. The homeland is given a place in the constellation where it is acknowledged and appreciated' (Ulsamer, website 1).

In constellations of persons who left or had to leave their country of birth, a representative for the native soil can be positioned in the constellation. The representative will often perceive clear feelings of power and relaxation. The client usually feels a strong connection with the representative of the native soil or homeland. In my experience, the country of birth of one's parents or even grandparents may also turn out to be a great source of power. There may be a flip side too, when the parents' or ancestors' country of birth is rejected. We often hear this echoed in the opinions of Hindustanis. A 50-year-old woman, born in Suriname and already many years in the Netherlands once told me, 'What is it you want with India, they are treating women so backwardly there; me, I don't feel connected and I don't want to go there either.' In a workshop, a Hindustani mother, married to a Dutchman, related how her son, a drug addict, was angry, blaming her for having married a Dutch man, and that he was deeply unhappy about living in Holland. Ulsamer (website 1) writes: 'A difficult situation arises for the children and grandchildren of immigrants. Some reject the parents' homeland – they want to "turn away" from the old homeland and "turn toward" the new'. Through this rejection they lose an important part of their roots and strength. Then, an appropriate statement that has a healing effect is: 'I acknowledge you as the homeland of my parents and give you a place in my heart'. Thus, the child gains strength through the recognition of his/her roots.

Marianne Franke-Gricksch is a German teacher and therapist who specializes in systemic thinking and acting, and is a pioneer in working with parents, teachers and students. She too remarked (2006: 170-81) that adolescents who have been born elsewhere should first learn to respect their own fatherland before they can muster respect for the new land. After a question by a teacher about a class of 16-18-year olds from various countries where there's unrest and insecurity, Franke set up a constellation where she positioned, after a few steps, a representative for the land of origin behind each representative for a student. The adolescents are asked to bow for their fatherland, however, hard that may be. Then they turn around to face the teacher, who says: 'I see your fatherland standing behind each of you'. As a teacher, one has to look at and bow to the fate of the child and his/her family system. And one may support them from an appropriate position, within the limits of a teacher's task. (Franke-Gricksch, 2006: 171-81).

Another example presents the case of a Hindustani woman who carried two migrations in her history and experienced a remarkable reconciliation with her native soils. She had been living in the Netherlands since her childhood and had strong ties with Suriname, her country of birth. In her constellation, representatives for the Netherlands, Suriname and India were positioned. The representative for Suriname was standing next to her, warm and familiar. The representative for India, the country of her forebears, was standing at a considerable distance and motioned to her lovingly and declared: 'I have a lot to offer, if you come closer'. The representative for the Netherlands bowed for Suriname and their shared history. The client then connected to the Netherlands, and honoured her new fatherland with a bow. Finally she stood opposite India, touched and thankful. After a deep bow she turned around and leaned backwards. With Suriname and India at her back, as a source of nourishment, and the Netherlands next to her, she heard sounds of a distant past and the facilitator whispering: 'Two motherlands and one fatherland'.

Early Death of those Close

After completing the contract period with its oppression, exploitation, many diseases and malnutrition, Hindustani families worked hard to eke out a living as a smallholder farmer, a middle man, a trader, or politician and intellectual (Bakker et al., 1993: 111). Apart from pride at what has been achieved there is also considerable silent grief and unprocessed, adopted mourning that was passed on from generation to generation. Working with Hindustani clients, the large number of close ones who died early is conspicuous. Prior to a family constellation, clients are asked about the composition of the family of origin, whether there were early deaths, stillborn babies or children who died prematurely, or if there had been abortions. A genogram or family tree serves to tap into a host of factual information, which is where deceased members of the family come into the picture.

It is often the case that families do not count deceased children as members of the family. 'Everybody belongs', is one of the laws of systemic work, and deceased children have their position in the family. In a constellation, a Hindustani woman chooses two representatives for her brothers, who are standing next to her. 'How does it feel to stand beside your brothers like that?' The facilitator knows about her younger brother who died in an accident and positions a representative for him in the children's line-up. 'How does it feel now in the children line-up?' She emits a sigh, 'it's so much better now, for all concerned'. Taking up the own position in a children's line-up is so clarifying, relieving and empowering, and therefore this ordering principle is almost always applied in family constellations.

When a sibling dies, the surviving children feel guilty for living, even to the point that it seems like a part of the surviving sibling is dying too. This may lead to a life without direction, or feeling empty. As Ulsamer (website, 3) puts it: 'Siblings of the deceased display an inclination to die themselves, which is expressed by the sentence "I will follow you". If someone is burdened in this way and he later has children, the children sense this burden and want to relieve the parent of it by taking it on themselves ("better me than you").' The inclination to die shows itself through disease or sickness in the family member, or through dangerous activities or behaviour such as excessive drug-use or engaging in dangerous types of sports. In constellations, we often see that a mother who has lost a child tends to lose her clear focus on the surviving children. The children will sense this, which in turns reinforces their guilt of being alive themselves. A child feels too guilty towards the parents to fully live a happy and fulfilled life, for fear of somehow disrespecting their parents' grief. (Payne, 2006: 75-6). Another entanglement surfacing in constellations is the reaction of children who are carrying their mother's or father's unexpressed grief.

Finally, I want to shed some light on what Indra Torsten Preiss (2003: 48) calls 'concealed suicide'. We are looking at concealed suicide when a child unconsciously wants to follow in his grief, a deceased family member who was consequently excluded for whatever reason, such as severe alcoholism, or drugs or medicine abuse. His childish, naive assumption, or magical love, is that he may help the family member. In a constellation, the representative of the deceased member of the family will pronounce the following to the child: 'This is my fate, not yours. You live, and I want you to live and make something of your life.' Whereupon the child says: 'I am staying'. The child thus honours the fate of the other and, if necessary, asks the blessing of the deceased to freely devote himself to his own wishes and goals. The representative of the deceased then responds: 'Thank you for your love. Now live your own life'. This serves to break through the unconscious identification and a shift takes place from magical love to knowing love (Veenbaas, 2002: 305).

A constellation is a powerful tool to bring relief to the processing of unprocessed loss. In a constellation involving a father who died early for instance, the client may hold the representative for the deceased father and pronounce the words: 'Daddy, I missed you so much'. Only after having held the deceased person, one may be able to let go of him. The father then blesses his son saying, 'You have my blessing, live your life.'

Only when the dead have been honoured and received a position, and mourning taken up, only then the client can allow himself to stop following. This is the only way to prevent the pattern from repeating itself throughout the system.

Loss and Mourning over a First Forbidden Love

Apparently lighter subjects may take their toll just as well. A good example is fledgling love between two young people who been banned from being together, due to differences in religion, background (class, caste, skin colour) or for other reasons. Family constellations show that the grief over a first love has a deep impact on those involved, on their relationships later in life and on ensuing children. Forbidden loves among Hindustanis are most often connected to questions of honour. The idea of falling in love and choosing one's own partner has for a long time been nearly impossible for Hindustanis, for both boys and girls (Sewradj-Debipersad, 2001: 74). Inter-ethnic and inter-religious relationships have led to a lot of trouble for those involved. Another example is inter-caste marriages, which, even today, is met with little acceptance, with a higher caste partner being preferred by someone from a lower caste. In the era of indentured labour, men out-numbered women, which resulted in women having more freedom in the choice of a partner (Boedjarath, 2013, unpublished). This changed over the following decades, and girls tended to be married off at an early age. The newly married girl continued to stay with her parents after the wedding ceremony, probably until her first period. Since the 1940s, child marriage has disappeared, and with the introduction in Suriname of the *'Huwelijksbesluiten Hindoes en Mohammedanen'* (Marriage Regulations Hindus and Muslims) of 1941, marriages performed by a pundit or imam are legally recognized. Before, marriage was seen as a family affair, and not as an individual or personal matter. The honour of the family was paramount, and mainly connected to a girl's honourable behaviour. She was responsible for having an impeccable reputation, lest serious repercussions would follow such as being taken out of school and forced to marry. Mainly men who are now over 50 and who grew up in Suriname had this experience: 'If your uncle saw you walking down the Chinese [store] with a Creole classmate to get a sandwich, he would snitch on you, and your father, who wouldn't want to lose face in front of his cousin would give you a good hiding.' The higher classes apparently were less affected by social control and were less sensitive to the notions of shame and honour, because among them mixed relationships were more common (De Koning, 1998: 173).

The movie *Wan Pipel* (*One People*), about the love of a Creole man for a Hindustani woman, caused quite a stir in the mid-1970s in Suriname. The film meant a dream about future Suriname for many, as it showed young people of all ethnic groups would build a new Suriname together. Unfortunately this proved too difficult for conservative elements in the Hindustani community, as the female actor was harassed and abused into emigration (De Koning, 1998: 169).

There are many harrowing stories of forbidden loves in Suriname. A young Hindu woman fell in love with a Muslim boy. Her father had the boy locked up by friends in the police force and had his daughter committed to the state psychiatric clinic. Here she was administered (unthinkable today) electroshocks. The woman never quite recovered, and despite the fact that both she and the man later married other partners and are now living in the Netherlands, the longing is still there. Her father asked to be forgiven on his deathbed. Another young Hindustani woman with a forbidden Muslim lover was forced to come to the Netherlands with her mother, while her brothers and father beat up the boy. In the Netherlands, too, girls were punished or abused because they fell in love with the 'wrong' partner. A young Muslim woman was beaten severely with the metal tube of a vacuum cleaner so that she will not see a Hindu boy. If she did, how would her father possibly face the mosque board? Regrettably, there are also stories of early loves fatally ending in the suicide of one or both of the partners. Nowadays, it is not uncommon anymore for young people who were pressured by their parents to get married, to divorce in little over a year, because the situation has become unbearable. A young woman I was coaching once told me she wanted to prove to her parents she could have a relationship with a Hindustani man. She started a relationship with a divorced man, a proud Brahmin by caste, a person her environment told her she should be happy with, as he was of a higher caste. She held out no more than three months, and to this day she still indignantly recalls how she had allowed him to humiliate her. Slowly, the views on choice of partner are changing and we see various degrees of freedom of choice, from total freedom to 'matchmaking with consent' and chaperoned or unchaperoned dating. There are now various mixed relationships, ranging from traditional marriages in line with religious traditions, to cohabitation and living together. A 'mixed relation' deserving special attention is lesbian and gay relations.

In systemic work and family constellations, everyone who has an impact on the system belongs; and in chronological order at that. In new systems of romantic relationships too, former partners, and indeed the first (forbidden) love take an important position. When earlier partners are not acknowledged, an unconscious identification may occur, with a child taking up the (forbidden) lover's position. If the child takes up the place of a former love, with for instance the son representing the mother's first love, he becomes the father's rival, and is not able to accept his father as a father (Hellinger, 2002: 121). A client in a workshop may then come up with the question why he doesn't seem to be able to start a relationship, or why he can not open up in an existing relationship. Other symptoms like vague complaints and fatigue may also be indicative. In one constellation, a client, a woman with roots in India is next to the father. This is the place where the father's partner, the client's mother, should be positioned. The mother is standing elsewhere in the Field, and the father has no contact with the mother. The facilitator asks various questions and examines, together with the client, what lies beneath the entanglement. In the end, this turns out to be the father's first love. His parents disapproved of the girl as she was of a different caste. A representative for this first love is positioned and the father starts beaming. After a number of healing phrases and rituals, in which the father first connects to the first love, the representative addresses the client: 'Live your own life;

thank you for making room for me. Now your father and I can say goodbye. Go now, you are free. . .'. The daughter pronounces to the father: 'I have nothing to do with that other woman. This is my mother.' The client can thus return to her role as a daughter. The father thanks his first love and points to his partner: 'This is my current partner, my wife. Look at us kindly if we are happy in our relationship'.

Weeks after, the client relates:

> It has certainly resulted in the stifling and entangling strings having loosened. The bond with my parents remains, but the position I am taking is now different. I am a child and I stay their child. I am growing and learning to recognise the mechanism. My brother, who was also present at the constellation, is very supportive. That's how I am becoming important to myself, too. This disentangling on an energetic level in family constellations, I really believe in that. It has been a more profound way of looking, feeling and experiencing.

Working with family constellations shows how 'relationships that have not been ended well negatively impact later relationships' (Torsten Preiss, 2004: 102). If someone has been in relationships before, the chances of a deep, happy and sustainable relationship is greater when all earlier partners have been honoured, and when they enjoy respect, gratefulness and love.

CONCLUSIONS AND RECOMMENDATIONS

How can we heal emotional loss? This article brings experiences of loss among Hindustanis into sharper focus and approaches the subject based on a systemic perspective and the healing potential of family constellations. Systemic work is a method that understands the individual in the context of the interrelated system of the collective, such as a family. Unprocessed events in earlier generations may have a negative bearing on many subsequent generations. People may suffer the grief of unprocessed loss that was unconsciously transmitted from one generation onto the next, in the family system of origin. This inter-generational loss becomes visible through the family constellation process, a form of short-term therapy and supervision that positions the individual in the context of the family. A constellation is a powerful tool to bring relief to the processing of unprocessed loss.

Those not familiar with family constellations might be interested, but also bewildered. Indeed, how may an ancestor who died fifty years ago play a role in a constellation? The explanation is that we are all a part of the Field that connects everyone with everything and where time plays no role. Almost anything that influences a person, whether it is another person, an emotion, a fate or a group of persons, can be represented by a person. This representative tunes in to the Field and the person he represents, and surprisingly he 'knows'; his bodily experience, his emotions and his inner images are in accordance with the situation at hand. This process, called 'representative perception', is as simple and natural as breathing, and does not require special knowledge or training. It does not take a special mental or spiritual state either. As the Surinamese proverb goes: *Ondrofenie na sabieso* (experiencing is knowing).

Thus a 66-year-old Hindustani woman who was representing a daughter in someone else's constellation could experience what it is like, as a daughter, to feel one's father's arms around her, something she longed for years. As it so happens, she was used to having long conversations with her now deceased, strong and strict father, but she could not recall him ever holding her.

Rituals do not just have a symbolic, but also a powerful psychological and social function in the constellations. Hindustanis know the power of rituals all too well. The family constellation, including its supportive rituals, may contribute to uncovering and processing unprocessed loss among Hindustani people, and serve to reconnect with the resilience of the ancestors and the nurturing force of the 'Mother Country' to improve the descendants' everyday life today. We can teach our children about the native soil of their forebears, which allows them to really take root in the new country. By accepting what happened in the past, we may sense the greatest freedom.

A family constellation offers endless potential, for new insights, a change of perspective, and a beginning of a solution for the problems one experiences. Both the scope of the method and the enthusiasm for the therapy are growing all the time. Constellations have moved on from being solely applied to addressing personal problems to resolving conflicts and offering solutions in organizations, and even between countries. For Hindustanis in both Suriname and the Netherlands, and all over the Diaspora, establishing a balanced connection with both the past and present may prove very beneficial. Through constellations, we connect with the flow of love in families. Constellations make us aware we belong to the family system and remain a part of it, with no exclusions. We can connect with our history and honour our forebears. The resilience of our ancestors and parents should inspire us. In the words of Ahmed Kathrada, speaking on the occasion of the opening of the Robben Island Exhibition:

> While we will not forget the brutality of apartheid, we will not want Robben Island to be a monument to our hardship and suffering. We would want it to be a triumph of the human spirit against the forces of evil. A triumph of wisdom and largeness of spirit against small minds and pettiness; a triumph of courage and determination over human frailty and weakness; a triumph of the new South Africa over the old. (Kathrada, 2004: 344)

REFERENCES

Bakker, E. et al. (1993), *Geschiedenis van Suriname. Van stam tot staat,* Zutphen: Walburg Pers.

Bhagwanbali, R. (1997), *Contracten voor Suriname. Arbeidsmigratie vanuit Brits-Indie onder het indentured-labourstelsel 1873-1916,* Den Haag: Amrit.

Bhatia, T. (2001). 'Media, Identity and Diaspora: Indians Abroad', *Studies in the Linguistic Sciences,* 31: 269-87.

Boedjarath, I. (2013). *Gender-specific Problems among Surinamese Hindustanis: Suicide and Alcoholism.* Unpublished.

De Koning, A. (1998). 'Als jij Ram bent . . . Veranderingen in het leven van Hindostaanse vrouwen in Paramaribo vanaf de jaren vijftig', in *Van Gya en Boodheea tot Lachman en Djwalapersad, Grepen uit 125 jaar maatschappelijke ontwikkeling van Hindostanen,* ed. M. Hassankhan and S. Hira. Den Haag: Amrit.

Edrisi, M. (2010). 'Wegkwijnen in ontheemding. Heimwee bij migranten', *Maandblad Geestelijke volksgezondheid*, 65: 669-83.

Francke-Gricksch, M. (2004). *'Jij hoort bij ons'. Systemisch denken en handelen voor ouders, leraren en leerlingen.* Translated by M. Wentink. Groningen: Het Noorderlicht.

Hassankhan, M.S. (2013). '*Kahe Gaile Bides* – Why did You Go Overseas? An Introduction in Emotional Aspects of Migration History: A Diaspora Perspective', in Kumar Mahabir (ed.), *Caribbean Issues in the Indian Diaspora*, New Delhi: Serials Publications, 3-35.

Hellinger, B. (2001). *De verborgen dynamiek van familiebanden*, Utrecht: Altamira-Becht.

—— (2002). *De wijsheid is voortdurend onderweg*, Groningen: Het Noorderlicht.

Hellinger, B. et al. (2010). *Leven zoals het is*, Groningen: Uitgeverij Het Noorderlicht.

Hira, S. (1982). *Van Priary tot en met De Kom. De geschiedenis van het verzet in Suriname, 1630-1940*, Rotterdam: Futile.

Kathrada, A. (2004). *Memoirs*, Cape Town: Zebra Publishing.

Majumder, M. (2010). *Kahe Gaile Bides, Why did you go overseas? Source book of the Bidesia project*, Amsterdam: KIT Publishers.

McTaggart, I. (2010). *Het veld.De zoektocht naar de geheime kracht van het universum*, tr. by G. Grasman. Deventer: Ankh-Hermes

Payne, J. (2006). *'The Language of the Soul: Healing with Words of Truth*, Forres: Findhorn Press.

Ramdas, A. (2000). *De Papegaai, de stier en de klimmende bougainvillea*, Amsterdam: De BezigeBij.

Sheldrake, R. and P. Smart (1998). 'A Dog that Seems to Know When His Owner is returning: Preliminary Investigations', *Journal of the Society for Psychical Research*, 62: 220-32.

St. Joseph's Women's Health Centre. (2007). *'Loss of home'*, accessed 30 April http://www.attachmentacrosscultures.org/impact/index.html#1.

Sewradj-Debipersad, R. (2001). *Emancipatie van Hindoestaanse vrouwen: een beschrijving van de veranderingen in het leven van Hindoestaanse vrouwen in Suriname vanaf 1873*, Paramaribo: Cerdes.

Torsten Preiss, I. (2004). *Familieopstellingen in de praktijk. De systemische dynamiek achter relatieproblemen, opvoedingsproblemen en ziektes*, Utrecht: Servire en Kosmos.

Ulsamer, B. 'International Similarities and Differences in Family Structure and Family Problems – First Results of the Family Constellation Method', accessed 30 April 2013. http://www.ulsamer.com/international_similarities.html.

Ulsamer, B. 'Order in Love' accessed 30 April (2013). http://www.ulsamer.com/order_in_love.html.

Ulsamer, B. (2009). 'Trauma Work and Family Constellations: Irreconcilable or Complementary?' Last modified 26 August 2009. http://www. systemic-familysolutions.com/articles_trauma.html.

Van Aartsen, J. (2011). 'Welkomstwoord door burgemeester Van Aartsen bij de Indiase Diaspora dag, Pravasi Bharatiya Divas, 25 september 2011'. Last modified 28 October. http://www.denhaag.nl/home/bewoners/to/Welkomstwoord-door-burgemeester-Van-Aartsen-bij-de-Indiase-Diaspora-dag-Pravasi-Bharatiya-Divas-25-september-2011-1.htm.

Van Dijk, R. (2006). 'Cultuur, migratie en psychoanalyse; enkele kanttekeningen', in W. Gomperts and G. Veen (eds.), *Migratie en Psychoanalyse*, Assen: van Gorcum, 60-8.

Van Kampenhout, D. (2001). *Beelden van de ziel. Over de werking van de ziel in sjamanistische rituelen en familieopstellingen*, Haarlem: Altamira-Becht.

—— (2007). *De tranen van de voorouders. Opstellingen en rituelen bij collectieve trauma's*, Haarlem: Gottmer.

Veenbaas, W. and J. Goudswaard (2002). *Vonken van Verlangen. Systemisch werken - perspectief en praktijk*, Utrecht: Phoenix.

Veenbaas, W., I. Baarspul-Schipper, S. Reinalda and M. Broekhuizen (2007). *Passe-partout*. Utrecht: Phoenix.

CHAPTER 7

Socializing for Educational Success

ANITA NANHOE

INTRODUCITON

The worldwide economic crisis demands interventions and cuts to prevent further economic problems. In the Netherlands the education sector is also affected by the world economic crisis. The limited resources have led to severe cuts on education budgets (OC&W, 2012). The (planned) cuts are a major disadvantage to immigrants and lower class people (SCP, 2011). Their chances to climb the educational ladder are limited even more so than already due to the fact that non-Western immigrants are affected more by the (planned) educational changes than Dutch students because of their greater distance to the educational system (SCP, 2011). Among these immigrants, women are most vulnerable. This happens in a country that has a history of at least two hunre years of educational policy to increase chances of educational success of women, minorities and lower class people (Nanhoe, 2012).

In times of economic crisis research on successful educational careers of lower-class native and non-native people[1] is more necessary than ever. This kind of research offers an underutilized information source for measures to fight educational disadvantages of

[1] The Central Bureau for Statistics (CBS) defines 'non-native' as: 'A person resident in the Netherlands, who is born abroad or at least has one parent that is born abroad'. Non-natives who are born in a foreign country belong to the first generation. Those who are born in the Netherlands, but have at least one parent who is born abroad, belong to the second generation. The non-natives in this research are all born abroad.

minorities. This chapter concentrates on relevant matters in the gender-related upbringing of Dutch academics of Moroccan and Hindustani descent, and of native Dutch academics from lower socio-economic backgrounds in the Netherlands. Indicators for the socio-economic background are the educational level, the financial income and the occupational status of the parents (Sadiraj and Groot, 2006). The educational level of the parents is an important indicator of the educational success of students. Highly educated indigenous parents appear more capable to support the educational careers of their children than lower educated parents, as higher educated parents are more familiar with the educational system, with the demands of the educational system and the opportunities to make the most of the educational career of their children (Smith and Driessen, 2002). The educational level of parents is also directly related to the degree to which a student is raised in a stimulating home environment. Household income – defined as the income of the parents – is another indicator of socio-economic status. The occupational level, the third indicator, also gives some information about the network and thus the social capital of the parents. Parents working in lower valued professions have other networks than parents who work in higher rated professions (Sadiraj and Groot, 2006). The three indicators are not unrelated. A high level of education affects the employment opportunities and thus income. However, the level of education does not guarantee a suitable or successful result in employment. The professional level does not always guarantee or match a good income. Although the three indicators are associated with each other, the income level is most commonly used as an indicator of socio-economic status (Sadiraj and Groot 2006). In case of research on educational issues, however, the educational level of parents dominates all indicators. In this study, the socioeconomic status of the family is converted from a combination of the three indicators: the education and occupation of parents and their household income, with an emphasis on the educational level. A low socio-economic background involves those with parents who have completed no more than a mulo- (or mavo) education, who work for uneducated or lower educated people and have a low income.

BACKGROUND

The databank of the Centrum Bureau for Statistics (CBS) and available reports give us insight into the educational position and achievements of Dutch people of different descent. However, since the educational performance of the various Surinamese is registered under one category 'Surinamese', the statistics in this section apply to the educational performance of all Surinamese ethnic groups, not specifically the Hindustani.

Moroccans and Surinamese as well as other non-Western immigrants experience a disadvantage when compared to native students (SCP, 2011; Rijkschroeff et al., 2003). This does not mean that the educational performance of the immigrants does not improve. There is indeed progress, but the native students perform much better and show more progress (SCP, 2011; Rijkschroeff et al., 2003). This is why the progression of the Moroccan and the Surinamese students has not resulted in catching up with the native students. In 2000, as many as 67 per cent of Moroccan and 49 per cent of the Surinamese population between 15 and 65 years was not in possession of a start qualification[2] compared with 36 per cent of the indigenous population. In 2000, 6 per cent of Moroccans, 14 per cent of the Surinamese and 21 per cent of the natives had an academic qualification. A decade later in 2012, 48 per cent of the Moroccans, 39 per cent of the Surinamese and 29 per cent of the indigenous population had no start qualification yet. The percentage with an academic qualification has risen to 13 per cent of the Moroccans, 21 per cent of the Surinamese and 29 per cent of the indigenous population (see Table 7.1).

The start qualification shows that the gap between the Moroccan and the Surinamese population relative to the native population has reduced, but it is still considered significant. The backlog has increased at the academic level. The question of what it takes to break the inequality thus remains topical.

[2] According to the Dutch government job prospects require a minimum educational qualification. This is at least a HAVO, VWO or MBO qualification at level 2 (Van Tilborg and Van Es, 2004). The Dutch government calls this minimum the start qualification.

TABLE 7.1: PERCENTAGE OF POPULATION WITH A START QUALIFICATION OR AN ACADEMIC QUALIFICATION

	No Start qualification in 2000	No Start qualification in 2012	Academic qualification in 2000	Academic qualification in 2012
Moroccans	67%	48%	6%	13%
Surinamese	49%	39%	14%	21%
Natives	36%	29%	21%	29%

Despite the increased backlog at the academic level the statistics also show that a growing group of Moroccans and Surinamese have achieved an academic degree (for higher education or university education) (SCP, 2011). The successful educational careers of immigrants are an underutilized resource in measures to promote their educational upward mobility (Conchas, 2006). More insight into the process towards successful educational careers will provide a platform for policy-makers to focus on the upward mobility of immigrants, and for a more conscious upbringing to educational success.

METHODOLOGY

The starting point in this research is the reproduction theory of Bourdieu, with the concepts of 'habitus', 'field' and 'capital'. The habitus is a result of ongoing socialization and includes both individual and collective behaviour patterns that form during the socialization process in fields and subfields (Paulle, 2006; Bourdieu, 1990, 1992; Throop and Murphy, 2002; Bourdieu, 1984). Bourdieu sees people as carriers of a group culture which belongs to a certain class. Within each (sub)group certain opinions, preferences and habits are learned and transferred from an early age. Thus, the habitus of people from lower classes therefore differ from the habitus of people from higher classes (Van der Stoep, 2005; Bourdieu, 1990). The habitus is also transferred from generation to generation, making the class structure reproduce itself (Bourdieu and Passeron, 1990). Bourdieu (1989) distinguishes between economic, cultural and social capital. 'Economic capital' refers to the availability of finances and property (Van Esch, 2010; Rijkschroeff et al 2003, Downey 1995, Bourdieu 1989). Cultural capital is the sum of cultural goods and values that are passed from one generation to the other (Bourdieu, 1977). According to Bourdieu (1986) internalized cultural capital consists of attitudes, preferences, customs, language and use of language. But also cultural goods, such as art, books, computers, music and diplomas. Social capital, according to Bourdieu (1986), is that part of the social network that is targeted to mobilize by the individual in order to achieve certain goals.

Bourdieu stresses the educational system as a central institution that maintains, legitimizes and reproduces inequalities in society (Bourdieu and Passeron, 1990). According to him, the education system is based on the middle class standard and assumes the presence of the cultural capital of the middle class in all pupils (Kahlenberg, 2001; Paulle, 2006; Bourdieu, 1990). Pupils from the lower class, unlike students from the middle and upper classes, often don't have the desired cultural capital and therefore start with a disadvantage to their teaching career (Paulle, 2006; Crossley, 2003; Parham, 2002; Sullivan, 2001; Bourdieu, 1973). Bourdieu provides no explanation for the upward mobility of members of the lower class to academic spheres. And he pays little attention to the influence of ethnic, migration-related and gender socialization in the course of a teaching career (Nanhoe, 2012; Delhaye, 1991). This is an important gap, as many researchers in addition to the class of origin, also designate gender and ethnicity as key concepts in explaining educational disadvantage (Veenman and Heij, 2008; Pels and De Gruijter, 2006; De Haan and Elbers, 2005; Van Ours and Veenman, 2005; Almaci and Van Craen, 2004; Driessen, 2001). If the early socialization takes place in another country or in a family with parents who've spent much of their socialization process in another country, it is expected that the habitus has internalized rules, dispositions, frames of meaning and (gender) success definitions that fit within the ethnic group and the position of that group in the country of origin. This (gender) habitus may differ from the habitus of natives. After migration a socialization process in the new field starts, which may have different rules than in the old environment. This study pays attention to ethnic and gender-related factors, as well as changes in these factors in the migration context.

The empirical study was performed among Moroccan, Hindustani and native Dutch academics from lower socio-economic backgrounds. The methodology in this study was the retrospective biographic interview. Each respondent was interviewed according to the biographical interview method, supported with a dynamic topic list in which new insights were integrated. During the interviews we searched for factors in the upbringing that positively affected the educational success according to the respondents.

The retrospective biographical interview method gives respondents the opportunity to tell comprehensively about their lives and to give all the information they consider important and relevant (Matthys, 2010). In this way, events in the lives of the respondents come into view, as well as the context in which these events took place and the interpretation of the respondents (Giddens, 2005; Tierney, 2000). They can also explain their problems in their own voice and explain how they reacted and dealt with these problems. This interview method provides the opportunity to achieve innovative information as well as changes in time and circumstances as described by the respondents (Wester et al., 2010). All discussions were transcribed literally; the transcriptions served as the basis for data analysis.

The recruitment of respondents took place with the aid of the so-called snowball method. This means that all respondents were asked to provide names and addresses of other potential respondents till the intended number of respondents was obtained. Verbatim transcripts of the interviews were analysed with the qualitative data analysis programme Atlas-ti using the topic list and the Bourdieuan capital concepts as the interpretive framework.

RESPONDENT CHARACTERISTICS

The respondents in this study were 18 Moroccans, 20 Hindustanis and 17 natives. All Moroccan and Hindustani respondents belong to the first generation of immigrants. All respondents had completed an academic degree in the Netherlands: 38 had completed a college education (12 Moroccans, 15 Hindustanis and 11 natives) and 17 a university education (six Moroccans, five Hindustanis and six natives). All respondents were from low socio-economic backgrounds. Their parents were not educated or educated to a maximum of a four-year mulo (or mavo).[3] The occupations of parents were unskilled, low-skilled or of lower office jobs. Among the respondents 31 were women and 24 men (see Table 7.2).

TABLE 7.2: ETHNICITY AND GENDER OF THE RESPONDENTS

	Moroccans	Hindustani	Native	Total
Women	12	9	10	31
Men	6	11	7	24
Total	18	20	17	55

The age of the respondents during the interview varied from 25 to 60 years. The migration age of the respondents varied between 0 and 24 years. The number of children of Moroccan families of origin varied from five to ten with an average of seven children. The family size of the Hindustani respondents varied between one and twelve children, with an average of five children. The indigenous families were relatively small with lesser number of children ranging between one and eight, with an average of three children.

Gender Related Factors in Economic Capital

Limited economic capital is a direct outcome of a low social-economic status. One of the consequences is the inability to pay educational fees and to provide adequate studying facilities such as a room to study or a computer. Nevertheless, these consequences do not always lead to the same results in the three groups since the respondents differed in their definition of family income and division of financial responsibility.

[3] Mulo and mavo in the Dutch educational system are comparable with the tenth grade in High School in the American school system. It is a form of Junior Secondary School.

Twelve out of the seventeen native Dutch respondents came from families with one-and-a-half incomes, in which the father had a full-time job and the mother had a part-time job. The other respondents had one working parent. This combined with a small number of children meant that respondents in families with one-and-a-half incomes had a relatively favourable financial starting position. Parents often contributed to a substantial proportion of the education fees.[4]

All Moroccan respondents considered their father's income to be the family income. In the cases where parents contributed their limited means to education fees, the preference was to pay for the education of the sons. But most Moroccan respondents were responsible for investing in their own education at an early age. Many of them had a part-time job early on, which meant that education fees did not impact or no longer impacted the family income. As a result, continuing education depended primarily on the respondents′ own willingness to invest and motivation to study as demonstrated by the following respondent:

> Everyone had to take care of themselves. So all my brothers went to work very young to pay their own tuition. We learned that very young. I followed that example. I had a job on my 13th. (. . .) I paid my own tuition since my 15th. I could keep the rest of my salary myself, for the fun stuff. So we had to pay our own expenses, but that was just for yourself, not for others. You had to provide your own cost. My father was responsible for the basic needs at home. (Moroccon female, 27 years)

For 12 out of the 20 Hindustani respondents, the family income consisted of the parents' income as well as that of the children, even after they left home (married). In some families, only the oldest child contributed, depending on the gender. In other families, it was normal for all children to contribute. In all, ten respondents structurally contributed to the family income themselves during their study. These incomes went to the family household and were

[4] In the Netherlands students have to pay tuition for all kinds of education, also for public education. The amounts are especially high for higher and academic education.

used to pay fixed costs, including education costs of the younger children.

By comparison, the (younger) native Dutch respondents had a relatively smaller number of children and the prioritization of an educational career for both their sons and daughters was equal because of their one-and-a-half incomes. Obviously, the native Dutch had a financial advantage over the Moroccan and Hindustani respondents. However, as a result of the division of financial responsibility, broader opportunities to study also developed for the Moroccan and Hindustani respondents. For those students who were not able to cover all needs financially, libraries were a substitution for a room to study and student grants and subsidized jobs compensated for the inability to pay student fees, especially for women who managed to continue their educational career later in life.

Gender-related Factors in Cultural Capital

The most important success factor within the cultural capital is that education plays a prominent role in child-rearing. A central question therefore is: how does child-rearing lead to achieving different levels of educational qualifications? The answer to this question differs according to ethnicity and gender. The answer also appears to change in relation to how long respondents have been residing in the Netherlands.

The native Dutch respondents were all brought up to achieve educational qualifications. Their parents saw education in the light of career prospects for their children, but also as a vehicle for self-development. Fifteen of the seventeen native Dutch respondents were brought up to choose the direction and level of education which would make them happy in their further lives. Whereas almost all native Dutch parents tried an approach tailored to their children, most parents with a foreign background wanted their sons to achieve the highest possible level of education, with the goal to take advantages of opportunities on the labour market because of their role and responsibility as breadwinners. Hindustani parents initially did not have any concrete education level in mind. Moroccan parents wanted their sons to follow a technical vocational course. None of the respondents' parents considered an academic educational qualification important partly because they did not consider that goal achievable and partly because parents were unfamiliar with the long-term benefits.

Gender differences played a role in all three groups of respondents, although in different degrees. For native Dutch women older than forty-five years education had lower priority in their upbringing, while younger women gave it higher priority because they grew up in an age when women were expected to develop through edu-cation as equally as men. The native Dutch working class environ-ment has transformed in the past forty-five years with regard to being open to an educational career, in particular for women. The position of education, however, was not consistent in the upbringing of younger respondents (younger than forty-five years old). The further the older children in a family climbed the educational ladder, the more parents realized that higher education was also achievable for their own children. This mainly increased expectations with regard to the younger children.

There was a different situation among the Moroccan and Hindustani respondents. Whereas the men among them were mainly prepared for a role as head of the family and breadwinner, the women were expected by their parents and family to prepare themselves primarily for a role as housewife and mother.

Where participation in education was given high priority in the upbringing of six Moroccan men in this study, it was not considered necessary for the Moroccan women for their future perspectives. For instance, eight of the twelve female respondents were from families in which the daughters initially did not go to school in Morocco. In the Netherlands, all girls did go to primary school, but secondary education was not required for five of them and was even undesirable for a few of them. An exception was made for domestic science schools, which suited the traditional expectations of a woman's role.

One respondent was not allowed by her father to continue her studies after secondary school. By following a dual educational route, she could continue to study, while her parents thought she was working for a wage.

In total, five Moroccan women had to steer carefully to be able to continue studying. They persevered, in spite of the dilemmas they faced on their way to gaining an academic qualification. Their own resilience or perseverance was the decisive factor. Personal strength was an important success factor, which partly explains why one successfully continues an educational career and another does not (see also Pels and De Gruijter, 2006). Bourdieu would probably explain the characteristic as the result of the socialization in the educational environment, as the internalization of success definitions which are typically encouraged in the educational environment. But it does not explain why these respondents were willing to make sacrifices for their educational careers. They paid a significant price. One respondent was divorced from her husband and suffered from health problems as a result of the great burden and two women left their parental homes with bad relationships. Some respondents indicated that their chances of marrying a Moroccan partner had been reduced because of their success in education and two respondents had lost the close relationship with their fathers.

Seven Moroccan women were brought up in families where it was normal for daughters to participate in education. These respondents were not put under pressure to perform well, but were generally given the freedom to determine their own educational route, in contrast to the Moroccan men, because the priority remained their qualities and duties as a housewife. For the female Moroccan respondents, their educational careers were accompanied by other very demanding roles. In the parental home, they helped with housework and caring for younger siblings, which left them little time to study. Educational institutions and libraries were legitimate alternative places to go, to escape household tasks. This was advantageous for their educational careers.

During or after the study, some parents changed their opinions and gender-related considerations became a reason to stimulate the participation in education of their daughters. Some Moroccan respondents were encouraged (secretly) by their mothers to follow further education. According to the findings of Van Pels (1998) and Pels and De Gruijter (2006), mothers often act as the agent behind change and emancipation when it comes to their daughters. In one case, it was the father who stimulated further education arguing that it would increase his daughter's ability to cope if she got divorced. In the Netherlands, he noticed an increase in the number of divorces after which women had difficulty making ends meet. He wanted to prepare his own daughters for this.

One Moroccan man also pointed out in his story the consequences of further education for Moroccan women: their chances of getting married were endangered, because women should preferably have a lower education than their husbands (see also Hooghiemstra, 2003). Two female respondents confirmed this image: they risked being rejected by Moroccan boys because of their higher education, especially if they locked housewife skills. Even academically trained women were expected to place their role in taking care of the home and children above that of their career. The care of children was given preference over childcare in a crèche (see also Pels and De Gruijter, 2006). Academic qualifications (and career ambitions) appear to be in conflict with the main success definitions for Moroccan women.

Educational qualifications were not required for the Hindustani women for their future as housewife and mother. Nevertheless, most of them were stimulated to get qualifications. The gender-related differences in upbringing become apparent from the significance of having qualifications. For Hindustani men, qualifications are mainly to do with the labour market and their future role as breadwinner. Higher education for women was not always so that they could find a job. According to this respondent:

> During my college time the marriage proposals poured in. It was a very strange effect. My mother told me that they got a proposal from people who had never seen me. They proposed because they heard that I was in college. But my parents didn't find him suitable for me. (. . .) My cousins were less fortunate. They were in junior college when they got marriage proposals. They had a lighter skin color, so the proposals came very early. But when they got married they had to prematurely terminate their studies. Once you were married

you had to be the daughter-in-law, you had to cook, play housewife and bear children. So you had to terminate the study. They didn't mind as they were brought up this way. You had to get married as soon as possible after your 18th and you will be taken care of. The education would have no function anymore, because you have already achieved the main goal. (. . .) I've seen more girls this way. They attend the first year at college or university and then wait for the wedding date. After that they terminate the study (Hindustani female, 37)

The parents of three Hindustani women saw education as a pastime until marriage, which would also increase their chances in the Hindustani marriage market. Other parents also experienced better chances of finding a good husband as a result of better education. Daughters appeared to be a greater concern to parents – especially to mothers – than sons. This concern appears to be based on the weaker position held or formerly held by Hindustani women in Suriname. After marriage, many women used to live with their in-laws. Women were dependent on their husbands and possibly their in-laws for an income after marriage. Divorces were taboo and very unfavourable for women as far as their income was concerned. After divorce, there was no breadwinner in the family. It is against this background that the parents – the mothers in particular – of six Hindustani women in this study did not just see qualifications as useful and desirable for their position in the labour and marriage market, but also as a sort of guarantee for (economic) independence. In other words, a means to provide for their own livelihood should these daughters end up on their own and have to take care of themselves and possibly their children completely on their own (see also Pels and De Gruijter, 2006; Distelbrink, 2000). It were the mothers who had experienced abuse and/or hunger in particular, who persistently insisted on educational qualifications for their children. For instance, one mother found every time she tried to get a divorce that she was unable to feed her children, which gave her no choice but to return to her husband with her children. All her daughters had wait until they had educational qualifications before starting a family. She explained her story:

Actually, my father did not even want me to attend elementary school. (. . .) The more he stimulated me to stay home, the more my mother encouraged me to try harder at school. As soon as my mom got the chance, she told me: 'Don't you act crazy. Do your best at school.' And very often, when I grew up, I saw that my mother was beaten by him when she argued for the children. But she continued to do it. (. . .) The junior college had to be paid. He didn't want to, but my mother stood up for me. Then again, we had thunder in the house. But that was the same every time that I went to the next class. And I did it very well. When my friends succeeded at school, their parents were happy, but my father was never happy. My mother was, she was always happy when I went to the next class, but she could not show it. (. . .) At a certain moment I wished to marry my boyfriend. But my mother refused to agree with the relationship as I had not yet finished my study.' After dealing with so many problems at home, I just could not marry him against her will. So I continued the study and unfortunately my relationship with him did not survive. (Hindustani female, 60 years)

Another respondent had a mother who even did not think it necessary for her daughters to marry. This mother was forced into an arranged marriage at a young age, which she felt had impeded her development. She wanted her own daughters to get the opportunity to develop fully, in spite of other expectations from her own social background. The father of a third respondent told his daughters that their husbands would respect them more if they had qualifications.

In spite of being stimulated to follow education, all Hindustani women indicated that their room for manoeuvre was restricted. Participation in education and part-time jobs were their main activities. Those who were the eldest in the family had alongside their household chores, a duty of care towards the younger children. The school and library were legitimate places for Hindustani women to visit. For the respondents themselves, there were also places where they met their peers.

CULTURAL CAPITAL AND CHANGING AMBITIONS

Educational ambitions of parents changed over time. Growing familiarity with the education system and the opportunities offered were the first factors contributing to this change. Familiarity develops as a result of high educational achievements of the older children, but also as a result of the socialization of the respondents and their parents in Dutch society. One respondent complements this position:

> As time passed and my brothers still studied alongside their jobs, my dad sometimes asked them why they worked at daytime and still went to school in the evening. Why they made their lives so heavy while they already had good jobs. And then my brothers explained to him that if they wanted a promotion at work, they would only have chances if they had the right educational qualifications. I think that was the time when my father came to realize that, okay, those are things you really need to relate to each other. (. . .) You can only have expectations when you know that there are possibilities. And for that matter my parents raised my eldest sister and brother with the message that they'll have to work hard and be good for their family. And school was not so much the target. It was fine if you had an education, but it was also fine if you didn't. And actually only later, perhaps only with the youngest three children, they were like: 'Our children can study. And there are possibilities here. It might be expensive, but they can also work and still have the opportunity to study'. I think they started to realize it then and as a consequence the expectations got higher. (Moroccan female, 26 years)

The second factor which contributed to changing ambitions was the increase of educational opportunities through migration, including accessibility of schools and enforcement of compulsory education. The women with a non-Dutch background benefited the most. Partly through the relative increase in the number of divorces among Moroccans and Hindustanis in the Netherlands, the parents of two Moroccan and six Hindustani women wanted them to have qualifications in case they needed to be independent.

A third factor was that families gained status and prestige through their children climbing the educational ladder. As a result, in time academic qualifications became a source of competition within families and the ethnic community and became more and more important in child rearing. The educational goals became higher for men in particular as espoused by another respondent.

> 'I like to mention that status surely plays a role. Because I can still remember that the fact that I went to the university brought my parents status. They told the family that I went to the university and that's also how my family talked about

me: 'She is smart. She is a university student and she is educated'. In the phase when it was difficult for me to study, I noticed the disappointment in my parents, but also in the family, so my sense of shame grew. Later it all came good and now it's still: 'She has finished university'. (Hindustani female, 34)

The fourth factor is the relationship between academic qualifications and the marriage market. Starting a family (from the age of 16 years) was among Moroccans as well as Hindustanis – both for men and women – slightly postponed to allow time to follow further education. Among Hindustanis, there was a notion that academic qualifications improved the marriage opportunities of both men and women. But there was a discrepancy on this point between the stories of the respondents and the respondent characteristics. The respondents said their chances of a good marriage partner increase as a result of high qualifications. However, the respondent characteristics showed that five out of the nine female respondents had a non-Hindustani partner. The other four did not have a partner. The presumption that the Hindustani respondents expressed is however: the higher the education, the better your chances of marriage. There is a similar pattern among Moroccans: high academic qualifications give Moroccan men a better chance at finding a partner, but the Moroccan women say they find it more difficult to find a partner because they have high qualifications.

A fifth factor was the normalizing role of close relatives (*siblings*). Especially among the Hindustani respondents where over time the siblings set the norm for each other at a minimal hbo-level (hbo – Higher Vocational Education). This normalization by siblings did not happen as often among Moroccan respondents and hardly took place at all among native Dutch respondents.

In sum, academic qualifications in the background environment of the respondents with a non-Dutch background have won huge amounts of ground as a result of various factors. In the process of their socialization into the new society, they have integrated, achieving possible academic success and including it into their cultural capital in a shorter amount of time than the native Dutch working class. The marrying age has been postponed both for Moroccan and Hindustani respondents so that they can study. But sometimes, marriages do go ahead before the study is completed. We see gender differences in the consequences here too. Marriage is a legitimate reason for women to end their study before finishing. For men, marriage is never a reason to end their study.

SUCCESS PROMOTING FACTORS IN SOCIAL CAPITAL

For all three groups of respondents, social capital was of essential importance for educational success. Respondents named parents, siblings and other relatives as sources of social capital within their background environment. The contribution of the Moroccan and Hindustani parents was mainly an emotional one. They had only little experience of the Dutch education system, which meant they were unable to support their children with the content of their education. All Moroccan and Hindustani respondents attached great value to the emotional support of their parents, even those that did not get any.

The norms set by parents were also significant. Moroccan and Hindustani parents set participation in education as a norm, even though Moroccan parents expected their sons more than their daughters to seize the educational opportunities as much as possible. Parents also expected their children to get through to the next grade and imposed sanctions if the children did not meet these expectations.

The emotional support and the sanctions of the parents stimulated the respondents to continue studying. Negative values formed on the other hand a restriction to educational progress, as the educational careers of various Moroccan and a few Hindustani women show. The involvement of the parents was particularly important to the children with low secondary school recommendations who took a longer route to reach further education.[5] Parents created room by repeatedly postponing the marrying age.

[5] Crul (2000) differentiates three school routes: (1) the direct route: pupils with an upper general secondary education (havo) or pre-university education (vwo) recommendation after primary school; (2) the indirect route: pupils with an average recommendation after primary school who go on to do upper general

In addition to parents, siblings also played an active role in the educational career. None of the native Dutch respondents mentioned the active involvement of their siblings, not even when/if they were specifically asked about it. However, siblings did have indirect influence on the educational career, as role models mainly.

On the other hand, 12 Moroccan and 13 Hindustani respondents said siblings played an important and active role in their educational careers. Their roles varied from supervision to steering to mediation. In addition, ten Moroccan and six Hindustani respondents named siblings as their role model.

Siblings sometimes let go of gender-specific success definitions for their sisters before their parents did. Three Moroccan and one Hindustani women had siblings who mediated between them and their parents to put off their marrying age and give them permission to follow a different education than domestic science. In my field research, one respondent said:

> I was one of the best students in the class, but the teacher gave a very low college advice. I guess he did not expect much from me because he never got to know me. I wasn't used to speaking to adults and certainly not to men. My mother and my sister went to the parents' evening to talk to the school. To ask if he could give me a higher advice. To the school my older sister went to. My sister thought I should try that and she persuaded my mother. My mother did not know what to do, so they took my sister to the parents' evening. My sister talked to the teacher and he agreed with her. So she got me a higher college advice. (Hindustani female, 37 years)

Brothers who did not live with the family often helped their sisters by offering a room in their home to study. In the homes of two Moroccan respondents, their study was a legitimate reason to stay at their brother's house.

Hindustani siblings appear to have played an even greater role in taking over the upbringing of their siblings. Nine Hindustani

---

education (havo) or pre-university education (vwo) after the first year at secondary school; (3) the long route: young people who receive a low recommendation for secondary school, who manage to get into further education by working their way up through the whole Dutch education system.

respondents had siblings who advised at crucial moments about the education route or even took over the decision-making and discussed the progress of the study with tutors, the entry into or continuation of a course and the recommendation for further education. A few respondents had parents who delegated all education-related decisions to the older children. Three respondents had brothers or sisters who took them into their homes, monitored their academic performance, supervised them and helped steer their way through the academic route and learning behaviour. Siblings contributed fully or partially to the education fee of four of the respondents. Another contribution was by setting a norm. Both younger and older siblings raised higher professional (hbo) education to the norm. This may or may not be accompanied by great social pressure.

Nine native Dutch, two Moroccan and three Hindustani respondents said other relatives were role models for them. Role models in the family circle enjoy status and prestige because of their academic achievements. Nevertheless, Moroccans and Hindustanis mention the use of academic qualifications as a competitive tool for status and prestige within the family circle and even within the broader community they belong to, more than native Dutch respondents. This competition formed a motivating force for ambitions in further education, both for the respondents and their parents. The urge to be competitive in the Netherlands caused parents not to re-inforce their gender-related objections to an educational career for their daughters.

Active involvement of the family can have either a positive or a negative effect. Five Moroccan women experienced a restrictive family influence. In their families, education for girls had no priority. Negotiations, mediation by tutors and concessions (domestic science instead of pre-university education [vwo]) were necessary to continue studying. Among Hindustanis, mediation by relatives meant that more room was created for an educational career for daughters. Also the competition within the family for status and prestige through qualifications (of children) contributed to making room for an educational career.

Outside the social environment, teachers and peer groups were important sources of social capital. The teacher's role proved to be of greater importance for non-native schoolchildren, because they usually had fewer information sources available at home, and their families frequently failed to appreciate higher educational qualifications. For them, extra investments by the teacher also turned out to be important, for instance with regard to the progress to higher education or language acquisition. A teacher's outreaching attitude to the parents was also a success factor. For instance, teacher's investments in parent understanding could create parental support for an educational career so students, especially Moroccan girls, could study without causing conflict situations.

Both fellow students and other peer groups were important for a student's educational career. Positive social contacts with fellow students contributed to the student's wellbeing and study motivation. Besides, fellow students could be a source of information and help, and act as discussion partners regarding the contents of the lessons. Fellow students also display behaviour to be copied. The class composition turned out to be very important for learning languages, standards and behavioural codes. Association with fellow students from comparable social environments also turned out to promote success. A major prerequisite here was that upward educational mobility as a mutual objective was displayed both through ambitions and study behaviour.

CONCLUSION

This study shows that Moroccan, Hindustani and indigenous academics who originally were disadvantaged students have completed a successful educational career thanks to factors in their upbringing. It also appears that the Hindustani and Moroccan students to compensate for their lack of 'capital' need a wider network within their home environment than native pupils. They need, as do native students, the support of parents, but in addition they also need the help of brothers, sisters and other family members for their educational success.

Within the economic capital, the groups' different visions on the origin of the family income and the division of financial responsibilities appear to be essential for success. In Dutch native families, the family income is usually generated by one full-time and one part-time job, and the fact that they have relatively fewer children gives them a favourable starting position. Parents often pay a considerable part of the education expenses. According to the Moroccan respondents, their family income equals their father's income. However, these respondents have been responsible for paying for their own education from an early age, causing many of them to take on extra jobs. Moroccan students will therefore, more than the other groups, dependened on their intrinsic motivation and perseverance.

According to the Hindustani respondents, different family members contributed to the family income. Among the Hindustani respondents both parents and siblings bear all family expenses, which also hosts the educational costs. Older siblings often take (partial) responsibility for younger siblings.

Within the economic capital we see that the diverse composition of household income and a broad financial responsibility distribution creates educational opportunities. But we also see that immigrant parents with limited resources give priority to the educational career of sons above that of daughters.

In cases where the parental home lacked a quiet place to study and a computer, libraries offered an alternative. Student grants were a condition to study for most of the students. Subsidized jobs with paid training created (second chance) opportunities for many respondents enabling them to study, especially for those who came to the Netherlands later in life, and for women who managed to continue their educational career later in life.

Within the cultural capital the main success factor is the importance given to education in the children's upbringing. Achieving educational qualifications was a target in the upbringing of nearly all men. Generally, the ambitions with respect to the educational level desired for sons differ for each population group. Whereas native parents set customized educational goals, non-native parents usually aspired for the best possible results, initially anything above their own educational level. Frequently, the parents of all respondent groups did not aspire to academic educational qualifications for their children, because these were considered unachievable or because the parents were not familiar with the long-term results.

Gender differences occur in all the three respondent groups, but in different gradations. Among the native respondents, gender differences are age-related. Women younger than forty-five years grew up with the idea that they should develop and blossom through education, just like the men. However, the first generation Moroccan and Hindustani women's parents' message was that they should primarily prepare for a role as wife and mother. For these parents, educational qualifications were primarily an emergency solution, in case their daughters should unexpectedly have to fend for themselves. Hindustani women more often received parental support for their educational ambitions than Moroccan women. The (academic) educational careers of Moroccan women were more frequently accompanied with damage to important relations and declining marriage chances.

Parents' ambitions are raised as they realize that higher educational qualifications are also achievable for their children. These changes in ambitions for daughters are greater than those for sons. Growing familiarity with educational opportunities, integration and women's emancipation increase the importance of educational qualifications in the upbringing. Within the own population of the Moroccans and Hindustani respondents, a growing competition arose with educational qualifications of both sons and daughters as commitment for status and prestige. This ensured that parents also encouraged their daughters to gain higher educational qualifications. Parents also became increasingly aware of the economic benefits of high educational qualifications. This appears important when considering the use of the already scarce economic capital. In addition, we see an emancipation process among the Moroccans and Hindustani in which women were prepared with educational qualifications as 'emergency' for a possible need for independence. The importance of educational success in upbringing is gradually growing, but does not replace other upbringing targets. Marriage is often postponed to achieve educational targets; daughters, however, are also expected to become successful wives and mothers, with all duties involved. Despite this heavy burden on women, the non-native respondents' families have made a huge step forward within a relatively short time (in comparison with the native respondents' families).

The upbringing goals and their changes directly influence the support respondents experience in their social environment. Both for the schoolchildren and their social environments, understanding of the possibilities proves to be a success factor in educational careers of boys and girls. Besides, the acceptation by the social environment of success definitions other than those of wife and mother also turn out to be a major success factor in women's education careers.

Within the social capital we see that the emotional support of parents for a teaching career is of great interest to all students. Native students also have benefits from the practical support of their parents. Among Moroccan and Hindustani students this practical support by parents is often lacking. Still, for many respondents, the fact that at least one parent encouraged his or her educational career was of major importance. The contribution of siblings compensates to a large extent the lack of practical support from the parents. Siblings take over upbringing tasks from their parents and accompany their parents to school for parent-teacher-talks, where they provide essential and critical input. Siblings stimulate educational achievements, act as role models, and strengthen competitiveness. Their standards are higher than those of their parents.

Among Moroccans and Hindustanis, other family members function as information sources and role models; they also have normative functions. After their stay in the Netherlands, educational qualifications tend to become a source of competition within families and the social environment. Not all students were able to rely on their home environment for the necessary resources. It is mainly the Moroccan women who lacked support from their home environment for an educational career. These students were among the most disadvantaged students and more than other students to rely on resources in the education system. However, given the austerity of the education system, the success promoting factors within the upbringing have become more and more important.

Teachers are an important source of social capital, especially for non-native schoolchildren, because they usually have fewer information sources available at home, and their families frequently fail to appreciate higher educational qualifications. Teachers' investments in parent understanding can create parental support for an educational career for especially (Moroccan) girls. Peer groups are important also, for example, as source of information and help, as discussion partners and as role models.

The interviews show there is one very special success factor relevant for immigrants. This is a personal property which can be described as innate strength. This concerns respondents' willpower and perseverance to achieve their ambitions. This property explains why under the same conditions, one individual perseveres whereas another quits. Innate strength also explains why some Moroccan women chose a career in education, contrary to all expectations of their social environment; for this, they often pay a very high price. This inner strength is something we can place as a part of cultural capital. People who migrate do this to achieve a better live standard and they are willing to fight for it. After all, migration from one to another country is a huge step and it is not taken easily. Immigrants fight for better living standards and raise their children while teaching them to fight also.

REFERENCES

Almaci, M. and M. van Craen (2004). 'Verweesd, verdwaald, verloren? Allochtonen in het Vlaams universitair landschap'. *Tijdschrift voor Onderwijsrecht en Onderwijsbeleid* 5 (2-3): 123-34.

Bourdieu, P. (1973). 'Cultural Reproduction and Social Reproduction', in R. Brown (ed.), *Knowledge, Education and Cultural Change.* Papers in the Sociology of Education, London: Tavistock Publications, pp. 71-112.

—— (1977). *Reproduction in Education, Society and Culture,* Beverly Hills: Sage.

—— (1984). *Distinction: A Social Critique of the Judgement of Taste.* London: Routledge.

—— (1986). 'The Forms of Capital', in J.G. Richardson (ed.), *Handbook of Theory and Research,* New York: Greenwood Press, pp. 241-58.

—— (1989). *Economisch kapitaal, cultureel kapitaal, sociaal kapitaal; Opstellen over smaak, habitus en het veldbegrip.* Amsterdam: Van Gennep.

—— (1990). *The Logic of Practice.* California: Stanford University Press.

—— (1992). *Pierre Bourdieu; Opstellen over smaak, habitus en het veldbegrip.* Amsterdam: Van Gennep.

Bourdieu, P. and J.C. Passeron (1990). *Reproduction in Education, Society and Culture,* London: Sage Publications.

Conchas, G.Q. (2006). *The Color of Success: Race and High-achieving Urban Youth,* New York: Teachers College Press.

Crossley, N. (2003), 'From Reproduction to Transformation: Social Movement Fields and the Radical Habitus.' *Theory, Culture & Society,* 20 (6), 43-68.

Crul, M. (2000). *De sleutel tot succes; Over hulp, keuzen en kansen in de schoolloopbanen van Turkse en Marokkaanse jongeren van de tweede generatie.* Amsterdam: Het Spinhuis.

Delhaye, C. (1991). 'Discussiedossier: Het symbolisch geweld van Bourdieu; Bedenkingen rond habitus, symbolisch kapitaal en tijdseconomie vanuit een gender-perspectief.' *Rapporten en perspectieven omtrent Vrouwenstudies,* 3: 129-47.

Downey, D. (1995). 'When Bigger is Not Better: Family Size, Parental Resources and Children's Educational Performance.' *American Sociological Review,* 69 (5): 746-61.

Driessen, G.W.J.M. (2001). 'Ethnicity, Forms of Capital, and Educational Achievement.' *International Review of Education,* 46 (6): 513-38.

Esch, W. van (2010). *De kleur van het middelbaar beroepsonderwijs: Een overzichtsstudie naar allochtonen in het mbo.* Den Bosch/Amsterdam: ECBO.

Giddens, A. (2005). *Modernity and Self-identity: Self and Society in the Late Modern Age,* Cambridge: Polity Press.

Haan, M. de and E. Elbers, (2005), 'Peer Tutoring in a Multiethnic Classroom in the Netherlands: A Multiperspective Analysis of Diversity', *Comparative Education Review,* 49 (3): 365-88.

Kahlenberg, R.D. (2001). *All Together Now: Creating Middle-class Schools through Public School Choice,* Washington, D.C.: Brookings Institution Press.

Matthys, M. (2010). *Doorzetters: Een onderzoek naar de betekenis van de arbeidersafkomst voor de levensloop en loopbaan van universitair afgestudeerden.* Amsterdam: Aksant.

Nanhoe, A.C. (2012). *Mijn ouders migreerden om erop vooruit te gaan: Onderwijs en de dynamische habitus; Succesbevorderende factoren in de onderwijscarrière van Marokkaanse, Hindostaanse en autochtoon Nederlandse academici uit lagere sociaal-economische milieus in Nederland.* Antwerpen: Garant Uitgeverij B.V.

Ours, J.C. van and J. Veenman (2005). *Age at Migration and Educational Attainment of Young Immigrants*, Discussion paper. Tilburg: Center Tilburg University.

Parham, J. (2002). 'Teaching Pleasure.' *Experiments in Cultural Studies and Pedagogy*, 5 (4): 461-78.

Paulle, B. (2006). *Voorbij de oude debatten; Een voorstel voor 'economische' desegregatie van het onderwijs.* www.volkskrant.com/bijlagen/essay_paulle.pdf, retr. 1 maart 2006.

Pels, T. (1998). *Opvoeding in Marokkaanse gezinnen in Nederland. De creatie van een nieuw bestaan.* Assen: Koninklijke Van Gorcum.

Pels, T. and M. de Gruijter (2006). *Emancipatie van de tweede generatie; Keuzen en kansen in de levensloop van jonge moeders van Marokkaanse en Turkse afkomst.* Assen: Van Gorcum.

Rijkschroeff, R., J.W. Duyvendak and T. Pels (2003). *Bronnenonderzoek integratiebeleid.* Utrecht: Verweij-Jonker Instituut.

Sadiraj, K. and I. Groot, (2006). *Sociaal-economische status in vereveningsmodel zorgverzekeraars: wat zijn de mogelijkheden?* Amsterdam: SEO Economisch Onderzoek.

Smit, F. and G. Driessen (2002). *Allochtone ouders en de pedagogische functie van de basisschool.* Nijmegen: ITS.

Sociaal en Cultureel Planbureau (SCP) (2011). *De sociale staat van Nederland 2011.* Den Haag: SCP.

Stoep, J. van der (2005). *Pierre Bourdieu en de politiek van het multiculturalisme.* Zwolle: Uitgeverij Kok.

Sullivan, A. (2001). 'Cultural Capital and Educational Attainment.' *Sociology*, 35 (4), 893-912.

Tierney, W.G. (2000). 'Undaunted Courage; Life History and the Modern Challenge', in N.K. Denzin and Y.S. Lincoln (eds.), *Handbook of Qualitative Research*, Second Edition, London: Sage, pp. 537-53.

Throop, C.J. and K.M. Murphy, (2002). 'Bourdieu and Phenomenology: A Critical Assessment', *Anthropological Theory*, 2: 185-207.

Tilborg, L. van and W. van Es., in samenwerking met Glaudé, M. and F. Verbeek (2004). *Werk in uitvoering: de evaluatie van de RMC-wet in 2003*, Amsterdam: Faculteit der Maatschappij- en Gedragswetenschappen, SCO-Kohnstamm Instituut.

Ministerie van Onderwijs, Cultuur en Wetenschappen (OC&W) (2011). *Tweede Kamer der Staten Generaal, Vergaderjaar 2010-11, 31.288 nr. 160, Hoger Onderwijs-Onderzoeks- en Wetenschapsbeleid, Beleidsnotitie Studiefinanciering 'Studeren is Investeren'.* Den Haag: Ministerie van OC & W.

Veenman, J. and C. Heij, (2008). *Immigrant Gender Convergence in Education and on the Labour Market*, Rotterdam: Erasmus School of Economics.

Wester, F., K. Renckstorf, and P. Scheepers, (2010). *Onderzoekstypen in de communicatiewetenschap*, Amsterdam: Kluwer.

PART 3

RELIGION, ARTS AND IDENTITY

CHAPTER 8

Slavery and Indentured Labour from the Perspective of Art Studies

J.S. (MITRA) RAMBARAN AND
R. SAFDAR ZAIDI

INTRODUCTION

In 2012, we were involved in translating a novel about indentured labour from Urdu to Dutch, a work that took us seven years to accomplish. The second author (Zaidi) wrote three songs for the novel, which transmits the feeling of migrants at that time and the emotions of the people when they arrived in Suriname, facing new circumstances. He thought that the Indian poetry reflected the history. For instance, ghazals of the last Moghul king of India, Bahadur Shah Zafar (1775-1862) are famous for recording the political unrest and injustice of the English colonization process (Kanda, 2007). While the author (Zaidi) was writing the songs about the departure, he tried to find authentic songs for the occasion, but they could not be found. At that moment he started questioning as to what happened to the original songs. Indians surely must have brought their songs from India and should have written and composed new songs in Suriname. This subject kept us engaged in a discussion regarding finding the facts about authentic Indian songs and lyrics.

Before indentured labour, the majority of the world was captured in slavery; for Suriname the Dutch slave trade existed for three hundred and fifty years (Emmer, 2006). In the USA, a Dutch vessel of a private company brought the first group of black people to Virginia in 1619 (Rose, 1999). The question mentioned above continued to remain in our mind unsolved; but we discovered that a lot of literature has been written concerning the role of art and culture in slavery. The spirituals and blues are melodic history of the pain and miseries encountered by black people in the south of North America. Small (1987, 191) stated that:

> It has been said that if gospel is the present-day paradigm of Afro-American religious musicking, so blues is of secular. It would be more true to say that blues and gospel are twin modern aspects of that ritual of survival which is the musical act . . . there is a good deal of quite secular enjoyment of both spirituals and gospel music, so in blues . . . there is a strong element of what can only be called the religious (see Moore 2002, 2).

In this paper we will address the blues, since it is assumed that West African slaves would have brought them to the Americas. (Moore 2002: 2). It is a well-known fact that the lyrics of the blues are written by slaves, who elaborated their lives under the agency of slavery. A famous phrase says *that history is written by the conquerors or by the masters.* However, in the case of 'the blues', the history is written by the slaves. The blues reflects the socio-political scenario, as do the ghazals of Bahadur Shah Zafar. Further research on Indian traditional music brought us to an interesting article written by Peter Manuel, who addressed the alhā, birhā and *Rāmāyan* songs brought by indentured labourers to the Caribbean. (Manuel, 2012). From these three music styles, we chose to keep our focus on the birhā. If we want to dig out the history from poetry, we may discover some facts which history probably could not register.

THEORY AND METHODOLOGY

Our main focus is the way in which slavery and indentured labour are seen from the perspective of art studies. Are the blues and the American-African spirituals not similar to the birhā and *Rāmāyan* that our forefathers brought with from India and incorporated in Suriname in their new lives? In this paper we argue that the birhā similar to the blues. A literature study on the blues and birhā, focusing on similarities in the two music appearances is used to show this. We used a thematic content analysis to study the way the songs were used, the musical form, the socio-political circumstances, the content, the poetry and message of the songs. We wanted to discover patterns and recurring themes relating to the purposes, meanings, and functions (Kinney, 2012: 398).

COMPARATIVE STUDIES

Of course, Suriname is not the only country where indentured labour came after the abolition of slavery. There are enough comparative studies about African and Asian cultures in the Diaspora (Shepherd, 1996). There are also different perspectives and it is often said that it is not possible to compare slavery and indentured labour. In fact, it is a very sensitive issue. However, due to the poor quality of life and sheer intensity of work, both indentured labour and slavery have much in common. The manner in which identity (James, n.d.) and culture of the labourers, was snatched is different. Others claim that the trans-Atlantic slave trade and colonial plantations were hardly interrupted by the abolition of slavery. Indeed the Indians were able to maintain their identity to some extent. Walcott gives the example of playing Ramleela in the village of Felicity in Trinidad (1992, as cited in Kale, 1998: 1). It is also a reality that through the creation of blues in North American, Afro-Americans established a visible identity within the world of music and songs. This paper focuses on the circumstances that people endured during slavery and indentureship. When people in pain open their hearts in music and release their souls out in melody, they create an everlasting impression of jubilee.

INDO-CARIBBEAN MUSIC AND SONGS

As stated earlier, we were in search of authentic Indian songs and music. Desk research brought us some information about a study in British Guyana of protest songs (Vatuk, 1964) and a case study of Indians in Trinidad who are fusing different musical traditions like combining the sitar with the steel pan. Also we found a brief description in an American encyclopedic history about songs like bhajans, or instruments like the harmonium, dholak and dantāl. But it was all about Trinidad, Fiji or British Guyana. We hardly found any literature written about Suriname. There was a Bidesia project between 2005-7, involving the Bhojpuri region of India, Suriname and the Netherlands. The project entailed collecting oral heritage. But research on the role of birhās was limited probably, because of the merit we give to the traditional Hindustani music. Finally we found an article by Peter Manuel (2012), which gave us guidance for this paper. It is also interesting to know what is being studied in the Caribbean area when it comes to Indian music, because the circumstances of indentured labour were the same for the whole region (Vatuk, 1964: 220-3).

Ramnarine (2001) describes the way in which the development of Indian-Caribbean music tradition took place, starting with chutney. The author speaks about the way in which influential chutney songs refer to the imagery of the boat: the different ships that sailed from India to the 'New World', and offer reminders of the historical and economic circumstances. In the text of the song there is a obvious evidence for this (Ramnarine, 2001: 51-2). The 'Bengalee Baboo' was the protagonist of the nineteenth century texts produced in Calcutta. Ramnarine concludes by saying that in this respect, chutney can be compared to Indian models from the nineteenth century, especially from Calcutta, which was the location of the main 'coolie depots', from where Indian migrants to the Caribbean began their journeys (Ramnarine, 2001: 53).

Manuel points out that 'in Suriname, where Indians still speak Hindi, Indian folk music thrives' (Manuel, 1995: 214). He refers to the loss of the Hindi language among the Indo-Caribbeans, and wonders how people in Guyana and Trinidad are crazy about Hindi films and film songs. On his journey he describes the tradition of the Hosay commemoration and the tassa drummers with the taziya. He discusses the way Indians have left behind the Hindu-Muslim enmity, and how music plays a role in building a bridge between the Afro-Caribbean and the Indo-Caribbean, as sung by Drupatee[1] in 1989 'Indian Soca' (Manuel 1995, 214).

[1] Drupatee Ramgoonai, the first Indian singer in the calypso tents, became one of the most popular singers of chutney soca (Niranjana, 2006: 98). The chutney soca singer Drupatee from Trinidad should not be confused with Drowpati, the pioneering female baithak gáná singer from Suriname.

Blues

A lot of literature has been written about blues. Resources (Moore 2002, 2; Manuel 2012, 118) reveal that in the nineteenth century the field hollers used a call to communicate. They worked individually in the fields in comparative quiet and such call had practical use. They used it to ease the repetitive actions, or to call instructions to animals. They also used it as communal expressions – one field hand picked up the call from another, and so on. We found that authors labelled the blues as signifying, and the way it is manifested in music, through historicized adaptations of the 'ring shout', realized as call-response textures (Moore, 2002, 10). Coming back home after a long day of work, without any pause; the tired male and female slaves suffered from the pain of their sores and wounds they received during their work in the harsh environments of slavery. These wounds were treated to allow the body to heal, but not their souls and hearts. The only therapy for these miserable souls was God, but actually it was not. According to the downtrodden folks, God was only for their masters, He had nothing to do with slaves. The only support for their painful souls was songs and music. It was music without instruments but created by the soul. When songs and music are created out of the depths of the heart and soul, they do not depend upon traditional instruments. They used whatever they could to create a sound, for example a spoon, fork or piece of wood. These were transformed to produce a joyful composition that eased the soul.

David Evans stated that, 'between 1890 and 1910 new sounds; meaning melodic-, instrumental-, and verbal – began to penetrate the repertoire of African American music' Moore, 2002: 20). The new sounds came from spirituals, functional songs of work and play, narrative folk ballads, banjo tunes and instrumental dance music. These music forms were all blended together slowly and transformed into a distinct genre of music called the blues. The first discovery of the blues by W.C. Handy in 1895, is mentioned by several authors (Moore, 2002: 25; Lawson, 2007: 40; Hamilton, 2007: 19-21). They all describe the impact that the song 'Going Where the Southern Cross the Dog' had on Handy and the unforgettable way the guitar was played with a knife.

Guido van Rijn (Moore, 2002) stated that blues belonged to the oral tradition. Access to these lyrics can therefore be highly problematic. Folklorist Alan Lomax recorded many blues' songs (Roodenburg and Grijp, 2005) and transcribed them, but could sometimes not recognize the words. Thomas (1997) emphasizes Sterling Brown's theory of the blues to combine the musical form with poetic expression. When Brown analysed the blues, he discerned the poetic approach was similar to nineteenth-century literary verse (Thomas, 1997: 2). The author discusses how Brown's poetry, for example, the poem he wrote for Ma Rainey, reflects African-American folktales. A crucial way to recognize blues music is the way it is composed to sound. Graeme M. Boone (Moore, 2002) describes the stanza in a scheme of chords, beats, band and lyrics. Through the songs, the southern African-Americans delivered messages of being poor and a long way from home. They speak of racism and discrimination, and living below poverty level (Moore, 2002: 89-90).

In his essay, Lawson (2007) notes that old blues singers like John Estes and new singers like Elvis Presley sang about the same thing: love, loss and escapism. The same issue was addressed in the book *Blues, Ideology and Afro-American Literature* written by Baker. Blues lyrics are usually set either in three-line or quatrain-refrain verse forms. In the three-line verse form, the second line repeats the first, sometimes with a slight variation, while the third completes the thought with a rhyme (Titon, 1990: 4). For this paper we focus on a blues written by Al Smith and Luther Dixon, and performed by Jimmy Reed in 1961.

I'm gonna get me a boss man
One who's gonna treat me right
I work hard in the day time
Rest easy at night

Big boss man, can't you hear me when I call?
Can't you hear me when I call?
I said you ain't so big, you're just tall that's all.

(http://www.lyricsmode.com/lyrics/j/jimmy_reed/big_boss_man.html)

Harry Shaw stated in his introduction that when Jimmy Reed sings this song, he is singing out of the direct or indirect experience of most black people. Shaw concludes that 'The shared common heritage of slavery, freedom, field work, house service, and so on, is part of the collective experiential background for black people' (Shaw, 1990: 2). Gradually the music of these slaves became famous. The aristocracy did not allow their kids to listen to the music of these slaves. They did not realize that they could make people slaves but could not enslave their hearts and souls that were released in music. This music became well known in various forms as blues.

Birhā

In Hindi language 'birhā' means separation, while a poetic word 'firaq' is equally used in the same manner in Urdu poetry. Birhā is widely used for the painful separation of the beloved. In Indian culture, love has a wide aspect such as love with god, love with the goddess, love with the mother, love with the village, love with pets or with the homeland. Mirabai's[2] (AD 1498-1557) birhā's and bhajans are a great treasure of Hindi literature, which she wrote in love of god Shri Krishnaji.

Nothing is really mine except Krishna.
O my parents, I have searched the world
And found nothing worthy of love.
Hence I am a stranger amidst my kinfolk
And an exile from their company,
Since I seek the companionship of holy men;
There alone do I feel happy,
In the world I only weep.
I planted the creeper of love
And silently watered it with my tears;
Now it has grown and overspread my dwelling.
You offered me a cup of poison

[2] Mirabai was a princess who become a saint and played a key role in the preaching of Bhakti ideology.

Which I drank with joy.
Mira is absorbed in contemplation of Krishna,
She is with God and all is well!

http://www.bharatonline.com/uttar-pradesh/culture/music/birha.html

People of India have created birhā lyrics to reflect love affairs and other social issues, such as separation from the village or river or complaining against oppression. According to Hassankhan (2013: 27 n.5) this is also mentioned by Brij Lal in 1983 and Marina Carter in 1995. Manuel (2012) notes that George Grierson, a folklorist, linguist and civil servant in the British Raj, wrote the first article on Bhojpuri folk songs in 1886. He published several scholarly works on the dialects and peasant life of Bihar, on Hindi literature, on bhakti and on linguistics (Manuel, 2012: 118). He was also the author of an official report on migration in 1883 (Arya, 1968: 2). Manuel (2012) argued that in the above-mentioned article, Grierson depicted a genre of the North Indian rural music called birhā. This music was very popular during the time of the indentured labour and it is no surprise that this music and songs were brought to the Caribbean, along with other forms of songs such as alhā (Manuel, 2012: 118) which were of less religious nature, and those of Kabir, and those based on a religious character, such as Tulsīdāsa (Arya, 1968: 10).

Manuel (2012) refers to Henry (1988, 150-3) who mentioned that the rustic original form of Bhojpuri birhā is a field holler, called the kharibirhā. The Ahir peasants used it to communicate with other peasants who were some distance away. The term kharibirhā can also comprehended as solo singer, perhaps accompanied by one or two more singers, who shout out the final verse words and sings a narrative text of undetermined length (Manuel, 2012: 118). This is also emphasized by Arya (1968) who stated that the Ahirs seem to have created the Indian birahā but in Suriname it has become the vehicle of creative poetry. He also points out that some birahā were also work songs, for instance the dhobiyabirahā, song no. 73 of the washermen. According to him, the birahā needs special attention:

It can be composed by any person on any subject. It is like a protest song, because it breaks all the social rules. Or it can praise a person, a practise or a custom. In former days birahā competitions were held and two parties were singing, competing with each other in questions and answers. It may be sung on a dholak or without any instruments at all (Arya, 1968: 29).

Arya (1968) drew in various music instruments that he encountered during his visits to Suriname.

The birhā is divided into three parts: firstly the dohā or the sumiran, where a verse from Kabīr, Tulasīdāsa or any other is used. The second part is lacārī or alcārī, which is the main composition on any topic and is faster in beat. The final part, the jācanī or bisarjan, rounds off the song, sometimes by thanking the deity or introducing the singer (Arya, 1968: 29-30). The author claims that these songs must be regarded in light of a long literary tradition in India. He recorded 100 songs from Suriname, in various styles. He transcribed them, translated them in English and stored the taped copies at the Instituut voor Oosterse Talen of the University of Utrecht (Arya, 1968: 4).

The question of whether indentured labour was volunteered or forced is a common discussion among the historians. The emotions of indentured labourers might help in understanding this. In the birhā songs, the labourers' emotions were recorded:

Ab se khabardar raho bhai
Teri bigri baat banjai
Kalkutte me bharti karke bhej diye jab bhai
layeutare Surinam me dipumein bhatkhawai
Teen mahine jalyandafar me lakh jhaperek hai
Shri Ram nagar ki charcha krake Surinam giye pahunchai
Har savera nambulakar bakarane baat sunai

(Be careful, your bad fortune will come to an end.
From Kalkatta, we were sent to a depot in Suriname where we were fed rice.
After a three month long difficult journey by ship,
we reached Suriname,
which we had earlier taken to be Shri Ram's land.
As soon as it is morning, the bakara [white man] called us).

(Majumder, 2010 in *Kahe Gaile Bides*: 151-8)

In the last line of the birhā above, it clearly shows that the writer experienced some kind of fraud when he/she was recruited as a labour. The recruiting agency may have mislead the labourers and used religious affiliation as an attraction to make the overseas journey (see also Vatuk, 1964: 223). The word 'kalapani' (black water) is well-known in India and used metaphorically. The British colonists used the Andaman and Nicobar Islands as an open prison to house rebels and other criminals. Crossing or entering the 'black water' was a taboo (Bannerjee, 2010: 1) because according to orthodox ideology, travellers travelling in or across the black water would lose their caste. Anderson (2009) explains what happened if the coolies heared about *kalapani.*

> If magistrates used the words kalapani, 'the coolie is apt to lose all self-possession'. 'Says the coolie to himself, when he hears a Magistrate Saheb talking to him of kalapani – 'Kya! Ham ne kya kasur kiya, ke hamko kalapani sunate hain?' ('What! What wrong have we done, that [he] speaks to us of kalapani?'). Migrants told him how as a result they 'escaped' from recruiters ('Tab bhagjata')

In birhā the folk song writers expressed their emotions about crossing the black water.

Pal ke jahajua men roi-dhoipaithai ho
Kaisi hoi kalapani par revidesia
Jiara dirae Ghat Kyan nahi aaehó
Baita din kaibhae mas re videsia.

Weeping and sitting in the ship with a sail,
anxious to know the journey to the fearful place
the heart is sinking and the mind is disturbed
as the destination is not visible.

(Majumder, 2007 in *Kahe Gaile Bides*: 151)

In this 'birhā', the writer reflects the fear and concern in crossing the black water. Manuel states that 'most of the North Indian music heritage brought to the Caribbean – primarily Trinidad, Guyana, and Suriname – consisted of folk genres that were predominantly text-driven, in that their expressive interest lay primarily in lyric content rather than purely musical dimensions' (Manuel,

2012: 115-16). The last remarks worth mentioned here is that Vatuk (1964: 223) as well as Arya (1968: 31) and Manuel (2012: 117) emphasize that the texts of songs in Suriname, Guyana and Trinidad are mostly derived from centuries-old songs, like the one of Mirabai in the beginning of this section. However, after the indenture period, the birhā in India evolved into a totally different musical genre (Manuel, 2012: 118). Nowadays there is no resemblance between the Indo-Caribbean birhā and its South Asian counterpart (Manuel, 2012: 122).

DISCUSSION AND CONCLUSIONS

In conclusion, we would like to discuss the similarities we found on six items. First, when we compare the birhā with the blues we discovered that the description of how the songs were used is the same: the field hollers used a call to communicate with others who were not nearby (Moore, 2002: 2; Manuel, 2012: 118). Secondly, the musical form is very simple, as seen in the appearances of the songs. Blues lyrics are usually set either in three-line or quatrain-refrain verse forms (Titon, 1990: 4). Birhā has three parts: the start, the second part is the composition and the final closing of the song (Arya, 1968: 29-30). Also the call-response textures can be found in both musical forms (Moore, 2002: 10; Arya, 1968: 29). Thirdly, the socio-political circumstances in the two music traditions are similar. These songs are from the nineteenth century and are filled with notions of imperialism. They cry out for better treatment because of maltreatment and severe work (Shaw, 1990: 2; Majumder, 2010: 157). Fourthly, the content of the two musical entities are the same in terms of authenticity, bitter honesty and the people's voice (Thomas, 1997: 1-2; Manuel, 2012: 124). Fifthly, the poetry in both musical traditions, from the perspective of the colonial masters are seen as childish (Manuel, 2012: 118). That is why Thomas (1997) describes the theory of Sterling Brown to 'elevate the poetry and to create a 'national literature' for black Americans'. (Thomas, 1997: 2). Finally, the messages of the songs reflect loneliness; lost love; homesickness; and discrimination. We see evidence for this in Moore, 2002: 89-90) and Majumder (2007, in *Kahe Gaile Bides*: 157).

If Roodenburg and Grijp (2005) can compare two music cultures such as the blues and the Dutch ballads, can we not also do the same for the blues and the birhā? Countries like Trinidad and Guyana have almost lost the Bhojpuri Hindi language. In fact, it has only been preserved in Suriname. Usarbodh Arya has recorded 100 songs and stored it in the University of Utrecht. Is there a possibility for a literary research on these songs?

Can we broaden this research to the development of the 'baithakgáná' and presently chutney in Suriname and the Netherlands, which are influenced by the Caribbean chutney?

Much research from various aspects (literary, musicology) has been done on the blues; can birhā also get the attention of the researcher for a intensive study regarding its literary and musical aspects?

During the colonization era, mostly the colonial powers engineered the history. We have limited resources for history written by enslaved or colonized people. Mostly people from the opposition were not allowed to record historical events. But the cultural arts are an actual source for the study of historical events. In this paper, we have seen where the blues and birhā have recorded political and social events. By studying the academic papers, using music and analysis of songs, we are convinced that comparing these musical traditions based on the six items we used will give us more insight into the similarities and differences. However, further research is necessary to see if other authors have made the same comparison. With this paper, we want to encourage more Hindustanis to continue studying art and literature. This can help bring out our legacy in 'baithakgáná' and 'Kabir' verses – which are still alive in the Indian diaspora, on an academic level.

GLOSSARY

Ahirs	Who, nowad ays in India prefer to be called Yādavs. They are a traditional cowherding caste, low-to-middle in rank, but proud of their traditional image as virile and martial (Manuel 2012, 118).
Alcārī	See lāchāri.
Alhā	The alhā-khand, a martial epic (Manuel, 2012: 116).
Baithakgānā	Form of folks songs, sung individually or in groups with specific instruments: dholak, har-monium and dhantāl.
Bhajans	Religious songs.
Bhojpuri	Four border districts between the provinces of Bihar and Uttar Pradesh.
Bengalee Baboo	A parody of a Bengalee gentleman on his visit to England.
Bidesia	Foreign country.
Birhā	Spelled according to Arya (1968); song addressing separation from country, city, village and lover. It served as a vehicle for a wide variety of lyric themes, ranging from the pious to prurient, and from the traditional to the spontaneously composed (Manuel, 2012: 124).
Bisarjan	Final part of the song. See Jācanī.
Chutney	Funny teasing song. Chutney is the music and song (and now dance) composed and sung by Indian women originally behind closed doors and now in the competitive arena by both men and women (Ingram, 1997).
Ḏantāl	A metal rod struck with a clapper (Manuel, 2012: 130).
Dhobiyabirahā	The washermen's song.
Ḏholak	Drum; both sides are covered by hide.
Dohā	Hindi couplet in a standardized metre, which is sung in free rhythm, essentially to the same tune as the birhā proper (Manuel, 2012: 120).
Firaq	Song inspired by separation from lover.
Ghazal	Poetry written for lovers.
Hosay	Muharram festival in Trinidad, *Taziya* in Suriname.
Jācanī	Final parts of the song.
Kabir	Poetry of the mystic named Bhagat Kabir.
Kalapani	Black waters (Manuel, 2012: 126).
Kharibirhā	Field holler, consisting of one or more couplets sung fortissimo to a 'tumbling strain' quintessentially by an

	Ahir peasant seeking to commune with brethren some distance away (Manuel, 2012: 118).
Khāsfarmāis	Special requests – with the songs the relatives or the migrant expressed their feelings of affection or feelings of pain as a consequence of separation from their loved ones (Hassankhan, 2013: 24).
Lacārī	Subsequent lines centre around the tonic, starting with the sixth scalar degree below and continuing indefinitely (Manuel, 2012: 120).
Moravian Church	The name 'Moravian' identifies the fact that this historic church had its origin in ancient Bohemia and Moravia in what is the present-day Czech Republic.
Rāmāyan	The tale of Rama, the righteous prince (Manuel, 2012: 129).
Ramleela	Dramatic folk re-enactment of the life of Ram (Hassankhan, 2013: 29, n. 17). Staging war between Ravan (anti-god) and Ram (God of Hindu mythology).
Shri Krishnaji	Deity of Hindu mythology.
Soca	From Trinidad, the term 'sokah' (later spelled 'soca') was coined by Ras Shorty I (Garfield Blackman, formerly called Lord Shorty) around 1973, following his musical experiments in mixing East Indian elements with calypso (Guilbault, 1997).
Sumiran	Introductory invocations (Manuel, 2012: 144).
Tassa	Special drums used at taziya or Muharram festival.
Taziya	Replica of mausoleum of Imam Houssain.
Tulsīdāsa	A Brahmin poet, evidently residing in Banaras, wrote the *Rāmāyana* in a regional dialect – aliterary version of Avadhi, the idiom spoken to the west of the Bhojpuri area (Manuel, 2012: 129).

REFERENCES

Anderson, C. (2009). 'Convicts and Coolies: Rethinking Indentured Labour in the Nineteenth Century', *Slavery and Abolition*, vol. 30, no. 1: 93-109.

Arya, U. (1968). *Ritual Songs and Folksongs of the Hindus of Surinam,* Leiden: E.J. Brill.

Bannerjee, R. (2010). 'The Kala Pani Connection: Francophone Migration

Narratives in the Caribbean Writing of Raphaël Confiant and the Mauritian Writing of Ananda Devi', *Anthurium: A Caribbean Studies Journal*, vol. 7: Issue 1, Article 5, accessed 2 May 2015. http://scholarlyrepository. miami. edu/anthurium/vol7/iss1/5

Cooley, J. (1985). 'Blues, Ideology and Afro-American Literature: A Vernacular Theory', *American Literature*: 290-2.

Emmer, P. (2006). *The Dutch Slave Trade: 1500-1850,* New York: Berghahn Books.

Guilbault, J. (1997). 'The Politics of Labelling Popular Music in the English Caribbean'. sibetrans.com. http://www.sibetrans.com/trans/articulo/265/ the-politics-of-labelling-popular-musics-in-english-caribbean. (accessed 2 May 2015).

Hamilton, M. (2007). *In Search of the Blues: Black Voices, White Visions*, London: Jonathan Cape.

Hassankhan, M.S. (2013). *Caribbean Issues in the Indian Diaspora*, Kumar Mahabir (ed.), New Delhi: Serial Publications.

Ingram, A. (1997). 'What is Chutney Music?' http://aingram.web.wesleyan.edu/ chutney.html (accessed 2 May 2015).

James, A.K. and M. Suzuki (n.d.). 'African and Asian Cultures in the Diaspora, Indenture and Slavery cannot be Compared. They are Fundamentally Different . . .' http://www.academia.edu/2316489/INDENTURE AND SLAVERY CAN NOT BE COMPARED. THEY ARE FUNDAMENTALLY DIFFERENT. DISCUSS.

Kale, M. (1998). *Fragments of Empire: Capital, Slavery, and Indian Indentured Labor in the British Caribbean*, Philadelphia: University of Pennsylvania Press.

Kanda, K. (2007). 'Bahadur Shah Zafar and His Contemporaries', in K. Kanda, *Bahadur Shah Zafar and His Contemporaries*, Delhi: Sterling, 12-17.

Kinney, A. (2012). 'Loops, Lyrics, and Literacy: Songwriting', *Journal of Adolescent & Adult Literacy*: 395-404.

Lawson, R. (2007). 'The First Century of Blues: One Hundred Years of Hearing and Interpreting the Music and the Musicians', *Southern Culture*, 13, no. 3, Fall, 2007: 39-61.

Majumder, M. (2010). *Kahe Gaile Bides, Why did You Go overseas*, Amsterdam: Koninklijk Instituut voor de Tropen.

Manuel, P. (1995). *Caribbean Music from Rumba to Reggae*, Philadelphia: Temple University Press.

—— (2012). 'The Trajectories of Transplants: Singing Alhā, Birhā, and the Rāmāyan in the Indic Caribbean', *Asian Music*, vol. 43, Summer/Fall, no. 2: 115-54.

Moore, A. (2002). *The Cambridge Companion to Blues and Gospel Music*, Cambridge: Press Syndicate of the University of Cambridge.

Niranjana, T. (2006), *Mobilizing India: Women, Music and Migration Between India and Trinidad.* Duke University Press, accessed 2 May 2015. https://www.dukeu press.edu/Mobilizing-India

Ramnarine, T. (2001). *Creating Their Own Space: The Development of an Indian-Caribbean Musical Tradition*, Kingston: University of West Indies Press.

Roodenburg, H. (2005). *Blues en Balades: Alan Lomax en Ate Doornbos, twee muzikale veldwerkers*, Amsterdam: Amsterdam University Press.

Rose, W. (1999). *A Documentary History of Slavery in North America*, Athens, Georgia: University of Georgia Press.

Shaw, H. (1990). *Perspectives of Black Popular Culture*, Bowling Green State University Popular Press.

Shepherd, V. (1996). 'Indentured Labour in the Age of Imperialism, 1834-1922', *Economic History Review*: vol. 49: 860-1.

Thomas, L. (1997). 'Authencity and Elevation: Sterling Brown's Theory of the Blues'. *African American Review*, Fall 97: 409-16.

Titon, J. (1990). *Downhome Blues Lyrics: An Anthology from the post-World War II Era*, Chicago: University of Illinois Press.

Vatuk, V.P. (1964). 'Protest Songs of East Indians in British Guiana', *The Journal of American Folklore*, vol. 77, no. 305: 220-35.

CHAPTER 9

Fu Moimoi: Body Art as Identity Marker

HILDE NEUS

Is it truly so that we inhabit the earth? Ay!
Maybe for ever on earth?
Even the hardest rock splits asunder,
Even gold perishes, even precious feathers shred and fray.
Maybe for ever on this earth?
Only for a fleeting moment are we here!

(NETZAHUALCÓYOTL, 1418-72,
ALBERT HELMAN, 1992, *MEXICO ZINGT*).[1]

INTRODUCTION

We are celebrating and commemorating in 2013 the one hundred and sixty years of Chinese presence in Suriname, one hundred and fifty years of Hindustani immigration and one hundred and fifty years since slavery was abolished. The general tendency during this commemoration of crown years is to go back into the past and emphasize the dark pages of slavery and indentured labour. There is reason to be joyful. This year we celebrate the beauty of the inhabitants of Suriname, how they all came to this land with their different cultures and their different ways of displaying their heritage, and how the trajectories of several aspects were deployed into a general attribution of legacies to enhance different futures. We look at

[1] Helman translated the poem from a native language to Dutch. The English translation from Dutch is by the author.

their bodies and the beauty and di-versity of them, of the ways the people in Suriname make themselves look beautiful.

Albert Helman, who wrote several books on Suriname's culture, defined culture as the ways in which a group of people approaches another group, known or unknown, shows itself and behaves itself as the way it is.[2] Culture is already available once there are two people present. One can identify culture as a marker of being, that is, oneness and identity. Culture is something by which one is influenced directly after birth and is passed on from generation to generation. Helman also states that each culture has its own specificities. Each group (or individual) tries to hold on to its special features, but also tries to exchange aspects inter-culturally. Within the process of acculturation, one sees exchange and acquisition of certain elements to the point of culture loss. One notices gains as well (Helman, 1977b: 8-10). Adornment is usually seen as low culture, although some golden jewellery is so very intricately made and expensive that it eventually evolves into high culture.

Over the past decades research has been conducted in the arts and humanities on how bodies and embodiments are remembered, refigured and resituated. How was the body seen in the past, how is it reviewed today and how would it develop into the future?

The intersection of body, institution and memory in art history or cultural studies can be the ground for research into the body as imagined, historicized and made part of the cultural process, accessed from both material and intangible angles. The body is part of a group and a society and decorations on the body might attract, or induce disgust in some spectators. The body is overtly represented in art as of old and modern forms. The human shape was one of the first images represented by human beings.[3] But the body can also be perceived as a piece of art in itself because of its decorations.

[2] Albert Helman (pen name of Lou Lichtveld 1903-96) was minister of Education and Community Development from 1949-51.

[3] The oldest art forms found in Suriname are the petroglyphs, incisions on rock, often depicting human forms, for example, at Werephai near Kwamalasamutu.

In this paper, it is emphasized that Suriname has a number of ethnic groups with a different historical past and various cultural and religious backgrounds. Amongst the indigenous peoples (the Amerindians) we already see variations in that they arrived in Suriname along different trajectories and routes. Each group came to the country with its own way of expressing identity through body art. Even within the group people might distinguish amongst themselves by different patterns in decorating the body not only in age groups but also between the sexes.

This paper examines the various types of decorating the body and discusses the variations amongst the Chinese immigrants (1853), former slaves (1863) and contract labourers from India (1873). This is because in 2013 these three groups commemorate a jubilee. But the identity markers of other ethnic groups in Suriname will also be discussed. This research does not touch upon clothing as a marker, although it is obvious that each group had its own habits and peculiarities in this area as well.

Structurally, this paper addresses five ways of adornment: make up, tattooing, piercing, jewels, hairstyles and nails. The different ethnic groups of which Suriname is constructed all came with their peculiarities in body ornamentation. In modernity, these specific habits are now applied by all groups. This is not limited to Suriname, but is a practice that occurs in the diaspora worldwide. This paper researches the elements various peoples brought to Suriname with respect to body decoration. What were the varieties of ways they applied and how these elements were distributed over time amongst the different ethnic groups and how nowadays individuals of all these groups use them intertwined. We will conclude that there are no longer identity markers of a separate ethnic group.

In Suriname, body art is a form of nation creation. This is a collective effort to create a nation which is based on solidarity, mutual respect and a harmonic alignment between the ethnic groups and their cultures (Menke, 2008: 21). From the bottom up, representatives from different ethnic groups share their forms of body decoration. Even though these used to be specific markers for one individual group, in modern days it may be concluded that all groups apply these decorations. This is also a result of the modern ways in which we communicate; all is made visible on the internet and we are subject to influences worldwide.

The argument in this paper is that all ethnic groups had their own identity markers when they arrived in Suriname, albeit in the mode of make-up, tattoos, jewellery and hairdos or nail decoration. Over the years, however, groups have adapted to other customs and started using each other's ways of decorating the body. This is a tendency in modernity that all groups use more or less the same forms of body art. This manner of distinction among ethnic groups has thus become less and less an identity marker but an expression of fashion.

This paper was originally written for the brochure of an exhibition that was planned in Fort Zeelandia by the Suriname Museum Foundation. Due to lack of expertize and finances the plan was not executed in 2013 but will be in near future. This means that the artifacts discussed in this paper are limited to the collection of objects belonging to the museum and the customs described as linked to these artifacts are not outside the scope of the exhibition.

MAKE-UP

Make-up was a way of beautifying oneself and self-identification as a distinctive person that is as old as the world. In the decorations left behind in Egyptian pyramids we recognize face enhancement by paint. We know about berries to redden ones lips for a seductive pout, charcoal to blacken one's eyes for a sultry look. And the proverbial milk to bathe in to gain a perfectly smooth skin. There are powders, creams and oils to enhance beauty and these elements are also related to ethnic groups. The making-up or painting of bodies might be an identity marker of old.

Loose and compact powder used to be only available in light tones, but nowadays special make-up is designed for women of colour, a famous brand is for instance 'Iman', created by a former top model from Ethiopia, a celebrity coloured women can identify with (http://www.imancosmetics.com/ visited in April 2013). This brand advertises on the internet with make-up that will be used in the musical *Motown* (black soul music) and present slogans as:

'meet your match' and 'find your shade'. Another well-known brand locally available in Suriname is Black Opal. This industry for brown and tanned skin, especially in India and the United States, is big business. This can be measured by the money involved, but also by the amount of information and advertisement scattered in the media and on the streets.

While choosing a partner, creoles tend to prefer lighter skinned lovers to obtain lighter skinned babies with 'better, straighter' hair. This was the tendency between the 1900 and 1950. By the time the 1960s set in 'black is beautiful' found its way into Suriname, especially with darker skinned people (Helman, 1977a: 62). Within the nationalistic movement, people became more self-conscious and succumbed to the Black is beautiful movement that was introduced here from the United States.

Some men and women used the practice of bleaching their skin in an attempt to upgrade their social position. Still, creams are sold in the shops locally to whiten your skin. There are products available for women as well as for men. These are also used by people of Hindustani descent, because some elements of this ethnic group still tie caste (higher social standing, i.e. Brahmins) with skin colour: the lighter skin, higher the position in society. This might for some people still be a selecting tool for choosing a life partner.

For a totally different purpose, descendants of slaves (Maroons as well as Creoles) use *pemba* during religious and cultural ceremonies. This is a kaolin formed into a clay ball and dried. Once it is mixed with water, one can apply it to the face (mostly) or other body parts. At special ceremonies, the entire body can be smeared with kaolin. This is not done for beautifying objectives but to be closer to the spirits and deities. Kaolin contains a lot of vitamins and minerals and is also eaten.[4] The practice of painting the body with white chalk was also used in East Africa by the Masaai (Fisher, 1987: 19).

[4] Eating kaolin is tied to the eating of 'dirt', earth that contains vital vitamins and minerals to compensate the lack of these in the food that slaves used to eat. Some women eat it still, while pregnant. This should not be overdone, because it can cause constipation.

Women from India traditionally applied kohl or kayjal on the rims of their eyes to make them look bigger. This is a practice they brought to Suriname. Charcoal was burned in a small round metal containers. The fine black powder was mixed with ghee or castor oil and used to draw the lines to create a mysterious effect. This procedure was not entirely harmless; in some cases it is led to lead poisoning. Today, one can go to the store and buy kohl in several shades in the form of a pencil.

The process of body painting with henna has also become much easier. In days gone by a close female relative used to apply the henna on the body with a small spatula. Now you buy small sachets with henna colouring, cut of the tip and pinch it to release a thin line of ready-made henna and draw the decorative lines on hands up to the elbow, or feet up to the ankle. Some stores in Suriname even sell booklets with patterns and motifs that can be copied. Henna is a tropical plant whose leaves contain lawsone (the Latin name is *Lawsonia inermis*). People use this natural tinting agent to dye skin, hair, leather silk or wool. The plant is in use since the Bronze Age, and today it is grown in India for commercial purposes. The fresh henna leaves do not provide colour, they have to be crushed, dried and pulverized. The powder is then mixed with lavender or eucalyptus oil and applied to the skin thus leaving long lasting patterns in a reddish-brown hue. The powder can be mixed with lemon juice or strong tea, but these patterns are not as durable. For best results, one leaves the mixture on the skin for as long as possible. There are warnings against the use of the so called 'black henna' which only needs to stay on the skin for an hour, but can cause severe allergic reactions. Henna is supposed to bring 'barakah' or good luck and beauty, and is especially popular amongst young brides. The applied pattern often contains the initials of the groom, hidden in the intricate drawings. The marriage is supposed to be lucky if he is able to detect his name. In the Indian diaspora especially women use this product, worldwide, and Suriname is no exception. Modern women also put mehendi drawings on other non-traditional body parts like the back. During the marriage ceremony, Javanese people tend to colour their skin with turmeric which gives a yellowish hue (Joanna Assad, 2013).

Eating food that does not seem appropriate for a person may

cause pigment spots on the skin. In literature we find the example of Maureen who shows such a *lostoe* spot on the lower arm. She explains that her mother had a craving for raisins during her pregnancy, but they were not available at that moment. This idea of some kind of allergy might in fact be an individual food taboo, a *trefu.* This naturalistic attribute derives from the word *tereifa,* which is Hebrew for unclean. Slaves observed that their Jewish masters did not suffer from skin problems and so they copied the stringent food laws (Endt-Meijling: 2006, 63).

A lot of natural produce can be applied on the skin to purify or clarify. Traditionally eggs were used or avocado and yoghurt, but also cucumber or aloevera for burned skin. For a long time these products were not in vogue because of the influence of modern beauty products available in stores. But nowadays we see a revival of natural ways to treat skin. Some Suriname women produce soap and other skin products, and market them as a specific Surinamese item, like mango soap. Beauty can also be a representation of tradition and authenticity (Van der Pijl, 2005: 120). In Suriname several beauty pageants are organized yearly. Most of them have ethnic groundings in which several markers of identity are shown, like make-up, jewllery, hairdo's and so on. Some of them are: Miss Indigenous, Miss Maroon, Miss Hindustani, etc.

TATTOO

Tattoo is a permanent form of make-up. Traditionally in Suriname we see this kind of body decoration only with the Amerindians. They smear their body with a natural red substance, which they deem healthy. They also decorated with ornamental patterns using *kusuwe* or a bluish dye that they apply with thin sticks into geometrical patters, especially along the nose and the back (Helman: 1977a, 52). A strong colouring device is indigo, a natural plant which was also grown in Suriname for export purposes. A plot of land north of Paramaribo, owned by Governor Jean Nepveu (1719-79), was called Blauwgrond (blue ground) because of its use as an indigo plantation.

In her famous work *The Vindication of the Rights of Women,* Mary Wollstonecraft wrote that:

The attention to dress, therefore, which has been thought a sexual propensity, I think natural to mankind. But I ought to express myself with more precision. When the mind is not sufficiently opened to take pleasure in reflection, the body will be adorned with sedulous care, and ambition will appear in tattooing or painting it. So far is this first inclination carried, that even the hellish yoke of slavery cannot stifle the savage desire of admiration which the black heroes inherit from both their parents, for all the hardly earned savings of a slave are expended in a little tawdry finery (Furguson, 1992: p. 90).

A typical form of permanent marking is scarification. Maroon girls use scarification to attract the opposite sex. Men and women used to practise scarification, but it was discontinued when they were converted to Christianity (*Encyclopaedie van Nederlandsch West-Indië*, 1917: 162). Elder people, but also girlfriends make small but numerous scarification on and near erogenous zones of the body of young girls. These are of eminent importance to one's love life, but the operation is painful and needs to be repeated several times to enhance the pattern. The cuts are made near the corners of the mouth, between the breasts, surrounding the navel, on the nape of the back and especially on the inner thighs. The incisions are filled with the ash of charcoal and this leaves keloids. These patterns are called *kamba* or *kamemba* (the Ndyuka call this *kokoti*). They are a sign of beauty and attraction as well as sexual arousal for a man and woman not just by seeing them, but caressing them with fingertips and recognizing the pattern and knows the meaning of it. Aluku women have a keloid tattoo styled as a naked figure also seen on aluku wooden objects. The copper nails with which woodcarving pieces are trimmed remind the man of the caresses of the *kamba* (Helman, 1977a: 57, 150).

With the immigration of contract labourers from India, other tattoos were imported. People from British India came to Suriname with different religious backgrounds (Hindustani, Muslims, etc.). Their faith dictated the ways in which they decorated their bodies. Permanent garnishing of the body has been a common ritual in several areas in India. In early civilizations it was used to show the social rank and status of the wearer. But mostly tattoos have the function of warding off evil powers. These powers are constantly lurking nearby and might master inattentive, unprotected people and cause misfortune, illness or even death. Tattoos are permanent, so it gives an unremitting protection. These tattoos are often placed during initiating rituals or to welcome adults as members of a certain group. Women have their faces, hand and legs tattooed with lines and dots in a geometrical pattern. Turmeric paste is rubbed into the wounds with castor oil and black kajal paste. Also the black extract from oil lamps is used (Maesao. 2008).[5] This practice is becoming less and less in India. At times we still see elder Hindustani women in Suriname who have tattoos on the inner side of their arms.

Glitter tattoos are applied at children's parties or festivals, often by stencilling. These can be washed off easily. Nowadays in some beauty salons or tattoo shops in Paramaribo it is possible to have your eyebrows or lip lines permanently defined by tattoo. This process is fairly costly; in the tattoo shop you have to pay 500 srd for a set of fake permanent eye brows. Eye lashes can be painted, but this is not a tattooing process. Dwight Sussenbach, a great promoter of tattoos, organized a tattoo conference in 2012 to popularize this way of embellishment and published a magazine *Urban Art* (2012, nr 1). It would be a mode of Creolization when artists who use ethnic letters in their paintings, like Marcel Pinas (Afaka, a religious maroon letter system) or Sunil Phoeljoen (Devanagari, the Indian Alphabet to write Hindi or Sanskrit) would generate designs for tattoos linked with the different cultures in Suriname.

PIERCING

Initially in Suriname, piercings were only visible within the Amerindian group. The Kali'na pierce the lower lip, ear lobes and sometimes the nasal septum to put in feathers. According to Helman, Caribs also use pins, fish or other bones and thin pieces of wood (Helman, 1977b: 53). The kali'na put a needle through the lower lip. Archaeological excavations at the Kwatta Tingiolo site yielded a pre-Colombian body ornament made out of bone (Versteeg, 2003: 155). This object was probably used as a nose

[5] The pages in this book are not numbered.

piercing. This form of decoration is still perceived by a lot of people as a notion of native and primitive. This was expressed in illustrations of black Africans, also in children's books (Kapelle, 2008: 55). In a 2013 television programme that was meant to show how white people perceive the local population in the island of Curacao, a white man remarks: 'They should be grateful to our ancestors [. . .] otherwise they would still live in the Ivory Coast [. . .] with a bone through their nose and wearing skirts made out of straw.'[6]

This perception or form of low culture can be transformed into high culture by way of upgrading the materials. Although Abbé Dubois, a missionary, referred to the nose piercing initially as 'having a hideous effect in the eyes of Europeans, but when one becomes accustomed to it, gradually it seems less unbecoming for the face'. Immigrants from India perceived the nose ornament (*nath*) as the most seductive one. These can be tiny studs of gold or a small precious stone pierced through the top of the nostril. Large round hoops that circle the cheek with strings of pearls or beads that dangle with every movement make a woman especially attractive. For women nose rings became mandatory when they got married. The custom of boring the nasal septum was distinctly Arabic (Bala Krishnan, 2004: 175).

Piercing seems a modern form of adorning the body and is applied to any extremity, even nipples. But mentioning of them can be found in ancient literature. Even the *Kamasutra* describes *apadravya*, penis piercing (Thorne 2011: 14). Socially widespread and accepted nose and ear piercings are not so much identity markers anymore, just a beautifying object. Piercings through other body parts however can be an expression of membership of a gothic cult. One informant of Lebanese descent explained how her grandmother used to place a rolled up money bill in a hole in her earlobe and carried it around (*Joanne Assad*, December 2012).

Samantha de Jong (alias Barbie), a Dutch reality star, was filmed with her baby daughter of seven months. The child was wearing earrings, which in the Netherlands caused an outcry of indignation

[6] Quote of a *makamba* in NTR-programma 'Hollandse maatjes' (uitgezonden zat. 30 mrt 2013, shown as 'Uitzending gemist').

on twitter. Several people deemed it child molestation (Internet *Algemeen Dagblad*, 25 March 2013). In Suriname it is common practice for all ethnic groups to have the ears of their newborn daughters (and even sons) pierced. Belly button piercings are also very fashionable these days.

JEWELLERY

Jewellery is an important identity marker, used for beautifying, as well as a form of religious expression. The site at Tingiolo, mentioned earlier, yielded some objects (primitive valuables) from before Columbus: a number of finely decorated hangers used by the Amerindians made out of shell, stone or bone. Kwatta was also a production area of detailed frog shaped carvings made out of nephrite, a greenish stone (Versteeg, 2003: 151-75, Davis, 1982: 41).

Stedman (Journey to Suriname 1796, reprinted in a popular Dutch version in 1988) is a good source on jewellery worn in the eighteenth century. He writes about the way young men try to woo coloured young women: 'A large number of negresses follow their own intent and refuse to accept the gold with which men try to seduce them, although they might accept a glass of brandy, a broken pipe, or even nothing at all' (Stedman, 1988: 14). At their arrival in Suriname the soldiers were offered a dinner at which they were served by an endless number of mulatto and black girls, all, to the ways of the land, were naked up to their middle, but wore clothing made of the finest Indian linen, and were decorated with golden chains, medallions, beads, necklaces, arm bands and nice smelling flowers (Stedman, 1988: 12). Stedman's lover, Joanna, was also wearing jewellery; her hair was decorated with flowers and golden pins; she was also adorned with a necklace and golden arm and ankle bands with a golden clasp. On her hat made out of felt, a silver lily was attached. These jewels were a gift from her mother who was the mistress of a planter to whom she had always shown much loyalty (Stedman: 1988, 16). Captain Fourgeoud, the head of Stedman's batallion, wrote in a letter regarding the raid of a maroon village: 'Aan de zeijde van de Tweede kost grond hebben wij een mooijedoode Boschneeger gevonden zeijnde met coraalenomringet [. . .]' (1775).[7] This indicates that the Maroons kept to the tradition of wearing necklaces.' Beijer (*Suriname in deszelfstegenwoordigentoestand*, 1823) also mentions the ornaments of European women and 'the better class of mulatto's': 'The ladies there love and know how to dress in style. They bedeck themselves with real beads and garnets. Nice coloured stones and real pearls are seldom seen.' Benoit, a Belgian traveller to Suriname, made exquisite drawings of Creole, Amerindian and Maroon men and women. These drawings show the distinct ways in which they adorn themselves (Benoit, 1980).[8] These decorations at times were so rich that the government published laws on placards (15 August 1777) to inform the population about what was allowed: 'Slaves, albeit mulattos, Indians or Negroes without distinction are only permitted to wear stockings, shoes, decorated hats or any gold or jewelry, unless they are golden earrings, necklaces and bracelets closing with a small golden locket'.

This law creates the impression that at times slaves were bedecked too richly, according to the white legislature. How important jewellery was to the Creole women, is expressed in this *odo*, a proverbial saying: *Minaabia-peri: mi e brenkilekigowtunalibismaai.*[9]

The art of fine jewellery making in Suriname is nowadays mostly confined to Chinese and Hindustani craftsman. They work the gold found in mines in Suriname or neighbouring countries (also silver). Filigree is an often applied technique to enhance all kinds of jewellery. We see this procedure often executed in Hindustani earrings and hangers. Most of the designs and decorations are adapted from their home countries and according to Helman there was little or no Creolization within their craft. One of the few exceptions was the pair of earrings with black curly feathers of the *powisi*, a hokko bird (Helman, 1977a: 155). We also see natural

[7] At the side of the Second Field we found a beautiful dead Maroon who was surrounded by beads.

[8] We need to take into consideration that the copper plates were imprinted in black and white and sometimes pencil-coloured by hand. The colours may not be realistic.

[9] I am a pearl, I shine like gold in the eye of the beholder.

stones or seeds worked into chains and also the stones of the *koebi* fish. These are white and irregular and this sea bass keeps its balance in the water because of them. According to some, these stones have magical powers and can be attributed to the *watraingi*, a deity (*Winti*) that is connected to the rivers.

The *pepiet* is used widely: a small clump of gold is made into a hanger or into earrings. Much sought after nowadays is the *alakondre* chain, with different patterned pieces of golden chain and different colour beads (Italian glass, red or black garnet in between, and sometimes a *pepiet*).[10] The chain can be custom made and even though it is often used as a celebratory and religious object (to Creole and Maroons), people from all ethnic diversities wear them. One can add a golden anchor, a bow and arrow, an eagle, or a cutlass. The intricacy of the chains and the weight of the complete chain dictate the price.

Jewellery often is a tribute to the *Winti*. The Creoles wear special clothing or decorations during religious celebrations to protect themselves from evil. When a child is born, the family tends to present gold chains with an engraving of the child's name. A new born can be protected against *Ogriai* with black stones (polished garnet). Most of the time these beads are kept together with a golden pin. A *boei* is often a bracelet which has a special predicate of protection. Maroons often wear them on the upper arm. These are personalized attributes within the Winti culture (Endt-Meijling, 2006: 62-71).

Many women from British India came by boat to Suriname, wearing only their clothes and jewellery. These were a much coveted form of investment. Some beautiful old photographs are stored in the archives and depict the abundance of these adornments. Mostly the necklaces were fabricated out of silver and enriched with coins and tassels made out of coloured threads of cotton or silk (Reeser, 2012: 71). People from India love an abundance of decoration, especially women. Gold jewellery and trinkets were already

[10] *Alakondre* means of all countries, mixed. This is especially telling since the chains are so varied, but also because people from all ethnic groups in Suriname wear them.

mentioned in the Vedas and were worn back in the day to exhibit prosperity. When women in India were no longer entitled to inherit, gathering gold was the only way to own movable property and often the only way to save money.[11] Gold was just available to the richer castes. Once in Suriname, many women bought silver or golden coins or jewellery with their first savings. This was also done by lower class women, even though succession rights in Suriname were equal to men and women.

Brides wear a special wedding sari and are adorned with jewellery for this occasion, mostly consisting of a set for head, ear and hand ornamentations. Gold has a purifying effect and holy power and that is why every family makes sure a bride looks shiny and radiant and thus attractive to her future husband. This is essential for her life's happiness. Hindustanis keep to their wedding traditions, although these are modernized and often copied from Bollywood movies.[12] Body decoration especially is rich and colourful.

Lately I saw a photograph of a new born-baby of Hindustani descent. It was wearing a thin black cloth band tied on its arm with a knot in the middle. This was a practice often used amongst the descendants of slaves (Creole and Maroon) who applied these straps to ward off evil. At times a piece of dried umbilical cord was

[11] Indian Succession Act, 1925, states that everyone is entitled to equal inheritance, barring exceptions to Hindus, Sikhs, Jains, Buddhists and Muslims. Under the act, the daughter of a person dying intestate would be entitled only to one-fourth of the son's share, or Rs. 5,000, whichever is lesser. This amount is also termed as Streedhan and this entitlement excludes the women from any further right in seeking a proper division of the properties of the deceased. The bias and gender deprecation is the only factor that the Indian women and daughters are isolated and remain dependent on the male heirs for their share and right in the seeking distribution of the property and giving rise to differences in the families and long legal battles. (http://www.lexorates.com/articles/inheritance-and-succession-rights-of-women-and-daughters-under-personal-laws).

[12] In 2008 this was visualized in the exposition 'Bidesia' in the Suriname Museum. It is clear that a lot of attention is given to and money spent on wedding rituals.

kept in the knot. Some women even mention the use of dried and powdered earthworms (Maria Maisi [Aucaanse], April 2013).

Jewellery was a much coveted way of saving money. And if one ran out, one could pawn the gold or silver to obtain cash. This used to be done at pawn shops (*pantioso*), but nowadays people trade their gold with the Volks Crediet Bank (VCB). Every now and then, this bank advertises in the newspapers to publicly sell off non-reclaimed jewellery. Cauri shells, used as a form of payment in Africa, are often braided into hair or applied in jewellery. In Suriname it has lost its valuable quality.

As an example of Amerindian decoration Helman mentions the *kweju*, a skirt made out of seeds. Nuns imported beads to the area in the nineteenth century. The ones for dancing were decorated with tassels and seeds that made a noise. (Hindustanis wear ankle bands with little copper bells and Maroons tie strands of seeds around their ankles to emphasize the movement of the feet and add additional noise.) Trios wear woven bands under the knees, called *sepu*. This also became a practice with the Maroons. Only men often enhance these with tassels, very long ones at that, during a dance. Trio and Wayana can be seen with strains of black beads or seeds on the upper arm or ankle and ties made out of natural fibre. In modern days silver and copper rings are worn. Earlier only the women used to wear earrings, but you see them now on men too. They wear long strains of beads across the torso that are enhanced with colourful feathers or the beaks of a toucan, and bracelets can be graced with a monkey's tail and decorated with parrot feathers (Helman, 1977b: 51). The museum houses a large collection of necklaces and bracelets, among others with the nails of an armadillo or one made of braided human hair. Helman states that ornamenting is subject to the loss of culture. People tend to wear cheap plastic jewellery now and do not create their own anymore (Helman, 1977a: 156). Lately we see an upsurge of own produce with local materials, especially seeds, for sale at craft markets.

HAIR

Amerindians remove body hair, their own or the hair of others. This removal can be part of the love ritual, as in removing fleas. And they eat what is edible. They pull out all body hair, except for the hair on their head which they wear long, men as well as women. They grease it and often wrap it up in a decorated tube made of palm leaves or wood. The Wayana part the hair in the middle, so it falls alongside their face. The Trio cut it gradually alongside the face and the Akurio have bangs over the ears. It should be stated that different tribes wear their hair in a totally different style, without a specific distinction between men or women, although men's hair is often shorter and mostly women wear it in braids (Helman, 1977: 51-3).

For Hindustanis hair is an important ritualistic attribute attached to the birth of a child.

Simantonnayan is the ceremony of the parting of the hair of a pregnant woman and this takes place within the fourth month of pregnancy to make sure all things go well. When the child is forty days old, its hair is shaven at a ceremony called *mundan sanskar*. The hair is wrapped in a ball of dough and thrown into running water (Endt-Meijling, 2006: 71-2). A married woman puts *sindhur*, red powder, on the forehead and in the parting of the hair to indicate she is married. A dot (*tika*) in red, white or yellow is placed on the forehead. *Tika* stickers are available in the shops now. These can be glued to the skin and be easily removed. Javanese women often comb their hair in a bun. At celebrations these hairdos are trimmed with golden pins, coins and colourful flowers. Jewish people do not think much of adornment. However, some groups distinguish themselves by wearing a long string of curly hair alongside the face. This is practiced mostly by men.

Afro-Surinamese people pay a lot of attention to their hair. Natural Afro hair is not treated by hot combs or irons or chemical products (perms, straightener or relaxant) to remove the strong curl as to reach a straight effect. Afro hair has the shape of a spiral and often is difficult to comb. There are lots of varieties of this hair, different structures and feels. This dictates also the pattern of braiding.

In the 1960s and 1970 the 'black is beautiful' movement was introduced to Suriname and it became fashionable to wear Afro hair. This was discontinued, but is now visible in the streets again. A fierce promoter of 'natural hair' is Mireille Liong-A-Kong, who has published books on this topic (*Going Natural, How to Fall in Love with Nappy Hair*, 2011), organizes gatherings and regularly publishes articles on how to keep this hair in shape. She also has a website that says: 'Motivated by the hair and scalp issues that a majority of Black women are dealing with, Liong started writing with the purpose to redeem the beauty of natural hair in the hope to decrease these problems.'[13]

Maroons from both sexes used to pay a lot of attention to their hairdo. Only women plait the braids, a job that may take hours. A man can ask any women to braid his hair, even if she is married. Such a request could lead to a romantic relationship. A number of beautiful wooden Afro combs are deposited in the depot of the Suriname Museum. Combing the hair is easiest with a special comb attached a ladle and a number of long teeth. By pulling the comb through the hair it stands up and one can model it by patting it with an open hand. The wooden combs in the Suriname Museum were mostly made by the Maroons. The comb can vary because of the decorations of wood carving and the addition of decorative nails.

Men were expected to fabricate a number of wooden objects, amongst them *prodokankan*, especially as a present to their prospective wives or lovers. They were also sold to people from outside the village. Some combs (for instance the one a first husband made for his girl) are entwined with colourful yarn that is twisted through the upper part of the teeth and end in a woolly plume. In earlier days raffia from the Maurici palm was used to this purpose (Price and Price, 1999: 154, 161, 196-8). Father Richard Abbenhuis described information on the wooden combs in the early 1960's. The plank is called 'idi' [*sic* = head] and the teeth 'tiefie' [sic]. The plank was smoothed by a knife. First, the teeth are cut, because they easily break off. Mostly they are round, but can also

[13] going-natural.com/mireille-liong-a-kong/

be oval or six sided. A normal comb is about 30 cm long and 10 cm wide, but some ornamental ones are much bigger. The Saramaka burn the teeth to make them stronger and less sharp. Unfortunately, only 54 known carvers still practise this trade (Crabasi, 2008: 5).

Nowadays most people use combs made out of plastic, even in the interior. Also combs with iron teeth were available. Nevertheless, the wooden comb is still popular when braiding hair. They are the best for parting and dividing. Abbenhuis (who did his research among the Aucans) called this: *a breinangawiewieriegieing* [*sic*]. The braiding is an imaginary and decorative language in itself. There are four types of braiding:

(a) *Paataede* (or *kaapataa*) is braiding flat against the head; this shape is also called *moelala*or centipede
(b) *Pito* are small standing up braids
(c) *Toshatawan* are small braids tied together
(d) *Kwikwi 'ba* or *bakafinga* is a style where the hair is parted in the middle, pulled to the side and braided against the side of the face.[14]

The Suriname Museum boasts a number of old photographs of these different hair designs. Every style has its own variations. They are also very trendy. Fashion is translated as *piisi* (pleasure), which is telling. Young people introduce a new trend and after much lamentation and discussion elder people reluctantly follow (Helman, 1977b: 55).

Hairstyles which were fashionable in 2013 were called Balotelli (after the Italian black soccer player) or Mohawk.[15] Rasta people still definitively wear their hair as an identity marker. It grows in dreads and may be covered by a crocheted hat or wrapped up in a piece of cloth (often in Rasta colours of red, yellow and green).

Hair is a very important identity marker. This is remarkably illustrated by Gillion Grantsaan, who took an image of (then) Queen

[14] This information is obtained from Polini Cairo and Maria Maisi (Aukan), April 2013.

[15] This information is obtained from Joanne Assad, April 2013.

Beatrix and portrayed her with an Afro Hairdo (Kolfinao, 2008: 339). This had a political impact of 'black power' as well as artistic consequences. It also showed that by wearing Afro hair it was possible to make an intentional politicized statement in the 1960s. This hairstyle has now completely lost its added meaning.

The Chinese immigrants who arrived in Suriname from 1853, mostly male, were in the habit of wearing their hair in a long plait. We see this in drawings by Arnold Borret (1848-88) who made an album of water colour paintings in 1882 (Hoefte and Medendorp, 2003: plates 97 and 149). This hairstyle was introduced at the beginning of the seventeenth century by Emperor Nurhaci who declared it compulsory for all men in the places he had conquered to wear the Manchu style as a sign of submission to the Qing dynasty. This practice was discontinued in the early 1910s with the fall of this dynasty. During this era, the long plaits also disappeared in Suriname.

A ritual which is still in place with the Chinese is a 'hairdresser' who visits the house of the bride and the groom on the evening before the wedding. Each chooses his/her own lady, a person who is well acquainted with the family and who lives a healthy and prosperous life. She combs the hair three times, and during this ritual each time expresses a wish:

(a) a good beginning of the marriage and a good life
(b) that they may grow into old age, with 'grey' hair, together
(c) that they may have a large family.[16]

It seems in Suriname, hair has become more important to the Chinese part of the population. They open Chinese barber-shops and wear styles that are globally fashionable.

Hair is nowadays the most distinctive and easy way to change one's appearance. It can be coloured, permed, uncurled, falsified with wigs and weaves with real or synthetic extensions. This is a big industry, expressed in a big diversity of products, manpower and women workforce. False eyelashes are used to seduce men,

[16] Information provided by Elly van Lierop, who is married into a Chinese family.

only women wear them, unless the male is a cross dresser or transvestite.

NAILS

Chinese people of high rank used to grow extremely long nails. This was a sign of wealth, expressing the fact that one did not perform any manual labour. Nowadays a man with some or all of his nails grown long can still be seen on the streets. Rumour has it that they use this nail to dig out the wax from their ears, or scratch body parts otherwise unreachable, like the back and the spot in between the shoulders. A man of Creole descent told me it was used to break the hymen of virgins, he was probably bragging.

A relatively small, but important way of showing off ones fashionability nowadays is the use of false and painted nails. Women wear long nails, not so much to indicate their pedigree, but to show they are in vogue. Nails are elongated by acrylic or gel to form false parts. All kinds of colours are applied and they can be enhanced by painting patterns, adding sparkling elements or even little beads or studs. Some styles are distinguished by a name that indicates a certain identity, like French tips; these are nails with a natural coloured polish and white tips. This type of decoration is perceived as chic. Women devote websites and bring out little design booklets that show examples of techniques and decorations of nail styling.

CONCLUSION

Material cultural heritage with displays of body decoration is abundantly available in Suriname's artistic expressions. For instance, the dioramas by Gerrit Schouten (1779-1839) on show in the Suriname museum expose Amerindian and Creole jewellery, hairdos and scarification (Neus and Van Putten, 2008: 17, 24). The detailing on the paper figurines is extraordinary and beautiful. These showcases (made in 1831, 1838 and one not dated) are some of the fine examples of documenting body adornment as identity markers in the past.

Nowadays young people dislike wearing specific costumes or

body decoration, except during special celebrations on specific days. Only in very isolated communities are certain attributes still uniform, and to the outside world suggest hard-core symptoms of a drive to distinction (Helman, 1977b: 51).

Representations, or images, as Wekker states, are no innocent reflections of reality, but constructions. They are carefully crafted to help create a certain reality. That is why some elements of the representation should be stressed, while others should be eradicated. Meanwhile, it is important to present this image as the reality (Wekker, 2004: 540). We can conclude that the stressing or eradicating of certain symbols in the body emphasis happen unconsciously. Many of these representations, or outer expressions used to have a specific meaning. As Appiah indicates: 'We are so familiar with this sort of symbolic act that we do not reflect upon it [. . .]. Many symbolic ritual acts are not arbitrary signs, but acts that draw their meaning from the non-ritual signification of relevantly similar performances' (Appiah, 1992: 112). The interpretation of the symbolic value of body adornment is often lost to us. But we do see Maroon girls still wearing *panji* in the villages and some Amerindian people wear traditional clothing or jewellery in the normal setting of everyday life. Rastafarians distinguish themselves by wearing their dreadlocks extremely long, often covered up by a crocheted hat in red-yellow-green or a tied wrap. Incidentally we can see a Sikh in the Suriname streets; the men who practice this faith do not cut their hair and wrap it up in a turban. These are definitely examples of identity markers. It is easy to distinguish and change visible identity by ways of choosing one of the five discussed body enhancers above. One can also take on a different identity by wearing a mask. This is illustrated by a statuette of a Dutch garden gnome. Artist Remy Jungermann puts one in an installation, but made the gnome wear an African mask, thus changing the identity in a stunning way (Kolfinao, 2008: 340).

Most modern people change their body art with the flow of actuality, changing hair and make-up colour and style, jewellery, and painting their nails every other day. Tattoos are permanent and less volatile, and – at a price – can also be removed by laser treatment. The value of the materials applied, styles, practices and intricacy executed dictate class distinction and identify prosperity and success. But they are no longer attached to ethnic pluralism as distinctively emphasized identity markers.

REFERENCES

Abbenhuis, Richard (1961). 'Aantekeningen mbt het houtsnijwerk van de marrons' (unpublished document, Suriname Museum Foundation)

Appiah, Kwame Anthony (2006). *Cosmopolitanism: Ethics in a World of Strangers.* New York: W.W. Norton & Company.

Bala Krishnan, Usha and Meera Sushil Kumar (2004). *Indian Jewellery. Dance of the Peacock.* Mumbai: India Book House.

Benoit, P.J. (1980). *Reis door Suriname. Beschrijving van de Nederlandse bezittingen in Guyana.* Zutphen: De WalburgPers (Original edition 1839).

CRABASI (2008). *Suriname Maroon Tembe: A Means of Living* (A Survey on the Last of the Tembe Carvers). Paramaribo: Crabasi; Craft & Art Business Association, Suriname

Davis, Mary L. en Greta Pack (1982). *Mexican Jewellery.* Austin: Universtity of Texas Press.

Benjamnins, H.D. and J.F. Snellemans (eds.) (1914-17). *Encyclopaedie van Nederlands West-Indië's,* Gravenhage: Martinus Nijhoff.

Endt-Meijling, Martha van (2006). *Rituelen en gewoonten.* Bussem: Uitgeverij Coutinho.

Fisher, Angela (1987). *Africa Adorned.* London: Collins Harvill.

Furguson, Moira (1992). 'Mary Wollstonecraft and the Problematic of Slavery', in *Feminist Review,* no. 42.

Helman, Albert (1977). *A Facetten van de Surinaamse samenleving.* Zutphen: De Walburg Pers.

Helman, Albert (ed.) (1977b.) *Cultureel Mozaïek van Suriname.* Zutphen: De Walburg Pers.

Hoefte, Rosemarijn en Clazien Medendorp (2003). *Arnold Borret. Suriname. Gezichten, typen en costumen.* Leiden: KITLV Uitgeverij.

Kapelle, Jeroen en Dirk J. Tang. (2008). *Zwart.* Harderwijk: Uitgeverij d'jonge Hond.

Kolfin, Elmer and Esther Schreuder (eds.) (2008). *Black is Beautiful: Rubens to Dumas* (Cataloqueexposition Nieuwe kerk Amsterdam) Zwolle: Waanders Publishers

Maes, Ignace en Riet Vanderbranden (2008). *India, Orissa before Monsoon.* Schoten: Uitgeverij Bai.

Menke, Jack (ed.) (2008). 'Ethniciteit tussen natievorming en natiecreatie in Suriname', in *Natievorming en natiecreatie in Suriname*. Paramaribo: SWI.

Neus, Hilde en Laddy van Putten (2008). *Gerrit Schouten. Met meesterhand vervaardigd. Tekeningen en diorama's in het Surinaams Museum.*Paramaribo: Stichting Surinaams Museum.

Pijl, Yvon van der (2005). 'Missverkiezingen en de articulatie van etnische identiteit', in *Oso*, year 24, nr. 1.

Price, Sally and Richard Price (1999). *De kunst van de marrons. Culturele vitaliteit in de Afrikaanse diaspora.* Amsterdam: KIT.

Reeser, Pepijn (2012). *Verzamelaars en Volksopvoeders. Musea in Suriname 1863-2012.* Leiden: KITLV.

Stedman, John Gabriel (1987). Reize naar Surinamen. Zutphen: De Walburg Pers (Original edition 1796).

Sussenbach, Dwight (2012). 'Urban Art', nr. 1, Paramaribo.

Thorne, Russ (2011). *De Bodypiercinggids.Complete gids met traditionele en eigentijdse piercings.* Kerkdriel: Librero.

Versteeg, Aad (2003). *Suriname voor Columbus.* Paramaribo: Surinaams Museum.

Wekker, Gloria (2004).'Sranan, Swit' Sranan', in M. van Kempen, P. Verkruijsse and A. Zuiderweg (eds.), *Wandelen onder de palmen.* Leiden: KITLV Uitgeverij.

CHAPTER 10

God at the Fore-deck and at the After-deck

JOOP VERNOOIJ

INTRODUCTION

In this paper, I will try to clarify the complex and formal relationship between church and state in Suriname. I can distinguish various historical phases. The ideas about free or forced migration and Diaspora are a constituent in the history and the historiography of Suriname. The majority of the ancestors of the Surinamese people reached Surinames via the sea. I use this specific title because religion was, and is, a very important issue in the life of the migrants and in the Diaspora, sometimes at the fore-deck and sometimes at the after-deck. They came with hope for the future (at the fore-deck) and with reverence and suspicion (in the backyard). It is a symbolic and imaginary terminology of us, for the God of the waters, rolling and floating as long as possible, at last entering a harbour. It is a matrix of life in Suriname itself. The proverb 'when you are eating with the devil, you need a long fork' can be applied here as the historiography of these issues in Suriname can be complex.

AUTOCRACY AND EXCLUSIVISM

First, I have to define the terms 'state' and 'church'. We understand religion as the invisible, intangible, transcendent world; a faith with a practical performance like churches, places, leadership, a hierarchy, rituals and so on. They are all in the public space. In this case, we have to speak about a colony of the Netherlands, where different groups were brought with their own respective cultures.

The idea of a state is recent in the sense of state creation and nation building in Suriname. The colony was a project, an initiative from outside, in this case, from Western Europe. The first seamen had to find out rules and norms because the colonizers started in a new environment, without administration, in the tropics, 8,500 km from Holland. These were far away neighbours with another language, without any contact with the small number of locals, called Amerindians, or more specifically, the Caribs and Lokonon. The name of that part of the Latin-American continent was Wild Coast. The Dutch also took possession of Recife-Pernambuco (1630, Brasil), and parts of the Caribbean, e.g. Tobago (1630), Curacao (1635), St. Eustatius (1643), and Essequibo (1658).

A special genre of literature was developed for the Dutch during the sixteenth and seventeenth centuries. It was the genre of the Vademecum. People engaged in merchandising overseas could read and study some books from ministers of Calvinistic origin on how to Christians overseas. Vademecum books like *Christelijcke Zeevaert (Christian Sea Shipping)* of Adam Westerman (1611); *Geesteliick Compas (Spiritual Compass)* (1617) and *'t Geestelykroer van 't coopmans-schip (Spiritual Helm of the Merchant Ship)* (1638) of G.U. Udemans; and *de Godvreezende Zeeman (God-fearing Seaman)* (1709), guided the sea people on a Christian way to new lands and continents, in addition to new religions. The message was the conversion of all new people to Calvinistic religion. The government was concerned about religion but the ministers had to collect their own money in the seventeenth century. Later on, the Board of the Colony sent money to the ministers and churches. By then the Calvinist minister of Middelburg (Zeeland), Bernard Smytegelt (1665-1739) had published his sermons. He implied that the people of Zeeland stole from the (robbed) slaves and that was a sin for him. He was one of the first opponents of slavery in the Netherlands. The ministers in Suriname knew of his books.

Suriname, with a surface area of 163,000 sq. km is situated on the northeast coast of South America. In 1651, the English from the island of Barbados took possession of the piece of land to establish plantations, using enslaved labourers from West Africa, where Islam and Christianity dominated. In 1667, Suriname was conquered by the province of Zeeland. In 1683, the Geactroyeerde Societeit van Suriname (Chartered Society) consisting of three shareholders took over the colony. The shareholders were the city of Amsterdam, the province of Zeeland and the family Van Aerssen van Sommelsdijck. In the meantime Jewish people, Sefardic (Spanish and Portuguese Jews) and Askenazic, came in as plantation owners and introduced sugar production. They made their own marriage arrangements and enjoyed other privileges. During the eighteenth century, Suriname was a prospering colony but also faced internal warfare with the Maroons. In 1760, a peace treaty was signed. In 1816, the Dutch government took over Suriname as part of the Kingdom of the Netherlands. This lasted until 25 November 1975 when Suriname got its independence.

The Calvinist church was something like a state-church. In Suriname, the first minister was Cornelius Caletus who functioned on behalf of the classis[1] (region) of Amsterdam (Joosse, 1996: 36-7). Initially, it was forbidden for Catholics to have public jobs; this was made clear in the Charter of 1683. A member of the Calvinist church board was also a member of the colonial board. The colonial board expelled a Calvinist minister (J. Kals, 1733) who was making trouble in the church and in the colony around 1730. The colony published a notification on the reverence of Sunday (1669), and introduced a new translation of the Bible (1775), and regulations against the misuse of the name of God (1669).

In 1735, the Moravians got permission for missionary work because of the lobbying of Count Ludwig von Zinzendorf in Amsterdam. The missionaries were carpenters, tailors, bakers, butchers, etc. They were in fact artisans working under very bad health conditions. They did not have mutual communication and contacts with the sending organization. In 1741, the evangelical Lutherans from Amsterdam were allowed to build a congregation. In 1785, the Catholics were allowed to do the same but under certain conditions. One of the conditions was that the Catholic community

[1] Classis is region: union of local preachers; a technical term in protestantism.

had to pay for the orphans and poor people in the (Calvinist) Diakoniehouse (Almshouse), where the orphans of the Catholics found a place. That was impossible for the poor and young congregation, and in 1792, after a couple of years, the community was closed. It was reopened in 1817.

One special phenomenon in the time of slavery was the system of manumission. Since 1733, on the occasion of manumission (the process of giving freedom to an enslaved by the owner) the new freed man/woman had to be educated in a recognized religion (the first draft had an article with the text of a Calvinist Christian religion). Between 1832 and 1863, 6,364 persons got manumission and many became members of the Moravian (and later of the Catholic) church. These churches used the new language of the enslaved, Sranan, in their services while the Calvinist and Lutheran churches were churches for the whites (owners, administrators, the military cadre and the colonial board) (Jones, 1981; Lampe 2001; Van Raalte, 1976).

The churches in Holland and in Suriname were not especially involved in the abolition of slavery, like the Anti-Slavery Society in Great Britain and the United States of America. These were involved even after the abolition of slavery in the British (1834) and French (1848) colonies in the Caribbean. Some sort of resistance came from Niels Otto Tank, the Praeses of the Moravians. He was born in Norway in 1800 and became a missionary when he visited the Netherlands. He came to Suriname in 1842 and became Praeses, the administrative head of the Moravians in 1846. On his visit to the Netherlands in 1847, and his visits to the Caribbean, he wrote a public letter to the slave-owners in Suriname in 1848 about the bad treatment of the slaves, but he was not against the system of slavery. In fact, he, as well as the Moravian church actually possessed slaves. One slave of his got by manumission the name Niels. A group of owners protested by letter and later on he had to recognize his dubious position in the Netherlands. He did not return to Suriname. Some Moravians saw him as a protester against slavery, but others saw him as a danger to the society. He was not a reformer (Lenders; Lampe). The board of the colony, comprising owners, was happy with the protest letter of the owners. The successor of

Tank in Suriname apologized (Lampe, 2001a). There was a commotion in the society. The churches in Suriname did not take any actions against slavery and there were little exception in the Netherlands. The Lutheran theologian and professor in Amsterdam, H. Miliës, wrote against slavery in his book *Can a Christian be Owner of Slaves? (Kaneen christen eigenaar van eenslaafzijn?*) (Fafié: 67-75). According to him, slavery was a violation of human rights. Later on, the theologian and poet Nicolaas Beets (1814-1903) wrote *The Liberation of the (Slaves De bevrijding van de slaven,* 1856).

The first important step in the process of emancipation was the abolition of the slave trade by the English in 1807, followed by the Dutch in 1814 and 1818. Slaves came in illegally (3,000 every year from 1819-26) (Ten Hove, 2013). The total number of slaves from West Africa in Suriname, until 1863 was around 450,000. Groups of slaves fled to the interior and formed small groups of Maroons with their own authority, territory and language.

After the abolition of slavery on 1 July 1863, the colonial government imported contract labourers for the plantations from British India to replace 32,972 slaves of private owners and 649 slaves of the government. Approximately 34,000 Indians were imported. In addition to this, about 33,000 labourers from Java were introduced in Suriname. They brought with them Hinduism and Islam and the population became multi-religious and multi-cultural. After the abolition of slavery, a kind of parliament with limited rights was introduced in Suriname. The small group of Jews, with their own religion, had an exceptional position in Suriname for a long time. They had power and they were owners of plantations, administrators, members of the Koloniale Staten, lawyers, medical doctors, etc. This group was very influential, with its own juridical cadre for marriage. Today, this group has nearly disappeared (140). For more than three centuries, the colony had a Calvinist signature and from the beginnings until 1975, only one governor was a Catholic, J. Brons, from 1944-8 (Brons, 1946).

The government combined power with care as it mandated that a percentage of the taxes be reserved for the poor (sugar). The government started a leper centre (Voorzorg and Batavia) and a centre for senior citizens and sick persons (Boniface). The colonial government introduced the system of orphanages in 1865. During the first two centuries, a small number of missionaries worked in the city of Paramaribo and in the interior with the Amerindians and Maroons. The colony was in Statunascendi, and the development of the peoples in the interior was forgotten. Later on, the government was more flexible in that field. The relation between different Christian churches was not always friendly and peaceful. In public, the Calvinist church was in trouble with the other Christian churches and the Protestant churches were in trouble with the Catholic church. The government was part and inside of this situation.

For the Moravians, the establishment of the Hague Society (Haagsche Maatschappij) was welcome. This organization, of some elite, was launched in 1828 as an initiative to promote the religious civilization of the African people, especially by the Moravians. The Haagsche Maatschappij was not an action group against slavery but a group for emancipation. For the Haagsche Maatschappij and other groups involved in the fate of the slaves, the leading idea was that Evangelization work by the Moravians would emancipate the slaves. The culture of Christianity would make them human beings; civilized people like themselves. Emancipation meant synchronization because the civilization of the Dutch elite was the norm. For nearly forty years, the Maatschappij, with a division in Suriname, converted nearly 200,000 persons under the Moravians (Zeefuik: 171). Since 1817, the Catholic mission was a part of the Congregatio de Propaganda Fide, for the missions all over the world. The representative of the Pope and Roman institutions was the vice-nuncio of Brussels and The Hague. Later on, the Society for the Propagation of the Faith (1822) and the Society of the Children (1843) collected money for the universal missions. In this period, the Franciscan sisters of Roosendaal (Brabant, Holland) came to Suriname to work for the promotion of education and to run a girls orphanage (1856). The position of women was diffuse; the slave society was matrifocal but the men had the power. In short, the government was autocratic as a characteristic of being a colony. The Calvinist church was like a state-church. In this climate, the churches were dependant on the goodwill of the government.

IMMIGRATION AND MULTICULTURALITY

After 1873, the image of Suriname changed. Shortly before abolition, the government contracted Chinese labourers for plantation work. They and other newcomers from Asia made Suriname multicultural and multi-colour.

Most of the time, the governors of the colony, as representatives of the Dutch government, had to move between the churches because they were active in social life. One example of this was seen in 1880. The Moravians had to cancel their use of Verbontoe, a manner of religious marriage from the period of slavery, when it was forbidden for slaves to marry legally. The Moravian church introduced ecclesiastical marriage, which was not recognized by the government as a legal form of marriage. The Moravians changed their policy in 1880, and ordered the official way of marriage for the government and the church. The Moravian members refused, on the basis that such a marriage was too expensive. In addition, they did not have birth papers.This was necessary for the administration. As a result, the government decreased the money for the Moravians. The whole affair brought commotion in the society, but in the end, it became quiet (Lenders: 337-46).

The newspapers of the Christians *Protestantenblad* (1903) and the Catholic *De Surinamer* (1894) followed the acts of the government and the parliament. A black page in the history of the churches was the initiative for a new Roman Catholic leper centre in 1892-3. The governor agreed with the apostolic vicar Mgr. W. Wulfingh concerning the planning of a central leper centre in Suriname, guided by nuns. The Protestants, hearing about the planning of this centre, protested and wrote a letter to the Queen. Wulfingh was so disappointed he cancelled the initiative. However, he erected the Roman Catholic leper centre Gerardus Majella in Paramaribo, while Groot Chatillon was for the public; the Protestants established Bethesda. It was a challenging project, new for ecumenical cooperation. However, the time was not ripe.

In that same time, there were riots against the high taxes in the district of Para. The governor was Jonkheer Maurits de Savornin Lohman (1889-91). He was publicly on the side of the Moravians, disappointed by the Calvinist and Lutherans. He was re-baptized in the Moravian Church and was anti-Semitic. He sent military people to the predominantly Moravians districts and this brought a heavy split in the society, which led to the resignation of the governor. Later, a new situation developed. The governor Arnoud Baron van Heemstra (1921-8) had to reduce the expenses for education. However, he faced a lot of opposition via newspapers, as well as the papers of the churches. He had to leave the colony as he was not well equipped to deal with the situation. The apostolic vicar Th. Van Roosmalen, always busy to find subsidy of the government for his schools, refused to welcome the governor in his home, on his trip to say farewell to the people. In the meantime, the schools and boarding schools of the Moravians and the Catholics were fighting with the governmental schools and even with the upcoming Hindu and Muslim schools, especially in the districts (provinces) where they lived on the former plantations.

In 1890, the government introduced the koelie school for children of immigrants, where they received education in their own language (Gobardhan-Rambocus: 142). The school laws in Suriname said that youngsters had to go to school. That was unusual for the East Indian immigrants, because many of the youth helped in the rice fields. To make education more attractive, the government introduced schools for boys and girls in the districts where a concentration of immigrants lived. In a later stage, the parents wanted schools with the Dutch language, and in 1940, the dessa schools for the Javanese followed (Gobardhan-Rambocus: 353). In 1927, the Hindustani immigrants protested against the policy of the Roman Catholic Church, to build new schools in Hindustani living areas. The immigrants wanted government schools and this happened (Gobardhan-Rambocus: 294).

Regarding marriages, the government made special rules for an immigrant's marriage in 1907. It recognized the position of people other than the Creoles (descendants of the enslaved). That was clear in the issue of the marriages of Muslims and Hindus. In 1940, the governor, with experience in Indonesia introduced new marriage laws for the Muslims and Hindus. The most important thing was the recognition of the religious marriage as a civil marriage.

However, this measure was criticized by many on the basis that it introduced juridical inequality between the citizens. In this period, the government continued a policy of giving preference to the Calvinist church.

Not only was the subsidy for orphans arbitrary, it was also the same for the subsidy for education. In 1898, the government gave the public schools 10,000Sf, and the confessional[2] schools only 50,000. In that year, of the 100 pupils, 27 attended the public school and 73 the confessional schools (in 1889 the numbers were 32 and 68). When the government saw that the Moravians and Catholics did good work (education, medical service, employment) it had to recognize that and had to subsidize them, but in moderation and scanty measure. The colonial government neglected the people of the interior. Missionaries built their schools and churches at the cost of the churches and the government did not pay for education and medical service in the interior.

We can mention a change of mind here. The orientation of the Roman Catholic Church towards the respective cultures of the different groups was growing. In the 1980s, a priest translated the Catholic catechism in the languages of the Caribs and the Lokonon. Some priests learned the languages of the immigrants (Hindustanis and Javanese). Around the turn of the century, the provisional statute of 1915, of the Catholic Redemptorist missionaries, dealt with the behaviour of the missionaries on plantations and in the interior. The advice was not to condemn all the cultural habits and customs that seemed wrong.

The missionaries needed *benevolentia* (benevolence) because they had to work *ex caritate* (charity) and in obedience with the apostolic vicar. The migrants changed the character of Suriname. First, the Chinese organized their small school (Gobardhan-Rambocus). The Chinese migrant organization Kong Njie Tong Sang managed a school from 1887-90. The *Statuta* of the vicariate of 1921 spoke about the colony of Hindustanis, also a colony within the colony (116) and special orders for a girl. When they wanted to baptize,

[2] Confessional: typical in Suriname: the schools of religious institutions as opposite to the public or governmental schools.

the family had to promise that she was free of the Indian customs (115). The Church found a priest from England willing to go to the West Indies. The church also wanted special attention for the Portuguese. When the apostolic vicar W. Wulfingh had the feast of his twenty-five years of priesthood and twelve and a-half years of bishop, the church was decorated with banners in the different languages (Portuguese, English) and this included the languages of the Amerindians.

In that period, the board of the Moravians gave Th. Wenzel (1901) the opportunity to prepare for evangelization for the British Indians at Alkmaarwhile. H. Bielke (1909) was going to work among the Javanese. In addition, the Catholic Church started with categorical pastoral with the Hindustanis (1904), with their own boarding school (Rajpur) and Giryapur for agriculture and a lumber factory for the Maroons at Tamarin (Cottica).

In 1921, the Catholic Church started the evangelization for the mission under the Javanese. The weekly *De Katholieke Waarschuwer* of 1891, published in Dutch, Negro-English and English had information about the Chinese church in Romanized Chinese. The system in the Catholic Church was the same; the same formula but in different languages. Therefore, the Roman Catholic Church translated the standard catechism in Hindustani language *Katholik-Dharm ka Prashnontar Surinam Vicariat* (1924). Most of the time the governors of the colony, on behalf of the Kingdom of the Netherlands, had to move between the churches, because they were active in social life. In the meantime the schools and boarding schools of the Moravians and the Catholics were in a struggle with the governmental schools and even with the upcoming Hindu and Muslim organizations especially in the districts (provinces) where they lived.

In these times, the migrants came to form self-organizations. Some of these were secular while others were religious in nature. The secular organizations were Suriname Immigrants' Association – SIV (1910)[2] and the Surinamese British Indian Association Echtti-

[2] The Surinamese Immigranten vereniging of 1910 was renamed Bharat Oeday in 1922. It was originally for Indians and Javanese, but soon it became an Indian (Hindustani) organization.

haraur Hak (Freedom and Justice) of 1911. The religious organizations were originally at the local level, attached to temples or mosques, such as the Himayatul Islam at Welgedacht C (1902). National religious organizations were founded around 1929-30 such as the Suriname Islamic Association – SIV (1929), the Arya Dewaker (1929), the Sanatan Dharma (1929), the Khilafat Anjuman (1931) and the Perkoempoelan Islam Indonesia (1932). Special attention must be paid to the fact that Javanese Muslims were divided as East prayers (wongmadepngetan) and the West prayers (wongmadepngulon) according the the direction of the qibla in Mecca (Towikromo).[3] Later the migrants erected umbrella organizations such as the Perhimpunan Ahmadyyah Islam, the Federation of Islamic Communities, the Asjafia Islam and the Foundation of Islamic Communities. In 1918, there was already the socio-cultural group, Tjintoko Muljo (Emancipation in Bad Times) and in 1933, there was the Nabawi Mosque in north Paramaribo (Towikromo). During and after the Second World War, there was a political awakening, which resulted in the foundation of cultural and political organizations, such as the Hindostaans-Javaanse Centrale Raad (1945), the Liga of Hindustanis (1946), and the Kaun Tani Persatuuan Indoneua (KTPI) (1946).[4]

The Protestants and liberal people saw the growing influence of the Catholic Church and started a hidden and public action against it, since it had opened schools in predominantly Hindostani and Javanese villages. Organized action against this policy led to the

[3] For the people in Indonesia the direction of the face for the salat is west (location of the Qaba in Mecca), while for Suriname the direction is east. Many Javanese retained after arrival in Suriname the west as the direction for their prayers.

[4] Other parties were the Pergerakan Banga Indonesia Suriname (PBIS) (1949), the Hindoe Partij Suriname, theHindostaanse Oranje Politieke Partij, the Verenigde Hindostaanse Partij (VHP) 1949 as Vatan Hitkari (party for promotion of National Welfare), later theProgressive Reform Party. The Creoles came to the launching of the Nationale Partij Suriname in 1946, like de Progressive Surinamese People's Party (PSV, 1946) of the Roman Catholic priest J. Weidmann P.S.V. Weitmann, 1975.

school fight (de schoolstrijd) of the years 1928 to 1932. People were talking about the Roman danger. There was a mixture of ethnic, racial, political and religious organizations, sometimes with a hidden agenda. Self-organizations created their own leaders and that were good for self-esteem in the colonial society. That was the foundation of political organization until now.

For the Catholics, there were funds of the Society of the Propagation of the Faith, the Society of Childhood (S. Infanta) and the Papal Society of St. Peter (St. Pieters penning as it was called in Dutch), and later the Indian Mission Society (1912) with her Association for Education. The Catholic Church got money every year from the Hofbauer Liefdewerk in Holland for the care of the lepers and since 1940, the Petrus Donders Stichting of Suriname got gifts from private people, for example the De Gruyter chain of shops of Den Bosch. The Zeister Zendings Genootschap had connections in the *Suriname Zending* and to the Moravians. In this period, the monopoly of the Calvinist religion made place for the presence of more churches. The government was conscious that Suriname was a country with more cultures and religions and it was its duty to care for unity in diversity.

In 1942, the four old, colonial Christian churches – the Dutch Reformed, the Evangelical Lutheran, the Moravian and the Roman Catholic churches – decided to cooperate especially in the field of ethics and good customs, because the American soldiers brought in dance, movies, music.[5] The Committee of Christian Churches (CCK) did not invite the umbrella organizations of Hindus and Muslims. There were even more Christian churches like those of the Adventists, the Baptists, the Salvation Army, the African Methodist Episcopal Church which were not so prominent and socially relevant, but with their own leadership. These were not dependent on the money of the government.

[5] During the war Suriname was the main producer of bauxite, a product used for the production of aluminium. Aluminium was the raw material for planes, used in the war. For this reason the US government stationed a part of its army in Suriname in order to guarantee the production and export of bauxite.

However, a new phenomenon was a vivid folk and religious heritage of the Afro-Surinamese, the Hindus and the Muslims, which was different from that in India/Pakistan or from Java. The Christian churches (Moravians and Catholics) had different approaches to the Hindus and Muslims and to the African heritage. There was some appreciation for Hinduism and Islam as world religions, but they perceived African heritage as superstitious, devilish and bad-one that ought to be eradicated. The government found in some churches a counterpart. The autocratic character of the government was not strict; some churches created elements of social relevance and power. The young society became multicultural and the churches were teaching the government how to deal with multiculturalism.

NATIONALISM AND INDEPENDENCE

When contract labourers wanted to stay in Suriname, they got a small piece of land.[6] Many people accepted the land grant and so a group of small agriculturalists emerged. In the middle of the twentieth century, elements of nationalism came up. The new laws for Muslim and Hindu marriage of 1940 were significant for the concept of unity. This period was fundamental and essential for the colony. After a period of self-organizations of the immigrants, the religious organizations as the SIV (1929), the Arya Dewaker (1929), the Sanatan Dharma (1929), the Khilafat Anjuman (1931), Perkoempoelan Islam Indonesia (1932) were founded. Very important to self-awareness and political awakening was the movement *Boss in Own House* (Baas in eigenhuis) which came after the announcement of Queen Wilhelmina of the Netherlands in 1942, concerning the change of relations within the kingdom. The union *Wie Eegie Sanie* (Our Own Sake) of Surinamese students in the Netherlands, promoted independence.

[6] Getting a piece of land was not included in the contract, but it was common practice to attract immigrants to settle in Suriname, especially since 1895. Those who abandoned their right of free passage received 100 Dutch guilders and as stimulus, they could get a piece of land on easy terms (Hassankhan, 1993 or De Klerk, 1953).

The creation of the diocese of Paramaribo in 1958, was important for the consciousness of independence as it recognized the growth of the Catholic community to adulthood. According to the Roman laws and customs, after a long period, Suriname was an apostolic prefecture (1825-52) and an apostolic vicariate (1852-1958). An example of change is the fact that the number of non-Catholics at the 24 schools in Paramaribo in 1958 was 22.3 per cent of the total pupils. This was shown by the inspector for the Roman Catholic schools, Father Herman van Nimwegen. In total, it was 41 per cent of the 16,759 pupils of the Catholic schools (Van Nimwegen, 289). In 1963, the Moravian church became an independent part of the Unitas Fratrum. Already in 1967, the CCK agreed to the common recognition of baptism.

The people's groups organized themselves in terms of culture and religion because the government did not understand them. A sort of assimilation was the introduction of the Indonesian type of village with a *lurah* as leader and head. Later on, in 1970, the introduction of national holidays like Holi/Phagwa and Eid ul Fitr/Bada opened a new perspective. The Christians lost the second Eastern Day and Maudy Day. The people changed the second Eastern Day with Ascension Day. The monopoly of Christianity decreased. In fact, the Creoles more than the other parties, wanted independence and most of the Creoles were and are Christians. It is always a policy to create coalitions for the administration of the government. In that time the nationalistic Creole Party of National Republic (PNR) won more and more support and joined the old National Party Suriname for the administration. After the election of 1973, the new government announced that Suriname would become independent in 1975. This caused unrest in the society and tens of thousands of people migrated to the Netherlands. The number of the Surinamese diaspora in the Netherlands is presently estimated at 350,000 persons (Choenni).

It is remarkable that even now the Catholic Church wanted to organize categorical pastoral for the different people's groups. In 1956, a Chinese priest came to Suriname (until 1972). Another came in 1967 and yet another in 1964. In 1965, two Indian priests arrived and in 1974, a priest came from Indonesia. An issue for the nationalists was the differentiation of the Moravian and Catholic churches for the population groups according to the (boarding) schools, categorical (ethnic) centra, special prayer books and literature. The churches recognized the danger of segmented churches and tried to minimize the splits. A good example is seen on the day of national independence, 25 November 1975, when there was the participation of all religious leaders, for example, the Hindu pandit was the prayer leader for the Moravians, and the Pentecostal leader was the prayer leader in the Catholic cathedral. It was a proof of dedication to the new age, closed by an important letter of the CCK to the nation. During this time the relations between the government and the churches was relatively quiet, both of them searching for new ways to engage the people.

FRAGILE SOCIETY AND COOPERATION

After independence, Suriname made a choice for a national army and some Surinamese living in Holland came back to join the Surinamese National Army. After some disciplinary problems within the army, it was forbidden for a group of soldiers to enter the garrison. During the day, they stayed in the city within their own centre. In that, time the government was careless and there was the delay for a year and a half, of monthly social security money for families (children) and seniors (above sixty years). The government failed to provide public support and as a result, the wives and other family of the military organized prayer meetings. The CCK was involved in the awkwward position of the military. The central question of the conflict was the founding of a trade union within the army, which according to the government was not allowed.

On 25 February 1980, a group of 15 soldiers held a coup and took over the government. The CCK and umbrellas of Hindu organizations and the Majlies Moesliemien Suriname (umbrella organization of Muslim organizations/associations) reacted in protest. They gave the coup the benefit of the doubt because it was a good moment for changing the social order and to start the war against poverty. In 1981, the CCK organized meetings under the title, *Being*

Christian in the Revolution. The Christian churches were conscious of their feeble socio-political involvement and saw the need for internal renewal. In the meantime, there were some actions of destabilization in the society (Archief der kerken, 1983).

Some people of African origin sought a solution for the confrontation between African and Christian elements in their culture by practicing a second religion since the colonial government rejected their African religious heritage. Communities of Hindus and Muslims (Hindustanis and Javanese/Indonesians) took the opportunity to build up the structures and contents of their religions. During the 1980s, representatives of religious organizations launched the Interreligious Council in Suriname (IRIS, 1989). This was an umbrella organization of all recognized religions but it was a bridge too far for some Christian and Muslim groups. The Moravian Church (EBG) and the SMA, a Muslim umbrella organization were not members of the IRIS.

A remarkable distinction has been developed between the official religions, according to the old religions aligned with the colonial powers, and the folk religious concepts and practices, created in the Surinamese context. In that framework the real impact of the official religions in political and socio-economic affairs was a point of research for critics with a perspective to the future and to the past. In this time, the group of Javanese *kejawen* – Javanism with the emphasis on the old Javanese *adat* in opposition to the Islam – organized themselves. They started the Sasi Suro, the month of fasting, which began in March, organized by the Federation Javanism in Surinam (*De Ware Tijd*, 15 April 2002). The churches used the languages of the people such as Asewatono, Siswatana, Suk Dhaam, Apinti and manari. While it was a mixture of cultures, the churches were fundamentally European with some so-called adaptations.

After independence, the CCK was more active in providing development aid and in the process of democracy. The CCK published open letters to the government and the parliament (1978 and 1979) about the fact that the rich became richer and the poor became poorer in spite of democracy. The CCK and the umbrella of Hindu and Muslim organizations protested in December 1982, following a military act in which 15 important citizens were killed.

What is remarkable is that some members of these umbrella organizations were high-level members of political parties. The atmosphere in the country was grim and the churches asked the people to work together for a new Suriname without violence and poverty (Archief der Kerken 1983; Tjon-Liem-Sang).

The military government expelled a Dutch priest after he called the president (military commander) a murderer and burned 15 candles. Some civilians protested publicly. The expulsion was correct as, according to the law, he was foreigner who had insulted the highest authority. In spite of troubles, the CCK helped the government during strikes of trade unions, helped to formulate a new constitution and also and during the internal war (1986-92) and in peace negotiations.

New evangelical movements came up after the 1960s. Normally they followed the government and were financially independent. The current president made the bishop of an Evangelical church his personal advisor and many of the Pentecostals followed him without public criticism. The suspicion is that the president was not at home in the old Christian church because his Catholic Church was too critical. There is another phenomenon where the Moravians and the Catholic Church worked with many missionaries from abroad, especially from Germany and the Netherlands. The Second World War significantly diminished the number of Moravian missionaries. The shortage of vocations for religious life in the Netherlands minimized the presence of Dutch missionaries in the Catholic church. Lay people and people from Suriname were their substitutes. However, both the churches had to reduce their activities, for example in the area of education and medical services. Non-governmental organizations and the government took over activities with which the churches built up their social relevance and showed the power of foreign money (care for the lepers, boarding schools for the youth of the interior, education and social work).

The churches are managing now, based on the former image that they built. The Catholic church was called a school church, or a children's church (Vernooij, 2012). Even now, the churches have to look for tasks to preserve their image. They have to show their social relevance by dedication to tasks other than the old fashioned ones. Now it is more important to be democratic, social, just and transparent than to have a lot of institutions and buildings, based on predominantly foreign money and always focused on the quantity of members, and institutions. There is the need for quality of life for everybody. During the so-called internal war (1986-92) between the two parties, on one side the national army and on the other side the opposition, helped by people from Holland, or the army against the guerrilla, the fight was fruitless and there were many victims on both sides and the damage of projects in East Suriname. This was ended by negotiations and peace in 1992. The CCK was active in helping the army and the government reach peace. The new government, independent of Europe, found a new Caribbean and Latin American context such as CARICOM (Caribbean Community) and UNASUR (Union of South American Nations). The churches were looking for help and cooperation.

REALITY AND RESEARCH

After the period of two military coups and internal war, the people were confused and tired. The churches themselves were tired of the mutual rivalry, now reflecting their position in the society in the midst of more religions. In this period, the churches and even the Hindu and Muslim organizations with their own schools, boarding schools and centres for the aged, underlined firmly human rights and the ethics of party politics. Both the church and state avoided public polarization. The churches shed their amateuristic initiatives and develop a mentality of tolerance.

The process of decolonization was thus full of surprises for them. The restoration of democracy was important, but a good part of the people followed the military. Of course, the elite saw the damage to the old structures, the Dutch juridical cadre and the old ties of trade. The members of the churches tried, in the grimy times of the military dictatorship, to design a new sort of policy without patronage and corruption and with real democracy. Immediately after the military coup in 1980, the CCK organized a congress under the title 'Being Christian in the Revolution'. The military leaders had promised a war against poverty. That was attractive for many church members and they wanted a revolution within the churches. A small group of scholars and theologians published *Amen* (1988), a reflection on creed in the Surinamese context, and *Christelijk Geloven and Politiekhandelen* (Christian Belief and Political Action) in 1989. In 1999, the CCK and the IRIS published their *NU: Samenverder (Now Together Forward)*, a programme for national restoration. The issue of good governance was a topic, but not for the man on the street and members of the old (ethnic) political parties (Sjak Shie, 2000).

The Catechetical Center of the Diocese of Paramaribo was busy promoting ecumenism among the Hindus and Muslims. It gave training for catechesis for the Roman Catholic schools and made study materials for them. Change of mind was important. The churches discovered their paternalistic and patron role and tried to communicate their positions. Both of the churches (Moravian and Catholic) started bureaus of projekt planning in the 1970s for community development in the interiors. The social projects would be a social network for building up a new society through new employment in self-help projects, work for women and communication with the people of the interiors.

The convents of the religious congregations were closed due to the shortage of religious workers (from Holland) as well as the many (ethnic) boarding schools. The Dutch element of the (Catholic) church diminished. Their jobs in medical service and in the schools were taken over by Surinamese. A process of Surinamization took place, avoiding the metaphorical image of a hydrocephalus. In all periods, there was no attention paid to religious arts inside and outside the buildings, or songs and literature. There were some trials, but generally, this field of religion had no attention paid or support. Therefore, the church missed the opportunity to strengthen its own identity.

After independence and military rule, the country had to find its own system of sound and transparent governance in democracy. Leaders knew the richness of multiculturalism. The former system of ethnic political parties was not relevant anymore. Labour and production were the pillars of the new society with possibilities in agriculture (rice), oil, gold, wood, bauxite, and tourism. However, a colonial mentality (mental slavery) was vivid; neo-colonialism unraveled itself. The Dutch heritage in Suriname, more and more regionally oriented, has decreased. The state was and is in statunascendi after three centuries of dependency. In early times, the colonial government neglected the people of the interiors. Missionaries built their schools and churches at the cost of the foreigners. The government learned to take up tasks in the field of social and medical service. Now the religions had time for mutual exchange and focusing on the quality of life. In fact, every ethno-cultural or religious group was/is a minority. That is not a guarantee that the relation between nation and church will be sound always. A good marker in the field of dialogue of religions was the launching of the Interreligious Council in Suriname, the IRIS of 1989. It was a combination of Hindu, Muslim and Christian religious representatives. During the period 2005-10, the representatives of the Afro-Surinamese religion applied for official recognition by the government. The minister in charge of religious affairs asked the IRIS for advice, but the advice did not come (private communication with Maurits Hassankhan, former Minister of Interior Affairs). An important act of the IRIS was the production of an ethical code for politicians in Suriname. The IRIS is an institution like the CCK, trying to win an important part of the society as a block to fight against the government when the society is in crisis, but also working together with the government for the benefit of the nation (Tjon-Liem Sang, 2005).

Recently, the participation of the (Dutch) Catholic bishop and other church leaders in a protest rally in the capital of Paramaribo against the amnesty law of the parliament (for the actors of the killings of December 1982), was the motive of the head of state (also accused of the killings of 1982) to demonize him in his public speech.

As per the census of 2012: Roman Catholis form 21.6 per cent; Lutheran's 0.5 per cent; Pentecostal 11.16 per cent; Moravian 11.16 per cent; Reformed 0.7 per cent; Other Christians 3.2 per cent; Hindu Sanatan 18.0 per cent; Hindus Arya 3.1 per cent; Other Hindus 1.2 per cent; Islam Sunni 3.9 per cent; Islam

TABLE 10.1: THE RELIGIOUS AFFILIATION IN SURINAME IN 2004 AND 2012

Religion	2004	2012
Christian	40.7%	48.4%
Hindu	19.9%	22.3%
Islam	13.5%	13.9%
Others/none	10.2%	12.3%
Unknown	15.7%	3.2%
Total	492.000	541.638

Source: *Population Census*, Algemeen Bureau voor de Statistiek, Paramaribo; 2013, 26.

Ahmadyah 2.6 per cent; Other Islam 7.3 per cent; Jehovah's Witness 1.2 per cent; Javanism 0.8 per cent; Other religions 0.9 per cent; none 7.5 per cent; Unknown 3.2 per cent.

The Census of 2012 introduced two new issues: Javanism and Winti (Afro-Surinamese). What is remarkable is the Moravian Church scoring lower than the Pentecostals. According to other census, Muslims consist of more people than traditional groups of Sunni and the Ahmadiah. The sections unknown were growing during the years. It is a puzzle to explain the numbers unknown, probably due to a new calculation system. The issue of Christians in the Census of 2012 is due to the growth of the Pentecostals. The number of Hindus and Muslims is naturally increasing. Until now, the number of Christians is predominant.

The government is looking to function better on behalf of the people. The processes of development, first at an infrastructural level, were and are very slow in tropical areas, especially as until now, clientism and patronage were important in the society. In addition, the churches were victims of the times; with lower budgets and more diverse. They had to finish some social projects. That was not a problem because the government tried to build up new institutions. Surinamese replaced the Dutch for education and medical work. The people created the saying 'there are more houses than churches'. In the first place, the families needed help. The exchange between Surinamese in Holland and in Suriname led not to a mass secularization and a generation conflict, because members of the churches preserved their heritage and Christianity was seen sometimes as a varnish. The Surinamese were more religious and busier with church activities than the Dutch in Holland. To be religious and a member of one of the religious institutions in Suriname is part of the identity, ethnicity, culture, and heritage.

The Christian churches with their work for care and emancipation missed the real Surinamese touch and experienced the need to become real Surinamese churches. They discovered that people had the right to get help without having membership of a church. A good and recent example of what can happen in Suriname can be seen in the case where the former commander-in-chief, Desi Bouterse, now president of the republic, converted from Catholicism to a Pentecostal church and nominated the bishop of the Pentecostal church as a personal adviser (and on the payroll of the government). It is clear that the old churches protested and that their behaviour was consequent. The president was not amused. However, the traditional relations were preserved in the ever-small society.

CONCLUSION

The government learned, after an autocratic period at the start of the colonization, a more democratic and a nationalist approach to the groups, surviving under the motto: unity in diversity for quality. The government is young, vulnerable and fragile and does not have all the tools as a very young country, with the heritage of slavery and colonialism. Caring, assuring, emancipating and combining are the issues, but in every period, they are not consequent and transparent. It is the culture of a young nation with a colonial heritage. Migrants found a place to live, partly with their own culture, religion and language, helped by the socio-economic and political context. Some like the idea of the diaspora aligned to the mother country. Perhaps it is a phase of coming home for so long as possible. It is not a diaspora with homesickness. It is behaviour for activity and multiculturality.

Over the centuries, the churches learned ecumenism and dialogue of religions. They discovered the fragility of European Christianity and were called to Surinamize catechesizing, liturgy (empirical) theology and an own and unique way to be religious in Suriname with slavery and contract labour in their pocket and luggage. The quest of hermeneutics of the gospel came up and they learned how to interpret the gospel in the Surinamese context. The quest for ethnicity and culture, always issues in Suriname, changed. The people discovered that ethnicity and culture are dependent on time and place. The population mixed more in terms of ethnicity and culture, which are always changing and are more than folklore. The introduction of Krishna Janmashtami and Gita (Geeta) Jayanti are interesting festivals but these are based on the past in India.

The churches did not reach the level of full emancipation thereby connecting people. Nevertheless, men within the churches were talking about ending the remarkable pampering of the Christians (the Creoles) by all sorts of developing projects. The churches are on the way to equality, convinced of their own rights. Especially so the Catholic Church that tried to shape its own world, an ultramontanic (Rome-oriented) image. The meaning of social projects was an indirect method for evangelization and recruiting. Now the churches learned not to work in rivalry and competition, but to look for cooperation, for respect for men and women, for the implementation of human rights, for liberation from colonialism and imperialism for a meeting of just and responsible people. It is a continuing game; a policy for political affairs to gain supporters. Nevertheless, the case of Suriname is an experiment of multiculturality at different levels. It is a future model of a society with citizens from all over the world. This model must have a chance in the future.

Uniformity is always the basis of governmental policy, but the society is enabled by multiformity. The government installed a commission to study the national holidays. For many citizens there are too many holidays with too many reasons for such. It is possible that Christians will have to give up some holidays in comparison with other religious and ethnic groups. The racial political parties have more and more branches but the inter-ethnic group of the National Democratic Party won the elections in 2010 and 2015. It has a future.

REFERENCES

Algoe, Kirtie. (2009). *Suriname: schip van diversiteit met een boeg van saamhorigheid. De invoering van Holi en IdulFitr als nationale feestdagen in Suriname.* Paramaribo: Stichting Wetenschappelijke Informatie.

Algemeen Bureau voor de Statistiek (2007). *Statistical Papers 5. Godsdienst/ Geloofsovertuiging.* Paramaribo. 6-7.

—— (2013). Resultaten Achtste (8e) Volks- en Woningtelling in Suriname. Paramaribo.

Bakker, Eveline, Leo Dalhuisen, Maurits Hassankhan and Frans Steegh (1993). *Geschiedenis van Suriname.* Walburg PersZutphen: 85-91.

Bakker, Freek and Jan Veltkamp (2010). *Surinaams Hindoeïsme,* Paramaribo: Suriname Informatie 2.

Boone, A. and J. van Ekeris (1991). 'Zending tussen woord en daad. Twee hoofdstukken uit de geschiedenis van gereformeerd piëtisme en zending'. Kampen: Uitgeverij De Groot Goudriaan/ Stichting Studie der Nadere Reformatie.

Brons, Jan (1952). *Het rijksdeel Suriname.* Haarlem, Bohn.

Choenni, Charietje and Chan Choenni (2012). *Sarnami Hindostani 1920-1960.* Woesteling, identiteit en gemeenschapsvorming in Suriname. KIT, Amsterdam.

Comité Christelijke Kerken (1983). 'Documenten van het Comité Christelijke Kerken in Suriname vanaf 1975'. *Archief der Kerken,* 38 (Amersfoort): 1-20.

Doe, Erik van der, Perry Moree and Dirk Tang (2009). 'De smeekbede van een oude skavin en andere verhalen uit de West', Zutphen: Walburg Pers. *Sailing Letters Journaal II.*

Evangelische Broedergemeente Suriname (1963, 2007). Handboek van de Evangelische Broedergemeente in Suriname, Paramaribo.

Exalto, John and Jan-Kee Karels (2001). *Waakzame wachters en kleine vossen. Gereformeerden en herrnhutters in de Nederlanden, 1734-54.* Uitgeverij Groen Heerenveen.

Fafié, Th. (2000). Henricus Christiaan Miliës (1810-68): Luthers hoogleraar te Amsterdam ern aanklager van de slavernij. En God Bleef in Mokum. Amsterdamse kerkgeschiedenis in de negentiende en twintigste eeuw, Eburon: 57-76.

Gobardhan-Rambocus, Lila (2001). Onderwijs als sleutel tot maatschappelijke vooruitgang. Een taal- en onderwijsgeschiedenis van Suriname, 1651-1975, Zutphen: Walburg Pers.

Gooswit, Sylvia and WonnyKarijopawiro (1997). Tayup en Jangrung in Suriname. Een Javaanse dansvorm, Paramaribo: Cultuurstudies.

Hassankhan, Maurits (1993). 'Immigratie en integratie van contractarbeiders', in Lila Gobardhan-Rambocus and Maurits Hassankhan (eds.). *Immigratie en ontwikkeling*. Paramaribo.

Herderlyke en vaderlyke brief, houdende aan de bloeyende hervormde gemeente, binnen deze stad vergadert,totontdekkinge van, en waarschouwinge tegen de gevaarlyke dwalingen van die lieden, dewelke onder den naam van hernhutters bekend zijn. Geschreven van de predikanten en ouderlingen des kerken- raads van Amsterdam, Amsterdam (1738).

Hove, Okke ten and Frank Dragtenstein (1997). Manumissies in Suriname 1832-1863, Utrecht: Bronnen voor de Studie van Suriname, 19.

Hove, Okke ten (2013). 'Vrije arbeiders', in Suriname. WiRutu 13 (Tijdschrift voor Surinaamse Genealogie): 24-37.

Jansen van Galen, John (2013). Afscheid van de koloniën. Het Nederlandse dekolonisatiebeleid. 1942-2012. Amsterdam/Antwerpen: Atlas Contact.

Jones, J. (1988). Kwakoe en Christus. Een beschouwing over de ontmoeting van de Afro-Amerikaanse cultuur *en religie met de Hernhutter zending in Suriname*. Brussels.

Kent, John (1986). Ontmoeting tussen christendom en Afro-Suinaamse godsdienst. Zicht zending. Zeist: Zeister Zendings Genootschap, 87-94.

Klerk, Cor de (1951). Cultus en Ritueel van het Orthodoxe Hindoeïsme in Suriname. Amsterdam: Urbi et Orbi.

—— (1953). De immigratie der Hindostanen in Suriname. Amsterdam: Urbi et Orbi.

Krüger, J. (1953). De weg van het Evangelie tot de Hindoes. Gemeenschap, 1/4, November. Paramaribo.

Lampe, Armando (2001a). *Mission or Submission? Moravian and Catholic Missionaries in the Dutch Caribbean during the Nineteenth Century*. Vandenhoeck and Ruprecht. Göttingen: 66-87.

Lampe, Armando (ed.) (2001b) *Christianity in the Caribbean: Essays on Church History*. University of the West Indies, Kingston, 126-53 (Christianity and Slavery in the Dutch Caribbean).

Lenders, Maria (1996). Strijders voor het Lam. Leven en werk van Herrnhutter Broeders en-zusters in Suriname, 1735-1900. KILTV Leiden.

Mingoen, Urmie (ed.) (1999). De EBGS in de 21ste eeuw. Uitdagingen in het nieuwe millennium, Paramaribo: EBGS.

Mitrasing, Frits (1990). Van Immigratie tot integratie 1890-1990. Het Javaans segment, Paramaribo.

Mungra, Harrie (1996). Katholiee Onderwijzersbond. 75 jaar strijd. Beschrijving van de vakbondsstrijd van de Katholieke Onderwijzers Bond van 1921-96. Paramaribo.

Nadere trouwhartige waarschouwinge, tegen de verleidingen der hernhutters; door den kerkenraad van Amsterdam voorgesteld, aan de gemeente in die stad, en aan allen, die hunne zaligheit, naar Gods Woord, met vrezen en beven, in den Heere Jesus Christus, zoeken, Amsterdam, 1750.

Nimwegen, Herman van (1958).R.k. onderwijs en opvoeding in Suriname. Het Schoolbestuur. Tijdschrift ten dienste van het R.K. Bijzonder onderwijs, 26 (10 oktober): 288-90.

Nurmohamed, Mustafa (1985). De geschiedenis van de Islam in Suriname. Gedenkboek Surinaamse Moesliem Associatie. Paramaribo.

Ort, J. (1990, 1963). Surinaams Verhaal. Vestiging van de Hervormde kerk in Suriname (1667-1800), Zutphen: Walburg Pers.

OSO, themanummer Religieuze specialisten. Utrecht jaargang 18/2 (1999).

Panda Beraad (1988). Amen. Overpeinzingen bij het Christelijk geloven in Suriname. Paramaribo: Katechetisch Centrum.

Pandaberaad (1989). Christelijk geloven en politiek handelen. Paramaribo.

van Paramaribo, R.K. Mannenvereniging (1911) Beschouwingen over den Economischen en Financieelen Toestand der kolonie Suriname. Paramaribo: J.Timmerman (overdruk van De Surinamer)

Prasne (2008). Arya Samaj in Suriname en Nederland in de 20ste eeuw, Den Haag.

Progressieve Surinaamse Volkspartij (1975). Weidmann. Priester Politicus. Vakbondsleider. Paramaribo.

Raalte, Jan va (1973). Secularisatie en Zending in Suriname. Over het secularisatieproces in verband met het zendingswerk van de Evangelische Broedergemeente in Suriname. Wageningen: H.Veenman en Zonen B.V.

Ramsoedh, Hans (1990). Suriname 1933-44. Koloniale Politiek onder Gouverneur Kielstra. Delft: Eburon.

Roosmalen, Th. Van (1921). Statuta Vicariatus Apostolici Surinamensis. Paramaribo: Randag. Appendix I. De Hindostanis.

CCK/IRIS – Samenwerkingsverband (1999). Nu Samen verder. Programma voor nationaal Herstel aangeboden aan de bevolking van Suriname en haar leiders, Paramaribo.

Sjak Shie, Peter (1990). Een gesprek tussen mensen; over de dialoog tussen de godsdiensten, Paramaribo: Panda Cahier 23.

—— (1996). Waar het v isioenontbreekt verwildert het volk (Spr. 29.18). Paramaribo: Panda Cahier 31.

Sjak Shie, Peter (2000). Als een nooit opgdroogde kreek (Amos 5, 24). 25 jaar kerken in Suriname (verslag van de conferentie, 11 November 2000 te Amsterdam), Amsterdam: 5-22.

Soemosentono, Jacob (1999). *Politieke Emancipatie en participatie van de Javanen in Suriname.* Paramaribo.

Statuta Vice-Provinciae Surinamensis C.SS.R. Paramaribo (1915): Randag.

Surinaamse Inspraak Orgaan (2006). Religie en integratie. Extreme religieuze denkwijzen en bereidheid tot respecteren en uitwisselen van normen en waarden. Utrecht.

Tjon-Kiem-Sang, Paul (2005). De beminde kinderen van één Vader zijn wij. Vastenbrieven van Monseigneur Aloysius Zichem. Paramaribo.

Towikromo, Yvonne (1997). De Islam van de Javaanse Surinamers. Amrit Den Haag: 35-6.

Vernooij, Joop (2012). De regenboog is in ons huis. De kleurrijke geschiedenis van de r.k. kerk in Suriname. Valkhof Pers Nijmegen.

Vijay. Orgaan van het Comité Viering Divalifeest, oktober (1969), nr. 3.

Wongsodikromo, Jenny-Flier (2009). Terugblik op honderd jaar Javaanse zending, Paramaribo. P.

Zamuel, Hesdie (1996). Het Lam en Zijn Navolgers, Paramaribo.

Zeefuik, Karel (1973). Hernhutter Zending en Haagsche Maatschappij 1828-67. Een hoofdstuk uit de geschiedenis van zending en emancipatie in Suriname. Utrecht: Elinkwijk.

Zeister Zendingsgenootschap (1935). 2 Eeuwen 1735-1935. Herdenking Suriname Zending Zeist.

Zimmerling, P. (1999). Nikolaus Ludwig Graf von Zinzendorfund die Herrnhutter Brüdergemeine. Geschichte, Spritualität und Theologie. Holzgerlingen.

PART 4

INDIAN MUSICAL TRADITIONS AND IDENTITY

CHAPTER 11

The Dhantal's Irreverence: Off-beat as the In-between Time of Indenture

ANANYA J. KABIR

INTRODUCTION

The world of Caribbean percussion is, in many ways, a magic-realist one. It was forged through the traumatizing and profoundly alienating processes foundational to global modernity – the movement of peoples across the Indian and Atlantic Oceans to the Americas. Like the mysterious amassing of butterflies in an episode in Gabriel Garcia Marquez's *One Hundred Years of Solitude*, Caribbean percussive traditions and instruments are manifestations of proliferation, mutation, bringing into the world of pleasurable sound unexpected source materials. These materials include not just skin and wooden frame to create myriad variations on the drum, but also crates and storage boxes, seeds, gourds, and tree trunks, wooden sticks used in shipbuilding, and a range of metallic objects purloined from everyday use, from oil drums to ablution vessels to spoons. These converted objects sound out of resistance and pleasure to the punishing rhythms of plantation life through an equally bewildering profusion of modes. They are not just slapping with hand or stick, but scraping, shaking, and bringing together two metallic surfaces to resonate against each other. To the latter category of Caribbean percussive instruments, technically called 'struck idiophones', belongs the subject of my essay, the dhantal.[1]

[1] Such incidents are described in profusion in historiographic literature of slavery as well as of the history of Afro-Latin music-making. For an example

In this article I offer a series of speculations based on the dhantal's sound. My understanding of the sound, purpose and specialness of this peculiar instrument, rooted yet rootless (for reasons that will be fully explicated below), is heavily shaped by my overall understanding of the Caribbean as a crucible of global modernity through its rhythmic profuseness. I have taken inspiration from the extensive body of scholarship that argues in Caribbean rhythm cultures and modes of resistance to plantation life are historical (like use of drums during slave revolts)[2] and philosophical (like African derived polyrhythm).[3] However, it should be noted that these formulations base their readings of rhythm as resistance on the African heritage of the Caribbean. The possibility of an Indian contribution to the richly resistive and utopian rhythm-scape of the Caribbean has been ignored. The obvious reason for this lacuna is that most such readings are heavily influenced by or arise from the same intellectual space that gave rise to Paul Gilroy's formulation of the 'Black Atlantic' (Gilroy, 1995). The Indians are made up of a longer journey that crossed two oceans as well as the seething waters around the Cape of Good Hope (*pagla samundar* – 'mad sea'). Thinking of the Indo- and Afro-Caribbean in creative dialogue asks us to conjoin the history of the Atlantic to the history of the Indian Ocean. In doing so, it not only expands our notion of the transatlantic fruitfully to the transoceanic; it also allows us to bring insights from two different scholarly domains to shed new light on old problems, or even, to problematize new ones. This desire to bring together the histories of two oceans and two Diasporas through the humble instrument, the dhantal, is central to this article.

---

of the former, see Vincent Brown, 2008; for one of the latter, see Peter Fryer, 2000.

[2] Two iconic examples are Antonio Benítez-Rojo, 1996, and Édouard Glissant, 1997.

[3] See Francesca Orsini (2002) for a comprehensive account of this process.

A THOROUGHLY DIASPORIC INSTRUMENT

The dhantal (dantal, dandtal) is used in music-making by Indian diasporic communities formed during indenture labour in Mauritius and Fiji. However, the preliminary scope of this paper restricts my discussion to its role, both musical and philosophical, in the Indo-Caribbean. The dhantal is most associated with Trinidad's chutney music. Since the early twentieth century, 'chutney' has denoted music derived 'primarily from a specific set of folksong sub-genres . . . which share the use of fast tempo, simple refrain-verse structure and light, erotic Bhojpuri texts' (Manuel, 1998: 21-42). The dhantal, harmonium and dholak provide its core instrumentation. The dhantal also appears in Suriname and Guyana in similar musical company and contexts (Arya, 1968: 8-9). Its form is extremely simple: 'a metal rod struck by a U-shaped clapper' (Manuel, 1998: 26). Tina Ramnarine writes that

> The top of the rod is tapered to a fine point to allow greater resonance and the end is shaped into a circle which rests on the ground, table, or other surface, when it is played. Its length is around a metre. . . . The dhantal is usually made by the player for personal use but can also be commissioned via puja shops which sell articles associated with religious ceremonies (1998: 1-22).

In chutney music, Peter Manuel asserts that:

> providing a fast, danceable rhythm is a primary requirement. Most chutneys are sung in the standard quadratic North Indian folk metre (called kaherva in that country). The dholak players, most of whom would be considered remarkably skilled in India itself, provide lively accompaniment, and are supplemented by the dantal, which is able to play fast rolls and damped or ringing tones. (1998: 29)

The presence and importance of the dhantal in Indo-Caribbean music has led to the assumption that it is 'derived from the Bhojpuri region' from which most of the Indo-Caribbeans came (Manuel, 1998: 26). Yet the dhantal's provenance is mysterious and its putative Bhojpuri origin is but one of several hypotheses. Similar idiophones under the generic names of kartal and manjira abound in north India, but nothing precisely like the dhantal is seen. Caribbean commentators have thus pressed for an autochthonous origin theory, finding the dhantal's origins in objects used in quotidian plantation life, including rods used to yoke oxen, horseshoes, and cooking implements (Ramnarine, 1998: 6).

Despite romantic desires to see it as an 'ancient Indian instrument which has been held in the biogenetic memory of Indian-Caribbean populations', there is as yet no evidence to prove 'whether the first migrants brought the dhantal with them, or whether they and their descendents [*sic*] only started to play this instrument in the Caribbean' (Ramnarine, 1998: 8). In a testimony from 1910, we hear that the original migrants went home from the cane fields to sing to 'sitar', 'sarangi' and 'majeera', but that they did not (as yet) have the dhantal with them (Mahabir, 1985: 58). At any rate, this testimony reveals an early establishment of the dhantal within music for recreation (see also Mohkamsing, 2013). This function of the dhantal, together with its non-ascribable origins and incorporation within Indo-Caribbean music, is what leads me to theorize, through it, the irreverent sound of diaspora – an irreverence that also compels us to think seriously about the interruptive power of pleasure and happiness within the capitalist machine of the plantation.

AN IRREVERENT SOUND

It is with this broader intention that I draw on Afro-Caribbean-based understandings of the resistive potential of rhythm within the plantation as repressive space in order to speculate on the dhantal's 'irreverence'. The title of my article immediately raises the question, and that is, irreverence towards what? A partial answer is suggested in my subtitle: 'off-beat as the time of indenture' (in course of the paper I will unpack its full significance). The ruptured genealogy of the dhantal is sonically reproduced in its persistent 'dhin-CHAK' sound, which fills the space in between the dominant beats of the tala, or the rhythm cycles which structure all Indic musical compositions. That is, the dhantal marks not the beats that mark out the division's constituent of each tala, but the off-beat. In Indo-Caribbean music, the most common talas used are eight beats (kaharva, e.g. dha-gi-na-ti-na-ka-dhin-na) and seven beats (e.g. dha-dhi-na-dhi-na-dhi-na). It is the dhantal's job to sound out the gaps between the sounds these vocables ('theka') represent, and which would typically be marked out by the major percussion instrument – the tabla, or, in the case of chutney or baithakgana, the dholak).

Not only that the dhantal can attain a level of loudness greater than the instruments keeping the beat but also the insistent sounding of the off-beat, by an instrument that would be categorized, like the maracas or the guiro, as 'minor percussion', contains the sound of irreverence. The tala demands fidelity and precision to its constituent beats. The dancer, listener, singer or musician does not dodge the tala in quite the way as African-derived rhythm systems invite us to do. Rather, we are schooled to find the dominant beats and inscribe them on our bodies by clapping our thighs or using our thumbs to count the grooves on our fingers in time to the pattern we discern. When the beat corresponding to the start of the cycle – the sam – is reached, we mark that recognition as the commencement of the cycle with a decisive body movement, such as a diagonal upward sweep of the head or the hand. This is the kinetic hegemony of tala that the dhantal subverts.

The dhantal's irreverence is directed towards tala's twin demands: congruence of kinetic expressivity with the beat, and kinetic acknowledgment of the som as the pinnacle of rhythmic satisfaction. This almost mystic convergence of semiosis, kinesis and rhythm is well illustrated in, for instance, Nusrat Fateh Ali Khan's rendition of the qawwali, *Haqq Ali* where the voice meanders through vocables mingling percussive and melodic patterns to arrive without fail on the sam with the word, 'haqq' (truth). It is not the place here to demonstrate the play with resistance and hegemony that the great Nusrat Fateh Ali Khan achieves through his mastery of the sufi genre of qawwali; but I do want to contrast this mode of asserting 'truth' through rhythm to the alternative possibilities that reside in evading the beats leading to the som, that are sounded in the dhantal. In this assessment of sonic alternatives we need to move from the formal to political levels implicit in the dhantal's irreverence towards the tala. A metonymic broadening out of the dhantal's sound enables us to consider an assortment of irreverent practices which that sound participates in historically and in the contemporary moment. Methodologically, it requires moving between diaspora and homeland, between the indentured and colonial past and the postcolonial, post-indentured moment, and between the contemporary national public spheres of Caribbean nations with Indo-populations, and India itself.

THE BHOJPURI LEGACY

The lever that allows this movement back and forth across space and time is the Bhojpuri language world, which also was, and is, a kinaesthetic world. The Bhojpuri region, straddling two post-independent states of India (Uttar Pradesh and Bihar) produced a globally-dispersed language that cannot be recognized qua 'language' thanks to the nationalist pressure of Hindi (and Urdu)[4] and whose marginalization is also implicit in the absence of a place-name, 'Bhojpur' corresponding to the adjective 'Bhojpuri' despite this region having given the world, through the outward migrations of its people, an expressive, exhilarating dance and music repertoire. Bhojpuri transoceanic migration through the routes of indentured labour has been accompanied by migration to Indian cities before and after independence. This migratory profile of Bhojpuri identity has left its trace in the lyrics and mood of song genres such as the biraha and the bidesiya whose formulaic expressions of separation and longing, pressed through the sieve of Bollywood song, have arguably given rise to a coded vocabulary of melancholia for post-Partition South Asians as much as traumatized indentured labour communities.

Some work on the 'affective trajectory' of the emotion known as 'viraha' (separation – Sanskritized rendering of 'biraha') is slowly putting together the pieces of this affective puzzle (Sangari, 2011: 256-87).[5] What still demands attention, however, is the 'happiness effect' of this rhythmic repertoire, and the insistent marginalization

[4] On biraha, bidesiya, and other folk song genres, see Scott Marcus (1987): 93-113; Catherine Servan-Schreiber, 1999; Arya, 1968; and Edward O. Henry, 1988.

[5] See the lyrics in George Grierson, 1886 a: 196-246 and 1886 b: 207-67; Henry, 1988; Marcus 1987 and Arya, 1968.

of this effect by nationalist impulses in colonial and postcolonial India. The explicit and ribald content of Bhojpuri song lyrics, drawing attention to female sexual pleasure, breasts and pubic hair, male and female genitalia, amorous kissing and embracing, and transgressive sexual desire is accompanied by dance styles that, unlike 'classical Indian dances', centre on the Bakhtinian lower body realm of the pelvis and movements on the off-beat.[6] Cross-dressing figures such as the *launda* (boy dressed as and dancing like a woman) embody the alternative subjectivities that flourish in this rhythm world.[7] These were the subjectivities that, like the devadasis (temple dancers), paraiyars (low-caste drummers from south India) and a whole host of other non-elite groups, marginalized by both caste and class, were written out of an anti-colonial nationalism which shaped the present through its dream of an ancient past achieved via a trajectory of Sanskritization (Soneji, 2011; Arun, 2007: 81-104; Morcom, 2013).

The aspirational Brahmanism that this process sanctioned has left its mark on the soundscapes and kinetoscapes – from the 'classical' to Bollywood – deemed acceptable to the nation's elite

[6] See the lyrics in George Grierson, 1886 a.: 196-246 and 1886 b: 207-67; Henry, 1988; Marcus, 1987 and Arya, 1968.

[7] On the *launda*, see, Henry, *Chant the Names of God*, p. 196: 'a launda (female impersonating dancer and singer) . . . may dance opposite a male dancer playing a male role . . . the launda is a young man who has learned how to look and move like a woman. His coiffured hair has been allowed to grow to a suitable length, or he may wear a hair-piece. He wears a padded brassiere and all the garments and jewellery worn by a well-dressed village woman, including ear and nose rings, hair ornaments . . . and the choli, sari and underskirt. He knows how to beautify his eyes, lips, finger and toenails, and feet. He sings with a peculiar timbre, a falsetto which is intended to represent a woman's voice . . . the laundas' performances range from pleasantly sensual to lewd. The launda circles and turns with gyrating pelvis, often one hand on his hip and the other behind his head. He might also lean back with his bent legs spread and arms in the air, jerk towards his leering, slightly crouched and pelvis-thrusting partner, with hand at crotch level motions with his upraised thumb. At low-caste gatherings women sometimes cluster near or around the band and dance with other women, or rarely, male kin, in this style.'

(Chakravorty, 2000-1: 108-19; Tewari Jassal, 2007: 5-40). The accompanying marginalization of Bhojpuri rhythm culture within postcolonial India, and that culture's survival and development of fresh forms of irreverent self-expression, is a story being explored by anthropologists and ethnomusicologists. This work fits into a larger body of scholarship on rethinking the creation of dominant cultural forms in India through the selective mobilization and appropriation of some groups' music and dance traditions (Henry, 1988: 196; Soneji, 2011; Arun, 2007; Morcom, 2013). There is inevitably an interest too in how the technologies of sound reproduction, processes of globalization, and economic deregulation in India enable those groups, such as the consumers and producers of Bhojpuri rhythm cultures, to propagate the sounds and moves of their own irreverence towards elite and urban hegemonies. (Manuel, 2012: 223-36; Vishal Rawlley, 2007; Tripathy, 2012; Fernandes, 2012).

SONIC SUBALTERNITIES

The dhantal's irreverence, as manifested in its off-beat, is a sonic clue towards the recovery of subaltern histories of resistance and difference that have been elided through the creation of master narratives of 'Indianness'. Nowhere is this more evident than in the coming together of Brahminical asceticism towards the body, Gandhianaskesis, and the persistent valourization of celibacy through the figure of the 'Brahmacharya'. As Sanjay Srivastava notes, 'this (Gandhian-brahmacharya) sexual landscape – or rather a landscape where sexuality is an unspoken spectre – is only one of many social topographies, and a fuller picture must include other, 'little' traditions that are too frequently regarded as aberrations' (Srivastava, 2004: 15; Chatterjee, 2012: 945-62). In retrieving, through the dhantal, the sound of the off-beat, often silenced by the Sanskritization that tala performs, we also retrieve what these aberrant 'little traditions' may sound like. But the dhantal also makes us move to new temporalities of indenture. It exploited the off-beat to sound out indenture's 'in-between time' – to borrow and extend a concept articulated by Homi Bhabha (Bhabha 1994).

Indeed, Sudesh Mishra's work on the radically interruptive significance of 'girmit' for capitalist temporalities and subject-formation helps us extract the full philosophical valence of the dhantal's offbeat as the 'in-between time' Bhabha offers as the site for the emergence of new postcolonial subjectivities. 'Girmit' is the Bhojpuri rendition of the English word 'agreement'; while 'agreement' described the process of indenture, 'girmit' was how the indentured labourers (girmitiya) appropriated and transformed the capitalist normativity of the word. To Mishra, 'it is not time but being itself that is expended in the five or ten years of indentureship, leading to the eventual transformation of the desiring subject into a traumatised body' (Mishra, 2005: 15-36). And yet, in girmit forms of play and sociability, 'new and emergent forms of association', unimaginable outside the interruptive moment of girmit emerged. Mishra uses photographs of tazia processions in Fiji to argue for these counter-social formations that, like the tazia itself, came into being through the labour of workers outside of the plantation economy. These processions took place around the Muslim festival of Muharram where the tazia is a delicate and decorative structure constructed out of bamboo and paper.

The paper and bamboo tazia and its attendant processions offered a flexible expressive repertoire that covered 'religious celebration, aesthetic performance, immoral revelry and political insurrection', (Mishra, 2008: 71-94) its 'short-lived nature' epitomized the potential for 'a more enduring arrangement along the same lines' (81). Nevertheless, this radical potentiality did not pass into the actuality of post-indenture social formations, which, according to Mishra, ultimately capitulated to the pressures of bourgeois capitalist time. The dhantal's irreverence is the sonic equivalent to the tazia's flexible expressive repertoire (Mishra, 2008: 86) but it also unfreezes the moment captured by the tazia and then the photograph as its remnant. The off-beat that repeats the interruptive moment ad infinitum performs and memorializes an immanent counter-history based on counter-economies of pleasure on the plantation. This counter-reading exemplifies what has been recently articulated as 'a postcolonial ekphrastic methodology', or the freeing of reified historical moments through postcolonial readings that would return the frozen moment to a new historiographic dynamism (Brock, 2011: 102-45).

TEMPUS INTERRUPTUS

Sudesh Mishra ends his evocative ruminations on the girmit's subversion of capitalist temporality with a return to the sound of the word as it forms in the labourer's mouth:

> As *girmit* emerged from the sense of an apocalyptic betrayal (after Vijay Mishra) of a general intentionality for a time positive, hence its general applicability as a sign for all that occurred in its aftermath, so the *girmitiya* came into being as the subject of *girmit*, as that being whose beingness was fired in the furnace of a terminated intentionality. There was no *girmitiya* before the time of *girmit*, no self-nominating subject with a name that induced a host of affects while designating an era, an odyssey as well as an ordeal, no subaltern agent with a reproof so tellingly mutated on the tip of the tongue and so marvelously expelled from the back of the throat that its very echo – sublime, guttural, and spondaic – constitutes an entire inexhaustible archive. (Mishra, 2005: 31)

What is so compelling about the dhantal's off-beat *tempus interruptus* is that it, too, is a sound created through the resisting body whose infinitive iterativeness can actualize the potential that Mishra finds lost with the cessation of the diaspora's tazia processions. 'It is all the fault of Empire!' cries the magistrate hopelessly in Coetzee's novel *Waiting for the Barbarians*. 'Empire has created the time of history!' (Coetzee, 1980: 146). The off-beat as in-between time encodes the radical subjectivities created by indenture's interdependence of work and play figured on the transhistorical, transoceanic body of the girmit who occupies but also blasts out the 'time of history' that may well have been created by Empire,[8] but

[8] Mishra ends his evocative ruminations on the girmit's subversion of capitalist temporality with a return to the sound of the word as it forms in the labourer's mouth: As *girmit* emerged from the sense of an apocalyptic betrayal (after Vijay Mishra) of a general intentionality for a time positive, hence its general applicability as a sign for all that occurred in its aftermath, so the *girmitiya* came into being as the subject of *girmit*, as that being whose beingness was fired in the

which today is sustained by postcolonial nationalist hegemonies in homeland and in diaspora alike.

---

furnace of a terminated intentionality. There was no *girmitiya* before the time of *girmit*, no self-nominating subject with a name that induced a host of affects while designating an era, an odyssey as well as an ordeal, no subaltern agent with a reproof so tellingly mutated on the tip of the tongue and so marvelously expelled from the back of the throat that its very echo – sublime, guttural, and spondaic – constitutes an entire inexhaustible archive' (Mishra, 'Time and Girmit', 31). What is so compelling about the dhantal's off-beat *tempus interruptus* is that it, too, is a sound created through the resisting body, whose infinitive iterativeness can actualise the potential that Mishra finds lost with the cessation of the diaspora's tazia processions. This counter-reading could exemplify what has been recently articulated as 'a postcolonial ekphrastic methodology', or the freeing of reified historical moments through postcolonial readings that would return the frozen moment to a new historiographic dynamism; see Richard Brock, 2011: 102-45.

REFERENCES

Arun, Joe C. (2007). 'From Stigma to Self-Assertion: Paraiyars and the Symbolism of the Parai Drum', Contributions to Indian Sociology, 41: 81-104.

Arya, Usharbudh (1968). *Ritual Songs and Folksongs of the Hindus of Surinam*, Brill: Leiden: 8-9.

Benítez-Rojo, Antonio (1996). *The Repeating Island: The Caribbean in Postmodern Perspective*, trans. James E. Maraniss, Duke University Press: Durham, NC.

Bhabha, Homi (1994). *The Location of Culture*, Routledge: London and New York.

Brandily, Monique (1984). *Dandtal*, Macmillan: London.

Brock, Richard (2011).'Framing Theory: Toward an Ekphrastic Postcolonial Methodology', *Cultural Critique*, 77.1: 102-45.

Brown, Vincent (2008). *The Reaper's Garden: Death and Power in the World of Atlantic Slavery*, Harvard University Press: Cambridge, MA.

Chakravorty, Pallabi (2000-1). 'From Interculturalism to Historicism: Reflections on Classical Indian Dance', *Dance Research Journal*, 32.2: 108-19.

Chatterjee, Indrani (2012). 'When "Sexuality" Floated Free of Histories in South Asia', in *The Journal of Asian Studies*, 71.04: 945-62.

Coetzee, J.M. (1980). *Waiting for the Barbarians*, Penguin: Harmondsworth.

Fernandes, Naresh (2012). 'Colloquial Music Reflects Changes in Rural Indian Romance', Notes on the World's Largest Democracy: *New York Times*, India Ink. http://india.blogs.nytimes.com/2012/06/20/colloquial-music-spawns-a-culture-of-romance/.

Fryer, Peter (2000). *Rhythms of Resistance: African Musical Heritage in Brazil*. Pluto Press: London.

Gilroy, Paul (1995). *The Black Atlantic: Modernity and Double Consciousness*, Harvard University Press: Cambridge, MA.

Glissant, Édouard (1997). *Poetics of Relation*, trans. Betsy Wing, University of Michigan Press: Ann Arbor.

Grierson, George (1886).'Some Bihari Folk-Songs', *Journal of the Royal Asiatic Society* 16: 196-246.

—— (1888). 'Some Bhojpuri Folk-Songs', in *Journal of the Royal Asiatic Society*, 18: 207-67.

Henry, Edward O. (1988). *Chant the Names of God: Music and Culture in Bhojpuri-Speaking India*, San Diego State UP: San Diego.

Mahabir, K. Noor (1985). *The Still Cry: Personal Accounts of East Indians in Trinidad and Tobago during the Period of Indentureship (1845-1917)*, Calaloux Publications: Tacarigua: 58.

Manuel, Peter (1998). 'Chutney and Indo-Trinidadian Cultural Identity', in *Popular Music*, 17.1: 21-42.

—— (2012). 'Popular Music as Popular Expression in North India and the Bhojpuri Region: from Cassette Culture to VCD Culture', *South Asian Popular Culture*, 10: 3: 223-36.

Marcus, Scott. (1987). 'The Rise of a Folk Music Genre: Biraha', in Sandria Freitag (ed.), *Culture and Power in Banaras: Community, Performance, and Environment, 1800-1980*, University of California Press: Berkeley, 1987: 93-113.

Mishra, Sudesh (2005). 'Time and Girmit', in *Social Text*, 82: 15-36.

—— (2008).'Tazia Fiji! The Place of Potentiality', in Susan Koshy and Radhakrishnan Rajagopalan (eds.). *Transnational South Asians: The Making of a Neo-Diaspora*. Oxford University Press: Oxford: 71-94.

Mohkamsingh, Narinder (2013). 'The Dhantál Enigma', Paper presented at the conference Legacy of Slavery and Indentured Labour, 6-10 June 2013, Paramaribo: University of Suriname.

Morcom, Anna (2013). *Illicit Worlds of Indian Dance: Cultures of Exclusion*, Hurst, London.

Orsini, Francesca (2002). *The Hindi Public Sphere 1920-1940: Language and Literature in the Age of Nationalism*, Oxford University Press: New Delhi.

Ramnarine, K. Tina (1998). 'Brotherhood of the Boat: Musical Dialogues in a Caribbean Context', *British Journal of Ethnomusicology*, 7: 1-22.

Rawlley, Vishal (2007). 'Miss Use: A Survey of Raunchy Bhojpuri Music Album Covers', in *Tasweer Ghar: A Digital Archive of South Asian Popular Visual Culture*, www.tasweerghar.net/2007/vishal/index.html.

Sangari, Kumkum (2011). '*Viraha:* A Trajectory in the Nehruvian Era', *in* Kavita Panjabi (ed.), *Poetics and Politics of Sufism and Bhakti in South Asia: Love, Loss and Liberation*, Orient Blackswan: Delhi: 256-87.

Servan-Schreiber, Catherine (1999). *Chanteurs Itinérants en Inde du Nord: La Tradition Oral Bhojpuri*. L'Harmattan: Paris.

Soneji, Davesh (2011). *Unfinished Gestures: Devadasis, Memory and Modernity in South India*. University of Chicago Press: Chicago.

Srivastava, Sanjay (2004). *Sexual Sites, Seminal Attitudes: Sexualities, Masculinities and Culture in South Asia*, Sage, New Delhi, 15.

Jassal, Smita Tewari (2007).'Taking Liberties in Festive Song: Gender, New Technologies and a 'Joking Relationship', in *New Contributions to Indian Sociology*, 41.5: 5-40.

Tripathy, Ratnakar (2012). 'Music Mania in Small-town Bihar: Emergence of Vernacular Identities', *Economic and Political Weekly*, 67.22: 58-66.

CHAPTER 12

The Role of the Tassa Drum Ensemble in Trinidad and Tobago's Cultural Identity Formation

SATNARINE BALKARANSINGH

Travelling through time and space, the drum has been one of the most visible icons in the development of cultures and civilizations. A drum can be either a hollow cylinder or a kettle or tea-cup-shaped receptacle, over which is stretched a skin of an animal or velum. Its hollow interior provides the acoustic resonance. It is beaten with either a stick or the hand. It can be fashioned out of wood, clay or metal (James Blades, 1970: 104). Drums are used in ritual worship, in festive celebrations and in battle. Their sounds can convey messages over long distances.

The Europeans' encounter with the 'New World' and particularly the Caribbean, in the fifteenth century created a very interesting history of plunder, exploitation, trade, commerce, migration and the transfer of art and culture. In contemporary times, this history plays itself out in various permutations and combinations of socio-economic, geo-political and hence, cultural constructs in the affected countries. The drum has been present in this history of cultural assimilation and integration.

The Republic of Trinidad and Tobago is part of this history of exploitation and migration. Various races have populated it. It inherited several diverse, cultural characteristics, icons and musical instruments, one of which is the percussion instrument of the performing arts, the drum. The drums of Trinbago are many and diverse. They are the gifts of our cross-cultural pollination. They include the maracas (chacchac), sambura and earliest versions of Tambour Bamboo of the first peoples of Kairi (Balkaransingh, 2014: 15-24); the tambourine, castanets, bass drum, timpani and sneer drum of Europe (http://www.drumjourney.com/ world/ index.htm); and the djembe, conga, tumba and bongo of Africa (Ahye, 1978). From Arabia and Syria came the tambourine, also called the doffor duff. The Chinese brought their bass drum (dagu) played with two sticks for their dragon dance. The Indians, in the 72-year period of Indian immigration and continuing migrations to Trinidad, brought a vast array of percussion instruments. These include the dholak, tabla, naal, damru, kartaal, pakhawaj, dandataal (dantāl), dhap, dafri, nagara, khol, majeera, mridangam, tappu,[1] and the Tassa ensemble of dhol, naqqara/nagara, tasha/tassa and jhanj.[2] Trinidad also invented a percussion instrument out of the steel drum, the Steelpan, the only musical invention of the twentieth century (Blake, 1995: 58-65).

After a period, these drums enhanced multiplicities of and even created new vibratory frequencies, rhythms, tempos, and moods within the various rituals, festivals and performative traditions. This family of instruments has established a unique legacy of music in Trinidad and Tobago's cultural landscape. However, none of these drums has been able to consolidate a unique cultural identity while simultaneously welding a common national identity as the Tassa drum ensemble (also referred to as the tassa drums). This paper highlights the unique role of the tassa drumming in Muharram, or the Hosay commemoration, forging an indispensable part of Indo-Trinidadian and national identity in our twin-island State.

[1] Tappu is a tambourine-type (dhap), resonant and loud percussion instrument. It is suspended by a single strap, from the shoulder and played with two sticks of different sizes. Personal observation by author in Trinidad, 2006.

[2] Narsaloo Ramaya (. . .). *East Indian Traditional Music: Art & Culture,* vol .1, no. 3, Trinidad: Trinidad and Tobago Printing and Packaging . Some of these instruments were identified by Ramaya, the rest have been identified by this author through over forty years of primary and secondary research, including interviews and various old photographs in Trinidad.

THE CHANGING CULTURAL LANDSCAPE OF TRINIDAD AFTER THE EMANCIPATION OF SLAVES – INDIAN IMMIGRANTS AND MUHARRAM OR HOSAY

Following the abolition of slavery in 1834, many attempts were made to locate alternative sources of labour for the colonial plantations, which were the mainstay of the territories' economies. The slaves were finally emancipated in 1838. In keeping with the new socio-economic realities and the continuing demands for labour supply on the plantations, but on different contractual terms and conditions of work, the initial triangular slave trade shifted geographic focus from Africa to Madeira, with China and India as the primary sources of labour supply. Madeira and China, to a lesser extent, became the new collection and transhipment ports for indentured labour bound for Trinidad and the Caribbean. Trinidad was then a separate geo-political entity from Tobago. The two were unified for administrative purposes in 1898.

From 1845, Indian indentured immigrants began arriving in Trinidad to work on these plantations. They comprised a cross-section of peoples from various geographic locations in India. They brought a composite of religions, rituals, festivals, performative traditions and other socio-economic values. These represented a rich array of cultural values and lifestyle. However, according to Lloyd Braithwaite's analysis, they were consigned to the lowest rung of the ladder with the free Africans slightly above them in this highly stratified society (Braithwaite, 1975: 34-6). Ironically both these groups shared a common historical encounter of bondage and deprivation, though in a sequential manner.

One of the first major events that the East Indians publicly observed in this new landscape was the observances of the Muharram rituals. The Tassa drumming was an integral aspect of this commemorative event. Masud-ul-Hasan (1987) explains that Muharram is an observance of a series of events that occurred during the month of Muharram within the Islamic calendar. The events ended in the martyrdom of Hussein, the grandson of the Prophet Muhammad (Masud-ul-Hasan, 1987: 158-60). Imam Hussein was ambushed and slain by rival claimants to the fledgling Islamic Caliphate (leadership). He, together with 71 members of his travelling party to Kufa, were ambushed and massacred at Karbala on the banks of the Euphrates River in Mesopotamia (today's Iraq).This event, which occurred in AD 679 is referred to as the Battle of Karbala (Masud-ul-Hasan, 1987). These events happened over a ten-day period in the first month of the Islamic calendar of Muharram, hence the name Muharram. These events continue to generate tremendous passion and have had major implications for religion and the Islamic world. Schisms were created in Islam. Two major sects emerged – Shia and Sunni (Masud-ul-Hasan, 1987; Matthews, David, 2003: 1-9; Korom, 2003: 22-4). The annual observances of this series of events in the month of Muharram in Trinidad came to be called Hosay.

Kelvin Singh, in his book *Bloodstained Tombs: The Muharram Massacre 1884* (1988), notes that during the annual observance of Muharram in Trinidad the mourners in the street processions would shout, 'Hassan', others responding with 'Hussein' (Singh, 1988: 6). These rituals were subsequently referred to locally as 'Hosay'.

While Muharram or Hosay is Islamic in origin, Jaffri (1979) notes that the Muharram or *Ta'zieh* procession in India, 'commands the utmost respect from Muslims and non-Muslims alike'. It later became a pan-Indian celebration, observed by Shias, Sunnis and Hindus alike (Jaffri, 1979: 222-7). As such, it was introduced to Trinidad as an 'Indian thing'. By 1847, just two years after the commencement of Indian immigration to Trinidad, and after the landing of just ten shiploads of 'bound coolies' to the island, totalling 2,637 (Deen, 1994), these indentured labourers had commenced to observe the rituals through public processions. These public processions of Muharram or Hosay included the parade of *Tadjahs* (mausoleums), of the martyrs, Hassan and Hussein venerated by the Shia sect of Islam, on the streets of the town of San Fernando. Tassa drummers accompanied the procession.

An 'Englishman,' commented then in a the newspaper: 'I saw their heathen temple carried on men's shoulders, heard their yelling, witnessed their dancing, gestures and other things connected to their pagan ceremonies. . . .'[3]

The Tassa drumming was not mentioned in that news report even though it was an indispensible feature of the widespread Muharram rituals of Mughal India prior to the 1850s (Sharar, 1975: 140-52). This was more so in the province of Avadh (which the British wrote and pronounced as Oudh or Oude), especially in Lucknow, the capital city. A large number of East Indians came from this region of India. The Tassa drumming within the San Fernando procession would have resulted in the reported 'dancing' in the streets. This public procession, replicated in parts from India, had travelled through the streets of San Fernando to commemorate the Muharram, as the ancestors of the immigrants had done for centuries in the various cities of their homeland of India (Sharar, 1975).

MUHARRAM AND THE TASSA DRUM ENSEMBLE

Muharram

Singh (1988) quoted documentary evidence to show that the Muharram rituals had begun to attract a wide cross-section of the population. The *Trinidad Sentinel* newspaper of 1867 reported that 'Negro involvement in the celebration was also quite evident from the 1850s onwards' (Singh, 1988: 7). The procession comprised Indian immigrants, both Hindus and Muslims (of Shia and Sunni sects) and some Africans. The Muharrram observance was a combination of several distinct yet interrelated events. These comprised the singing of *marsiyas* or dirges, on the martyrdom of the grandsons of Prophet Muhammad, Hassan and Hussein; the playing of Gatka, a martial art of fencing, or mock combat, using long staves (Hakka

[3] The *Trinidad Spectator* and *Port of Spain and San Fernando Advertiser*, Saturday, February 1847, referred to in Brinsley Samaroo's 'The First Hosay, 1847', presented at an international conference on Hosay/ Muharram entitled 'Hosay/Muharram and Cultural Space'. 7-8 March 2008, University of Trinidad and Tobago.

sticks) and shields (Fennas); performance of the acrobatic Banaithe or swirling of sticks around the body, with fire on both ends of the sticks; and the playing of the mesmerising rhythms of the Tassa drums narrating the story of the events of Karbala in AD 679. This ensemble of drums – bass (*dhol*), kettle drums (*tassa*) and cymbals (*jhanj*) – were effectively used to vividly convey the various moods and emotions associated with the actual events at Karbala and the subsequent martyrdom of Hussein and all of the male members of his band of followers. The tremendous impact of this music continues while the other aspects of the Hosay – the Marsiya, gatka, jharoo and banaithe – have all disappeared from the observances today.

As the years progressed, Hosay, with its accompanying tassa drumming became an annual public procession on the streets of many of the towns and villages in Trinidad. The *Port of Spain Gazette* of 1859 carried an article on the procession in Port of Spain (Singh, 1988). It noted that, 'Negroes helped to carry the tazias on their shoulders and some participated in the drumming' (read tassa drumming) (ibid., 1988: 7). The tassa drumming was a peaceful means of welding an Indian and African cohesiveness, albeit temporarily. The initial mistrust that was created within the minds of the Afro-Trinidadians for these new arrivals from India became temporarily diffused during the Hosay commemoration. From the various news reports and opinions, it is clear that the antagonisms continued to be fanned by the ruling classes (ibid., 1988). They wanted to maintain the schism within the races to ensure that the lower working classes forged no alliances, for these could have major socio-economic and political repercussions, deleterious to the future governance of the country and the economy.

However, the message of deprivation and exile contained within the Muharram story and the power and the mood emoted by the music, of both the dirges and the tassa drumming, created and facilitated a common understanding of empathy and identification. Hassan and Hussein's pain related within Islamic religious history became the collective community's transient pain and suffering. This annual temporary togetherness, created by the emotional intent and inherent purpose of the occasion, demonstrated the potential power resident within group dynamics, just waiting to be harnessed and released. New identities were being created, based on the common denominators present, the theme of music and specific rhythms of the tassa drums. The working classes began to forge their new relationships.

THE TASSA DRUMS AND THEIR HISTORY

The exuberance and intoxicating rhythm of the Tassa drum reflecting the essence of the spirit of Trinidad and Tobago, has been captured most fittingly by one of our most famous sons of the soil, Mohammed Pharouk Alladin (1919-80). M.P., as he was affectionately called, is remembered as the 'Guru of painters' of Trinidad and Tobago in modern times. In his poem, 'Hosay Drums', M.P. captures a fleeting moment of his boyhood recollections of the drumming of the tassa ensemble in the Hosay in Dinsley village, Tacarigua where he grew up:

Jhim-Jhim, Jhai!
Jhim-Jhim, Jhai!
Bass drums booming,
Tassas rolling,
Jhanj clashing,
Jhai, Jhim-Jhim Jhai!
Ostads cutting
Ramnarh, Bholai,
Chicklan, Bejai.
Hosay!
Labui at the bass,
Ali Raj with the jhanj,
The boys, foolaying.
Rangtaka-tikki-tang,
Jhai

(Alladin, 1969: 33).

The Tassa ensemble, an assemblage of three north Indian percussion instruments is today a distinct genre of percussion music in Trinidad. It functions as both a stand-alone ensemble and as a rhythmic accompaniment to dance and other orchestration work.

The tassa ensemble usually consists of the dhol or bass, a tassa and a jhanj (Ramaya, vol. 1, no. 3). The dhol, a large double-barrel bass (referred to as base drum or *boom*), the tassa, a smaller kettle drum that provides the rhythmic variations, referred to in Trinidad as the 'cutter' from the Hindi word of *Katna,* meaning 'cutting' (Manuel, Peter, 2000: 10).[4] Then there is the second tassa which provides the 'rolls' or the African-derived '*foolay*' or *fula* sound. The *Fula* or 'foulay'/foule the tempo or laya 'rolling the beats in constant tempo or even accelerating them. The 'foule provides rhythmic variations and "counterpoint"' (Balkaransingh, 2010; Blake, 1995; Manuel, 2000). The dhol maintains this tempo and the cutter provides the variations and flourishes within this rhythmic structure. These drums are accompanied by the *jhanj* or cymbals. The rhythms emanating from the Tassa ensemble are varied, mesmerizing and intoxicating. The texture and tonal quality of the individual instruments are rich and full.

THE TASSA DRUMS IN THE TRINIDAD HOSAY

The Tassa drum ensemble is used to evoke emotions in the celebration of creation, bonding and reproduction, valour and benediction. It is no wonder that the Tassa drum ensemble assumed a position of prominence in the history of the development of Trinidad and Tobago. Today they are an indispensable feature of our rituals, pomp, pageantries, ceremonies and festivities. In fact, it is an ever-present icon in our performative traditions; a metaphor of the Indo-Trinidadian identity and presence, and indeed of the peoples of the cultural rainbow that is our twin island republic. Its language easily evokes the emotion of militancy and rebellion, of battle, victory and jubilation, celebrating bonding and identity as easily as it conveys the agony of pain and despair. Of these the ones most associated with militancy, rebellion, valour, battle and the agony of defeat are the Tassa drums in the annual Hosay observances in Trinidad.

[4] The Hindi verb is *kaatna* – to cut.

HISTORY OF TASSA

These drums have been used individually for centuries in India; the *dhol* for festivity, the tassa for summoning people at large to deliver important messages, or to announce the arrival of some important official or dignitary and as a percussion instrument in festive music.

These drums in Trinidad can be traced back to India. Emperor Akbar, during his reign (1556-1605), had *dhol, nakara* and *jhanj* players, among others, in his royal symphony and travelling entourage. The drums have been a part of the Muharram in India, especially in Lucknow, the former capital of the state of Oudh (Avadh), and later the territories of Avadh and Agra and currently the capital of the Uttar Pradesh. A significant portion of Indian immigrants came to Trinidad and the Caribbean from this area.

The famous essayist, historian and novelist, Abdul Halim Sharar (1860-1926) writing around 1875, on the Tassa instruments and their role in Muharram, both in Lucknow and Calcutta, recalls:

> In Lucknow bands there are usually three or four large dhols and at least one man, though occasionally two or three, beating tashas. There is also at least one man playing the jhanjh cymbals. . . . After the fortieth day of mourning there is a tazia procession in Lucknow known as the Bashu'stazia . . . the tasha players were the most skilled and were always introducing innovations into their music. . . . (Sharar, 2005: 151)

Sharar, who was part of the community that lived with Nawab Wajid Ali Shah after the British rulers exiled him to Calcutta in 1856, recalled:

> What greater proof can there be that the dhol and the tasha were played according to correct principles, than that Wajid Ali Shah, who was an incomparable musician, was an exponent of the art. I have seen him with my own eyes in Matiya Burj, coming out of Asmani Kothi with the procession on the seventh day of Muharram playing tasha which was tied round his neck. Expert singers carrying dhols accompanied him and he was surrounded by his court favourites. He played the tasha with such delicacy and skill that even people who did not understand music applauded him. I have also seen him playing the dhol. (Sharar, 2005: 151-2)

Matiya Burj still exists today in Kolkata.[5] In 1857, India's first war of independence occurred and Lucknow provided the heaviest resistance. After the war, many Indians fled India through the route of indentureship, bringing some meagre belongings, including their drums. As the Moghul Empire was systematically dismantled and its key players and representatives were dispersed to various locations, the Tassa drums accompanied their owners and continued to be used for the purposes for which they were created, in the new environments.

In Trinidad this trend had already begun since 1847 where the tassa drums accompanied the Hosay procession in the streets of San Fernando (Singh, 1988). And thereafter, they accompanied all of the Hosay processions throughout the country – Sangre Grande, Arima, Tacarigua, San Raphael, Tunapuna, Curepe, San Juan, Chaguanas, Princes town, Cedros and St. James.

THE FABRICATION AND PREPARATION OF THE DRUMS AND *JHANJ*

Dhol: The *dhol* is a large, hollow, barrel-shaped and double-mouthed wooden drum, approximately 18-20 inches long and 12-15 inches in diameter. The diameters at the mouths are the same. The mouths are covered with the dried and 'cured' skins of either goat or deer which is tightened with chords running across the outer side of the body. Due to its weight, the dhol or 'boom' is hung across the player's body by a strap going around the back. It is played using both hands. In one hand, a stout stick, the tip of which is wrapped in cloth, and called a *dagga*, strikes one surface, while the other surface (mouth) is hit by the open palm.

Tassa: The Tassa is a miniature kettledrum, the mouth of which is about 12-14 inches in diameter. It is made from either metal, clay or fiber glass. Previously it was made from metal or baked clay.

[5] The Wajid Ali Shah referred to above was the last Nawab of Lucknow (1847-56). A patron of the arts and himself a dancer and musician, he was deposed from office in 1856 by the British rulers and exiled to Calcutta (present-day Kolkata) where he took up residence at Matiya Burj.

Figure 12.1: *Dhol* drummers accompanied by Tassa drummers in procession on the day of Ashura in St James Hosay, Trinidad. The *tadjah* of Gulam Hussein's Hosay is in the background. Photo: S. Balkaransingh, 2006.

Figure 12.2: Tasha/Tassa. Photo S. Balkaransingh.

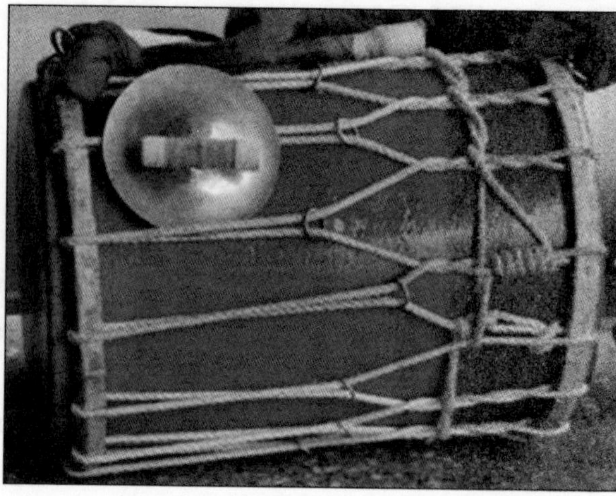

Figure 12.3: One side of a *jhanj* on a dhol or bass drum.

Jhanj: The *jhanj* is a pair of flat, brass or copper plates, approximately six to eight inches in diameter. These plates are heated at high temperatures and when malleable, uniformly sunk in the middle of the plates to produce the required sound when clanged together. The sunken portion is about three inches in diameter. A hole is drilled through the middle of each sunken plate, from which a piece of rope is attached and around which cloth is tied. The cloth pieces are held in each hand of the player and 'crashed' together with varying forces and pressure intensities on different parts of the plates to produce the required acoustic effects and evoke the emotive moods or *rasa*. Today stainless steel plates are being introduced instead of brass ones.

Drum sticks: There are basically two types of drum sticks; one for beating the dhol and the other, a pair, for beating the tassa. In the case of the dhol, the drum stick or *dagga* is locally referred to as the bass stick. It used for beating one side of the dhol. It is made from a stout piece of strong wood, usually from that of a guava tree because of its sturdiness. It can be approximately 12 inches long, giving it reach yet flexibility to strike the middle of the drum skin. The end that hits the skin is capped with cloth tied into the shape of a lawn tennis ball.

The pair of sticks, or *chopes* used for beating the tassa and naqqara respectively is made from thin strips of the *Roseau* shrub. The *Roseau* is preferred because of its spring. The ends of the drum sticks, the sides which hit the goat skin, are tipped with black waxed cloth. The *Roseau* is now a scarce commodity and as such it is being replaced by wild cane, bamboo strips, and now fibre-glass rods, capped with 'masking tape'.

RHYTHMS OF THE TASSA ENSEMBLE

The main method of measuring time in Indian music is called *taal. Taal* is a rhythmic cycle of fixed time-beats. Unlike Western music where the rhythm is linear, in Indian music (vocal and instrumental music and dance) the rhythm is cyclical. Each time-beat within this cycle is referred to as *matras* and can be reproduced through sound syllables called *bols*. The structure of the rhythmic cycle, the *vibhāg*, of each *taal* is clearly demarcated and can be demonstrated through claps (*tālis*) and hand waves *(khāli)* with the most dominant beat being the *Sama*. Each *taal* has fixed permutations and combinations of beats, referred to as *kaaydas* and *relas*. These *kaaydas* and *relas*, fitted within the structure of the *taal*, are learned and performed by the percussionist.[6]

However, in Trinidad today, the *taal* in the *tassa* rhythm comprises a set of distinct metres and ostinati now generally referred to as the 'hands'. While the technical term 'taal' is also used for the respective rhythmic patterns played on the tassa and other percussion instruments, e.g. the dholak, to accompany other types of local Indian music and dance, the term does not conform to the accepted, standard definition of the term 'taal' in north Indian music. This is partly because of lack of formal knowledge of the grammar and syntax of Indian music itself. The Indo-Trinidadian musician, trained locally, by rote, uses different terminologies to describe his technical terms. In the tassa drumming in Hosay, the use of the term 'taal' or '*hand*' conforms more to the folk method of drumming, of *barhti* or *barti,* where the drummer displays his

[6] Personal knowledge of music by the author.

virtuoso by playing intricate patterns, sometimes melodic, sometimes syncopated, within the *taal* or changing the tempo. This is similar to the *laggi* of north Indian music. Ethnomusicologist Peter Manuel explains, 'the tassa rhythms are complex . . . in which the lead cutter player performs flashy improvisations and guides the accompanying players through various rhythmic modulations by means of signal patterns' (Manual, 2000: 10, 30 and 75).

THE TASSA AND HOSAY IN TWENTIETH-CENTURY TRINIDAD

As more indentured Indian workers arrived in Trinidad, the Hosay processions, with their accompanying tassa drumming, grew in communities where workers lived. These areas included Sangre Grande, Cedros, and Chaguanas. Indo and Afro-Trinidadians stood shoulder to shoulder in the street processions, drumming out the various rhythms, enrapt in the solemnity, valour and later the piety of the occasion.

Moreover, the Hosay rituals fostered community involvement and a spirit of estate workers' camaraderie. It also encouraged a competitive spirit amongst workers of the various plantations. Issues involving race and class were subsumed by artistic creativity in tadjah and moon designing, construction and decoration, 'moon dancing' and tassa fabrication and playing. Hosay was used to foster community spirit, solidarity with the Muslims and to consolidate social and cultural identity (Korom, 2003: 100-4). This emerging alliance and the power of the drums were also a cause for concern. Singh (1988) noted that the Hosay processions involving thousands of indentured 'Coolies' and some blacks in the early 1880s, in the town of San Fernando, with their accompanying tassa drumming, created much fear and panic among the ranks of the planters and the colonial administrators (ibid.). It finally led to the famous Muharram/Hosay massacre by the military arm of the government on 30 October 1884. Forty-two buck shots were fired at point blank range; 16 persons were shot dead and more than 80 other persons were injured, according to 'official' records (ibid. 88-9). There are no official records of how many of these injured ones eventually died from their wounds incurred in this dastardly act. While the drums of Hosay were silenced in San Fernando for all times, they continued in other places until the 1970s. Today, they continue to beat out the rhythms of bravery, valour and lament in three different geographic location; the towns of Cedros, Curepe and St. James.

While the Hosay processions and their accompanying tassa drumming have been significantly reduced throughout the country, the gravitas of the occasion where it is still commemorated is kept especially in St. James, while in Cedros it has diminished. Today, it is common sight to witness Indo and Afro-Trinidadians side by side, in one Tadjah procession, completely enveloped and emotionally transported through the different rhythms of the drums. They tell the Muharram story of the deception of ambush, the preparation for battle, the actual battle and the mourning for the dead on the parched desert sands of Karbala. This mood is sometimes juxtaposed when different tadjah processions cross paths. The rivalry of the different groups is intensely played out in the rhythms. The moods emanating from these drum ensembles became tactile. Race issues recede into non-existence. Droplets of sweat flow. The energies of both the drummers and the mourners or *azadars* merge into a composite, pulsating energy. The intensity of the chemistry of the emotions becomes visibly apparent. During these sessions the separate identities of Indian, African, French Creole and other mixed races, whether as performers or onlookers, are subsumed. They merge into a oneness, assuming a unique national identity.

THE TASSA DRUMMING WITHIN THE HOSAY

The tassa drums are still played in Lucknow, for the Sunni tadjah processions, while the nagara still remains the official instrument of the Shia Muharram commemoration of Lucknow.[7] The *taalas* identified in the various 'hands' played in the Hosay in Trinidad

[7] Personal observations of Muharram processions in Lucknow, India in 2007 (Shia and Sunni processions) and Shia procession in 2009.

are basically three; a seven maatraa, an eight maatraa and a ten maatraa taal.[8] The seven beat or *saat maatraa taal*, is variously called *Ropak* (*Ropak*), *Deepchandi* or *Dhamar*, depending on the structure of the rhythmic cycle. While *Ropak* is the seven-beat *taal* *Deepchandi* and *Dhamar* are fourteen-beat rhythmic cycles each with a different rhythmic structure. There are marked differences in the accentuation, and hence, in the cadence and resultant tonal quality and emotion or rasa elicited from each taal. The *bols* for the seven-beat Ropak *taal*, are; *Tin Tin Na, Dhe Na, Dhe Na.* For Dhamar, fourteen beats are *Ka Dhi, Ta Dhi Ta Dha S, Ka Tit, Ta Tit Ta Taa S.* The *bols* for the eight-beat taal, known as *Kaharwataal*, are *Dha Ge Na Te, Na Ka Dhin Na* or variations of the cycle. The ten-maatraa rhythmic Cycle is academically referred to as *Jhap taal* with sound syllables, *Dhin Na, Dhin Dhin Na, Tin Na, Dhin Dhin Na.* Each *taal* has its gradations of *laya* or tempo; slow (*Vilambit*), medium (*Madhya*) and fast (*Drūtl*).

During the Muharram period in St James, the tassa ensembles is played in rehearsals, in the Hosay 'camps' or 'yards' of the Imambaras. They then accompany the processions on the streets for the four days, from the seventh to the tenth day. The tassa is still played in Cedros, the southwestern peninsula of the island, for the same days of the street processions and up to the 'drowning' of the tadjahs on the evening of the day of Ashura.

The different 'hands' played during the Hosay processions, the usage and moods evoked are classified in Table 12.1.

The Kabulkhana hand is played on the night of 'Small Hosay' when the son of Hussein was martyred on the battlefield at Karbala. It was also played on flag night, the day that Hazrat Abass, the person in charge of the security of Hussein's followers, had gone with a (white) flag in his hand, trying to make peace with the army of Yazid. He did this so that he could collect water for the women and children who had been thirsty for the nine days of the siege. In response, his hands were severed from his body. The *Chalta*

[8] Personal observations and confirmations with Trinidadian sitarist/musician Mungal Patasar and Indian musician and vocalist Ram Narayan Jha during the annual Hosay periods between 2008 and 2012.

TABLE 12.1: TASSA HANDS, INTERPRETATION, TEMPO AND USAGE, AND THE EMOTION EVOKED WITHIN THE TRINIDAD HOSAY/MUHARRAM

Name of Hand	Trinidad Interpretaiton of Hands	Tempo and Usage	Mood & Emotion evoked (rasa)
Kabulkhana	Drum of peace, also called 'dead hand'	Slow; processional for burial ceremony	Sadness, pain, agony, grief (*Karuna*)
Chalta Kabulkhana	Walking Kabulkhana; or 'fine hand'	Slow tempo (*Vilambit Laya*); walking in funerary procession; funeral cortege	Procession of a brave warrior; sad but valiant (*Karuna* & *Vir Rasa*)
Mahatam	War hand; war drum	Fast tempo (*Drūt Laya*); battle rhythm	Valour, aggression, conflict (*Rudra*)
Nabi Sarbat	Burial hand	Slow or funerary tempo (*Vilambit Laya*)	Lamentation, grief, (*Karuna*)
Teen chopa also called *Taachopa*	Sad hand; drum of sorrow (some call it drum of peace)	Brisk, lively; Jubilant; post-Karbala	Valour

Source: Prepared by Satnarine Balkaransingh through interviews between 2006 and 2010 from Abdool Karate (b.1929), Ameer Ali, Fareed Ali, Raiaz Ali and Darryl Merani of St. James Hosay 'yards' and Barboi Ganpat, Charitar Sinanan (b.1919) and Reish Baboolal of Cedros.

Kabulkhana or the marching drum is symbolic of movement; slow but valiant, fearing no one.

As the conflict with his enemies ensued and heightened, Hussein went into battle with his enemies. The rhythm and tempo shifts to the war hand, battle rhythm, or *Mahatam.* When it is realized that Hussein is no longer alive, the scene gives rise to grief, sorrow and lamentation. The *teen chopa* is performed. This tempo, according to master drummer Ameer Ali of the Gulam Hussein Yard, then shifts to the *Nabisarbat* or funerary hand (Ameer Ali, P.I., 2008-

10).[9] In St James on the day of Karbala, the last or tenth day of the mourning rituals, the *Nabisarbat* is played. This does not mean that the other hands are not played on a daily basis on the streets, but the main hands are those identified in the appropriate order.

Ameer Ali also indicated that some of the Hosay drummers in St James also allude to another hand, the *Tikora* or *Dingolay.* This is a locally named 'wedding hand'. It is a lively rhythm, played on festive occasions. Ali explained that the rhythm here is more jubilant. This 'hand' is played when the procession of moons and tadjahs are returning from prayers on the grounds of the Queens Royal College, back to their respective *chowks* for dismantling and eventual immersion into the sea (Ameer Ali, P.I., 2008). Other conventionalists and purists however discredit this 'hand' within the Hosay context, given the mood of the occasion. This view was also reaffirmed by Nawab Jafar Mir Abdullah by his public pronouncements in 2008, at an international Hosay conference in Trinidad[10] (Abdullah, 2003). The purists refer to another hand, the *Kalinda.* This hand is named after the martial art of the African stick fighters, an integral aspect of the annual pre-carnival celebrations. It is a marshal tempo, played, according to Ali when there used to be the chanting of marsiya in St. James (Ameer Ali, P.I. 2008).

In St James, the *Kabulkhana* and *Chalta Kabulkhana* rhythms were played when the elegies (marsiyas) were sung during the street parades of the tadjahs, during the Hosay procession. This rhythm is done in a slow speed (*Vilambit laya*). In Cedros, the drummers refer to two additional hands; the *nagara* and *tilana,* 'played after

[9] Ameer Ali [Personal Information (P.I.) during the Hosay periods of 2008-10]. Ali was the elder of the Asgarali Lineage of Gulam Hussein Hosay 'Yard' St. James, Trinidad.

[10] Jafar Mir Abdullah Nawab of Sheesh Mahal Lucknow, in March 2003 in San Fernando, Trinidad, spoke against any type of jubilation, or happy mood during this observance given the nature of the rituals and the grief associated with it. His pronouncements were made publicly both at the International Conference entitled 'Hosay/Muharram and Cultural Space' on 7-8 March 2008 held under the aegis of the University of Trinidad and Tobago. He also repeated this position on radio and television talk shows during his stay in Trinidad in 2003-8.

a messiah was sung' (Baboolal, 2006: 11). As a matter of fact, all the hands (five) are played on the streets in St. James on each of the four main days.[11]

Notwithstanding the views expressed by various individuals on Hosay drums, it is clear that during the Hosay procession the purity of the tassa vibrations transcends space, time, religious affiliations and class consciousness. These periods of musical engagements, even though for a few hours annually, evoke intense empathy. They become cathartic moments for the mourners, spectators, and participating drummers alike. There is a temporary psychic and psychological release from the constant pressure of daily life and the maintenance of the social status quo. After the Muharram period is over, the 'tension strings' of the tassas and Dhols are relaxed and slackened. Together with the Jhanj, the drums are hung up, to be used for the next year's Hosay. In Cedros, however, the forty days (Chihilum) Hosays (tadjahs) are built and processions are observed. Many of the St. James practitioners, especially the drummers, journey to Cedros annually to join their southern neighbours to participate in their road processions for Chihilum.[12]

OTHER DRUM 'HANDS' OF TASSA

While this paper deals mainly with tassa drumming in Muharram, there are two distinct patterns of tassa drumming; one for the commemorative Hosay or Muharram and the other for festive occasions. Tassa drummers identify five Hosay 'hands' and five festive 'hands'. The festive hands are used as indispensible aspects of weddings and other celebrations. They are heard on three consecutive days of a Hindu wedding; these are for the *matikor*, the *lawa*, the welcome (*milan*) of the groom's party and the farewell ceremony of the bride and groom. They then become part of the

[11] A.I. with Raiaz Ali on 24 May 1908. He confirms the rhythms and the order of precedence.

[12] Author's personal observations and interviews with members of the street audience and practitioners/drummers of St. James Hosay on 29 February 2008 in the Cedros 40-day Hosay rituals.

welcoming music for the bride and groom at the groom's home, following the wedding ceremonies. The rhythms of this drum ensemble change in accordance with the existing mood of the occasions. Today they are an indispensible feature of weddings, functions and major national celebrations.

Tassa drums have also been identified with the island-wide Ramleela celebrations whose genesis goes back to over one hundred and twenty-five years. The drum hands are used to highlight and convey the different emotions and moods being dramatized within the story of the epic. These include love, pleasure, celebration, hate and anger, war and battle, valour, mourning and compassion. These emotions transcend issues of race, creed and ethnicity. They are universal moods of humanity and as such all peoples can identify with them, irrespective of race, religion, class or social status.

RECOMMENDATIONS AND CONCLUSION

Tradition *vs.* Modernity in Tassa Drums Preparation

There are those who still maintain the traditional form of drum preparation – of skins, ropes, rings, and deer strips. However, the hemp ropes have been replaced by synthetic ones and the iron rings have changed to brass ones. The brass prevents the previous rusting and eventual bursting of the ropes during the process of stretching in the 'tuning' ritual. Today the 'kettle' superstructure of some tassa and nagara drums are still made from baked clay and to a lesser extent, metal, but there is a growing prevalence of fibreglass skeletons, covered with plastic, snare 'skins'. The synthetic 'plastic' skins are tuned by tightening nuts and bolts, instead of by the previous, small, open flames. The synthetic drums are also played with sticks using plastic tips. While the fibreglass drums with plastic coverings are lighter and less expensive, and less fragile, the texture and tonal quality (according to experienced tassa players) are not as rich as that of the original clay or metal and skin. There is the claim that quality and originality are being sacrificed on the altar of modernity. But the 'innovators' argue for the longevity and readiness of the instrument for performance, as no open flame fire is required to 'tune' the skin, just some tightening of nuts and bolts. Moreover the drum skin is not as easily susceptible to sudden bursting and tearing, which is a feature of the 'animal'-skin drums.[13]

The tassa ensemble has, since its first introduction in the Trinidad landscape, captured the spirit and imagination of both its performers and listeners. With the introduction of Muharram in Trinidad in 1847, the Indian immigrants had unwittingly started painting their indelible presence on the socio-cultural landscape of their new country of domicile. They had begun to establish a separate, though unique, identity interweaving it within a new national identity. This has continued over 167 years, in an unbroken chain. Not even the two world wars – which disrupted the other major public event of Carnival – interfered with the unbroken commemoration of Hosay and its tassa drums on the island. The tassa drums in the St. James, Cedros and Curepe Hosays are played by anyone who comes to participate in the ritual – Indians, Africans, and mixed races and both males and females. These drums are also played in the carnival masquerade bands and street processions, in parties and on almost all major public and private festive occasions. It remains a symbol of freedom and unity. It is a reminder of a common past of bondage and deprivation. The drum rhythms continue to provide the release from the deep-seated psychological bondage of a past of slavery and indentureship. This continuously goes back to the theme of deprivation running through the Hosay narrative and transcends issues of race, creed and religion. Moreover, the hypnotic qualities of the tassa rhythms speak a unique language, mesmerizing its audiences with the various emotions and flavours (*rasas*). It evokes the spirit of the story of the events of Muharram, constantly reinforcing cultural and religious identity. The spirit of the tassa drums constantly renewing the

[13] 'Mere Dash awards for five' *Sunday Guardian* Trinidad. 12 July 2009: P, B7. One of the plastic tassa-drum makers and performers of Trinidad is Vijay Rambir who has used his plastic drums extensively at home and abroad, performing with carnivalist Peter Minshall in his stage production to commemorate the bombing of Hiroshima in Japan during World War II.

collective common identities of the peoples of multicultural Trinidad and Tobago while simultaneously transcending issues of race, creed, religion and social status.

REFERENCES

Ali Mir Ahmed (n.d.). *Husain: The Saviour of Islam.* New York: Anjumane Aza Khana-Azhra.

Ahye, Molly (1978). *Golden Heritage: The Dance in Trinidad and Tobago.* Trinidad: Heritage Cultures Limited.

Alladin, M.P. (1980). *In Memory of Mohammed Pharouk (M.P.) Alladin (1919-1980*). Port of Spain, Trinidad.

—— (1969). 'Hosay Drums'. *The Monstrous Angel – Forty Poems*.

Balkaransingh, Satnarine (2014). *Kunuwaton: Culture and Cuisine of the Santa Rosa First Peoples of Arima, Kairi, Trinidad,* Arima Trinidad: Santa Rosa First Peoples, 15-24, http://www.drumjourney.com/world/index.htm.

Balkaransingh, Satnarine (2010). 'Trinidad Space Speaking through Indo-Trinidadian Rituals and Festivals: 1990-2009', Unpublished Ph.D. thesis, University of Trinidad and Tobago.

Blades, James (1970). *Percussion Instruments and Their History.* London: Faber & Faber.

Blake, F.I.R. (1995). *The Trinidad and Tobago Steel Pan: History and Evolution.* Port of Spain: Published by Author.

Braithwaite, Lloyd (1975). *Social Stratification in Trinidad: A Preliminary Analysis.* Kingston: ISER UWI.

Deen, Shamshu (1994). *Solving East Indian Roots in Trinidad.* Trinidad: H.E.M. Enterprises.

Forrest, G.W. (2006). *A History of the Indian Mutiny: Reviewed and Illustrated from Original Documents,* vol. III. New Delhi: Asian Educational Services.

Jaffri, Syed Hussein Ali (1979). 'Muharram Ceremonies in India', in Peter J. Chelkowski (ed). *Taziyeh: Ritual and Drama in Iran,* New York: New York University Press and Soroush Press, 222-7.

Kippen, James (2005). *The Tabla of Lucknow: The Cultural Analysis of a Musical Tradition.* Delhi: Manohar, p. 4.

Korom, Frank (*2003*). *Hosay Trinidad: Muharram Performance in an Indo-Caribbean Diaspora.* Philadelphia, Penn.

Manuel, Peter (2000). *East Indian Music in the West Indies: Tân Singing, Chutney and the Making of a Caribbean Culture.* Philadelphia: Temple University Press.

Masud-ul-Hasan (1987). *History of Islam (Classical Period 571-1258 CE)*, vol. 1, Lahore Pakistan: Islamic Publications Ltd.

Matthews, David (2003). *The Battle of Karbala: A Marsiya of Anis.* Delhi: Rupa and Co.

Ramaya, Narsaloo. *East Indian Traditional Music. Art & Culture*, vol. 1, no. 3. Trinidad: Trinidad and Tobago Printing and Packaging.

Sharar, Abdul Halim (2005 [1975]). *Lucknow: The Last Phase of an Oriental Culture.* Trans. and ed. E.S. Harcourt and Fakhir Hussain, New Delhi: Oxford University Press.

Singh, Kelvin (1988). *Bloodstained Tombs: The Muharram Massacre 1884.* London: MacMillan Caribbean.

CHAPTER 13

The Mike Men of Trinidad: Cultural, Social and Political Influences

PRIMNATH GOOPTAR

Traversing the tiny Caribbean island of Trinidad is a group of East Indian music lovers referred to as traditional DJs but better known as 'mike men'. They are cultishly fanatical about their airborne amplification systems, which are seen on the hoods of automobiles. Each mike car has two mega-horns amplifying music that can be heard miles away. Those enormous portable air raid warning megaphones are attached to the roof of the automobile with a hood rack system. The mike system consists of a record player, an amplifier, two horns or funnels, horn drivers, the microphone, a motor vehicle battery, a backup battery, an automobile hood rack and 78-RPM vinyl records.

ORIGINS OF THE MIKE MEN IN TRINIDAD

Early amplifier systems with small horns attached were brought into the country primarily for home usage. By the 1920s, larger wooden box systems were used to amplify sounds in public gatherings. The first horn-mike system was imported into Trinidad in the 1930s, but there was limited public usage (Ramdeowar Ramjattan, personal interview, recorded 14 February 2008. St. Augustine). However, with improvements in the systems, by the 1940s, their public use increased and the mike men became popular as 'announcers', used to amplify voices and songs. Those mike systems were considered 'loud and noisy instruments' because of the sheer power with which they blasted sound all around. People

Figure 13.1: Mike System bolted on to hood of motor vehicle, Trinidad. Personal photograph by author, 2010.

in the country had not, up till then, experienced such high levels of sound in public spaces and many, particularly from the wealthy and upper class, considered the instruments a public nuisance (Nanlal Ramcharan, personal interview, recorded 8 April 2009, Sangre Grande). They often objected to the loud mike system in public spaces and as a result, there was limited public use of such systems in the early days of its introduction into the country. However, by the late 1940s, the mike men found a niche in the market among East Indians and mike systems became popular at Hindu weddings and other East Indian events (Dolly Mahabirsingh, personal interview, recorded 22 March 2010, Rio Claro).

Until the mid-1950s, Hindu weddings were all-night affairs starting at 6 p.m. and ending at 6 a.m. the next morning. After 1955, the Hindu night weddings were phased out due mainly to disturbances that occurred during the wedding ceremonies. Those disturbances were sometimes violent. By the late 1960s, such weddings took place during the daytime, usually on a Sunday (Balliram Ramoutar, personal interview, 30 April 2009, Couva).

Entertainment at Hindu weddings before the 1950s consisted

largely of classical singing and dance dramas which lasted through the night.[1] There were no sound amplification systems available in those early years, and singers and actors in the dance dramas strained their voices to the maximum to be heard over the often noisy and boisterous wedding attendees. Wedding affairs then were open events and everyone in the village attended, even if not invited. With the advent of mike systems in the country, Hindu wedding hosts employed the mike men to amplify the voices of the local Indian classical singers and the dance drama personnel. Most mike systems came with one microphone, which was passed from one person to the other.[2] This amplification of sound at the Hindu wedding was a novelty for East Indians and the popularity of the mike man gradually spread among members of the East Indian community (Ramjattan). As his popularity grew in the wedding gatherings, he was commonly referred to as 'the mike man' because his main purpose for being at the weddings was to use the microphone to amplify the voices of actors and singers. Hence, due to regular use and for quick reference, the term microphone was shortened to 'mike'. John Jagroopsingh indicated that as the mike man arrived at locations where he played, members of the public were heard to remark 'the mike man reach', 'look the mike come', 'the mike passing (meaning, going by)', all in reference to the man with the microphone (John Jagroopsingh, personal interview, recorded 26 April 2013, San Raphael). In time, the operator of the microphone became known as the 'mike man'. The term 'mike man' passed into common usage and came to refer to the operators of the horn amplifier systems. Before long, the term 'mike' also came to refer to the large horns or funnels placed on the hood of automobiles and people pointed to the horns when referring to the mike. Thus, the term 'mike' which firstly referred to the microphone, came to refer to the horns and later to the entire system. The term 'mike man' which originally referred to the man who

[1] These dance dramas were classified as dances but were replete with dialogues, singing and dancing.

[2] Ramjattan explained that the one-microphone-system was largely because of the high cost of the microphones.

handled the microphone, came to refer to the owner of the mike system (Partap Sitahal, interview, recorded 22 March 2013, Brazil Village, Arima).

Randy Kissoon, president of the Mike Men Association (2012-13) said that every mike man gave his mike system a name. The names were written on the inside of the wide end of the horns and were supposed to reflect power and dominance of the owner. For example, 'names such as Dosti, Rafi, the Dragon, Sher Singh, Son of India, Bollywood, Guns of Navarone, Mount Everest, Janglee, Yahoo and Thunder were often seen etched on mike horns' (Randy Kissoon, personal interview, recorded 15 March 2013. Cunupia).

THE MIKE MEN AS INDIAN CULTURAL ICONS

The mike man made his greatest impact on Indo-Trinidadian weddings where he continually played Indian film songs. He played at Hindu, Muslim and Christian weddings and found a niche and in the process became identified with Indian film songs as his main offering (Kelvin Boodoo, personal interview, recorded 5 November 2009, Arouca). John Jagroopsingh, however, pointed out that although he played at various types of events, the mike man's most popular 'stomping ground' was the Hindu wedding.

During the early years of the mike man at the Hindu night wedding ceremonies there were breaks or intervals during the official entertainment programme (which consisted of classical singing and dance dramas) and the mike man made use of these intervals. He seized those opportunities to keep the audiences entertained with Indian film songs played through his mike system, much to the delight of wedding audiences. In this way, he began to popularize Indian film songs at Hindu weddings. East Indians loved the Indian film songs because they were very catchy, rhythmic and melodious and many people enjoyed listening to those songs through the mike systems during the intervals at the wedding nights (Narsaloo Ramaya, personal interview, recorded 5 May 2008, San Juan). Soon, audiences demanded Indian cinema songs for longer intervals at wedding nights and people looked forward to hearing film songs on the mike system during such intervals. Some people went to those night weddings and waited for hours for those intervals when the mike man played Indian film songs. As audience demands for the mike man grew at the Hindu night weddings, he began arriving early and entertained the first arrivals with Indian film songs from as early as 5 p.m. until the classical singers and dance performers took over the entertainment proceedings later in the evening. (Jagroopsingh, personal interview). In addition, he continued playing at intervals during the night. On occasions, at the Hindu night weddings, there were disappointments with the non-appearance of the dance drama troupe or the classical singers and the mike man was asked to fill the entertainment gap. This he did willingly and much to the delight of the fans in the audience. Many people, particularly the wedding hosts, were surprised that the mike man 'carried' the entire wedding night playing Indian film songs which the audiences enjoyed. Doolie Deoraj indicated when the local Indian classical singing sessions and the dance drama performances were in progress, many young people took little interest in them, but it was the opposite whenever the mike man played Indian film songs. Most people remained to hear the 'mike' songs and on special occasions when he played for the entire night, everyone stayed, enjoyed the songs and kept asking for more (Doolie Deoraj, personal interview, 22 March 2010, Princes Town). What started as a stop-gap measure to fill-in for an absent troupe or a group of singers, caught on, and by the early 1960s, the mike man was the preferred form of entertainment at Hindu weddings. The classical singers and the dance drama groups were pushed into the background.

When, by the mid-1950s, Hindu weddings became a daytime affair, usually on a Sunday, there was a vacuum left on the Saturday night between the Friday night *Haldi* ceremonies and the Sunday wedding rituals. The entertainment previously provided on the wedding night was to entertain the *Baratis* (visitors) from the bridegroom's entourage. With the shift in the wedding rituals from Saturday night to Sunday (daytime) many wedding hosts continued the tradition of entertainment for the visiting entourage during the wedding ceremony on the Sunday. However, this was not practical as there were concerns that the entertainment was a cause of disruption of the wedding rituals being performed. For many, a Hindu wedding was an excuse for elaborate entertainment and socialization so more people preferred to pay attention to the entertainment taking place than the wedding rituals (Mahabirsingh, personal interview).

In the initial wedding arrangements pre-1950s, because the wedding was normally held on a Saturday night, certain prenuptial ceremonies (*Haldi*) were performed on the night preceding the wedding which was usually a Friday night. With the shift of the wedding ceremonies to the Sunday (daytime), the prenuptial *Haldi* rituals could have been brought forward to the Saturday night, but most people decided to keep the tradition of the Friday night prenuptial arrangements. This left a vacuum for the Saturday night. Wedding ceremonies among the East Indians were known 'open affairs', and villagers, friends, families and well-wishers assisted the wedding hosts with cash donations or foodstuffs. At the time when such weddings were held at nights, villagers, friends and relatives came to the assistance of the hosts and cooked and fed all the visitors. This continued through the night. When the wedding was shifted to Sunday mornings, wedding hosts kept the tradition of cooking and feeding guests during the wedding day (Sunday). However there were difficulties with concluding the cooking chores on time, especially the preparation of the roti. To resolve the problem the wedding hosts prepared some of the food items during the 'free' Saturday night. Friends and relatives were invited to keep company with the cooks as they prepared food items (mainly roti) for the next day while others prepared various *tarkaries* (vegetable dishes) for cooking the next day. To keep the attendees 'lively and entertained 'people told stories, jokes and danced and sang among themselves. Eventually as the Saturday night gatherings grew, dance-dramas troupes and classical singers were invited to provide entertainment. As the event took on new proportions and people came not just to give company to the cooks, but to enjoy the entertainment, the Saturday night event became hugely popular and came to be referred to as the 'cooking night' (Deoraj Harrikissoon, personal interview, 22 March 2010, Princes Town). Eventually, from the mid-1950s to the late 1980s, the mike man was a popular choice of entertainment at cooking nights, especially in the lower income groups because around that time Indian orchestras had become fashionable in the cooking night circuit but they were a lot more expensive. So what began as entertainment to keep family, friends, well-wishers and the cooks in good spirits during the cooking nights, turned out to be a major event at Indo-Trinidadian weddings (Kissoon, personal interview). Largely, the Saturday cooking night entertainment eclipsed the actual wedding day event as many people preferred to attend the cooking night because of the entertainment value. This was because of the novelty of the mike system, its loud broadcasts and its seeming beacon call to all around that something unique in the entertainment world was taking place at the wedding house. Later, Indian orchestras gradually replaced the mike man at these events, but the orchestras needed the microphones from the mike man for amplification of their singers' voices. In this way, even though the mike man was pushed into the background when the Indian orchestra provided entertainment during the cooking night, he remained a necessary ingredient. In addition, he played Indian film songs during intervals, before the orchestra commenced playing music (usually 5 to 8 p.m.) and after the orchestra completed its entertainment programme (usually after 2 a.m. Sunday morning) and during the wedding day (Kissoon).

The mike man emerged without challenge as the key ingredient in the cooking night and people from near and far gathered at the wedding house to listen to the 'music from the mike'. However, playing the mike at Hindu weddings eventually turned out to be a challenge for the mike man as it grew from entertainment to the timely playing of relevant songs at the event. He learned to be skilled in his selection of appropriate songs according to the time of the night and the ceremonies performed during the several wedding rituals spanning from Friday night through Sunday evening (Hublal Ramkissoon, personal interview, recorded 22 March 2010, Rio Claro). He emerged as the star attraction of the cooking nights and thus became a cultural icon for East Indians.

During the early years of its development in the country the mike man was considered an outcast but but by dint of hard work and perseverance he created a cultural space for himself at the cooking night. Equally, the East Indians' love for Indian film music was a positive reinforcement for the mike man in the creation of a niche in the market. In time, he overcame all obstacles and emerged as an Indian cultural icon because of the music he played.

STOCKS, STARS AND STYLE

Kissoon, stated that 'the mike man played mainly in rural East Indian settlement areas of the country' and 'his stock in trade was Indian film songs played from 78 RPM vinyl records imported from India'. Correspondingly, Ramkissoon pointed out that the mike man's favorite Hindi film playback singers included Mohammed Rafi, Lata Mangeshkar, Hemant Kumar, Mukesh, Asha Bhonsle, Mahendra Kapoor, Manna Dey and Talat Mahmood. He went on, 'the mike man had a huge number of records (literally running into the hundreds) which he took to the cooking night and other functions'. At the wedding house (as with other locations where he played), the mike man was the centre of attraction. The celebrity status accorded to him created a stir among audience members at cooking nights and many felt compelled to become acquainted with the mike man (Ramjattan). Partap Sitahal, a mike enthusiast and avid cooking-night follower, remarked:

> There was a certain aura about the mike and the mike man, which caught the attention of audiences. Just to 'see' the mike passing was a huge achievement for many. To be waved at or talked to by the mike man as he passed, was an honor for the average villager as they ran out of their homes to the roadside when they heard the sound of the mike in the distance. He held a special, exalted position in the eyes of the villagers and the audience. From the moment he entered the village on Saturday evening playing his mike to the time he left on Sunday evening, he enjoyed celebrity status among the villagers . . . (Partap Sitahal, personal interview.)

Ramjattan, a mike man for more than sixty years confirmed Sitahal's assertion and added: 'Women ran out with flour (dough) in their hands, as they lined the roadside to see the mike. People waved to us and made us feel special as we passed through the villages. Wherever the mike man played in those days, he was the centre of attention, like a kind of star boy himself. People treated us special' (Ramdeowar Ramjattan, personal interview).

Baliram Ramoutar, a mike man for fifty years, stated that the mike man was the man of the moment at cooking nights and weddings and his wishes were instantly fulfilled by the hosts and those around him (Baliram Ramoutar, personal interview). Sitahal further pointed out that many people wanted to get close to the mike man, to befriend him, talk to him or to request a song. Just being close to him or being in his company was adequate for the average East Indian film music fan. For others, getting an acknowledgment from him, a knowing look or just a simple nod of the head meant a great deal. Sitahal also suggested it was a major talking point to tell their friends they knew the mike man, spoke to him, or requested a song which he played. When a requested song was played, the person requesting the song often hailed out the mike man with a 'thank you mike man', so that everyone present knew that he/she had requested that song. Sitahal recalled spending an entire night sitting next to a mike man, chatting with him and making special requests for songs not only on his behalf, but also on behalf of other friends who channeled their requests to the mike man through him. This was a great achievement for him as he (Sitahal) shared the centre of attention, sitting next to the mike man. Everyone who had an encounter with the mike man felt a sense of importance and this added to the evolving image of the mike man as an icon among the people. In this way the mike man gained in prominence and many sought to create innovations in the manner in which they performed their duties.

As he played at the cooking night there was a certain style, flair and individuality with which the mike man executed his duties. For example, many people admired the dexterity and panache with which he lifted the arm of the record player as he replaced the records on the turntable (Kissoon). However, while the mike man was adept at selecting appropriate film songs for Hindu weddings, he encountered some difficulty in providing the same level of service when he played at a Muslim or Christian cooking night. Both Ramkissoon and Kissoon admitted there were some relevant Indian film songs related to Muslim weddings but limited numbers that were applicable to Christian weddings. This was because most Indian movies focused on Hindu weddings and therefore most of the songs reflected those scenarios. Nevertheless, he played generic wedding songs on those occasions since he had a wide repertoire of Hindi film songs that were general in nature which were loved by all audiences, and he could made up for any deficiencies.

FROM ENTREPRENEURS TO IDENTITY MARKERS

While the mike man began his journey in Trinidad as an entrepreneurs, his mike playing routine assisted in the evolution of East Indian identity in the country. Whether he played his music as a hobby or as hired agent, his impact on East Indians was phenomenal. He came to be identified with playing Indian film music which formed the core of an evolving East Indian identity in Trinidad.[3] He was also hired to perform at several functions such as announcements of Indian movies at cinemas, weddings and Hindu religious occasions where he played mostly Indian film songs.

In the early days of cinema in Trinidad (1900-45) advertisements were usually done using storefront windows, posters at strategic locations, distribution of flyers by hired flyer-boys and newspaper advertisements. Most cinemas were located in urban areas and depended primarily on the walk-in crowd since transportation to and from outlying areas posed severe difficulties in terms of costs and availability at night-time. Before the advent of Indian movies in 1935 East Indians were not known to frequent cinemas. Cinema owners, in an effort to encourage East Indians to leave their comfort zone and attend the cinema in urban areas, sent flyer-boys into the villages to distribute flyers announcing the arrival of a new Indian movie. They left flyers at shops, doctors' offices, schools and other places. In addition, posters were stuck at village shops and other places, but these had limited success since many East Indians could neither read nor write in the English language.

[3] For a comprehensive discussion on this topic see Primnath Gooptar's Ph.D. dissertation 'The Impact of Indian Movies on East Indian Identity in Trinidad', UTT, 2012.

Ramesh Boodhoo, a former cinema owner indicated that cinema owners needed to find a different way to get their messages to East Indians and this was where the mike man made a significant difference (Ramesh Boodhoo, personal interview, recorded 15 May 2008, Sangre Grande).

Beginning in the 1940s, cinema owners exhibiting Indian movies employed the services of the mike man who went into the rural areas to advertise the movies. Boodhoo also indicated that every cinema that exhibited Indian movies had a mike man attached to it. Sometimes, depending on the popularity of the movie and the songs, three or four mike systems were hired by the same cinema to go into the surrounding areas and advertise the movie. The mike man went into predominantly East Indian villages and publicized Indian movies in a manner that no other medium could match. His remit was to attract East Indians to the cinema and this he did creditably (R. Boodhoo, personal interview). Kelvin Gajadhar pointed out that in the same manner in which people ran out of their homes to see and listen to the mike when it came to the cooking night or when it 'carried' the wedding,[4] they came out and stood by the roadside when they heard the 'cinema' announcements (Kelvin Gajadhar, personal interview, recorded 15 March 2013. Couva.) In advertising the Indian movie, the mike man played Indian film songs as a beacon call to attention, then cut into the song still playing softly in the background and spoke of the Indian movie being shown in the nearby cinemas. He drove through the villages very slowly, attracting maximum attention because of the sheer loudness of the music being played. As he drove along he distributed flyers relating to the Indian movie being shown. Many people felt encouraged to attend the exhibition of the movie at the cinema primarily because of the work of the mike man advertising the songs from the movie. In addition, Jagroopsingh pointed out that 'we were eager to hear the mike man play the songs from the movies and this was a great motivation for us to see the movies'. Sitahal added that without the work of the mike man publicizing

[4] 'Carried' the wedding indicates that the mike vehicle led the bridegroom's motorcade to the bride's home.

Indian movies in the villages, cinemas would have been hard pressed to get a decent crowd for Indian movies. He further mentioned that people 'remembered the songs that were played on the mike and it kept "ringing in our minds, ears"; it seemed to cast a spell upon us and until we saw the movie we were not satisfied'. By playing the film songs from Indian movies at several occasions, the mike man unknowingly encouraged the process whereby he was identified with Indian film songs and East Indians began to identify with the Indian film songs. Even as the mike man went about his business earning an income, he unwittingly made a tremendous contribution to the popularity of Indian film songs and the exhibition of Indian movies.

In those early years before the advent of Indian movies, the average East Indian was starved of Indian music and songs. The only source of songs and music for them was the mike man who endeared himself to the villagers with the playing of popular songs from Indian movies whether it was during announcements or at the cooking nights. There was a link between Indian film songs, the mike man and the people. Eventually people associated the mike man with Indian film songs. Later, during the 1950s and the 1960s Indian film songs became an identity symbol for East Indians in Trinidad (Primnath Gooptar, 'The Impact of Indian Movies on East Indian Identity in Trinidad', Ph.D. thesis, 2013, pp. 254-6).

The influence of the mike man also extended to several religious functions among the East Indians, mostly among the Hindus where he also played Indian film songs, but this time his repertoire was limited to religious songs from Indian movies. The cumulative effect of constantly bombarding East Indians with Indian film songs popularized those songs among them in a manner that had not been achieved by the traditional songs that existed in the community. Narsaloo Ramaya argued that largely because of the work of the mike man, Indian film songs gradually replaced traditional folk and religious songs at East Indian events. He noted that the average East Indian had been starved of any new identity connections with India and Indian movies were seen as an identity connection with India. The songs were catchy, rhythmic and 'modern' in the eyes of most East Indians who preferred to listen to the filmi songs rather than the traditional East Indian songs (Narsaloo Ramaya, personal interview).

By the mid-1950s the mike man had also become an indispensable part of the success of major Hindu religious activities in the Indian settlement communities. His contribution was a major input to the success in hosting community *Ramayan yagyas, Bhagwat yagyas*, monthly *kathas* and Ramleela and Phagwa celebrations. In addition, the mike man became a major influence in the success of community sporting events, bazaars and social gatherings. His contributions included announcing the event, providing a microphone for the speakers, such as pundits at religious ceremonies and announcers at sports meetings, and playing music on the occasion. For Hindu religious occasions such as *Ramayan* and *Bhagwat yagyas* the mike man arrived very early, by 5 p.m., at the location and began playing religious songs from Indian films. This, Sitahal suggested, was a wake-up call for villagers, reminding them that the *yagyas* was in progress and would begin very shortly that evening. Many people came early simply to listen to the religious songs played by the mike man (Jagroopsingh).With sports meetings, the mike system was an indispensable part of the proceedings as the announcer kept everyone abreast of what was happening on the field with the microphone supplied by the mike man. This was possible because of the wide reach of the horns and its loudness which could be heard above the noise on the sports ground. In addition, whenever there was a lull in the proceedings the mike man always filled in the gaps by playing Indian film songs (Sitahal).

Wherever he went, up to the 1970s, the mike man was a real star boy; he was the man of the moment, almost given celebrity status. Everyone wanted to know him, to meet him, to talk to him or just to be around him. People in villages where the mike man gave his services talked for days afterwards about meeting him, talking to him, nodding to him or simply listening to the film songs he played. Those who requested songs that he played, talked about the event for weeks afterwards (Kissoon).

SOCIAL IMPACT

While in the early days of his existence the mike man was largely popular among members of the East Indian community. His work was eventually noticed by other sections of the country and he was hired for several other activities including announcements connected with politics and government services. Even though many people considered the mike system 'noisy and annoying', it eventually became the mouthpiece of businessmen, politicians and many government utility services and performed valuable services in times of crisis to get information to the public in a timely manner and many people believed that it was due to the services of the mike man that many crises in the health sector were averted.

With the introduction of party politics in Trinidad and Tobago in 1956, the mike man became an integral part of political campaigns by the various parties. Since then to the present, the election season has been one of the most lucrative times of the year for the mike man (Kissoon). Although it is a short season, every mike system is utilized during an election campaign as candidates try to gain the upper hand over their opponents. Political parties and independent candidates, see the mike man as the best option to get their messages out to the people through 'roving mike announcements' or by using the microphone at political meetings. Usually the mike system remains on the motor vehicle while speakers at political meetings make their speeches on stage using the microphone provided. Often, the candidates were present in the vehicle speaking to the constituents as the automobile traversed the constituency. Again, at those political outings, the mike man played film songs, because that was his stock in trade (Kissoon).

With the introduction of the cassette recorders, and later digital recordings, the politicians no longer needed to sit in the roving mike vehicle and speak to their audience. They simply recorded their message on cassette tapes or CDs and the mike men played the recordings throughout the constituency. In most cases, particularly in the early days of the use of tape recorders, many people did not realize it was a recording and thought it was the candidate who had come to the area with the mike to personally give his message to them. The social and political impact of the mike man was phenomenal as he worked not only in traditional areas but in communities throughout the country. Through him the politicians were able to make contact with the people in an effort to gain their votes at election time (Sitahal).

In addition to politicians, numerous government agencies and businesses regularly made use of the mike man to get their messages out to the people at very short notice. For example, if there was an outbreak of malaria in a particular part of the country and there was a need for an urgent spraying with insecticides, the Ministry of Health, Victor Control Division, utilized the services of the mike man to inform residents of the schedule for spraying in the areas affected. Similarly, other utilities such as the Water and Sewage Authority (WASA) and the Trinidad and Tobago Electricity Commission (TTEC) utilized the mike man to inform residents of affected areas when scheduled works and interruptions of the utility services would negatively affect them.

By the late 1960s, many business concerns began using the mike systems to go into villages and surrounding areas to publicize sale events of their commercial enterprises. The mike man went into the areas announcing the sale events and distributing fliers to residents. It is important to note that when making those announcements the mike man played Indian film songs to get the people's attention. Most times, people were interested in hearing the Indian film songs played by the mike man rather than the announcements, which he was paid to make (Ramesh Boodoo).

A unique feature about the mike system was its ability to reach out to the public in a manner that other communication devices could not. The sheer loudness and carriage of the sound ensured that people within a wide radius took note of the messages being broadcast. In addition, the mike man went into areas where there was no electricity and broadcast his message to everyone. The message was heard by all within the catchment area at the same time.

Besides those announcements the mike man made his appearance during the death of a villager. From the inception of the mike man in Trinidad, people realized that the quickest way to get the message of a death in the village to surrounding areas was through the mike man. In those days when there were no refrigeration services to keep the deceased body for long periods, it was important to get the word out as quickly as possible as funerals were normally held within one or two days after death. In those circumstances, the mike man came to the rescue and made death announcements in the village and surrounding areas playing Indian religious film songs between the announcements (Ramjattan). Ramjattan expressed the view that in those early days of the mike man it was considered 'unjust and unwise' to charge the family of the deceased to make a death announcement so his contribution was universally accepted as community service and any mike man who asked for money in those days was frowned upon as trying to 'take money from the dead'.

The social and political impact of the mike man, therefore was remarkable as he sought to get their messages into areas that were not accessible to radio and other forms of public information. He communicated with the people, lived among them and played music for their enjoyment. As with other aspects of his routine, the constant playing of Indian film songs kept those songs alive among the people and in time the songs became commonplace among them and the mike man gained in status among East Indians.

CULTURAL INFLUENCE

The mike man was largely responsible for the spread and development of Indian film songs in Trinidad and Tobago. He was the repository of the largest collection of Indian film songs in the country and was a collector of old and rare Indian film songs which were considered prized possessions. There were Indian film songs in the possession of mike man that were never heard on the radio. It was the mike man who in the early days before the advent of radio, took Indian film songs to the people in the outlying areas, particularly in the Indian settlements and kept it alive among them (Ramkissoon). His job was a labour of love in the early days of the mike in Trinidad because the financial return from the letting of the mike system was very small. Nevertheless, he provided musical enjoyment for East Indians while giving expression to the East Indian identity in public spaces. The people in turn held him in high esteem (Ramjattan).

For many people the mike man will always have a special place in their lives because of the tremendous contribution he made to East Indian culture and the evolution of East Indian identity in Trinidad. Without the work of the mike man, Indian film songs would not have been as popular and widespread as they were in the 1950s, 1960s and 1970s. The work of the mike man kept Indian film songs popular among the East Indians and that popularity of film songs led to the identification of East Indians with Indian film songs and their spin-offs.

During the period under consideration, the mike man was the gatekeeper of Indian culture and Indian film songs in the country. Wherever he went, he played his stock-in trade (film songs) and thereby kept Indian culture alive among East Indians. The playing of Indian film songs by the mike man in the streets and other public spaces helped to build the self-esteem of East Indians who hitherto practiced their religion and culture in privacy. East Indians were not known to broadcast their culture and religion in public spaces but the coming of the mike man changed that and for the first time Indian songs were played regularly in public spaces for all to hear. The public space claimed by the mike man boldly encouraged East Indians to assert themselves at a time when they were struggling to claim an identity in Trinidad. That identity was indelibly linked to Indian film songs (Gooptar). The mike men collectively preserved one of the tangible heritage of the East Indians in Trinidad – Indian film songs.

CONCLUSION

The mike man was hired for various jobs and as he played Indian film songs in public spaces, he unwittingly claimed those open spaces for East Indians. The extremely loud cinematic expressions that emanated from the mike systems carved out new social, cultural and religious spaces for them (East Indians) and their continued consumption of film songs added significantly to the cumulative effect of their evolving East Indian identity in Trinidad.

During the period under study, East Indians in Trinidad struggled to claim their space in the country and Indian film songs afforded them the opportunity to do so. However, constant playing of those songs pushed into the background traditional East Indian songs and music and etched into the psyche of the East Indian, the 'modern' Indian film songs of the era. Indian film songs created an affirmative affinity between East Indians in Trinidad and India and assisted in their evolving identity. They identified with the film songs because those songs provided a link to their ancestral homeland, India, and the mike man who brought those songs to them became a cultural icon for them.

REFERENCES

Ben-Amos, Dan and Liliane Weissberg (1999). *Cultural Memory and the Construction of Identity.* Detroit: Wayne State University Press.

Dabydeen, David and Brinsley Samaroo (2006). *India in the Caribbean.* London: Hansib.

Dubey, Ajay Kumar (2003). *Indian Diaspora: Global Identity.* Delhi: Kalinga Publications.

Erikson, Erik H. (1974). *Dimensions of a New Identity.* New York: Norton.

Fong, Mary, and Rueyling Chuang (2004). *Communicating Ethnic and Cultural Identity.* Lanham, MD: Rowman & Littlefield.

Gooptar, Primnath (2013). 'The Impact of Indian Movies on East Indian Identity in Trinidad', Ph.D. Dissertation. UTT.

Klass, Morton (1961). *East Indians in Trinidad: A Study of Cultural Persistence.* New York: Columbia University Press.

Knigh, G. (ed.) (1993). *Ethnic Identity.* Albany: State University of New York Press.

Lash, Scott and Jonathan Friedman (1998). *Modernity and Identity.* Oxford: Blackwell.

Manuel, Peter (2000). *East Indian Music in the West Indies: Tān-singing, Chutney, and the Making of Indo-Caribbean Culture.* Philadelphia: Temple University Press.

Myers, Helen (1998). *Music of Hindu Trinidad: Songs from the India Diaspora.* Chicago: University of Chicago.

Ramnarine, Tina K. (2001). *Creating Their Own Space: The Development of an Indian-Caribbean Musical Tradition.* Kingston, Jamaica: University of the West Indies.

Saraswati, Baidyanath (1997). 'Civilizations and Settlement Societies: Cultural Development and Identity at the End of Twentieth Century'. *Interface of Cultural Identity and Development.* New Delhi: Indira Gandhi National Centre for the Arts.

Seukeran, Lionel Frank and Kenneth Ramchand (2006). *Mr. Speaker, Sir: An Autobiography of Lionel Frank Seukeran, the Silver-tongued Orator.* San Fernando. Trinidad and Tobago: Chandrabose Publications.

INTERVIEWEES

Boodhoo, Ramesh (1941-) is a former cinema owner/operator who spent most of his adult life in the cinema business. He owned and operated the Silk Cinema in Sangre Grande,15 May 2009, Sangre Grande.

Boodoo, Kelvin (1949-). Retired Machine Operator, 5 November 2009, Male, Arouca.

Deoraj, Doolie, Housewife, 22 March 2010, Female, 89 years, Princes Town.

Gosein, Siew (1918-). Male. Retired labourer. Mike man enthusiast and former *Indar Sabha* and *Raja Harischandra* dance drama artiste (1930s-60s). 18 March 2009, Mundo Nuevo.

Jagroopsingh, John (1939-) Retired Tractor Driver, 18 July 2008, Male, Brazil Village, Arima.

Kissoon, Randy (1954-) . . . Is self-employed and the owner of three mike systems. He is the current president of the Mike Men Association. He has more than 30 years' experience in the mike business. President, Mike Men Association, 15 August 2012, Male, Cunupia.

Mahabirsingh, Dolly (1932-) Retired Labourer, Housewife, 22 March 2010, Female, Rio Claro.

Ramcharan, Nandlal (1908-) Retired Labourer, 8 April 2009, Male, Plum Road, Manzanilla.

Ramjattan, Ramdeowar (1920-2012). Retired Caroni worker and mike man. He has more than 60 years' experience as a mike man, 14 February 2008, Male, St. Augustine.

Ramkissoon, Hublal (1949-). Religious and cultural activist and the owner of two mike systems. He is self-employed and repairs mike systems as a hobby. He has more than 40 years' experience as a mike man. His father was a mike man and he retains two mike systems used by his father in the 1930s and 1940s, 22 March 2010, Male. Tabaquite Road, Rio Claro.

Ramnath, James (1909-) Retired primary school principal, Lay Preacher, 15 May 2008, Male, Guaico, Sangre Grande.

Ramoutar, Balliram (1939-) is still an active mike man with more than 50 years' experience in the business. He has trained several young people in the mike business. Mike man, 30 April 2009, Male, Couva.

Sitahal, Partap (1946-) is a retired Machine Operator. He is a community, cultural, religious and political activist and a mike enthusiast, 22 March 2013, Arima.

Contributors

SATNARINE BALKARANSINGH is a musician, dancer, choreographer and producer who has scripted and directed many television and stage productions including several ballets. He functioned in several capacities in various government ministries in Trinidad and Tobago including Policy Planner, Director and Permanent Secretary. Balkaransingh holds a Ph.D. in Cultural Studies from UTT and is currently artistic director of the Kathak Kala Sangam, an adjunct lecturer and a consultant in strategic and policy planning for national development. E-mail: satbalkaransingh@gmail.com

NIRMALA BIRJMOHAN is a psychotherapist and health care psychologist. She has her own practice at the Mental Health Center (MHC) in The Hague. She specializes in system therapy and group therapy. She is also an expert in the treatment of Post-traumatic Stress Disorder. She is an adjunct lecturer at the Hogeschool Utrecht, Faculty of Education, where she lectures on dyslexia, auism, ADHD, multicultural aspects of education and adolescence development. She is also a student supervisor and coach. E-mail: Nirmala.Birjmohan@telfort.nl

INDRA BOEDJARATH is a psychologist and psychotherapist who specializes in trans-cultural and gender-specific psychotherapy and sexology. She works at the Care Express in The Hague, an institution for mental health care for youngsters and their families. She also has her own practice where she offers direct mental health care to adults. She is a Ph.D. candidate at Tilburg University working on the topic of suicidal behaviour among Surinamese Hindustanis. Email: i.boedjarath@xs4all.nl

PRIMNATH GOOPTAR is a writer/biographer and former educator. He has co-authored *Ranjit Kumar: Bridging the East and West* with

Bridgette Brereton and is the author of *Baal Joban: The First Indian Movie in Trinidad* (2013); *The Impact of Indian Movies on East Indian identity in Trinidad* (2014) and, *Cultural Persistence: 50 Years of the National Council of Indian Culture in Trinidad and Tobago (1964-2015)* published in 2015. He holds a Ph.D. in Cultural Studies (UTT). E-mail: pgoopta@hotmail.com

MAURITS S. HASSANKHAN is senior lecturer and Head of the History Department of the Faculty of Humanities, Anton de Kom University of Suriname. His main research interests are: *Indentured Labour in Suriname in Comparative Perspective*; *Ethnicity*, *Ethnic Relations and Ethnocentrism, Migration and Diaspora Studies*. His publications are in these fields. He compiled the Historical Database of Suriname in collaboration with Sandew Hira. He co-edited with Jerry Egger and Eric Jagdew, *Explorations in Historiography of Suriname. From Colonial History to History of the People.* (2013) E-mail: mauritshassan@gmail.com

RAHINA HASSANKHAN is an internationally certified NLP trainer and an expert in systemic career, family and organizational constellations and body work. She distinguished herself as an independent trainer in the development and teaching of (specifically adapted) training courses and coaching. She was manager at the Regional Bureau for Women's Emancipation, and a freelance trainer at ISIS Transcultural Leadership Institute. Presently she offers counselling and constellations to individuals, families and organizations through Raahi Training & Counselling. Email: info@raahi.nl

KUMARI JAYAWARDENA is a former Associate Professor in Political Science at the University of Colombo, Sri Lanka. She has written *Feminism and Nationalism in the Third World* (1986) and *The Rise of the Labor Movement in Sri Lanka* (1972). She co-authored with Rachel Kurian *Class, Patriarchy and Ethnicity on Sri Lankan Plantations: Two Centuries of Power and Protest* in the Series *Critical Thinking in South Asian History* (2015). She is presently Secretary of the Social Scientists' Association os Sri Lanka.

ANANYA J. KABIR is Professor of English Literature at King's College, London. She is a literary and cultural historian who works at the intersection of memory, embodiment, pleasure and post-trauma in the global South. She is the author of *Partition's Post-Amnesias: 1947, 1971 and Modern South Asia* (2013), and the director of 'Modern Moves', a five-year research project funded by a European Research Council Advanced Grant, which investigates the transnational history and popularity of Afro-diasporic music and dance forms. E-mail: ananya.kabir@kcl.ac.uk

RACHEL KURIAN is International Labour Economist at the International Institute of Social Studies of the Erasmus University Rotterdam. She works on issues relating to economic globalization, gender, human and labour rights, social justice, social exclusion and poverty. She has published on the situation of plantation workers, and in particular women workers throughout the world. She co-authored, with Kumari Jayawardena, *Class, Patriarchy and Ethnicity on Sri Lankan Plantations: Two Centuries of Power and Protes* (2015). E-mail: kurian@iss.nl

RADICA MAHASE holds a BA and PhD in History from the University of the West Indies, St. Augustine and a MA in Modern Indian History from Jawaharlal Nehru University, Delhi, India. She is the recipient of an Eric William Memorial Scholarship and a Government of India General Cultural Scholarship. She spent one year at the Centre for the History of Science, Technology and Medicine, University of Manchester, England as a Commonwealth Visiting Scholar. She is the co-author of *Caribbean History for CSEC* (2011). Her areas of research include Indian indenture ship, Indian Diaspora and South Asian Studies. E-mail: radica.mahase@gmail.com

ANITA NANHOE studied Developmental and Educational Psychology and Clinical and Health Psychology at the University in Leiden. She works at the municipality of Rotterdam on migration, emancipation, education and domestic violence. As a senior researcher she initiates and coordinates joint research on domestic violence for the four biggest cities in the Netherlands. She is Visiting lecturer at the Erasmus University, Rotterdam. E-mail: acnanhoe@hotmail.com

HILDE NEUS worked at the Suriname Museum Foundation and is currently Head of the Dutch Department of the Advanced Teachers Training College (OIL) in Paramaribo. She teaches Colonial and Modern Literature here. Her main interests are the history of Suriname, gender studies and literature. She published *Susanna du Plessis. Portret van eenslavenmeesteres*, a study on a cruel slave mistress (2003). E-mail: heneus@sr.net

J.S. (MITRA) RAMBARAN studied Health Science and Medical Anthropo-logy as well as Gender, Reproductive Health and Fertility and media. She is active in politics in The Hague and has experience in writing, film making and public relation via social media. E-mail: mitrambaran@gmail.com

LOMARSH ROOPNARINE is Associate Professor of Caribbean and Latin American Studies at Jackson State University. He has published numerous peer reviewed articles on Caribbean migration and identity. He is the author of *Indo-Caribbean Indenture: Resistance and Accommodation* (2007). *Indian Migration and Identity in the Caribbean* is his forthcoming book. E-mail: lomarsh.roopnarine@jsums.edu

NIVEDITA SINGH is a research scholar from Jiwaji University, Gwalior. She works on the visual aspect of Dalit culture. Her research interests include migration, sociology of marginalized groups and social change. Her other interests are writing articles on social issues and nature photography. Email: niveditasinghrt@gmail.com

TANYA SITARAM is Head of the Reading Room and Library, National Archives of Suriname. She is also the acting Head of the Public Service. She holds a Bachelor degree (BA) in Journalism and Communication and is presently completing her MA in History with a focus on women/gender history. She is Secretary of the National

Archives Council and the main narrator in a documentary about the uprisings of the Hindustani indentured labourers at plantation Zorg en Hoop in 1884 in Suriname. Email: tanya_svs@yahoo.com

JOOP VERNOOIJ was ordained as a Roman Catholic priest in 1967. From 1969 to 2001, he worked for the Roman Catholic diocese of Paramaribo. He studied missiology at the Radboud University of Nijmegen, from 2001 to 2005; he was Lecturer at the Radboud University. He is the author of *De Rooms-Katholieke Gemeente in Suriname* (*The Roman Catholic Church in Suriname*, 1998) and *De regenboog is in ons Hui* (The rainbow is our home, 2012). E-mail: vernooij.joop@gmail.com

R. SAFDAR ZAIDI studied life science in Delft and Business Management in The Hague. He is employed at the Embassy of Pakistan in The Hague. He is the author of *De suiker die nietzoet was* (The Sugar That was Not Sweet, 2013) which was translated as *Chini Jo Meethi Na Thi* (2014) and *Horticulture Chain and Network in India* (Nihon University, 2014). E-mail: zehrason@hotmail.com.

Index